From Bards to Biblical Exegetes

From Bards to Biblical Exegetes

*A Close Reading and Intertextual Analysis
of Selected Exodus Psalms*

DAVID EMANUEL

PICKWICK *Publications* • Eugene, Oregon

FROM BARDS TO BIBLICAL EXEGETES
A Close Reading and Intertextual Analysis of Selected Exodus Psalms

Copyright © 2012 David Emanuel. All rights reserved. Except for brief quotations in critical publications or reviews, no part of this book may be reproduced in any manner without prior written permission from the publisher. Write: Permissions, Wipf and Stock Publishers, 199 W. 8th Ave., Suite 3, Eugene, OR 97401.

Pickwick Publications
An Imprint of Wipf and Stock Publishers
199 W. 8th Ave., Suite 3
Eugene, OR 97401

www.wipfandstock.com

ISBN 13: 978-1-60899-548-6

Cataloguing-in-Publication data:

Emanuel, David.

    From bards to biblical exegetes : a close reading and intertextual analysis of selected exodus psalms / David Emanuel.

    xiv + 300 pp. ; 23 cm. Includes bibliographical references and index.

    ISBN 13: 978-1-60899-548-6

    1. Bible. O.T. Psalms—Criticism, interpretation, etc. 2. Intertextuality in the Bible. I. Title.

BS1430.52 E82 2012

Manufactured in the U.S.A.

To my wife, Emma, and our children,
who have sacrificed their time,
enabling me to complete this endeavor

אִשְׁתִּי כְּגֶפֶן פֹּרִיָּה בְּיַרְכְּתֵי בֵיתִי בָּנַי כִּשְׁתִלֵי זֵיתִים סָבִיב לְשֻׁלְחָנִי

(Adapted from Psalm 128:3)

Contents

Preface · ix
Abbreviations · xii

1 Introduction · 1
2 Remember and Obey: Psalm 105 · 26
3 Standing in the Gap: Psalm 106 · 87
   Excursus: The Book of Moses · 169
4 YHWH's Supremacy: Psalm 135 · 172
5 A Never Ending Love: Psalm 136 · 210
6 Conclusions · 242

   Appendix A: Psalm 105 · 265
   Appendix B: Psalm 106 · 267
   Appendix C: Psalm 135 · 270
   Appendix D: Psalm 136 · 271

Bibliography · 273
Scripture Index · 289

Preface

All of the biblical references in the present work are listed according to English Bible translations, and where variations exist between the Hebrew and English text, I have placed the Hebrew verse number (and chapter where necessary) in brackets afterwards. For the most part, the English translations found within the present study are my own. In the few places where I have deviated from this practice, the New American Standard version has been adopted. Instances in which this version is used are clearly indicated. As a matter of personal preference and in an attempt to remain true to the biblical texts, I have rendered the tetragrammaton, the name of God, as YHWH in my translations. For the most part, initial Hebrew quotations cited directly from the Bible are pointed; however, after this, I have chosen to omit the vowel points unless their presence is necessary for interpretation. Variances between the written tradition (*ketiv*) and the read tradition (*qere*) are indicated by parentheses and brackets. The *qere* is surrounded by square brackets and the *ketiv* is surrounded by parentheses. References to the BHS refer to the critical apparatus found on the relevant page of the verse being discussed. As a matter of interpretational preference, I have translated the Hebrew ים סוף either as "Yam Suf" or "Sea of Reeds," as opposed to "Red Sea," as it is frequently named in modern English versions.

The present study sheds new light on the work of biblical psalmists, specifically concerning the composers' skill in reworking their source texts into new contexts. More than simply cutting and pasting sections of the source material into a psalm, the psalmists demonstrated a tangible degree of exegesis during the work of composition. The present study emphasizes the psalmists' work as that of a biblical interpreter, one who reinterpretes and reapplies source material from one context, with one meaning, into a new context reflecting a different meaning. The study extends the field of inner-biblical interpretation to include more of the psalms. For the most part, scholars have focused on the work of the Law and Prophets when investigating instances of exegesis between source and target texts within the Bible. Although certain scholars have investigated isolated psalms concerning this phenomenon, the Psalter has generally been neglected. The present study's primary focus on the psalms, and its conclusions demonstrate that the Psalter constitutes a rich, and to date, unappreciated source for the research of inner-biblical interpretation.

To date, the majority of research on the selected exodus psalms has primarily focused on the literary-historical data found therein. Although researchers have indeed been diligent in identifying the selected psalms as a group, their efforts have focused primarily on the allusions to the exodus tradition to determine the origins and development of the tradition. In doing so, the psalms have remained undervalued as independent works that were woven together with a specific purpose in mind. The poetics employed within such works have seldom been noticed or fully appreciated, and few have highlighted the skill and careful consideration each psalmist invested in his work. As a response, the present research has focused on the aforementioned areas; consequently, it contributes significantly towards the understanding of the poetics involved in creating historiography, and further demonstrates that although the psalmists drew from a vast repository of literary strands, they were careful in weaving them together to form a coherent and unified literary tapestry.

Finally, my hope is that the present study sheds further light on the close relationships existing between individual psalms. Overall, the tendency for modern scholarship leans towards analyzing each psalm as an independent unit bearing no relationship to the neighboring works. The results of the present study clearly demonstrate, or at least further confirm, that concrete links, which cannot be explained by chance or coincidence, exist between the psalms. In certain instances, these links were both lexical and interpretive, while at other times, interpretive links were more evident. By revealing the aforementioned associations between the psalms, the present work results in a different perception of the Psalter's arrangement, forcing one to understand it as an example of biblical interpretation. In the same way that the psalmists reworked their sources, affecting the meaning therein, so too the arrangers and editors of the Psalter reworked the material in their possession to create new valances of meaning from older texts.

• • •

Preface

Four individuals deserve special acknowledgement for the start and completion of the present undertaking. David Forbes, my early teacher and mentor, was instrumental in steering me into a career change from Computer Network Analysis to Biblical Studies, and also directing me to travel to Israel for my studies. Doctor Zvi Sedan (Israel College of the Bible) provided further critical direction by introducing me to the field of Inner-biblical Interpretation and Allusion. For ten years I studied under Prof. Yair Zakovitch at the Hebrew University, and it is he who inspired me and guided me through my Masters and Doctoral studies at the Hebrew University. Finally, I must acknowledge the invaluable advice and encouragement provided by Prof. Benjamin Sommer, Jewish Theological Seminary. Since my graduation I have deeply valued his wisdom in a wide range of areas, both related and unrelated to biblical studies.

My greatest thanks, however, must go towards my patient wife, Emma, who has put up with two changes of continent and culture to accompany me on this academic odyssey. She has suffered well through my temperamental inclinations caused by late nights and early mornings working on my dissertation and its conversion into the present undertaking. Similarly, I am indebted to my five children (Naomi, Tamar, Natan, Jo'el, and Shai) because they have sacrifice precious "playtime with abba" to enable me to complete this work.

Abbreviations

1. JOURNALS AND LEXICAL TOOLS

AB	The Anchor Bible
ABD	D. N. Freedman (ed.), *The Anchor Bible Dictionary*. 6 vols.
BDB	F. Brown, C. Briggs, and S. R. Driver, *A Hebrew and English Lexicon of the Old Testament*
BHS	R. Kittel (ed.), *Biblia Hebraica Stuttgartensia*
CAD	A. L. Oppenheim et al. (eds.), *The Assyrian Dictionary of the Oriental Institute of the University of Chicago*
CBQ	*Catholic Bible Quarterly*
DBI	*Dictionary of Biblical Interpretation*
DJD	Discoveries in the Judaean Desert of Jordan
ETL	*Ephemerides Theologicae Lovanienses*
GHAT	Göttinger Handkommentar zum Alten Testament
GKC	E. Kautzsch (ed.), A. E. Cowley (tr.), *Gesenius' Hebrew Grammar*. 2nd ed. (1910)
HAT	Handbuch zum Alten Testament
HCOT	Historical Commentary on the Old Testament
HS	*Hebrew Studies*
HUCA	*Hebrew Union College Annual*
ICC	International Critical Commentary
IEJ	*Israel Exploration Journal*
ITL	International Theological Library
JBL	*Journal of Biblical Literature*
JM	P. Joüon and T. Muraoka (tr.), *A Grammar of Biblical Hebrew*
JNSL	*Journal of Northwest Semitic Languages*
JAOS	*Journal of the American Oriental Society*
JSOT	*Journal for the Study of the Old Testament*

Abbreviations

JSOTSup	Journal for the Study of the Old Testament Supplement Series
KB	L. Koehler and W. Baumgartner, *The Hebrew & Aramaic Lexicon of the Old Testament*
LSJ	H. Liddell, H. Scott, and H. S. Jones (eds.), *A Greek-English Lexicon*
NCB	New Century Bible
NIB	The New Interpreter's Bible
OTL	The Old Testament Library
RevQ	*Revue de Qumran*
SBLDS	SBL Dissertation Series
SBLMS	Society of Biblical Literature Monograph Series
TDOT	G. J. Botterweck and H. Ringgren (eds.), *Theological Dictionary of the Old Testament*
TLOT	E. Jenni and K. Westermann (eds.), *Theological Lexicon of the Old Testament*
VT	*Vetus Testamentum*
VTS	Supplements to Vetus Testamentum
WBC	The Word Biblical Commentary
ZAW	*Zeitschrift für die Alttestamentliche Wissenschaft*

2. GENERAL ABBREVIATIONS

ABC	Archaic Biblical Hebrew
IH	Israelian Hebrew
LBH	Late Biblical Hebrew
Ms(s)	Manuscript(s)
MT	Masoretic Text
SBH	Standard Biblical Hebrew
Tg(s)	Targum(s)

1

Introduction

Throughout the Psalter an array of prominent motifs and allusions to literary-historical events appear. Creation constitutes one such motif;[1] sometimes only a single verse vaguely alludes to it (see Pss 24:2 and 102:25 [26]), and in other instances it dominates entire works (see Pss 8 and 104). Similarly, the exile of Judah to Babylon in 586 BCE surfaces in numerous psalms (see for example Pss 79 and 137), as does the Davidic kingship, though it is far less prevalent. The latter receives attention in Psalm 132, which re-emphasizes God's promise to David to establish his descendants as perpetual heirs to the throne, and echoes events narrated in 2 Sam 7 and 8.[2] Aspects of the Davidic covenant also appear in Psalms 78 (see vv. 70–72) and 89 (see vv. 4, 21, 36, and 50). Another common tradition recurring in the Psalter is the exodus, the account of Israel's deliverance from Egypt through YHWH's miraculous signs and mighty works, and their journey through the desert to the promised land. This account, which effectively recalls the formation of the Jewish people, represents the most important tradition in Israel's history, and is undoubtedly the most prevalent[3] and influential tradition recorded in the Bible. It appears in all of the prominent biblical genres:

---

1. Among those psalms referring to creation are Psalms 8, 24, 33, 65, 74, 89, 102, 121, 134, 147, and 148.

2. Ps 89:18–38 [19–39] similarly displays knowledge of the Book of Samuel.

3. Exod 1–18 first recalls the events, and Numbers presents a detailed narrative of the desert itinerary. Moreover, both Leviticus and Deuteronomy are set within the context of the desert sojourn and frequently allude to it. In addition to the Torah, prophetic literature frequently alludes to various parts of the tradition (e.g., Jer 7:22; 31:32; Ezek 20:6). The motif is also pervasive in the New Testament (see Acts 7; Heb 11:27; and Jude 1:5), and pseudepigraphic material (see for example Jdt 5:10–17, Bar 1:19–22, and 4 Ezra 9:26–37; as well as the Dead Sea Scrolls 4Q422). Zakovitch, *And You Shall Tell Your Son*, discusses the overall concept of the exodus in the Bible in detail.

laws, prophetic literature, historiographical writings, and poetry, and influences a significant number of psalms.

Two important questions arise concerning this tradition in the Psalter: upon which sources did the psalmists depend? and, how did they redeploy their sources into the compositions we possess today? The latter question raises three further questions: did the psalmists rearrange the material at their disposal? did they alter the traditions in their source texts? and if they did what would motivate them to do so? The present study seeks to answer these questions, and additionally investigates how the editors and arrangers of the Psalter used the exodus psalms.[4] Concerning this issue, the study aims to reveal whether they were influenced by the contents of the psalms whilst arranging them, and if they sought to create new meanings from these psalms via their arrangement. When completed, the study will shed new light on how the psalmists and editors of the Psalter interpreted the material available to them.

For the purposes of this study, the terms "exodus motif" and "exodus tradition" relate to the sequence of events from Israelite literary history that record how YHWH *actively* brought the children of Israel from Egypt into the land he had promised their forefathers. The time span begins from Israel's oppression in Egypt, and ends when Israel arrives at the River Jordan. Within this definition of the motif, the study identifies numerous smaller events and motifs that it considers the more important sub-motifs and events defining the aforementioned period.[5]

In total, twenty psalms relate to the exodus tradition in one form or another,[6] and due to this relatively large number, further limitations

---

4. In certain instances, because the exodus psalms reproduce earlier texts and traditions, the work of the psalmist is very similar to that of the later writers of *Aggadaic Midrash*. The function of these later exegetes was primarily to explain texts, and their tasks included filling out lacunae, supplying interpretations of discrete texts, and providing concrete applications of abstract texts; see Sarason, "Midrash."

5. These motifs are: Jacob entering Egypt, multiplication of Jacob's descendants, oppression from Egypt, deliverance via the plagues, deliverance at the sea, bitter waters at Marah, the provision of manna, water from the rock, the battle against Amalek, the provision of meat, the giving of Torah, the golden-calf idolatry, Aaron and Miryam's rebellion, the initial rejection of the promised land, Korah's revolt, the bronze serpent, the early conquest battles (with Og and Sihon etc.), and the account of Bilaam and Balak.

6. Pss 22, 44, 66, 68, 74, 77, 78, 80, 81, 98, 99, 103, 105, 106, 107, 111, 114, 135, 136, and 147.

must be implemented in order to define a working corpus for analysis. Because a number of exodus psalms only contain vague or fleeting references to the tradition, they will be excluded from our corpus.⁷ Similarly, even though Psalm 114 reflects certain exodus events, the study excludes the composition because it does not recall YHWH's active involvement in leading Israel out of Egypt (see definition above).⁸ The remaining psalms (77, 78, 81, 95, 105, 106, 135, and 136), however, still present a corpus too large for the present study, and so it places two further restrictions on potential psalms. First, only those psalms *unambiguously* narrating at least three incidents associated with the exodus motif, as defined above including its sub-motifs, are accepted for further treatment. Second, only psalms dating to the second temple era are included. The latter adjustments enables a richer analysis because they raise the possibility of detecting sequencing transpositions the psalmists may have effected, and additionally raises the probability that the psalmists are in fact reusing early traditions. These final constraints further disqualify Psalms 77, 78, 81, and 95. After applying all of the aforementioned criteria, the remaining psalms are: 105, 106, 135, and 136.

RESEARCH IN RELATED FIELDS

In total, three areas of biblical studies are brought together in the current study. It intersects with the development of Psalms research overall, in addition to the field of Inner-biblical Interpretation and Allusion, and the following paragraphs provide some background to these areas of research with particular regard to how the present study relates to earlier research.⁹ Because part of this study focuses on the relationships

---

7. The psalms disqualified at this point are: 22, 44, 66, 68, 74, 80, 98, 99, 103, 107, 111, and 147.

8. This peculiarity in Psalm 114's portrayal of events has been noted by other scholars. Concerning this remarkable feature, Weiss states, "This absence of any theocentric interpretation of the historical event ... is surprising in the case of the psalmist ... because such an anthropocentric account of the exodus from Egypt has no parallel in the Book of Psalms" (Weiss, *The Bible from Within*, 357).

9. The following survey of Psalms study is not intended to be comprehensive for two reasons: first, space does not permit such a survey; second, much of the earlier research based on form criticism is not pertinent to the present study. For a more comprehensive survey on the modern developments in Psalms study see Eaton, "Psalms," and Johnson, "The Psalms," 162–209.

between juxtaposed psalms, which falls under the broader category of canonical criticism, a terse summary of related research performed within this specific field is included.

General Psalms Research

The most significant development in Psalms research emerged at the start of the twentieth century with the work of Hermann Gunkel.[10] As a guiding methodological principle, he stressed the importance of studying psalms on the background of their ancient Near Eastern context—associating the psalms with other Canaanite and Mesopotamian ceremonies and festivals. As part of this process he established form criticism and applied the form-critical approach to the psalms. Using this approach, he determined each psalm's life setting (*Sitz im Leben*), determining how ancient Israel used them in their original contexts. Gunkel's most important contribution to Psalms study was his classification of the psalms into five major genres (*Gattungen*): Individual Laments, Communal Laments, Hymns, Royal Psalms, and Individual Thanksgiving Songs (he also defined minor groups: Pilgrimage Songs, Wisdom Poetry, Communal Thanksgiving, and Liturgy). The determination of each psalm's form, structure, and setting constituted an integral part of his approach. The exodus psalms selected for the present study do not fall into any single category within Gunkel's form-critical taxonomy, though he generally refers to historiographic psalms as Legends (*Legenden*).[11] Psalms 105, 135, and 136[12] are Hymns, but Psalm 106 constitutes a Lament.[13]

---

10. Gunkel's primary form-critical work on psalms was completed by his student Joachim Begrich (*Einleitung in die Psalmen: die Gattungen der religiosen Lyrik Israels*, Gottinger Handkommentar zum Alten Testament, 1933); the fourth edition (1985) of which was translated into English by James Nogalski, see Gunkel and Begrich, *Introduction to Psalms*.

11. See Gunkel and Begrich, *Introduction to Psalms*, 247–49.

12. The definition of these psalms is unanimous; see, for example, Allen, *Psalms 101–150*, 53, 292, and 294; Weiser, *The Psalms*, 673, 789, and 792; and Terrien, *The Psalms*, 723.

13. Some questions arise concerning Psalm 106, but it is generally interpreted as a Communal Lament, see Gunkel and Begrich, *Introduction to Psalms*, 82, although a hymnal element is also recognized; see Allen, *Psalms 101–150*, 133, and Hoffman, יציאת מצריים, 133.

Introduction

Since Gunkel established the form-critical approach, most modern commentaries (and major works on the psalms) continued in a similar direction with various adjustments. Sigmund Mowinckel[14] specifically pursued the relationships between Israel's cult and the psalms. He reconstructed a theoretical Israelite New Year festival, utilizing the Babylonian *Akitu* festival as a paradigm, and subsequently related many psalms to this event. The remaining psalms he attributed to various other temple services. Similarly, Artur Weiser's commentary on the psalms[15] reflects an affinity with Gunkel's form-critical approach with respect to establishing the *Sitz im Leben*; however, he relates many psalms to a covenant renewal festival, a hypothetical festival derived from his study of the Law and Prophets. Kraus,[16] like Gunkel, determines each psalm's *Sitz im Leben* but refines and advances much of Gunkel's work by taking into consideration modern archaeological findings, especially those relating to *Ras Shamra*.[17]

The 1950s and 60s witnessed numerous scholars deviate from the form-critical principles established by Gunkel.[18] In 1969 James

---

14. Mowinckel, *The Psalms*, originally published in Norwegian as *Offersang og Sangoffer* (Oslo: H.Aschehoug, 1951), this work was later revised and translated into English in 1962.

15. Weiser, *The Psalms*, originally published in German as *Die Psalmen* (Das Alte Testament Deutsch 14/15, 1935), and translated into English from the fifth revised edition (Göttingen: Vandenhoeck & Ruprecht, 1959).

16. Kraus, *Psalms 1–59*, and *Psalms 60–150*, originally published in German in two parts, *Psalmen* (Biblischer Kommentar Altes Testament Band XV/1 and 2, Neukirchen-Vlugn: Neukirchener, 1966); translated into English in 1988 (from the fifth edition, 1978).

17. Of the more recent commentaries, the Word Biblical Commentary adopts an eclectic approach to Psalms study utilizing the methods described above, acknowledging the proposed New Year and covenant renewal festivals. Additionally it includes a cursory analysis of poetic forms found within the psalms. It still, however, directs most of its efforts towards determining the *Sitz im Leben*, and the commentary depends heavily on establishing form, structure, and setting.

18. With the discovery of the Ugaritic language, a number of scholars have studied parallels between Ugaritic poems and the poetry of the Hebrew Bible, especially the psalms. Avishur, עיונים, and Cassuto, *Biblical and Oriental Studies*, have compared a number of archaic poems from the Bible with Ugaritic literature. Perhaps the most relevant research in this field to Psalms study, however, has been the work of Dahood, *Psalms III*. The latter work largely consists of an interpretation and reconstruction of the psalms through the lens of Ugaritic literature. Though this line of research does not directly pertain to the present study, the works of the aforementioned scholars occasionally shed light on the interpretation and understanding of the selected psalms.

5

Muilenburg's seminal work, *Form Criticism and Beyond*,[19] sparked a new direction in Psalms study, rhetorical criticism. Instead of focusing on the psalm's historical function within the specific background of ancient Israelite cultic institutions, and the wider context of the ancient Near East, he advocated an holistic and text-centered approach to analyzing biblical texts. His methodology aims at uncovering the meaning of individual textual units, which could consist of psalms or other pericopae, and shows how individual verses and stanzas[20] all contribute to that meaning. Muilenburg recovered a new appreciation for the poetics employed in biblical compositions, demonstrating how poetic features contributed to the meaning and purpose of a given text.[21] At approximately the same time Muilenburg birthed rhetorical criticism, Meir Weiss pioneered total interpretation,[22] a development of *Werkinterpretation* and new criticism that similarly sought an holistic understanding and interpretation of each work. Like Muilenburg, Weiss stressed the importance of the literary work as a whole and the close reading of biblical texts; he likewise emphasized the importance of understanding how all aspects of a literary work contribute towards its meaning: words and phrases, images, sentences and verses, and literary units.[23] Supplementing the methodological direction of the aforementioned scholars is Wilfred Watson's outstanding contribution to Biblical

---

19. See Muilenburg, "Form Criticism."

20. Concerning terms for the division of psalms, I have primarily adopted those outlined by Watson, *Classical Hebrew Poetry*, 11–15, whereby "Stanza" defines larger textual divisions, "Strophe" constitutes smaller divisions that make up stanzas, and "Colon," which constitutes a half line of text.

21. Trible, *Rhetorical Criticism*, built on the work of Muilenburg by formulating methodological processes for applying Rhetorical Criticism to specific texts.

22. The original work was published in Hebrew (המקרא כדמותו, 1962), and the second edition published soon after that was almost identical, with the addition of work on Psalm 46 (Jerusalem: Mosad Bialik, 1967). The English version constitutes a revised, enlarged and fully updated edition of this work (*The Bible from Within: The Method of Total Interpretation*, [Jerusalem: Magnes, 1984]).

23. Even though the focus of this dissertation is not on the historical reality of the exodus tradition or its diachronic development, three works falling into this category deserve a mention because at some stage in their research they collect and analyze groups of exodus psalms: Loewenstamm, *Evolution*, Norin, *Er Spaltete das Meer*, and Hoffman, יציאת מצריים. Each of these works isolates and examines a number of exodus psalms in order to glean from them their renditions of the exodus motif. In each case, the fundamental purpose is to reconstruct various aspects of the tradition as a whole, recreate the historical setting, or trace the motif's diachronic development. As

Hebrew poetry, *Classical Hebrew Poetry: A Guide to Its Techniques*.[24] Watson not only classifies an array of poetic techniques, but also demonstrates their function, explaining how each one contributes to the meaning and purpose of poetic units.[25]

To date, few scholars have exposed any of the selected psalms to a verse-by-verse poetic analysis implementing the principles established by Muilenburg and Weiss.[26] One possible explanation for this reticence relates to the *borrowed* nature of historiographic psalms. Psalms recounting and retelling Israelite literary history could be viewed as *less poetic* than other psalms, and more akin to biblical narrative, thus less likely to yield rich results. The present study aims to fill this lacuna by poetically analyzing each of the selected psalms.

Inner-Biblical Interpretation and Allusion

To varying degrees, biblical scholarship has long recognized the idea of Scripture reworking Scripture.[27] Numerous commentators, including Gunkel himself, mention textual relationships in their analysis of biblical psalms, even if the attention afforded such connections is somewhat limited. Overall, such associations appear with no further comment or examination. Perhaps the first scholar to collect examples of this phenomenon and systematically order, analyze, and classify them was Michael Fishbane. In his seminal work,[28] he collected numerous exam-

---

a consequence of their approaches, any concept of each psalm's unity is ignored, and the exodus content alone is deemed most important.

24. See Watson, *Classical Hebrew Poetry*, in addition to the companion volume *Traditional Techniques*.

25. Two other scholars who have contributed to an improved understanding of Hebrew poetry deserve mention: Schökel, *Hebrew Poetics*, and Alter, *Biblical Poetry*. The present study periodically draws upon both of these works.

26. Scholars such as Zakovitch have conducted this type of analysis on other psalms, such as Psalms 78, "ויבחר"; Psalm 82, "Psalm 82," and Psalm 137, "על נהרות בבל." Another scholar deserving a mention is Ceresko, "A Poetic Analysis," who treated Psalm 105 to some detail, but did not perform a line-by-line analysis.

27. A wide range of commentaries—such as Hacham, ספר תהלים, McCann, *Psalms*, Tate, *Psalms 51–100*, and Allen, *Psalms 101–150*—note the various associations certain psalms bear with other biblical texts. None, however, continues to analyze further the relationships between the texts and sources. The topic is broadly treated with regards to biblical and extra-biblical contexts in a volume dedicated to Barnabas Lindars; see Anderson, "Historic Psalms."

28. See Fishbane, *Biblical Interpretation*, and *The Garments of Torah*.

ples of inner-biblical interpretation and classified them into four broad categories: Scribal Comments and Corrections, Legal Exegesis, Aggadic Exegesis, and Mantalogical Exegesis. Methodologically, Fishbane's first task was to identify an older source text, *traditum*, before questioning how the interpreters reused this material in creating an interpretation, *traditio*. In certain respects, Fishbane's work represents a development of the tradition-history approach to biblical studies. Instead of studying the development of oral and written folk traditions into a recognizable and broadly accepted canon, he traces the development of an existing canon into a broader canon inclusive of interpretational expansions.

Soon after Fishbane's contribution to the field of inner-biblical interpretation, Zakovitch[29] and Sommer[30] produced works on the same subject. Zakovitch approached the topic from a different perspective. He focused on interpretation instigated by redactors and editors of the Bible as they created new meanings from the texts they were responsible for arranging. Whereas Fishbane predominantly viewed the authors of the individual biblical books as interpreters working on earlier biblical texts as their source, Zakovitch leaned more to viewing the redactors as the interpreters with completed sections of text as their sources. His work collects numerous examples from the Bible but categorizes them differently, arranging them into groups such as songs interpreting prose, redactional layers interpreting each other, and speeches interpreting narrative. Sommer's work on biblical allusion builds, in many respects, on the work of Fishbane. For example, Sommer also first establishes an older work from which a later author drew, before analyzing the changes effected. Unlike the previous two scholars, however, Sommer examines in detail a smaller corpus of biblical literature, Isaiah 40–66. His methodological approach is firmly based on modern literary theory, especially the work of Ben-Porat.[31] Sommer's work discusses numerous biblical allusions between Isaiah 40–66 and the Torah,[32] Prophets, and Writings. Due to the variances in

29. See Zakovitch, מבוא לפרשנות פנים-מקראית.
30. See Sommer, *A Prophet*.
31. See Ben-Porat, "Poetics of Literary Allusion."
32. At this point, I would like to clarify that my use of the term "Torah" throughout the present study is somewhat flexible. The reader should note that the term does not always refer to the whole of the printed Torah editions in our possession today, and may simply refer to a text an author may have had that reflects modern printed editions.

Introduction

his methodology, Sommer's taxonomy of inner-biblical allusion differs from both Zakovitch and Fishbane, classifying the associations as echo, exegesis, influence, revision, and polemic.[33]

Each of the aforementioned works recalls, at some stage, isolated allusions involving the psalms. Zakovitch predominantly addresses them in his chapter on poetry interpreting narrative, and Fishbane occasionally mentions instances in which psalms reuse material from other biblical books. Because Sommer's work adopts Isaiah 40–66 as a working corpus, it predominantly views the psalms as sources, as opposed to texts that reuse older material. Of these scholars, none of them has dedicated efforts to investigating the inner-biblical relationships with a group of psalms as a working corpus. Consequently, the field of inner-biblical interpretation and allusion from the perspective of the psalms has, until now, been a neglected topic.

Juxtapositional Interpretation

Research concerning the juxtaposition of psalms[34] has predominantly developed along two lines: the general composition and structure of the Psalter, and juxtaposition of individual works through various principles of association.[35] Concerning the general composition of the

---

33. See Sommer, *A Prophet*, 20–30, in addition to the authors mentioned here, others have investigated further the exegetical aspects of intertextual relationships. Among these are Day, "Inner Scriptural Interpretation," who analyzed the relationship between Isa and Hos; Schoors, *(Mis)use of Intertextuality*, who discusses textual relationships involving Qohelet (Ecclesiastes); and Sarna, *Psalm 89*, who addressed intertextual relationships involving Psalm 89.

34. Broadly speaking, this category falls under the semi-recognized rubric of canonical criticism, a discipline that seeks to shed light on the formation of the biblical canon. For further discussions on this topic, see Sheppard, "Canonical Criticism."

35. With no specific reference to the Psalter, others have posited theories concerning the relationships between biblical sections. Cassuto, "Sequence and Arrangement," predominantly focused on association as a motivation for juxtaposition, noting that apparently random textual units, such as prophecies and laws, are grouped together by associated words or expressions (and sometimes ideas). He shows that the apparently unrelated laws concerning the eating of blood in Lev 17 and uncovering a father's nakedness in Lev 18:6 are in fact related by the common phrase איש איש appearing in 17:13 and 18:6. He similarly explains the positioning of the minor prophetic books Joel and Amos. In Joel 3:16 [4:16] we see the phrase וַיהוָה מִצִּיּוֹן יִשְׁאָג וּמִירוּשָׁלַיִם יִתֵּן קוֹלוֹ ("YHWH roars from Zion and from Jerusalem he utters his voice"), and in Amos 1:2 we see יִתֵּן קוֹלוֹ וַיֹּאמַר יְהוָה מִצִּיּוֹן יִשְׁאָג וּמִירוּשָׁלַיִם ("And he said, 'YHWH roars from Zion and from Jerusalem he utters his voice'"). Cassuto, "Arrangement of the Book of Ezekiel," also applies the principle of association to Ezekiel among other books.

Psalter, scholars such as McCann have recognized that the arrangers designed the book for a sequential reading that addresses the theological difficulties raised by the exile. Thus, the first three books reflect the failed Davidic kingship, culminating in Psalm 89, which laments the Babylonian exile; and the latter two books, beginning with Psalm 90, a song of Moses, reflect the desire to return to the desert model of national leadership, a theocracy, as a response to the failed Davidic covenant.[36] This line of investigation primarily focuses on determining the rationale for arranging larger groups of psalms, and the placement of individual units, though addressed in certain instances,[37] does not constitute a primary concern. Wilson's work on the arrangement of the Hebrew Psalter falls in line with this approach,[38] and he further asserts that titled and non-titled psalms played a role in determining the location of smaller psalm groups.

Numerous scholars have recognized principles of *association* as the guiding force motivating the editors of the Psalter in their placement of individual psalms. Two of the earliest scholars to address the issue seriously were Keil and Delitzsch.[39] They determined that the psalms were generally arranged through similarities of themes, common vocabulary, or common genres—referring to the incipit and not

---

36. Perhaps most representative of this view are McCann, *Psalms*, 660–64, and Wilson, *Shaping the Psalter*, though Terrien, *The Psalms*, 23, recognizes the pivotal nature of Psalm 89, depicting the failure of the Davidic dynasty, and the direction change that begins in Psalm 90. An eschatological agenda is also espoused by some, whereby the message of the Psalter points to a coming son of David (see Reddish, "Heaven").

37. For example, McCann, *Psalms*, 659–65, notes that Psalm 1, in addition to serving as a Wisdom Psalm, functions as an interpretive gateway into the Psalter itself. Other scholars such as Fohrer, *Introduction*, 295, and Eissfeldt, *The Old Testament*, 449, have observed this characteristic.

38. See, for example, his work on the function of Royal Psalms in the assembly of Books I–III, Wilson, *Royal Psalms*; see also Wilson, "Shaping the Psalter"; "Purposeful Arrangement"; *Editing of the Hebrew Psalter*; and "'Untitled' Psalms."

39. See Keil and Delitzsch, *Psalms*.

Introduction

Gunkel's formal definition.[40] McCann's work[41] devotes some attention to the principle of association in his interpretation of psalms. Similarly, Howard,[42] though dealing with a limited number of psalms, addresses how they develop certain themes when read consecutively.[43] One of the shortcomings of juxtaposition via association, however, is that it generally fails to answer adequately why certain psalms appear together in a specific order: why is A next to B, and not the other way round?[44]

40. Their taxonomy of association identifies three categories: External Association, constituting lexical similarities in which the arranger juxtaposes two psalms because they share a relatively rare word or phrase. Internal Association, depicting the similarity of subject matter between two psalms, a strategy concerned with common ideas expressed through semantic equivalences as opposed to lexical similarity. An example appears in Psalms 50–51, where both songs concern themselves with animal sacrifices. The third strategy, Community of Species, operates on a larger scale whereby the arranger assembles psalms according to their genre—not that defined by Hermann Gunkel's form-critical approach, but the type according to subscripts such as מזמור (*Mizmor*) and מכתם (*Miktam*). As an example, we see psalms entitled מזמור grouped together in Psalms 62–68, and משכיל in Psalms 52–55. Much of the scholarly literature on the psalms that address the issue of juxtaposition concentrates on these three guiding principles.

41. See McCann, *Psalms*.

42. See Howard, *Psalms 93–100*.

43. In addition to associative ideas, Goulder, *The Psalms of the Return*, suggests a model with respect to the positioning of the Songs of Ascent, whereby each psalm is sequentially arranged according to events in Neh 1:1—12:42. Thus, he raises the possibility that sequences of psalms may have received their order from corresponding events, or books, in the Bible. A related phenomenon concerns the Psalter's division into five books, which according to Jewish tradition corresponds to the five books of Moses.

44. Although not directly related to the psalms, the work of Alexander Rofé deserves some mention here because he raises additional possibilities for why psalms appear together in a specific order. Rofé, "The Arrangement," recognizes the possibility of texts organized according to chronological sequencing, the chronology expressed in the contents of certain books determines the order in which they appear. As an example, he adduces the ordering of the Torah and Deuteronomic history, which reflects a historical continuity from creation to the exile (in the Hebrew Bible). This historical continuity does not necessarily reflect the dates when the individual compositions were composed, but the historical content contained therein. Another strategy he identifies is that of sequencing according to size, from large units to small (or the opposite). The ordering of the classical prophets Isaiah, Jeremiah, Ezekiel, and the Minor Prophets demonstrate this strategy. Rofé also elaborates upon what is best described as a consideration, rather than a strategy. He recognizes a propensity among biblical authors to close sections of texts with words of comfort. We can see this principle at work in the book of Amos. The first nine chapters condemn Israel's behavior and speak of their judgment, but the last chapter speaks words of hope concerning their future. The

From Bards to Biblical Exegetes

The present study adopts a more detailed look between the selected psalms and their neighbors; in so doing, it hopes to uncover other rationales for the juxtaposition of psalms. The study aims to shed some light on why the editors placed certain psalms after others. It also seeks to uncover interpretive strategies present in the work of the arrangers and editors of the Psalter. In the same way that the psalmists may have viewed their historiographical sources as semantic units that could be carefully selected and arranged to reflect an independent agenda, so too the arrangers of the Psalter could have viewed each of the psalms with which they worked as similar semantic units which could be arranged to address specific issues. Concerning this potential layer of interpretation between psalms, Zakovitch[45] has treated the matter in his work on the psalms, as have Hossfeld and Zenger.[46]

METHODOLOGICAL CONSIDERATIONS

Methodologically, when analyzing various forms of intertextuality, two possible approaches exist: diachronic and synchronic. The first approach relies on the determination of an older source text that lay before an author whilst compiling his composition. Consequently, the inner-biblical associations appearing within the author's work generally constitute the result of his purposeful and cognizant work (thus an author-centric method). Fishbane,[47] Sommer,[48] and Zakovitch[49]

---

present study's analysis of juxtaposition considers all the aforementioned principles discussed by Rofé. More recently, Nasuti, "Sequence and Selection," discusses a range of potential sequencing strategies for the Psalter.

45. With respect to the psalms, Zakovitch, "ויבחר," applies more of an interpretive approach to his treatment of the relationship between Psalm 78 and its neighbors. The idea of interpretive juxtaposition receives further treatment in his work on inner-biblical interpretation (Zakovitch, מבוא לפרשנות פנים-מקראית). Concerning other biblical texts, Zakovitch's analysis of the Abraham narratives follows similar principles (Zakovitch, "Juxtaposition").

46. See Hossfeld and Zenger, *Psalms 51–100*.

47. Throughout Fishbane's monumental work he relies on the two terms *traditum* and *traditio* to refer to a source text and its reworked form, respectively; see Fishbane, *Biblical Interpretation*, 6–7.

48. See Sommer, *A Prophet*, 20–31.

49. For the majority of Zakovitch's important work on inner-biblical exegesis (Zakovitch, מבוא לפרשנות פנים-מקראית) he assumes the principle of a redactor, instead of an author, working with a pre-established text (see esp. 7–11). In principle, this constitutes a diachronic approach since it recognizes a composer working with an older

Introduction

each adopt a diachronic approach. The second approach, synchronic, disregards consideration for date and chronological authorship, and is thus *ahistorical*. Within these broader confines, an older text can influence the reading of more recent texts and vice versa, depending on the reader's interpretation (thus constituting a reader-centric approach).[50] The present study predominantly[51] adopts a diachronic method to inner-biblical allusion and exegesis,[52] and primarily refers to this approach as "biblical allusion."[53] Regarding the present study, the latter term describes the phenomenon of both inner-biblical allusion and inner-biblical interpretation.

In light of the methodology adopted by the study, isolating and dating the sources of the selected psalms is essential. Consequently, it conducts four stages of investigation for each psalm: first, a close read-

---

established text. In addition to these authors, Schoors, "(Mis)use of Intertextuality," adopts, and emphatically endorses, a diachronic approach, in which the determination of a source in relation to the author's work is essential.

50. Nielsen, "Intertextuality," and Tanner, *The Book of Psalms*, are proponents of this approach. In the first part of her four recommendations for responsible exegesis, Nielsen states, "that responsible exegesis involves not only a responsibility towards the possible intentions of an 'original author' or 'editor', but also a willingness to include meanings that were not intended but which arise in the dialogue with later intertexts" (ibid., 31). Further in the fourth recommendation she says, "that future texts will have consequences for textual interpretation" (ibid., 31). Though Tanner's work involves the psalms, her methodology differs from the present research, as does her working corpus.

51. Certain intertextual readings of a more synchronic nature are performed during the close reading, at a stage when the dates for the psalms in question remain undetermined.

52. For the present study, the primary difficulty involved relates to the successful determination of the sources for a specific text. Although this is relatively straightforward with many other biblical texts, it proves somewhat problematic with respect to the psalms in particular. Eslinger, "Inner-Biblical Exegesis and Allusion," rightfully raises this concern in his criticism of Fishbane, *Biblical Interpretation*. His ultimate response, however, is to abandon any attempt at determining the source in favor of following "the sequence of the Bible's own plot." Sommer, "Exegesis, Allusion and Intertextuality," who ultimately proposed that any difficulties in establishing a borrower–borrowed relationship should be resolved by careful argument as opposed to abandonment, subsequently challenged Eslinger's criticism of Fishbane's work and his proposal to abandon any quest to establish the direction of borrowing between texts. As far as the evidence permits, the present research adopts Sommer's recommendation.

53. This term is in accordance with Sommer's use of "influence and allusion"; see Sommer, *A Prophet*, 6–10. He contrasts this phrase with "intertextuality," a model adopting the synchronic approach.

ing of the psalm in question; second, a determination of the psalm's date; third, isolation of potential sources employed by the psalmist; and fourth, the analysis of inner-biblical allusions. The following paragraphs detail each phase; and each of the latter three stages is dependent upon it predecessor. The close reading, among other things, raises evidence concerning the date; unless the date is determined, it is impossible to establish if a psalmist appropriated material from a source or vice versa. Only after the sources are established can the study analyze how the psalmists reused them.

The close reading examines each psalm as an independent work written with a specific purpose in mind. Within this analysis, the methodology of Weiss plays an essential role.[54] After dividing each psalm into stanzas, the study shows how each stanza contributes to the meaning of the whole work. The analysis similarly conducts a verse-by-verse examination of the psalm revealing how each verse contributes towards the psalmist's overall scheme. During the close reading, understanding the psalm as a unique literary unit takes precedence over analyzing inner-biblical associations. This stage in the analysis concentrates on highlighting poetic features found within each psalm. The identification of repetition plays a key role in this part of the study, focusing on how the psalmist utilizes it in developing the psalm's meaning. In addition, the close reading explores the images adopted by the psalmists, comparing each author's deployment of words and phrases in the psalms with their use in other parts of biblical literature.

The diachronic nature of the present study demands a date for each of the selected psalms in order to determine the direction of borrowing between texts; however, numerous difficulties arise when dating psalms.[55] Perhaps the greatest problem is that very few psalms specifically mention people, events, or places that can be concretely located to a specific time period. To assist in alleviating the inherent complexities in dating, the current research primarily seeks to establish a *relative*

---

54. In addition to Weiss, *The Bible from Within*, the work of Watson, *Classical Hebrew Poetry*, plays an important role in the rhetorical analysis of the psalms in question. Various studies in the field of poetics in biblical narrative have also proved useful to the present study (see for example Sternberg, *Poetics*, and Berlin, *Poetics and Interpretation*).

55. It is interesting to note here that due to the specific difficulties in the dating of psalms, Sommer mostly avoids addressing instances of inner-biblical allusion with regards Isaiah and the psalms.

date for the core[56] of each psalm. The term *relative date* refers to the date of a psalm in relation to the exile and the potential sources employed. Thus, in determining the relative date, the study locates each psalm in the pre-exilic, exilic, or postexilic eras; and if the data permits, a further placement of the psalm is determined within the confines of its relative date. In addition to the psalms, dates must be found for the potential sources, and for the purposes of this study, the consensus of contemporary scholarship provides an adequate resource from which to work.[57] Due to the complicated redactional history of certain psalms, conflicting evidence concerning the date may arise revealing both early and late origins. Recognition of each psalm's earliest stratum is, therefore, important to this study for correctly assessing each work's dependencies.

Where necessary, the study divides evidence for dating the psalms into two tiers, *primary* and *secondary*, in order to resolve potential conflicts in dating evidence. Primary evidence constitutes more conclusive data and overrules secondary evidence when conflicts arise between the two; the primary evidence consists of linguistic data, and datable people, places, and events found in the psalms. A psalm specifically mentioning the divided kingdom, for example, would thus be deemed later than the event itself. Linguistically, the study compares each psalm's words and phrases with lexical elements appearing in Archaic Biblical Hebrew (ABH) corpuses,[58] or Late Biblical Hebrew (LBH) corpuses.[59] Concerning the latter, the study also adopts Hurvitz's approach for identifying LBH style and vocabulary. According to this methodology, words and phrases are only accepted as being late if they comply with three criteria: distribution, whether the lexical item appears in

56. Here I refer to the oldest unified section of the psalm, as opposed to the psalm as a whole, including glosses, verses, and even stanzas that a later redactor may have added.

57. Current scholarly research may prove insufficient when addressing instances in which one of the selected psalms sources material from another one. In such instances, the study attempts to determine the later of the two works involved.

58. Here, I depend on works such as Sáenz-Badillos, *A History*, Freedman, *Pottery, Poetry, and Prophecy*, and Kutscher, *A History*, for identifying ABH.

59. For the determination of LBH vocabulary, syntax, and morphology, I primarily rely on the work of a selection of scholars who have assembled lists of late features: Polzin, *Late Biblical Hebrew*, 123–50, Rooker, *Biblical Hebrew*, Sáenz-Badillos, *A History*, 56–63, Hurvitz, בין לשון לשון, and Kutscher, *A History*; though lexicons such as BDB, and KB also prove useful.

biblical books known to be late; extra-biblical sources, evidence of the item's use in post-exilic, extra-biblical literature; linguistic equivalence, identifying an equivalent word or phrase used in SBH that the later item replaced.[60]

Even though scholars generally consider linguistic dating as an objective methodology for determining the date, it also poses a number of pitfalls.[61] An example of which concerns isolated cases of late features within a large psalm. The identification of an isolated late word or phrase does not necessarily reflect the date of an entire work. For example, instances arise in which later redactors alter earlier texts; thus, the final work appears late, but in reality bears relatively early origins. Throughout the present study, care is taken to avoid this lexical pitfall by considering the broadest range of dating evidence, and refraining from jumping to quixotic assumptions based on a single word or phrase, especially in the longer psalms. The secondary evidence consists of evidence such as datable customs reflected in psalms; correspondence between the psalm's *message* and a political, cultural, or religious reality from the psalmist's era;[62] and thematic similarities between a psalm and

---

60. See Hurvitz, בין לשון לשון, and *Biblical Texts*.

61. It should be noted at this stage that in recent years a debate has arisen among the scholarly community concerning the reliability of dating texts linguistically. In 2008, the publishing of I. Young, R. Rezetko, and M. Ehrensvärd's *Linguistic Dating*, raised doubts over the possibility of any text being dated exclusively on linguistic grounds. In short, they assert that the phenomenon of Late Biblical Hebrew presents an alternative style available to certain authors and does not necessarily reflect chronological development. They explicitly state, "'Early' BH and 'Late' BH, therefore, do not represent different chronological periods in the history of BH, but instead represent coexisting styles of literary Hebrew throughout the biblical period" (see Young, Rezetko, and Ehrensvärd, *Linguistic Dating*, 2:96). In spite of their claims, it is still wise to include a discussion of linguistic evidence for evaluating the direction of borrowing for two reasons: First, no consensus from within the scholarly community has been determined concerning their findings. For example, Joosten's (forthcoming) review challenges the book's broad claims and methods, and Rendsburg's (forthcoming) analysis on late language in Haggai similarly refutes arguments found in Young, Rezetko, and Ehrensvärd's work. Second, the present study's primary intention is not to determine an absolute date for the individual texts, fixing them to a specific era in biblical history according to the diachronic evidence found within.

62. An example of this appears in Psalm 95, which speaks of coming into YHWH's presence in v. 2, and kneeling and bowing before YHWH in v. 6. Verses such as these reflect the probability of an extant temple at the time the psalm was written. Such evidence eliminates the possibility of an exilic date for the psalm because during the exile the temple lay in ruins.

Introduction

other texts with established dates.[63] Though the present study considers secondary evidence less compelling than the primary evidence, the importance of the secondary evidence rises when the psalm in question offers no primary evidence. In such instances, a preponderance of secondary evidence is used to locate the psalm to a specific era.

In determining the sources for the selected psalms, the study first determines the lexical associations, or markers,[64] between each psalm and other locations in biblical literature, irrespective of the direction of borrowing. After determining the associations between texts, it is then possible to establish the direction of borrowing between the psalm and text in question via the pre-established date, and thus establish the sources from which the psalm borrowed.[65]

Three factors play an important role in identifying associations between the psalms and other texts: lexical and semantic correspondences, contextual correspondences and multiple references. For our study, lexical and semantic correspondences constitute the most valuable evidence, and may consist of a rare word or root appearing in a limited number of texts, or a combination of words similarly limited in their distribution. It may also consist of a sequence of semantically corresponding ideas, even if the association lacks precise lexical cor-

---

63. More general guidelines for determining a psalm's date were adopted from Steck, *Old Testament Exegesis*.

64. A concept borrowed from Sommer, *A Prophet*, 11, who in turn adopted it from Ben-Porat, "Poetics of Literary Allusion," referring to an identifiable element or pattern in one text belonging to another independent text. A marker could consist of a poetic line, a sentence or phrase, a motif, a rhythmic pattern, or an idea.

65. Hays, *Echoes of Scripture*, 29–32, in his work on biblical echoes in the writings of Paul, proposes seven heuristics for determining biblical allusion: 1) availability, was the proposed source available to the author; 2) volume, the degree of correspondence between the two texts; 3) recurrence, the frequency with which the author cites from the source; 4) thematic coherence, how well does the allusion fit into the author's argument; 5) historical plausibility, could the author have intended the allusion and could the readers have understood it; 6) history of interpretation, have other readers recognized the claimed allusion; 7) sense, does the proposed reading make sense, and does it shed light on the reading. He additionally advises general satisfaction, with or without lucid confirmation from all of the above criteria. Even though I have not formally adopted these as guiding principles in the current research, they have played a role in determining the sources for the selected psalms. Additionally, Leonard, "Identifying Inner-Biblical Allusions," presents eight similar keys to the identification of inner-biblical allusions, which he then applies to identify the literary sources adopted by the author of Psalm 78.

respondence.⁶⁶ The second criterion, contextual correspondences, analyzes the degree of correspondence between a psalm's use of a word or phrase, and the source's use of the same word or phrase. As an example, if the word צור appears in the psalm and a proposed source within the context of God's provision of water in the wilderness, then the case for the proposed allusion is strengthened. On the other hand, if the same word appears in the context of the exodus in the psalm, but in the context of an individual's deliverance in the proposed source, then the case for an allusion is weakened.⁶⁷ This criterion reinforces instances in which weak lexical correspondences occur. The contextual correspondences are not essential to the determination of associations because in certain instances the lexical correspondence's precision negates the need for further confirmation. Moreover, instances may arise in which an author deliberately borrows from a source in order to transform it into a new setting, consequently creating unharmonious contexts.⁶⁸

The third criterion, multiple references, similarly solidifies lexical and semantic correspondences between texts. If the study reveals a potential marker, and a previous association has already been established between the psalm and this same potential source text, then the likelihood stands that the psalmist borrowed twice from the same location. As a result, the study would consider the *potential* source as a *definite* source.⁶⁹

Even after the study has identified the associations according to the criteria above, a need still exists to eliminate *pseudo allu-*

---

66. Day, "Inner Scriptural Interpretation," exemplifies this method of establishing a marker in his work on Isaiah's dependence on Hosea.

67. This corresponds with Hays, *Echoes of Scripture*, second criterion.

68. An example of this is apparent in Psalm 106:31, which contains the phrase ותחשב לו לצדקה ("and it was considered to him as righteousness"). With the exception of the psalm, the phrase only occurs in Gen 15:6. Though in this instance the lexical association is unquestionable, the contexts in which the verses occur differ significantly (even if they both contain the idea of reward).

69. This principle has been adapted from Jeffrey Tigay's work on literary borrowing. Though his article primarily focuses on parallels between the Bible and ancient Near Eastern literature, and methods of identifying if parallel material recorded in the Bible is borrowed from Canaanite or Mesopotamian literature, he argues that if a biblical text apparently refers to two separate locations in a body of ancient Near Eastern literature, then this strengthens the notion of the biblical author borrowing from the ancient Near Eastern text; see Tigay, "Evaluating Claims." Hays, *Echoes of Scripture*, 30, also recognizes the principle; see his third rule, recurrence.

Introduction

sions—sources creating the *impression* of literary borrowing. The *stock formula*,[70] a common phrase utilized by poets in specific situations, constitutes an example of this phenomenon. The words ידה, יהוה, כי, and טוב (to thank, YHWH, for, and good), which appear in both Ezra 3:11 and Jer 33:11, exemplify the notion; even though lexical agreement exists between the two, and Ezra 3:11 bears the later signature, any notion of Ezra directly borrowing from Jeremiah proves invalid because the phrase additionally appears in a variety of other places. Rather, at some stage in the development of Israelite oral or literary tradition, the phrase became a stock formula for opening songs of praise, and both authors subsequently adopted the formula. As a means of avoiding this methodological snare, the study exercises meticulous care to ensure the markers identified do not represent widely used stock formulas.

Another potential pitfall arises when we consider that certain psalmists worked with sources, either written or oral, that were familiar to them and their contemporaries but not reflected in biblical literature. In instances like these, the differences between the wording of a tradition in the psalm and that in the Torah tradition may simply reflect an *alternate tradition* from which the psalmist borrowed. Though the possibility for such occasions is relatively high, proving the existence of such alternate traditions presents a more complex problem. One method of establishing if such traditions existed is to search for signs of them in other biblical texts. Theoretically, oral traditions employed by the psalmists may be absent from the Torah, but reflected in other biblical books. In addition to other biblical traditions, extra-biblical accounts and ancient Bible translations may also contain traces of alternate traditions. Consequently, the discipline of textual criticism proves useful to the study. In certain instances, a Greek or Aramaic text could reflect an alternate Hebrew rendering that echoes or reproduces an alternate tradition.[71] Additionally, the possibility exists that oral sources and traditions may have been considered illegitimate for the Bible and excluded from MT, but committed to later writings such as

---

70. For more on this concept, see Watson, *Classical Hebrew Poetry*, 74–75, 81, who relates the formation of such phrases to the possible oral origins of Biblical Hebrew poetry.

71. Tov, *Textual Criticism*, 313–50, discusses textual criticism's contribution to literary criticism. Within this discussion, he reveals numerous examples of the Septuagint's vorlage representing texts differing from MT. Such sources could potentially echo, or even recount in full, alternate traditions.

pseudepigraphic texts from the Second Temple period, sectarian texts from Qumran, Ben Sira, the works of Josephus and Philo, and Rabbinic literature.[72] Consequently, such texts are considered important to the present study.

As part of the source analysis, the study briefly attempts to reconstruct the process of selection undertaken by each psalmist when he chose his sources. This part of the study uncovers the potential factors influencing the respective psalmists either to adopt or reject specific aspects of the exodus tradition. Of particular interest here are the rejected aspects of the motif that ostensibly comply with the psalm's central purpose.

Part of the analysis of biblical sources involves identifying the Pentateuchal sources with those of the proposed documents of the Documentary Hypothesis. Because it is not the intention of the present study to redefine these documents in any way, the study relies on the work of earlier scholars to establish which texts are associated to which sources. For the purposes of this research, the study tests each Pentateuchal source by comparing it to the work of two scholars who have independently determined the sources[73] of the Documentary Hypothesis. When the two selected scholars agree, the study accepts the indicated source. In instances where the selected scholars disagree, the study widens its scope to include additional scholars[74] to assist in identifying the source. As an example, if the two selected scholars agree that Exod 14:16 belongs to the P document, then the study adopts this decision. If one scholar claims it is P and the other JE, then additional scholars are introduced to aid the decision process. Due to the difficulties in identifying and separating the J and E sources, they are treated in the present study as a single document.

After all of the aforementioned analytical procedures are completed, the study investigates aspects of inner-biblical allusion and interpretation appearing within the psalm. To accomplish this, the study poses a series of questions, such as: what did the psalmist add, what did

72. Rabbinic literature is also consulted throughout the present study since it occasionally sheds useful interpretive light on the selected psalms.

73. The primary works selected for the study are Driver, *An Introduction*, 22–75; and Campbell and O'Brien, *Sources of the Pentateuch*. The later work depends on Noth, *A History*.

74. For the most part, Fohrer, *Introduction*, is referenced in disputed cases, although commentaries such as Tate, *Psalms 51–100*, are occasionally used.

Introduction

he omit, does reading the psalm affect the reading of the source, has the order of events been altered by the psalmist, how does the source affect the meaning of the psalm, does the author employ multiple sources to retell a single event, why has the psalmist added or taken elements away from his source's tradition? When analyzing the allusions, unlike the close reading, a greater emphasis falls on the source text. The close reading understands each psalm as an independent entity with its own unique purpose; however, when examining the allusions, the psalm's meaning is compared with the meaning of the source.

The primary aim of analyzing the juxtaposition of the exodus psalms is to uncover interpretive strategies the redactors of the Psalter may have implemented.[75] Methodologically, the first task is to isolate common words or phrases appearing in neighboring psalms. Obviously, certain words, like prepositions, frequently appear throughout the Psalter, and do not indicate a purposeful relationship. Other words, however, may only appear a limited number of times in the Psalter. In such instances, the likelihood exists that such words played an important role in the arranger's rationale for positioning the psalms. After identifying common key words and phrases between psalms, the study analyzes how each of the respective psalmists utilizes them.[76] When this is completed, the study attempts to uncover interpretative rationale for the positioning of the psalms. A slightly higher degree of conjecture and subjectivity enters into the discussion at this point, since ultimately no living or written witnesses survive that explain the redactor's thought processes as he worked.

SCOPE AND STRUCTURE

Scope

Since the number of selected psalms still constitutes a relatively large body of material, the study further narrows the scope of the proposed analysis. Within the close reading section, though a thorough analysis

---

75. The present study does not claim that the editors and redactors employed all of the potential strategies raised therein.

76. Ideally, the work on juxtaposition would not be complete without an exhaustive list of all common words and phrases appearing between neighboring psalms, along with a discussion on their relevance. Unfortunately, however, due to space restrictions, I have omitted such material and only opted to discuss the more obvious common words and phrases.

is performed, the study limits itself to focusing on poetics that directly contribute to the psalm's meaning. Consequently, it overlooks issues pertaining to formal poetic features, such as meter, and ballast variants.[77] Concerning the dating, as previously mentioned, the objective in the present study is to discover the relative date[78] of each work, and as a result avoids any attempts to determine an absolute composition date for each psalm.

The primary goal for the determination of sources is to establish the biblical texts employed by the psalmists in their retelling of the exodus. In a number of instances, the selected psalms may contain allusions to texts other that those related to the exodus narrative.[79] Even though these cases present interesting opportunities for investigating intertextual relationships, this study limits itself to determining sources for the exodus motif alone. This restriction bears implications for analysis of Pentateuchal traditions relating to the Documentary Hypothesis because only those relating to the exodus tradition are identified, thus limiting the breadth of data. On the whole, it must be made clear from the outset that due to space restrictions the discussions on the relationships between individual psalms and Pentateuchal sources has been restricted. Occasionally, during the close reading, however, the study does pursue the relationships between the psalm and other biblical texts. Another interesting area, overlapping the work on sources, concerns the relationships between the selected psalms and myths from the ancient Near East. At various points in the research, associations arise in which certain motifs from Ugaritic and Mesopotamian literature echo in the selected psalms.[80] Such cases are not analyzed to any great length in the present study.

Regarding the sections on allusions and juxtaposition, two more constraints need mentioning. The former section limits itself to discussing the connections between the exodus motif as it appears in the psalm and its appearance in the proposed source. Because the present

---

77. For more on these topics see Watson, *Classical Hebrew Poetry*, 87–143, 344–48.

78. See pages 11–12 for a definition of this term.

79. Psalm 105, for example, bears obvious associations with the patriarchal narratives and episodes from Joseph's life. Such instances, though intriguing, fail to fall within the scope of the present study.

80. An example of this phenomenon occurs in Psalm 106's portrayal of YHWH splitting the sea by rebuking it; see close reading for Ps 106:9.

Introduction

study relies on diachronic methodology, establishing how the psalmists use their sources, it avoids investigating the relationships between the psalms and later texts that may have appropriated material from them.[81] The study, however, in certain instances, does briefly discuss alternate traditions relating to the exodus motif identified in the section on sources, comparing them with the Torah. With respect to the analysis on juxtaposition, the primary concern for the present study is for the close[82] relationships between individual psalms. Even though the psalms themselves may indeed contribute to much larger arrangement strategies, such strategies do not constitute the primary objectives here.

Structure

The present study contains four chapters and a concluding section, where each chapter corresponds with one of the selected psalms: 105, 106, 135, and 136. For the sake of simplicity, the psalms are ordered according to their appearance in the Hebrew Bible. Each chapter is subsequently divided into seven sections. First a short section discusses the structure of the psalm. Due to the nature of the aforementioned psalms, subject matter constitutes the primary criterion for dividing each composition. Because most of the selected psalms retell the exodus account, points at which changes occur in time, space, or speaker form natural places for dividing the work. In addition to this, other formal elements are considered, e.g., structural markers such as refrains and repetition. The close reading, section two, performs a verse-by-verse analysis of the work in question and constitutes a significant part of the research. At this stage of the proceedings, the study concentrates on a poetic analysis of the psalm and devotes particular attention to repetition, images, and associations that verses may have with other texts in biblical literature. Attention is devoted to revealing how each verse contributes to the meaning of the psalm. By way of conclusion, section three ties in the main elements of the close reading and structure to define a primary purpose for the psalm under investigation. This section also attempts to

---

81. An example of this arises with 1 Chronicles 16's probable reuse of Psalm 105; see Dirksen, *1 Chronicles*, and Klein, *1 Chronicles*. For more on the relationship between the two works, see Butler, "A Forgotten Passage," and Hill, "Patchwork Poetry."

82. Here I am referring to the immediate neighbours of each psalm.

reveal how the psalm's important themes contribute to furthering the main purpose.⁸³

After the meaning is established, sections on dating and sources are presented respectively. The date, as mentioned earlier, is primarily ascertained via the identification of LBH within each psalm, although other means are also employed. Upon completion of this stage, the study suggests a plausible relative date for the psalm. Only upon successful completion of determining a relative date for the psalm can the sources be established. For the most part, the discussion on the sources focuses on clarifying instances in which multiple possibilities arise concerning a psalm's source. Cases in which the lexical associations are easily identified appear in the appendices and consequently not discussed at length. The final objective in this section is to crystallize a list of potential sources, biblical and alternate, employed by the psalm. In certain instances, it may not be possible to identify unambiguously a verse's specific source, when cases like these arise, the study does not pursue such verses in its analysis of allusions. An important underlying assumption concerning this part of the analysis is that psalms written after the exile are generally considered to postdate Torah traditions. After identifying the Pentateuchal sources, the study associates them with their respective documents according to those defined in the Documentary Hypothesis (JE, P, and D).

With the sources established, the section on allusions further questions the relationships between the psalm and its sources. A detailed look at the two contexts is performed here, and the study investigates how the psalmist has removed, added, or reordered his source material to conform to the meaning and strategy of his composition.

The final section on juxtaposition adopts a wider view of each composition, evaluating the relationships between the psalms and their neighbors. The first task in this section is to identify any possible signs of editorial activity in the arrangement of the psalms, as determined via lexical similarities between juxtaposed psalms. The section then analyses the semantic relationships between the psalms—those apparent from common words, and those created from the key themes

---

83. The underlying assumption for this section is that each psalm was composed with a single primary intention by the author. Even though certain psalms may have experienced varying degrees of redaction, the works as they appear in MT still display a single purpose in writing.

Introduction

of juxtaposed works. In this second phase, the primary goals is to determine how the meaning of the psalm changes from being read as a single independent work, to its meaning and function as part of a larger selection of compositions.

The conclusions at the end of the study directly return to the questions posed in this introduction, i.e., how the psalmists of exodus psalms used their sources, and how the editors of the Psalter arranged them. To address these matters, the conclusions discuss the sources employed by the psalmists, the arrangement of these sources in their respective works, and the motivations the psalmists had to alter or preserve data from their source texts. Following this, more general conclusions are drawn from the study concerning the psalmists' relationship to the exodus tradition, and their use of the motif.

2

Remember and Obey
Psalm 105

Psalm 105, a hymn of praise, recounts events from Israelite history from the days of the patriarchs to the fulfillment of God's promise to Abraham to give his descendants the land of Canaan. The primary concern of the psalm centers on the promise and its fulfillment. Throughout the psalm YHWH's faithfulness to his word constantly recurs, and at the end, the psalmist indicates the response YHWH desires from Israel: obedience to his laws. Two factors separating Psalm 105 from the other selected psalms are its inclusion of events from the lives of Abraham and Joseph. Particularly notable amid the psalm's recollection of events is the decidedly positive light shed on all that transpires concerning Israel. Unlike other similar works, such as Ps 106, instances of Israel's rebellious behavior are avoided, and the nation's relationship with God is idealistically portrayed at all times.[1]

STRUCTURE

Most scholars agree on Psalm 105's fundamental structure, but disagree on the precise details of each stanza. For the purposes of this study, the psalm may be divided as follows:

---

1. At this point, it is worth noting that 1 Chr 16:8–22 reuses Ps 105:1–15 with only a few alterations. The majority of the changes are stylistic and orthographic (e.g., פיו פיהו ["his mouth," 1 Chr 16:12 vs. Ps 105:5], עלילותיו עלילתיו ["his deeds," 1 Chr 16:8 vs. Ps 105:1], ישחק יצחק ["Isaac," 1 Chr 16:16 vs. Ps 105:9]). On at least three occasions (vv. 6, 8, and 12), however, the emendations could be described as interpretive. Even though these instances are discussed in the close reading of the psalm, they are confined to footnotes because they detail ways in which the Chronicler has adapted the psalm, as opposed to our psalmist adapting a source.

Remember and Obey

1. Summons to worship YHWH in light of his deeds (vv. 1–7)
2. YHWH's promise of land to Abraham recalled (vv. 8–11)
3. YHWH's protective intervention in the lives of the patriarchs (vv. 12–15)
4. The preservation of the promise in Joseph's life (vv. 16–22)
5. Israel's multiplication, oppression, and deliverance from Egypt (vv. 23–36)
    A. Israel multiplies and are subsequently oppressed by Egypt (vv. 23–25)
    B. YHWH delivers his people via plagues (vv. 26–36)
6. The desert wandering and fulfillment of the promise (vv. 37–45)
    A. YHWH's provision in the wilderness (vv. 37–41)
    B. Recollection and fulfillment of the promise (vv. 42–44)
    C. Injunction to obey in light of all YHWH has done (v. 45)

The first stanza of the psalm opens with an exhortation to praise YHWH for his deeds, with particular regard for those judgments he has wrought with his mouth. In total, four phrases appear in the opening section that portray his mighty acts: נפלאות ("wonderful deeds," vv. 2, 5), עלילות ("his deeds," v. 1), משפט ("judgment," vv. 5, 7) and מופת ("mighty acts," v. 5). No geographical limitations apply to these deeds; they are for proclamation among peoples (v. 1) and they fill the earth (v. 7). Remembrance of YHWH's mighty acts constitutes the primary theme of the psalm: from beginning to end, it recalls all he did for his people from the promise to Abraham to its fulfillment. The final two verses of the opening stanza highlight those whom the psalmist addresses, creating an intimate link between the patriarchs, and those of the psalmist's generation. Two notable stylistic features within the opening, which separate it from the remainder of the psalm, are the concentration of imperative forms and the frequent use of the divine name, which scarcely occurs in the psalm's remaining verses.

Section two (8–11) is marked by a shift in temporal focus, as the psalmist begins addressing the promise God made to the Patriarchs and his faithfulness to it. This promise dominates the remainder of the psalm, which further details its fulfillment. After God promises the land to Abraham, the remainder of the psalm is dedicated to its fulfillment. Each of the subsequent sections depicts instances in which a danger threatens the bearers of the promise, Abraham or his offspring, consequently endangering its fulfillment. An inclusion demarks the first three verses of the section, which highlights the eternal nature of the promise, and the psalmist closes the stanza citing words YHWH originally used to establish it (v. 11).

Each of the next four sections features the following components: a setting, characters introduced (except God, who is always present), a conflict threatening the recipients of the promise, and resolution of the conflict through God's intervention. A change in subject clearly defines each section. The first of these sections, stanza three (vv. 12–15), recalls the patriarchs' early sojourn in the land of Canaan. Although the psalm only dedicates four verses to this period, it is the only treatment of the patriarchs' lives found in the selected psalms. The threat of being abused and killed by the inhabitants of Canaan constitutes the danger presented within the stanza. In response to the danger, God intervenes with words of rebuke in defense of his chosen ones. His intervention forms the climax of each literary-historical account.

After the patriarchal wanderings, the psalmist recounts the story of Joseph, which is also unique among the selected psalms. The main events recalled are Joseph's sale into slavery, his time in prison, and subsequent promotion to being Pharaoh's second-in-command. The psalmist portrays all of these events with YHWH in total control of all that transpires. He is directly responsible for causing a famine, sending Joseph to prepare the way for his family, and releasing Joseph from prison. Joseph's imprisonment constitutes the threat to the promise in this section: If he dies then his family, the bearers of the promise, perish from starvation in Canaan. YHWH intervenes, resolving the threat by removing Joseph from prison and appointing him ruler over Egypt, second only to Pharaoh.

The fifth stanza (vv. 23–36) constitutes the longest and most detailed account of YHWH's intervention for the sake of his promise. Israel's miraculous multiplication is first mentioned in vv. 23–24, followed by God turning the hearts of the Egyptians against his people (v. 25), which represents the threat to the promise. God's intervention to deliver Israel consists of nine verses and represents the longest account of deliverance in the psalm. Despite the introduction of Moses and

Aaron as the human protagonists in this section, YHWH alone is responsible for the plagues. His mighty acts (מופתים), initially mentioned in the first stanza, links the two sections.

The sixth and final stanza (vv. 37–45) primarily depicts the Israelites' journey through the desert to inherit the promised land. The desert wanderings begin with the Israelites leaving Egypt with spoil from their captors. Here, death by hunger and thirst constitutes the primary threat to their lives. YHWH resolves the danger in the wilderness by guiding his people and providing them with food and water. Eventually, Abraham's descendants receive the land promised to their founding forefather. The recollection of the promise in v. 42 creates a link to the second stanza, along with the words אברהם, ארץ, and חק (Abraham, land, and law). Verse 45, the psalm's concluding verse, breaks away from reciting the literary-historical account to provide a rationale for the entire work.[2]

CLOSE READING

הוֹדוּ לַיהוָה קִרְאוּ בִּשְׁמוֹ הוֹדִיעוּ בָעַמִּים עֲלִילוֹתָיו[1]

Proclaim thanks to YHWH, call out his name, make known among the nations his deeds

The psalm opens with an exhortation to declare thanksgiving to YHWH, הודו ליהוה ("proclaim thanks to YHWH"),[3] which constitutes one of the features defining it as a hymn of praise. Verse one employs three imperatives to exhort the listeners to praise God, קראו, הודיעו, הודו ("make known," "call out," "proclaim thanks"),[4] each being a verb expressing vocal declaration.[5] On one hand, קראו בשמו ("call out his name") suggests invoking God and being involved with him in an act of

---

2. See close reading for v. 45.

3. The Septuagint moves "Hallelujah" from the end of Psalm 104 to the beginning of Psalm 105, creating a series of "Hallelujah" psalms that all begin with this exhortation.

4. In a similar way, Psalm 95 begins with numerous cohortatives encouraging the audience to offer praise.

5. For להודות as a verb of vocal declaration, see BDB 986, and Josh 7:19, which employ the noun תודה from the same root.

From Bards to Biblical Exegetes

worship.[6] On the other hand, this same expression bears the nuance of declaring and speaking out his name.

Within the present context, שם (name) is best understood as a reference to God's reputation. In Gen 11:4, the people of Shinar sought a reputation (שם) for themselves by attempting to accomplish something that would make them famous. Just as they sought to gain this reputation by building a tower (see also Gen 12:2; Josh 7:9), YHWH's fame in this psalm stems from *his* deeds, which are for declaration among the nations (הודיעו בעמים עלילותיו). The second colon introduces the idea of YHWH's jurisdiction over other nations besides Israel, a theme reflected numerous times in the remainder of the psalm.

God's mighty deeds, another central theme in this psalm, are represented in this verse by עלילותיו. When used of God, this word frequently refers to miraculous deeds YHWH performs to aid his people, as in Ps 77:12[13] where it parallels פעל (works/actions), another verb of action, וְהָגִיתִי בְכָל־פָּעֳלֶךָ וּבַעֲלִילוֹתֶיךָ אָשִׂיחָה ("I will meditate on all your works and on your deeds I will speak," see also Ps 66:5). The placement of the word at the end of the verse serves as an instance of delayed identification, a poetic device frequently used in this psalm to create suspense and heighten its impact.[7] Overall, the opening words of the psalm have a strong association with those of Isa 12:4, הוֹדוּ לַיהוָה קִרְאוּ בִשְׁמוֹ הוֹדִיעוּ בָעַמִּים עֲלִילֹתָיו ("Proclaim thanks to YHWH call out his name make known among the nations his deeds"), which speaks of a new song that the exiles will sing upon their return to Israel. This link between the two works specifically associates the words of the psalm with the occasion implied in Isaiah, a return from exile.

שִׁירוּ־לוֹ זַמְּרוּ־לוֹ שִׂיחוּ בְּכָל־נִפְלְאוֹתָיו ²

Sing to him sing, make music to him, speak about all his wonderful deeds

The exhortation to praise continues in v. 2, which parallels the opening verse with respect to syntax: Three verbs appear at the start of each verse, each verb is in the third-person imperative, each implies a vocal activity, and God's works constitute the object of each verb. It is possible to understand the repetition in the parallelism as an emphasis on

---

6. The phrase is similarly used in Gen 12:8 and 26:25, when Abraham calls on the name of YHWH after building an altar.

7. See v. 45, for example.

speaking out and declaring God's deeds. Of the verbs used in this verse continue expressing aspects of vocalization, שירו . . . שיחו . . . זמרו (sing . . . speak . . . make music), the first two suggest musical accompaniment and are commonly used interchangeably (see Pss 21:13 [14]; 57:7[8] for שיח as a verb of speaking). Job 7:11 contrasts לא אחשך פי ("I will not restrain my mouth") with שיחו (speak) and אדברה ("speak," see also Judg 5:10 and Prov 6:22).[8] The second half of the verse presents נפלאותיו ("his wonderful deeds") as another synonym for עלילותיו ("his deeds"), or God's deeds (both appear in Ps 78:11[9]); v. 1 employs עלילותיו and the two appear together in Psalm 78:11. The root פלא generally indicates something difficult to understand (see Job 37:5; 42:3) or a task difficult for a man to accomplish (see Deut 17:8). In the context of this psalm, נפלאות refers to the unique works YHWH has wrought on behalf of his people. In Psalm 78, this word frequently refers to the plagues sent against the Egyptians to facilitate the Israelites' deliverance (see also Exod 3:20; Ps 106:22).

3 הִתְהַלְלוּ בְּשֵׁם קָדְשׁוֹ יִשְׂמַח לֵב מְבַקְשֵׁי יְהוָה

Praise his holy name; let the seekers of YHWH rejoice

Verbal declaration continues in v. 3 with התהללו, meaning "to boast on the grounds of" or "to speak greatly of" (Ps 34:2 [3]), and further highlights the theme of proclamation as the last in a series of seven imperatives forming a perfect call to praise. YHWH's reputation, originally mentioned in v. 1, is further described here as holy שם קדשו ("his holy name") that is, unique and set apart from all others (see Gen 2:3). Additionally, שם marks the end of an inclusion that begins with v. 1, and which emphasizes the declaration of God's name. Each verb found within the inclusion constitutes an imperative of declaration. The first non-imperative verbal form appears in the second colon, where the psalmist's audience is introduced for the first time as מבקשי יהוה ("seekers of YHWH"). In all likelihood, this phrase is a reference to the Israelites (see Ps 69:6 [7]), or more specifically, to godly Israelites

---

8. The preposition ל could be rendered as "about," resulting in "Sing about him," referring to the acts he has performed. See Ps 98:1 for this understanding, as well as BDB 514.

9. Though Psalm 78 is not an integral part of the present study, it is frequently referenced in the present work because of their many similarities.

(see Zeph 1:6). The wish for happiness, ישמח לב (may he rejoice), for those who seek YHWH is echoed in Ps 70:4 [5], and contrasts with the string of imperatives previously mentioned. The change in mood corresponds with a change in subject to מבקשי יהוה ("seekers of YHWH"), and introduces a new theme, seeking YHWH, which is highlighted by the root בקש.

דִּרְשׁוּ יְהוָה וְעֻזּוֹ בַּקְּשׁוּ פָנָיו תָּמִיד ⁴

Seek YHWH and his strength, seek his face always

Verse 4 continues the change in direction from praising to seeking. Each colon in v. 4 parallels v. 3b; both contain verbs of seeking and YHWH's name (or a reference to him). Together they focus the attention of the listeners on him. The two synonymous phrases, דרשו and בקשו, both emphasize the action of seeking;¹⁰ they frequently appear in parallel (see Isa 65:1; Ps 24:6; Prov 11:27) and in exhortations to worship (see Deut 4:29; Hos 3:5, 7:10; Jer 50:4). As the verb's object, עזו ¹¹ signifies God's presence, understandable from its parallel with פניו, where his face equates to his presence.¹² An alternative way of rendering עזו is "God's strength to save," based on Exod 15:13, נָחִיתָ בְחַסְדְּךָ עַם־זוּ גָּאָלְתָּ נֵהַלְתָּ בְעָזְךָ אֶל־נְוֵה קָדְשֶׁךָ ("You led in your mercy the people you redeemed, you guided them with your strength unto your holy dwelling place," see also Pss 21:2; 66:3; 74:13). Interpreting it this way suits the psalm's context because the following sections speak of YHWH's great power in deliverance. The modifier תמיד functions both adverbially, meaning "continually," explaining how the listeners seek his presence, and adjectively, detailing the nature of God's presence, which is eternal.¹³ This eternal aspect of God's character echoes throughout the body of the psalm because it recounts God's endless faithfulness throughout a number of generations.

---

10. The Septuagint translates both verbs as ζητησατε ("to seek"), indicating they are synonymous in this context.

11. Here, the Septuagint reads an imperative form, which may have been influenced by the multiple imperatives found in vv. 1–7.

12. In addition to its use in Ps 78:61, וַיִּתֵּן לַשְּׁבִי עֻזּוֹ וְתִפְאַרְתּוֹ בְיַד־צָר ("And gave up his strength to captivity, his glory into the hand of the adversary."), where it signifies the Ark, the place where YHWH was present among the Israelites

13. Similar instances in which תמיד modifies that which immediately precedes it appear in Nah 3:19 and Ps 71:6; see Dahood, *Psalms III*, 52.

Remember and Obey

⁵ זִכְרוּ נִפְלְאוֹתָיו אֲשֶׁר־עָשָׂה מֹפְתָיו וּמִשְׁפְּטֵי־פִיו

Remember the wonderful deeds that he has done, his mighty acts and the judgments of his mouth

After imploring the listeners to seek God's presence, the psalmist now explains how to achieve it: by remembering his deeds. Verse 5 resumes the theme of YHWH's mighty deeds that began in vv. 1–2. The psalmist replaces verbs of seeking in the previous two verses with a verb denoting remembrance. In addition to remembering, זכר usually signifies acting in accordance with what one has remembered. Nehemiah 4:14 [8], אֶת־אֲדֹנָי הַגָּדוֹל וְהַנּוֹרָא זְכֹרוּ וְהִלָּחֲמוּ עַל־אֲחֵיכֶם בְּנֵיכֶם וּבְנֹתֵיכֶם נְשֵׁיכֶם וּבָתֵּיכֶם, ("Remember the Lord, great and fearsome, and fight for your brothers, your sons and your daughters and your wives and your houses") exhorts the exiles not only to remember and think about the Lord, but to let their recollections and thoughts be an incentive to fight. Similarly, Ps 78:42 chastises Israel for not remembering God's power, which is not to say they never reflected on his acts, but that they failed to act accordingly. In Ps 105, the appropriate consequence of remembering appears later in the psalm. Earlier in v. 2 the listeners are exhorted to sing and speak of God's magnificent deeds (נפלאות); it is only logical that here they are called upon to remember them. The word corresponding to נפלאות in the second colon is מפתיו ("his mighty acts"), which similarly often recalls the tradition of the plagues in Exodus.[14]

In the present context, the word משפט signifies deeds of judgment (see Isa 26:9; Jer 48:21; Ezek 39:21; Ps 7:6 [7]), referring to those instances in which YHWH intervenes to administer punishment or reward. With this understanding, משפטי פיו describes verbal acts of judgment, even though the phrase is unique in the Bible. By maintaining the words of MT, God's verbal judgments are emphasized. Such verbal judgments persistently recur throughout the psalm.[15]

⁶ זֶרַע אַבְרָהָם עַבְדּוֹ בְּנֵי יַעֲקֹב בְּחִירָיו

Seed of Abraham his servant, the sons of Jacob his chosen ones

---

14. See Exod 4:21; 7:3; 7:9; 11:9; and 11:10.
15. See vv. 8, 11, 15, 16, 19, 27, 28, 31, 34, and 42.

In v. 6, focus switches from the works YHWH has done to the psalm's audience and their relationship with him. The internal parallelism here dwells on the relationship between the patriarchs and the audience, thus strengthening the connection between the two. Here, the psalmist draws a direct correlation between his audience and Abraham, a relationship important to his overall purposes. The presence of Abraham[16] in this psalm separates it from the other historiographic psalms, which neither mention him nor echoes events in his life. Abraham's seed, זרע אברהם in this verse, naturally refers to the nation of Israel, paralleling בני יעקב ("sons of Jacob," see also Jer 33:26). The psalm accentuates Israel's unique status in various ways. In this verse, the emphasis manifests itself in the term בחיריו[17] ("his chosen ones," see also vv. 26 and 43), which together with עבדו ("his servant"), constitutes a word pair frequently found in Isaiah, where it similarly relates Israel to the patriarchs, וְעַתָּה שְׁמַע יַעֲקֹב עַבְדִּי וְיִשְׂרָאֵל בָּחַרְתִּי בוֹ ("And now hear O Jacob my servant, and Israel whom I have chosen," see Isa 44:1; 41:8; 45:4)[18].

הוּא יְהוָה אֱלֹהֵינוּ בְּכָל־הָאָרֶץ מִשְׁפָּטָיו 7

He is YHWH our God, in all the earth are his judgments

The psalmist now changes his perspective and identifies himself with his listeners via the third-person common plural pronoun אלהינו, which additionally establishes an intimate relationship between God and his people. His judgments, משפטיו, are further detailed in this verse. Previously they were verbal (v. 5), but now the psalmist states they are not limited by geographical boundaries, but exist in all the world (בכל הארץ). This alludes to the title Abraham gave to God when he mediated on Lot's behalf in Gen 18:25, הֲשֹׁפֵט כָּל־הָאָרֶץ לֹא יַעֲשֶׂה מִשְׁפָּט ("Will not the judge of all the world act justly"). In this context, God indeed serves as a judge of the whole earth because he executes his judgment on Sodom and Gomorrah. The same idea of God's deeds transcending

---

16. The Chronicler in 1 Chr 8:18 changes the reference here from Abraham to Israel. The most probable reason for this is to focus more attention onto his audience. Such a redirection of focus from the past to the chronicler's generation is similarly reflected in his changes to Ps 105:8, 12; see below.

17. See also 2 Sam 21:6 where it specifically describes someone that God has chosen.

18. This similarity in phrasing indicates a possible literary connection between Psalm 105 and Deutero-Isaiah.

Remember and Obey

national boundaries creates an inclusion for the opening stanza since v. 1 states that his deeds should be proclaimed to all peoples.

One of the main features found in vv. 1–7 is the intense repetition of the divine name. Four of its five occurrences in the psalm appear in v. 7 alone. Consequently, the psalmist establishes YHWH as the main subject for the remainder of psalm. After the opening section, the psalm generally refers to YHWH implicitly, via pronouns and third-person masculine singular verbs.[19]

8 זָכַר לְעוֹלָם בְּרִיתוֹ דָּבָר צִוָּה לְאֶלֶף דּוֹר

He remembers forever his covenant, the promise he determined for a thousand generations

Verse 8 begins a new section that is distinguished by a change in theme and time. The psalm now begins to focus on a covenant, and the temporal framework shifts to the past. In this section, the psalmist initiates that which he previously exhorted his audience to do: to proclaim thanks to YHWH, to talk about him, and to remember his deeds. In v. 5, the psalm instructed the Israelites to remember (זכרו) YHWH's mighty acts performed on their behalf; and now it shows how God remembered[20] (זכר) his covenant. The chiastic structure within v. 8 serves as an emphatic opening to the section and highlights through repetition the eternal nature of the covenant: לעולם : בריתו :: דבר : לאלף דור (forever : his covenant :: promise : for a thousand generations). The corresponding terms דבר and ברית here represent the important theme of God's covenant, or promise.[21] Furthermore, we can surmise that דבר further defines ברית not as a two-sided covenant but as a unilateral promise that YHWH alone is obliged to keep, such as that found in Gen 9:16,

---

19. The repeated plural imperatives, concentration of the divine name, reasons for praising him (in this case his wonders), and words of praise such as הודו ("proclaim thanks," v. 1), שירו (sing, v. 2), זמרו (make music, v. 2), and התהללו (praise, v. 3) constitute strong indicators for Gunkel's form-critical category "Hymn of Praise"; see Gunkel and Begrich, *Introduction to Psalms*, 22–34.

20. The chronicler here apparently adds a *wāw* to the word זכר, making the form an imperative addressed to his audience. Instead of God remembering his covenant, as recorded in the psalm, the audience is implored to recall the covenant that God made with them. As mentioned in the close reading for v. 6, this represents the Chronicler's desire to focus more intently on his audience.

21. Even though the term ברית stems from legal terminology, it does not necessarily bear this nuance in the present context.

35

("and) וְהָיְתָה הַקֶּשֶׁת בֶּעָנָן וּרְאִיתִיהָ לִזְכֹּר בְּרִית עוֹלָם בֵּין אֱלֹהִים וּבֵין כָּל־נֶפֶשׁ חַיָּה
when the bow is in the cloud, I will look upon it, to remember the everlasting covenant between God and every living creature"). Additionally, the word דבר bears the meaning "word," or "spoken utterance," alluding to one of the פיו משפטי ("judgments of his mouth") mentioned in v. 5. Thus, the promise mentioned here exemplifies one of YHWH's spoken judgments. Moreover, the God's promise is something that he has determined to fulfill, evidenced by צוה, which serves as a modifier expressing a degree of certainty concerning its accomplishment (see Ps 111:9).²² The deeds mentioned within the psalm continually recall YHWH's determination to fulfill the promise to Abraham.

אֲשֶׁר כָּרַת אֶת־אַבְרָהָם וּשְׁבוּעָתוֹ לְיִשְׂחָק ⁹

*Which he cut with Abraham, and his oath to Isaac*²³

Verse 9 continues by further detailing the covenant introduced in v. 8. The connection between the verses is primarily established by the relative pronoun אשר, and is subsequently strengthened by the breaking up of a composite phrase, כרת ברית ("cut a covenant," cf. Hos 10:4; Ps 89:3 [4]). The psalm specifically identifies the promise mentioned in vv. 8–9 with God's promise to Abraham in Gen 15:18 בַּיּוֹם הַהוּא כָּרַת יְהוָה אֶת־אַבְרָם בְּרִית ("On that day YHWH cut a covenant with Abraham"). In both passages, the particle את does not serve as a direct object marker, but the preposition "with" (see also Gen 6:13; 2 Sam 16:17). Abraham's name previously appeared in v. 6, where it linked the people of Israel with the patriarch. With that link established, its appearance here provides a degree of association between the promise made to the patriarch and the Israelites. Continuing to detail the covenant, the second colon recalls Gen 26:3, וַהֲקִמֹתִי אֶת־הַשְּׁבֻעָה אֲשֶׁר נִשְׁבַּעְתִּי לְאַבְרָהָם אָבִיךָ ("and I will establish the oath which I swore to Abraham your father") when

---

22. The only other place אלף דור occurs in the Bible is Deut 7:9, where it describes God's faithfulness to his covenant, although the covenant mentioned in Deuteronomy differs

23. This variation of the word יצחק stems from the phonetic similarity between צ and שׂ; see Kutscher, מילים ותולדותיהם, 104. In addition to its appearance here, it also appears in Jer 33:26; Amos 7:9, 16. One can be sure that it does not represent a diachronic alteration because when 1 Chr 16:16 reuses Ps 105:10 it employs the expected form יצחק, which occurs in both pre-exilic and postexilic texts Consequently, the change in representation probably represents a dialectal variant.

God reaffirms to Isaac the promise he originally made with Abraham. Appearing in this colon is a third synonym for the promise, שבועתו, meaning "oath" (see Deut 7:8; Jer 11:5), a word that further reinforces the connection between vv. 8–9.[24]

וַיַּעֲמִידֶהָ לְיַעֲקֹב לְחֹק לְיִשְׂרָאֵל בְּרִית עוֹלָם [10]

He established it for Jacob as an ordinance,
for Israel an everlasting covenant

Continuing to describe the promise, v. 10 recalls events in Gen 28:13 הָאָרֶץ אֲשֶׁר אַתָּה שֹׁכֵב עָלֶיהָ לְךָ אֶתְּנֶנָּה וּלְזַרְעֶךָ ("The land on which you are lying I will give to you and to your seed") when God appears to Jacob to reaffirm the oath he originally made to Abraham. By separating the patriarchs' names, Abraham, Isaac, and Jacob, which normally appear together, (see Num 32:11; Deut 34:4; 2 Kgs 13:23), the psalmist creates a stronger link with the previous verse. In the present stanza, חק refers to the covenant with Abraham, which was first introduced in v. 8.[25] Within the present context, ישראל refers to the nation of Israel because in vv. 10–11, each colon represents a separate generation in which the promise is preserved (ישראל . . . יעקב . . . ישחק . . . אברהם ["Abraham . . . Isaac . . . Jacob . . . Israel"]), from the patriarch Abraham via Isaac and Jacob to the people of Israel. In developing the relationship from the patriarch to the people, the psalm recalls v. 6, which also links the two entities. Moreover, the continuum represented here throughout the years exemplifies the promise's eternal nature, since YHWH preserved the promise from generation to generation. Reflecting that eternal nature is the last phrase of the verse, ברית עולם ("eternal covenant") that creates an inclusion with עולם בריתו ("his covenant forever") at the start of v. 8. Within this envelope, the promise's durability is demonstrated. At this stage, it is worth noting that the entire burden of maintaining the promise falls on YHWH; he must prove faithful in remembering the promise, and the people have no active role to play.

---

24. The two words שבועה and דבר appear synonymously in Num 30:3.

25. See also Josh 24:25 for a similar association between חק (law) and ברית (covenant).

From Bards to Biblical Exegetes

¹¹ לֵאמֹר לְךָ אֶתֵּן אֶת־אֶרֶץ־כְּנָעַן חֶבֶל נַחֲלַתְכֶם

Saying: "to you I will give the land of Canaan as a territory for your inheritance"[26]

After speaking generally about the promise, the psalmist now quotes the promise itself, alluding to Gen 15:18 לֵאמֹר לְזַרְעֲךָ נָתַתִּי אֶת־הָאָרֶץ הַזֹּאת ("saying, 'to your seed I will give this land'"). Although the psalmist probably had numerous texts before him that mention God's promise to Abraham, he specifically focuses on one aspect of the promise, the land, as opposed to fame and progeny. In doing so, he introduces the central concern for the psalm: YHWH's promise to give Abraham's descendants the land of Canaan. The psalmist's use of לאמר (saying) is slightly out of character for the Psalter because direct quotes within the Psalter are generally unmarked (see v. 15);[27] thus, it would appear the psalmist is pointing the reader to Gen 15:18. Although YHWH specifically made the promise to Abraham, its realization belongs to Abraham's descendants, including the psalmist's contemporaries. The verse's wording reflects this situation: The promise is phrased in the singular to Abraham, לך, but the fulfillment appears in the plural, נחלתכם,[28] encompassing the psalmist's contemporary audience. Appearing for the second time in the psalm is ארץ, which here only refers to the land of Canaan, as opposed to the whole earth in v. 7. The land of Canaan is bestowed to Abraham's descendants as a נחלה, an inheritance passed down from generation to generation, as Num 36:7 implies: וְלֹא־תִסֹּב נַחֲלָה לִבְנֵי יִשְׂרָאֵל מִמַּטֶּה אֶל־מַטֶּה כִּי אִישׁ בְּנַחֲלַת מַטֵּה אֲבֹתָיו יִדְבְּקוּ בְּנֵי יִשְׂרָאֵל ("So no inheritance of the sons of Israel shall be transferred from tribe to tribe, but the sons of Israel shall each hold to the inheritance of the tribe of his fathers"; see also Job 42:15). The act of giving land as an inheritance further exemplifies God's judgments going out into all the earth (בכל הארץ משפטיו), as mentioned in v. 7. YHWH's ability to be-

---

26. An alternative reading of this verse is possible by moving the pause to ארץ, rendering "I will give the land, Canaan as an everlasting possession," breaking the composite phrase ארץ כנען ("the land of Canaan") and creating a relationship in which the second colon explains the first.

27. See Meier, *Speaking of Speaking*, 33–50.

28. This is a common poetic device used to relieve monotony; see Dahood, *Psalms III*, 54, and Berlin, *Dynamics*, 35–50.

stow the land of one nation to another exemplifies his jurisdiction over the whole earth.

Section two closes here, establishing God's eternal covenant with Abraham as the main theme. Verse 10 explicitly states the eternal nature of the covenant by referring to it as a ברית עולם. The psalm further illustrates this fact in its remaining verses, which detail how the covenant began with Abraham and continues throughout the generations of his offspring. Also featured is more detail concerning how YHWH has fulfilled his promise.

בִּהְיוֹתָם מְתֵי מִסְפָּר כִּמְעַט וְגָרִים בָּהּ 12

When they were few in number, sparse and sojourners in it (the land)

Verse 12 opens a new section in the psalm with the central emphasis moving away from a description of the promise to the way in which YHWH has fulfilled it. In each of the following stanzas, it is possible to identify three entities: God, his chosen one(s), and a threat to the promise. God ultimately dominates and controls all situations and circumstances. The psalm portrays the chosen one(s) as flat characters[29] who are unable to save themselves,[30] and the threat usually manifests itself in the form of other nations, but also appears as the forces of creation. Verse 12 recalls when the patriarchs were small in number,[31] מתי מספר, and lived in the land of Canaan. Literally, the phrase means "small number," although the word מספר by itself may also simply be translated as "few" (see Isa 10:19).[32] Moreover, מתי מספר recalls Gen 34:30, וַאֲנִי מְתֵי מִסְפָּר וְנֶאֶסְפוּ עָלַי וְהִכּוּנִי (I am small in number, they will gather against me and strike me) which is one of the few times this expression

---

29. Although Psalm 105 is a poetic text, vv. 12–41 lend themselves well to a narrative analysis; consequently, terms from this sphere of study may be applied. The *flat* character is described in Berlin, *Poetics and Interpretation*, 23–41, and Ska, *Our Fathers*, 83–94.

30. This contrasts their role in the Torah where they speak, think, and act.

31. As with the Chronicler's change in Ps 105:6, here too it would appear that the psalmist seeks to switch focus from past generations to his audience. He achieves this by altering the suffix on בהיותם from the third-person plural to the second-person plural (בהיותכם).

32. The word can also refer to an individual or people in exile, as Ezra 2:2 suggests (see BDB 709), which could constitute a reflection of the psalmist's reality.

appears in the Torah.³³ Moreover, in Genesis it depicts an incident in which the inhabitants of Canaan threaten Jacob and his family. After his sons slay the inhabitants of Shechem, Jacob fears that the local people will hear about it and attack him and his family in retribution because they were relatively *few in number*. The notion of a threat fits well into the context of the psalm since the threat posed to Jacob also endangers the promise's fulfillment.

The Psalm portrays the patriarchs here as גרים, or sojourners without rights in a land.³⁴ By choosing this word, the psalmist emphasizes that the promise remained unfulfilled. The patriarchs begin in Canaan as journeymen and then move to Egypt before their offspring returns to Canaan. Only at this final stage, when the promise is fulfilled are they no longer גרים. The word also recalls Gen 23:4, גֵּר־וְתוֹשָׁב אָנֹכִי עִמָּכֶם ("I am a sojourner and an alien among you")³⁵ in which Abraham describes himself as a sojourner when he purchases a plot of land to bury Sarah. At this stage in his life, he has wandered from place to place with the promise of land still awaiting fulfillment. The pronoun בה in this verse refers to כנען (Canaan), previously mentioned in v. 11; it also determines the geographical starting point of the patriarchs. No mention is made of Abraham's sojourn from Ur because the author apparently desires to have the promise's origin and fulfillment in the same location, Canaan.

¹³ וַיִּתְהַלְּכוּ מִגּוֹי אֶל־גּוֹי מִמַּמְלָכָה אֶל־עַם אַחֵר

They walked about from nation to nation, from kingdom to another people

As a consequence of being גרים, or "sojourners," the patriarchs traveled from people to people. The verb התהלכו, meaning to wander about with no specific destination (see Ps 82:5; Esth 2:11), complements the patriarchal status of the גרים (sojourners), because they had not yet established a country of residence. Verse 13 recalls Gen 13:17, קוּם הִתְהַלֵּךְ בָּאָרֶץ לְאָרְכָּהּ וּלְרָחְבָּהּ כִּי לְךָ אֶתְּנֶנָּה ("Arise and walk about the land, its length and breadth, for I am giving it to you"), which speaks of God's command to Abraham to walk about the land and re-emphasizes God's

---

33. Outside of the verse quoted, the phrase never appears in connection with the patriarchs. Its only other occurrences are in Deut 4:27 and 33:6.

34. See BDB 157 and Judg 17:7–9.

35. Here, the related noun גֵּר, or "stranger," is used.

Remember and Obey

promise to give it to him.³⁶ Although גוי is a general term referring to a people or nation, here it specifically relates to those peoples living in Canaan because this was the region in which the patriarchs wandered.

The word ממלכה alludes to another incident in which the patriarchs faced danger. The only instance in which it appears with respect to the patriarchs occurs in Gen 20:9 כִּי־הֵבֵאתָ עָלַי וְעַל־מַמְלַכְתִּי חֲטָאָה גְדֹלָה ³⁷ ("For you have brought unto me and unto my kingdom a great sin"). These words are taken from an incident in Gen where Abraham's life was threatened by the king of Gerar. Once again, the threat to the patriarch represents a threat to the promise. Heightening the notion of a threat in this verse is the phrase עַם אַחֵר, which appears as a synonym for Israel's enemies in Deut 28:31–32, בָּנֶיךָ וּבְנֹתֶיךָ נְתֻנִים לְעַם אַחֵר ("your sons and your daughters will be given to another people"). The use of עַם אַחֵר in the psalm refers to the nations that stood as a threat to the promise, it also recalls the nations to whom YHWH's deeds were proclaimed in v. 1, הוֹדִיעוּ בָעַמִּים עֲלִילוֹתָיו (make known among the nations his deeds).

לֹא־הִנִּיחַ אָדָם לְעָשְׁקָם וַיּוֹכַח עֲלֵיהֶם מְלָכִים ¹⁴

He never permitted a man to oppress them, and reproved kings on their behalf

The allusion to the patriarchal families' vulnerability continues, but attention is now devoted to God and his ability to protect them. Despite the potential danger, YHWH never permits (לא הניח; see also Eccl 5:12 [11]; Judg 16:26; Lam 5:5) anyone to harm them. The merismus, אדם מלכים . . . ("man . . . kings"), highlights YHWH's prevention of anyone—from a single man, to many kings, implying all in between—from oppressing (לעשקם, see 1 Sam 12:3; Ps 62:10 [11]) the patriarchs. More specifically, the word מלכים points to two different events in the lives of the patriarchs, when they faced danger while in the presence of kings or other powerful individuals. To prevent people from oppressing the patriarchs, God had to intervene verbally and rebuke, ויוכח, those who threatened them. An instance of this occurs in Gen 31:42 (אֶת עָנְיִי וְאֶת

---

36. Josh 18:4 uses the same verb in the context of surveying a land before taking possession, which reflects Abraham's situation when God told him to survey the land prior to his descendants possessing it.

37. Together, the words גוי and ממלכה are well attested in biblical literature as a parallel pair; see for example Jer 51:20; Pss 46:6 [7] and 79:6.

יְגִיעַ כַּפַּי רָאָה אֱלֹהִים וַיּוֹכַח אָמֶשׁ, "my affliction and the toil of my hands God has seen, and he rebuked last night"), when Laban threatened Jacob's life. Furthermore, the root יכח recalls the incident in which the king of Gerar posed a threat to Abraham and Sarah. Unlike the instance in Genesis 31, however, the king was not reproved: וּלְשָׂרָה אָמַר הִנֵּה נָתַתִּי אֶלֶף כֶּסֶף לְאָחִיךְ הִנֵּה הוּא־לָךְ כְּסוּת עֵינַיִם לְכֹל אֲשֶׁר אִתָּךְ וְאֵת כֹּל וְנֹכָחַת ("I have given you brother a thousand pieces of silver; behold it is your vindication before all who are with you, and before all men you are cleared," NASB, Gen 20:16). Although the meaning of נכחת here refers to Sarah's vindication, the account itself speaks of God intervening on her behalf.

אַל־תִּגְּעוּ בִמְשִׁיחָי וְלִנְבִיאַי אַל־תָּרֵעוּ ¹⁵

Do not touch my anointed ones and to my prophets do no harm

Specific words of rebuke now complete the picture of God's protection that began in the previous verse. The psalmist employs chiasmus to create an emphatic conclusion to the section.[38] By employing the word נגע together with יכח from v. 14, the psalmist creates a semantic connection between the two verses.[39] Recalling Gen 20:6, the phrase אל תגעו במשיחי ("do not touch my anointed") echoes God's rebuke of Abimelech for taking Abraham's wife, (עַל־כֵּן לֹא־נְתַתִּיךָ לִנְגֹּעַ אֵלֶיהָ, "therefore I did not permit you to touch her"). The word also echoes an event in Isaac's life, when Abimelech charges all of his citizens to leave Isaac's wife alone: וַיְצַו אֲבִימֶלֶךְ אֶת־כָּל־הָעָם לֵאמֹר הַנֹּגֵעַ בָּאִישׁ הַזֶּה וּבְאִשְׁתּוֹ מוֹת יוּמָת ("And Abimelech commanded all the people, saying, 'the man who touches this man or his wife will surely die,'" Gen 26:11). Thus the psalmist with a single word references at least one event in each of the patriarchs' lives.

The corresponding terms, משיחי and נביאי, each bear a nuance of being "chosen," as do the words עבד and בחיר in v. 6. Ordinarily, משיח is reserved for priests and kings[40] (see Lev 4:5; 16:32; 1 Sam 12:3; Isa

---

38. For this function of chiasmus, see Watson, "Chiastic Patterns," 118–68.

39. In 2 Sam 7:14 both appear together synonymously, "אֲנִי אֶהְיֶה־לּוֹ לְאָב וְהוּא יִהְיֶה־לִּי לְבֵן אֲשֶׁר בְּהַעֲוֺתוֹ וְהֹכַחְתִּיו בְּשֵׁבֶט אֲנָשִׁים וּבְנִגְעֵי בְּנֵי אָדָם: ("I will be a father to him and he will be a son to Me; when he commits iniquity, I will correct him with the rod of men and the strokes of the sons of men," NASB).

40. Priests are anointed with oil (see Exod 29:7), that is to say oil is poured on their heads when they take office. Kings are similarly anointed, as 2 Kgs 9:3 indicates (see

45:1), and although the Bible doesn't explicitly call Abraham a king, instances arise in which he is described as possessing certain royal attributes.[41] Gen 14 portrays Abraham as a peer to the kings of Sodom and Gomorrah. Additionally, one could argue his superiority over these kings because he not only rescued the kings of Sodom and Gomorrah, but also defeated the confederation of kings that led the original assault. Gen 17:6 also associates Abraham with kingship because it declares that kings will come forth from his offspring, suggesting he somehow possesses royal blood. The parallel term to "king" in v. 15, נביאי, draws one's attention to the peculiar[42] verse Gen 20:7, וְעַתָּה הָשֵׁב אֵשֶׁת־הָאִישׁ כִּי־נָבִיא הוּא וְיִתְפַּלֵּל בַּעַדְךָ וֶחְיֵה ("Now return the man's wife for he is a prophet, and he will pray for you and you will live") where Abraham receives the title of prophet, the only occasion in the Torah where a patriarch is so designated. The use of נביא in Gen 20:7 emphasizes Abraham's intercessory role because God instructs him to intercede on behalf of the king of Gerar. In the second colon of v. 15, the phrase אל תרעו recalls another incident in which God verbally intervenes on behalf of the patriarchs. As mentioned in v. 14, God prevents Laban from harming Jacob in Gen 31:7, וְלֹא־נְתָנוֹ אֱלֹהִים לְהָרַע עִמָּדִי ("but God did not permit him to harm me").

Verse 15 brings the first literary-historical account to a climax. Initially, the section presents the patriarchs as being numerically small and vulnerable, and proceeds to raise the listeners' awareness of their vulnerability as the patriarchs wandered about the land of Canaan. In the final climactic scene, God verbally interposes himself for the sake of his promise. His intervention in these verses represents an example of the judgments of his mouth, משפטי פיו, mentioned in v. 5.[43]

---

also Ps 89:20 [21]). Abraham, however, never receives such an anointing.

41. The idea of Abraham's association with kingship appears in extra-biblical sources. *Gen. Rab.* XLIII 5 suggests Abraham was offered kingship of the world after his defeat of the four kings.

42. This verse is peculiar because it designates Abraham as a prophet, a title considered by most to be anachronistic, thus leading some to believe Gen 20:7 constitutes a later addition.

43. At this point the Chronicler ceases quoting from Psalm 105. It is worth noting that the meaning of the quoted section differs significantly from its appearance in Chronicles. This change in meaning is best described by Butler, "A Forgotten Passage," 41, who states: "By simply omitting the remainder of Ps CV, the editor has transformed the meaning of the old material to speak to a new generation, few in number, wander-

From Bards to Biblical Exegetes

וַיִּקְרָ֣א רָ֭עָב עַל־הָאָ֑רֶץ כָּֽל־מַטֵּה־לֶ֥חֶם שָׁבָֽר ¹⁶

He called a famine on the land, every staff of bread he broke

The beginning of the psalm's fourth section contains a second literary-historical account, the story of Joseph. This rendition of Joseph's life only covers the period of his descent into Egypt to his promotion to Pharaoh's second-in-command. Outside of the Pentateuch, this is the only reference to such events.[44] In recounting Joseph's story, the psalmist restricts himself to selecting and retelling events in a way that reinforces his overall aim of demonstrating God's direct intervention to save his chosen ones.

The psalmist again opens the narrative by setting the scene for the coming events with a reference to God calling a famine on the earth, ויקרא רעב. This once again recalls משפטי פיו from v. 3, since קרא is a verb usually associated with speech (see Exod 1:18; Jonah 3:4). This verse also recalls v. 7, בכל הארץ משפטיו ("in all the earth are his judgments"), a fact demonstrated here since the famine affects all of the earth. Although a famine is often considered a natural disaster, here the author attributes it to YHWH via the phrase ויקרא ("and he called"), contributing to the author's plan of portraying God's omnipotence, in good and bad situations.[45] The expression מטה לחם שבר ("he broke every staff of bread") constitutes an expansion of רעב in the first colon. It occurs in four other places in the Bible (Lev 26:26; Ezek 4:16; 5:16; 14:13) as a phrase depicting famine[46] caused by God's judgment; however, the idea of punishment is not appropriate in this context. One potential reason for selecting this somewhat peculiar term is that it contains the root שבר, which appears extensively in the Joseph narrative with different meanings (see for example Gen 41:56, 57; 42:1–3, 7, 10, 19).

---

ing between world powers, but armed with God's eternal covenant and his warnings to the nations not to harm his designated leaders."

44. This contrasts post-biblical literature, which has a tendency to expound upon the lacuna in Joseph's life; see Kugel, *In Potiphar's House*, 13–27.

45. This is not always the case, in Ruth 1:1, the author does not attribute the famine to God; rather, it simply happened as a natural course of events

46. The term מטה לחם is generally understood as the pole on which bread rings were hung to protect them from mice. Figuratively, the expression here implies a shortage of bread; see Milgrom, *Leviticus 23-27*, 2313–14; and Noth, *Leviticus*, 199.

Remember and Obey

שָׁלַח לִפְנֵיהֶם אִישׁ לְעֶבֶד נִמְכַּר יוֹסֵף ¹⁷

He sent before them a man; as a slave he was sold, Joseph

In addition to calling a famine, God sent a man, שלח לפניהם איש, to prepare the way for the patriarchal family. Verse 17 recalls Joseph's own words when he speaks of the same situation in Gen 45:7, וַיִּשְׁלָחֵנִי אֱלֹהִים לִפְנֵיכֶם לָשׂוּם לָכֶם שְׁאֵרִית בָּאָרֶץ ("God sent me before you to preserve for you a remnant in the earth"). Moreover, on various occasions the Genesis narrative describes Joseph as איש, as in 39:2, וַיְהִי יְהוָה אֶת־יוֹסֵף וַיְהִי אִישׁ מַצְלִיחַ ("Now YHWH was with Joseph, and the man was successful", see also 43:3–14). The second colon introduces Joseph specifically as a servant, and we can interpret his role as עבד (servant) in two ways.⁴⁷ On one hand, it refers to events transpiring in Gen 37:27, where the context indicates Joseph was sold as a *slave* although the word isn't specifically used. Additionally, Potiphar's wife describes him as such in Gen 39:17, וַתְּדַבֵּר אֵלָיו כַּדְּבָרִים הָאֵלֶּה לֵאמֹר בָּא־אֵלַי הָעֶבֶד הָעִבְרִי ("And she spoke unto him according to these words, saying, 'the Hebrew slave came unto me'"). On the other hand, עבד also indicates Joseph's position before YHWH, as his "servant" or "chosen one," a title previously bestowed upon Abraham in v. 6. Although Joseph was obviously sold as a slave, the psalm obscures the identity of those who sold him via a *nip'al* verb, נמכר, as opposed to the *qal* in Gen 37:27, לְכוּ וְנִמְכְּרֶנּוּ לַיִּשְׁמְעֵאלִים וְיָדֵנוּ אַל־תְּהִי־בוֹ כִּי־אָחִינוּ בְשָׂרֵנוּ הוּא ("Come let us sell him to the Ishmaelites, and our hand will not be against him, for he is our brother and our own flesh"). Consequently, the fact that Joseph's own brothers sold him is not conveyed in this rendition of events. By substituting איש in the first colon for Joseph's name, יוסף, the psalmist creates an instance of delayed identification, waiting until the last moment to reveal the subject's identity.⁴⁸

עִנּוּ בַכֶּבֶל (רַגְלָיו) [רַגְלוֹ] בַּרְזֶל בָּאָה נַפְשׁוֹ ¹⁸

They bound his feet with chains, and iron came over his neck

After describing his deliverance into captivity, the psalm now details Joseph's incarceration. His feet were bound, ענו (literally, "oppressed")

---

47. Zakovitch, אחת דבר אלהים, further explores the use of a single word purposely to serve dual meaning.

48. For another example of this concept, see Ps 112:6.

with chains, and his neck, נפש, with iron. Together, נפש and רגל (foot) constitute a merismus, expressing the fact that Joseph was bound from head to foot. In this interpretation, נפש has the literal interpretation of "neck," as in Jonah 2:4 [5].[49] "Neck" could also be used figuratively to express subjugation as in Jer 27:12 (הָבִיאוּ אֶת־צַוְּארֵיכֶם בְּעֹל מֶלֶךְ־בָּבֶל וְעִבְדוּ אֹתוֹ וְעַמּוֹ וִחְיוּ, "Bring your necks under the yoke of the king of Babylon and serve him and his people, and live").[50] Genesis provides no evidence supporting this description; consequently, one should understand it as an expansion by the psalmist intended to accentuate the threat to Joseph's life. If Joseph were to die at this point, his family would presumably also die of starvation, and the promise would remain unfulfilled. Joseph's binding, according to the psalmist's rendition, could represent two events. On one hand, it could refer to him being sold into captivity by his brothers, an interpretation that aligns the verse more with the previous one; on the other hand, it could represent his incarceration by Potiphar, after Potiphar's wife falsely accused Joseph of making a pass at her. The latter interpretation accords well with the following verses.

[19] עַד־עֵת בֹּא־דְבָרוֹ אִמְרַת יְהוָה צְרָפָתְהוּ

Until the time came for his promise, the word of YHWH refined him

Verse 19 continues the psalmist's interpretation of events in Joseph's life with a theological perspective on his suffering. Joseph remained in prison until God was ready to fulfill his promise, עד עת בא דברו ("until the time for his promise"), where the word בא additionally links vv. 18–19. By itself, the phrase דברו serves two functions in this context. In the life of Joseph, it refers to God's word, revealed to Joseph through his dreams that one day his siblings and parents would bow before him (see Gen 37:6–11). In the psalm's larger context, it alludes to v. 8, remind-

---

49. See also KB 2:711–12; and Isa 5:14 where it parallels פה, and forms the object of הרחיב.

50. It is also possible to read נפש as "soul," like ψυχὴ in the Septuagint. The word may additionally form part of an expression נפש . . . ענה meaning "to humble" (see Lev 16:31; Num 30:14; Isa 58:5; Ps 35:13). Understanding it like this suggests Joseph was humbled, adequately describing his state from the time he was sold to his promotion. The understanding of "soul" also suggests a threat to life, which is a recurring theme in the narrative accounts.

Remember and Obey

ing the listeners of God's promise to Abraham.[51] In this instance, the promise is being fulfilled since God is preserving his people through Joseph, as part of the process of giving land to Abraham's descendants. Verse 19 consists of a terrace pattern[52] with דברו ("his promise") corresponding to אמרת יהוה ("the word of YHWH"), a word pair found in Ps 147:15 (הַשֹּׁלֵחַ אִמְרָתוֹ אָרֶץ עַד־מְהֵרָה יָרוּץ דְּבָרוֹ, "Who sends forth his command to the earth; his word runs swiftly"), that similarly depicts an action brought about by God's spoken word. The poetic word אמרה represents another actualization of משפטי פיו ("the judgments of his mouth"). God's spoken word, אמרת יהוה, purifies and prepares Joseph, removing from him his presumed character flaws.[53] A similar process of perfecting occurred with Gideon's army in Judg 7:4. Concerning Ps 105:19, the psalmist may have been influenced by the wording of Ps 18:30 [31], הָאֵל תָּמִים דַּרְכּוֹ אִמְרַת־יְהוָה צְרוּפָה, ("God's way is blameless, the word of YHWH is tried") which similarly describes the purifying character of God's word. Nowhere in Genesis does any theological reason appear concerning Joseph's suffering in prison. Surely he could have continued working for Potiphar, and YHWH could have theoretically promoted him to be a ruler of Egypt from there! The psalmist answers this potential objection with the explanation that Joseph's incarceration constituted part of a divine plan to test and purify him through trials and tribulations.

20 שָׁלַח מֶלֶךְ וַיַּתִּירֵהוּ מֹשֵׁל עַמִּים וַיְפַתְּחֵהוּ

He sent a king and freed him, the ruler of the people released him

Verse 20 introduces a radical change in Joseph's fortunes as YHWH imposes his will on the situation. God intervenes to preserve his promise here, just as he did with the patriarchs. The dramatic turnaround recalls events in Gen 41:14, וַיִּשְׁלַח פַּרְעֹה וַיִּקְרָא אֶת־יוֹסֵף וַיְרִיצֻהוּ מִן־הַבּוֹר ("Pharaoh sent and called Joseph, and they hurried him out of the dungeon"). From the form of the verb שלח, one may derive two possible

---

51. This expression also refers to the dreams Joseph interpreted while in prison, as maintained by Humphries, *Joseph*, 207–9.

52. Watson, *Classical Hebrew Poetry*, 201–13, presents a useful overview of verse patterns.

53. Literally, the word refers to the process in which precious metals like silver and gold are refined of impurities, as in Zech 13:9, but this purging process may apply to people (see Isa 48:10).

subjects. On one hand, the subject could be Pharaoh, who sends for Joseph to release him (ויפתחהו), a reading well suited to the following verse. On the other hand, the subject could be God, so the verse reads as, "God sent for the king who then freed him." The latter interpretation conforms to the psalm's overall desire to portray God as omnipotent, and Pharaoh subordinate to his judgments. Although Pharaoh is a ruler of peoples, משל עמים, he is subject to God's bidding. Supporting this notion is the selection of the word מלך (king) as opposed to פרעה (Pharaoh), as recorded in Gen 41:14 because the former corresponds with the kings God rebukes in v. 14. Another recollection of earlier verses concerns the word עמים, which recalls v. 1, where the psalmist exhorts his listeners to declare God's deeds to the nations. The connection here implies that Joseph's release constitutes one of the deeds for declaration among the nations.

שָׂמוֹ אָדוֹן לְבֵיתוֹ וּמֹשֵׁל בְּכָל־קִנְיָנוֹ 21

He made him lord over his house and ruler over all his possessions

After setting the young Israelite free, the king appoints Joseph lord of his house, שמו אדון לביתו, recalling events in Gen 45:8, וְעַתָּה לֹא־אַתֶּם שְׁלַחְתֶּם אֹתִי הֵנָּה כִּי הָאֱלֹהִים וַיְשִׂימֵנִי לְאָב לְפַרְעֹה וּלְאָדוֹן לְכָל־בֵּיתוֹ וּמֹשֵׁל בְּכָל־אֶרֶץ מִצְרָיִם ("Now, therefore, it was not you who sent me here, but God; and He has made me a father to Pharaoh and lord of all his household and ruler over all the land of Egypt.") Previously, when Joseph's brothers spoke about him, they referred to him as the lord, אדון, of the land (see Gen 42:10, 30, 33; 43:20). The second colon in the verse parallels the first, repeating and emphasizing Joseph's exalted status. Corresponding with לביתו ("his house") is קנינו ("his possessions"), a phrase usually associated with livestock. Here, however, it represents all Pharaoh owned (see Gen 31:18; 36:6; Josh 14:4; Ezek 38:12).

לֶאְסֹר שָׂרָיו בְּנַפְשׁוֹ וּזְקֵנָיו יְחַכֵּם 22

To bind his officials as he pleases and his elders he makes wise

Joseph's elevated position after God's promise materialized is further explained in this verse, although here the psalmist apparently depends more on his understanding of the situation than on events narrated in Genesis. It is possible to understand לאסר as "to imprison" or "to bind," as in Ps 149:8 (לֶאְסֹר מַלְכֵיהֶם בְּזִקִּים וְנִכְבְּדֵיהֶם בְּכַבְלֵי בַרְזֶל, "To bind their kings with chains, and their nobles with fetters of iron"), which completes the role reversal that began in v. 18 with Joseph being bound and imprisoned. Here, he has authority to incarcerate Pharaoh's ministers, שריו, as he pleases בנפשו[54] (see Ps 35:25). Joseph's authority to imprison individuals is reflected in Gen 42:17 when he imprisoned his brothers. Perhaps more importantly, his authority to bind individuals is reflected in the binding and imprisonment of Simeon in Gen 42:24, וַיִּקַּח מֵאִתָּם אֶת־שִׁמְעוֹן וַיֶּאֱסֹר אֹתוֹ לְעֵינֵיהֶם ("and he took from them Shimon and bound them before their eyes").

Alternatively, לאסר could be corrected to ליסר,[55] "to instruct" (see Ps 94:10), creating an internal parallel with יחכם in the second colon, and emphasizing Joseph's role as an instructor to Pharaoh's ministers. Genesis 41:33–39 portrays Joseph functioning in this capacity, as he instructs[56] Pharaoh on how to manage the years of plenty and the years of famine. With these two understandings in view, the psalmist highlights the fullness of Joseph's authority in both the judicial and administrative spheres. Both of the aforementioned interpretations demonstrate aspects of authority, and reflect Joseph's new standing in contrast to his old. Adding to the previous section, vv. 16–22 reveal God's ability to reverse a dire situation. Joseph was not only delivered from his chains but also richly blessed, a turnaround dramatized by the chiasmus in vv. 18–22, בנפשו : משל :: משל : נפשו ([his neck : ruler :: ruler : as he pleases] vv. 18, 20, 21, 22 respectively), the one whose soul was ruled over now rules over other souls.

וַיָּבֹא יִשְׂרָאֵל מִצְרָיִם וְיַעֲקֹב גָּר בְּאֶרֶץ־חָם [23]

Then Israel came to Egypt and Jacob sojourned in the Land of Ham

With this verse, the psalm transitions into the third and longest recital of Israelite literary history, depicting a shift from individuals (the patriarchs and Joseph) to a nation. The stanza begins with Jacob and his family's move to Egypt and ends with the Israelites' expulsion by

---

54. A plausible alternative understanding appears in the Septuagint, which translates "himself," τοῦ παιδεῦσαι τοὺς ἄρχοντας αὐτοῦ ὡς ἑαυτόν ("To chastise his rulers at his pleasure"), meaning, Joseph did not need to consult with Pharaoh before he imprisoned one of his ministers; he could do it on his own authority.

55. As interpreted by the Septuagint (παιδεῦσαι) and Peshitta.

56. The notion of Joseph being renowned for his wisdom is also recorded in Acts 7:9–16.

the Egyptians. As with the openings of the previous sections, v. 23 sets the stage for forthcoming events by recalling Exod 1:1 (וְאֵלֶּה שְׁמוֹת בְּנֵי־יִשְׂרָאֵל הַבָּאִים מִצְרַיְמָה אֵת יַעֲקֹב אִישׁ וּבֵיתוֹ בָּאוּ, "And these are the names of the sons of Israel who came to Egypt with Jacob, they came each with his household").[57] The psalmist forges a connection with the previous sections via the word בוא, which portrays steel passing over Joseph's neck in v. 18 and the fulfillment of God's word in v. 19. Another link appears in the second stanza via the chiastic arrangement with v. 10: ישראל : יעקב :: יעקב : ישראל (Israel : Jacob :: Jacob : Israel). Unlike v. 10, however, both references here indicate the patriarch and not the nation. After entering into Egypt, Jacob settles in the Land of Ham, (גר בארץ חם). Just as the other patriarchs were few in number when they dwelt in Canaan, כמעט וגרים בה ("sparse and sojourners in it, v. 12), so too was Jacob's family when he dwelt, גר, in the Land of Ham. As a designation for Egypt, the term ארץ חם (Land of Ham) no doubt stems from the table of nations in Gen 10:6. The choice of this term may have been motivated by the psalmist's desire to include the word ארץ in an epithet, and in so doing develop it as a leitmotif.[58] It first appears in v. 7 as a description of the world, then in v. 11 as a designation for Canaan, and once again in v. 16 referring to the whole earth. As with Ps 78:51, recollection of חם brings with it a derogatory element since Ham, one of Noah's sons, was deemed guilty of shameful behavior (see Gen 9:22), and so the nation that bears his name may have been conceived as also sharing in his shame.

וַיֶּפֶר אֶת־עַמּוֹ מְאֹד וַיַּעֲצִמֵהוּ מִצָּרָיו [24]

He multiplied his people greatly, and strengthened them more than their enemies

After arriving in Egypt, the psalmist describes how God greatly multiplied his people (ויפר את עמו מאד), the sons of Jacob, recalling events recorded in Exod 1:7, וּבְנֵי יִשְׂרָאֵל פָּרוּ וַיִּשְׁרְצוּ וַיִּרְבּוּ וַיַּעַצְמוּ בִּמְאֹד מְאֹד ("The

57. There is an additional connection with Gen 15:13, כי גר יהיה זרעך בארץ לא להם ["For your seed will be strangers in a land that is not theirs"], which speaks of Jacob's move to Egypt. The declaration of the future in the Genesis reference, coupled with the fulfillment in Ps 105:23, is another example of God fulfilling his word. By alluding to this event, the psalmist is able to preserve the notion of God's word coming to fruition, and yet avoid the negative imagery of future enslavement mentioned in Gen 15:13.

58. For more on this concept, see Buber, דרכו של המקרא.

sons of Israel were fruitful and increased, and multiplied, and became exceedingly strong"; see also Exod 1:20). The psalmist's rendition of events, however, employs causative verbs as opposed to simple verbs. Exodus simply states that Israel multiplied, employing the *qal* form of פרה, whereas the psalmist reinterprets this to imply that God caused this growth (פרה in *hipʿil*). A similar difference appears with the stem עצם, which the psalm transforms to *hipʿil*, implying that God strengthened his people. In the psalmist's rendition of events, God's profile in literary history is elevated; he appears as omnipotent and in control of all situations.

Verse 24 represents a shift from the patriarchs and their families to the bearers of the promise as a nation. Consequently, it contains the first mention of עמו, which, with the third-person masculine singular suffix, means "his (God's) people." Previously עם referred to other nations—those to whom God's deeds should be declared in v. 1, dwellers of Canaan in v. 13, and the people whom the king of Egypt ruled over in v. 20. Here, for the first time it refers to Israel. As a result of God multiplying Jacob's sons, they become stronger than their enemies. The psalmist refers to the enemies in the current verse as מצריו, which presents a lucid reminder of their identity via its similarity with מצרים.

הָפַךְ לִבָּם לִשְׂנֹא עַמּוֹ לְהִתְנַכֵּל בַּעֲבָדָיו 25

He changed their heart to hate his people, and to conspire against his servants

Because of Israel's multiplication, the hearts of the Egyptians turn against them; however, their hatred has another origin: YHWH causes them to hate his people (לשנא עמו). In the same way that YHWH calls a famine on the land in v. 16, creating a problem for Abraham's descendants, so too he creates a difficult situation for them here. In presenting God this way, the psalmist again demonstrates YHWH's total control of all events. The image of God causing the Egyptians to hate his people reflects the situation in Exod 4:21, in which God hardened the heart of Pharaoh, which effectively increased the Israelites' oppression, (וַאֲנִי אֲחַזֵּק אֶת־לִבּוֹ וְלֹא יְשַׁלַּח אֶת־הָעָם) ["And I will harden his heart and he will not let my people go"] see also Exod 7:3). The previous object of YHWH's benevolence in v. 24, his people (עמו), is now the object of their enemy's hatred. Together, vv. 24–25 accentuate Israel's passive role in the proceedings; they never act on their own volition, but merely constitute the object of another's actions.

As a result of their hearts turning against Israel, the Egyptians begin to plot evil, להתנכל, against them in the same way Joseph's brothers plotted against him in Gen 37:18 (וַיִּרְאוּ אֹתוֹ מֵרָחֹק וּבְטֶרֶם יִקְרַב אֲלֵיהֶם וַיִּתְנַכְּלוּ אֹתוֹ לַהֲמִיתוֹ, "And they saw him from afar, before he approached them, and they conspired against him to kill him"). Exodus' account of Israel's sojourn in Egypt records various manifestations for the Egyptians' scheming: enslavement Exod 1:9-11, attempted murder of male children via midwives in Exod 1:15-16, and murder of male Israelite children in Exod 1:22. The reference to the Israelites in the second colon, עבדיו, recalls the titles bestowed upon Abraham (v. 6) and Joseph (v. 17). In each instance, the title represents the bearers of God's original promise to Abraham.

שָׁלַח מֹשֶׁה עַבְדּוֹ אַהֲרֹן אֲשֶׁר בָּחַר־בּוֹ [26]

He sent Moses his servant and Aaron whom he chose

In response to the threat created by the Egyptians, God sends his servant Moses, (שלח משה עבדו), and Aaron. This is probably an allusion to Exod 3:13-16, which recounts YHWH's commissioning of them both. The selection of Moses and Aaron as recorded here is unproblematic when compared with Exodus, in which Aaron's involvement only becomes necessary after Moses raises a series of objections to accepting YHWH's commission (see Exod 4). The idea of Moses as God's servant is widespread in the Bible, especially in Josh 1:1; 18:7; 22:5 (see also Num 12:8; Deut 34:5). Aaron, however, is never directly referred to as God's chosen one. The use of this title for Aaron here reflects Num 17:5 [20] when God affirmed Aaron's selection as high priest: וְהָיָה הָאִישׁ אֲשֶׁר אֶבְחַר־בּוֹ מַטֵּהוּ יִפְרָח ("It will come about that the rod of the man whom I choose will sprout"). More importantly, the two titles applied to Moses and Aaron here reflect those given to Israel in v. 6, זֶרַע אַבְרָהָם עַבְדּוֹ בְּנֵי יַעֲקֹב בְּחִירָיו ("Seed of Abraham his servant, the sons of Jacob his chosen ones") linking the two sections and creating a bond between the psalmist's listeners and their righteous forefathers.

Remember and Obey

שָׂמוּ־בָם דִּבְרֵי אֹתוֹתָיו[59] וּמֹפְתִים בְּאֶרֶץ חָם [27]

They executed against them (the Egyptians) his mighty works[60], and mighty acts in the Land of Ham

After receiving their commission from YHWH, Moses and Aaron,[61] now execute, שמו, his mighty works against the Egyptians. The present verse represents one of the few examples in which Moses and Aaron take an active role in the sending of plagues.[62] The normal portrayal in the psalms is that YHWH alone punishes the Egyptians. Verse 27 refers to YHWH's works with the peculiar phrase דברי אתותיו literally, "the works/words of his mighty acts," a phrase unattested anywhere in biblical literature. In order to make the verse more readable, it is possible to remove the form דברי.[63] Such an emendation, however, is unnecessary for two reasons. First, a similar form appears in Ps 145:5, דִּבְרֵי נִפְלְאוֹתֶיךָ, (lit: "words/matters of your wonders") which employs נפלאות instead

---

59. To improve parallelism within the verse, the BHS suggests reading במצרים ("in Egypt") in place of בם דברי. Such an emendation, however, contradicts the psalmist's overall schema; throughout his account of the sojourn in Egypt, he avoids the use of מצרים (Egypt), replacing it with synonyms and pronominal references such as ארץ חם ("Land of Ham") and גבולם ("their borders").

60. The phrase is somewhat tautological, and here it has been translated as a single word. A similar type of construction appears in Deut 33:19 וּשְׂפֻנֵי טְמוּנֵי חוֹל ["hidden treasures of the sand"]).

61. The Septuagint and Peshitta amend the third-person plural reading of שמו to the third-person singular שם. This change casts God in the role of primary instigator, which places the verse more in line with the psalmist's plans.

62. Within the overall context of the psalm, the fact that Moses and Aaron now execute the plagues is particularly remarkable. Elsewhere, the psalmist takes pains to emphasis YHWH as the lone actor (see for example vv. 17, 20, 24). The alteration raises the possibility that v. 26 constitutes a later addition to a psalm that attributes Israel's deliverance to YHWH. The motivation for such an alteration would have been to include Moses' role in the events because Moses, on the whole, plays an important role in Book IV of the Psalter (see the Excursus). After adding v. 26, the next task of an arranger would have been to harmonize his addition with the following verse, v. 27. This he would have done by adding a *waw* to the verb שם. The removal of the two aforementioned alterations, would hardly affect the psalm's development and flow, and the psalm would resonate extremely well with Exod 10:2 וְאֶת־אֹתֹתַי אֲשֶׁר־שַׂמְתִּי בָם ("and my signs which I have worked among them," see also close reading for Ps 135:9 in this volume).

63. As the Peshitta has done.

of אתות.⁶⁴ Second, by maintaining the phrase as it appears in MT, the word דבר (word) aligns the verse with the psalmist's emphasis on God's spoken judgments. Verse 5 introduces the idea with משפטי פיו, or "the judgments of his mouth"; v. 16 recounts God calling, ויקרא, a famine on the land, and in v. 19 it is the word of YHWH, דברו, that is fulfilled in Joseph's life. Thus, it would seem natural that the psalmist portrays the plagues in reference to YHWH's *words* in this verse.

The first reference to the Egyptians, בם, appears as a pronoun and thus delays their full identification until the end of the verse. Joseph's identification was similarly delayed in v. 17. The word מופתים appears in a context reminiscent of Exod 4:21, רְאֵה כָּל־הַמֹּפְתִים אֲשֶׁר־שַׂמְתִּי בְיָדֶךָ, "see all of the signs which I have placed in your hand"), which also uses the verb שים. Usually, the words אתות and מפתים indicate YHWH's "deeds" or "works." When used together, however, they also specifically relate to the plagues executed to procure Israel's emancipation from Egypt,⁶⁵ as Exod 7:3 demonstrates: וַאֲנִי אַקְשֶׁה אֶת־לֵב פַּרְעֹה וְהִרְבֵּיתִי אֶת־אֹתֹתַי וְאֶת־מוֹפְתַי בְּאֶרֶץ מִצְרָיִם ("But I will harden Pharaoh's heart that I may multiply my signs and my wonders in the land of Egypt," see also Deut 7:19; Ps 78:43). Repetition of the phrase ארץ חם creates an inclusion with v. 23, enclosing the buildup to the plagues. Overall, the psalmist is specific about the roles of both Moses and Aaron in this verse, explaining that YHWH performed the miracles, and the human intermediaries were merely vessels, pawns in the divine plot.

שָׁלַח חֹשֶׁךְ וַיַּחְשִׁךְ וְלֹא־מָרוּ אֶת־(דְּבָרָיו) [דְּבָרוֹ] ²⁸

He sent darkness and it became dark and it never disobeyed his word

The following description of the plagues is by far the longest and most detailed account of God's intervention to save his chosen one(s). The patriarchal and Joseph narratives are ascribed two cola each in vv. 15 and 19; but nine verses are dedicated to portraying YHWH's intervention. The expansion emphasizes how important the psalmist viewed this particular act of deliverance. Just as God sent, שלח, his servant Moses,

---

64. Both terms נפלאות and אתות should be considered interchangeable, because they represent standard biblical language for depicting miracles; see Zakovitch, *Concept of Miracle*, 11–18.

65. See Deut 6:22; Neh 9:10.

he now sends another messenger, darkness,[66] recalling Exod 10:21 (וַיֹּאמֶר יְהוָה אֶל־מֹשֶׁה נְטֵה יָדְךָ עַל־הַשָּׁמַיִם וִיהִי חֹשֶׁךְ עַל־אֶרֶץ מִצְרָיִם וְיָמֵשׁ חֹשֶׁךְ), "Then YHWH said to Moses, 'Stretch out your hand toward the sky, that that darkness will be over the land of Egypt, darkness which may be felt'"). Duplication of the root חשך could be indicative of the heavy darkness, which could even be felt, as reported above. The psalm relates the sending of the plague directly to God, he commands the darkness. In doing so, the psalmist continues accentuating God's omnipotence by portraying his domination over creation. After God commanded the darkness, it did not disobey his word, (לא מרה את דברו). By recounting that God's command of the darkness, the psalmist utilizes an image similar to v. 16, וַיִּקְרָא רָעָב עַל־הָאָרֶץ כָּל־מַטֵּה־לֶחֶם שָׁבָר, ("And he called a famine on the land, every staff of bread he broke") which involves another instance of YHWH manipulating creation to accomplish his goals. Repetition of דבר[67] here links v. 28 to v. 27 and perpetuates the notion of God's verbal judgments (משפטי פיו). Unlike the order of the plagues in Exodus, the psalmist has repositioned the plague of darkness from the penultimate to the first position. A possible rationale for this is that he sought to portray the plagues in an escalating order of severity

---

66. A long-standing problem with this verse concerns the identification of the subject of לא מרו. The Peshitta and certain Septuagint mss alleviate this discrepancy by removing the negative particle and making the Egyptians the verb's subject: "The Egyptians rebelled against his word." Such a reading provides God good reason to continue with the plagues since the Egyptians would not listen to or heed the first warning. In spite of this, it is perhaps best to remove a *wāw*, making "darkness" the subject of the verb, suggesting that it was obedient to God's command. This reading is in line with Codex Sinaiticus and the Vulgate, which both render the equivalent of מרה in the singular; see also Booij, "The Role of Darkness." Technically, as Keil and Delitzsch, *Psalms*, 146, suggest, all of the wording of MT could be preserved, reading Moses and Aaron as the subjects of מרו. This reading of the text draws our attention to the other instance in the Torah when this verb appears together with Moses and Aaron as the subject, i.e., Num 27:14. In this verse, God recounts how Moses and Aaron both rebelled against his word when they carried out his instructions to obtain water from a rock. By maintaining MT, it is possible to understand the author arguing that unlike the incident at Meribah, Moses and Aaron obeyed YHWH's command in this instance. Modern commentators have suggested other emendations. Kraus, *Psalms 60-150*, 308 and Allen, *Psalms 101-150*, 39 prefer amending מרו ("they rebelled") to שמרו ("they kept") and applying the verb to the Egyptians again. Dahood, *Psalms III*, 60, influenced by the Akkadian *amaru*, "to see," prefers reading אמרו. He also applies this verb to the Egyptians, understanding the second colon as a result of the first.

67. In an un-pointed text, דבר alludes to pestilence, a plague mentioned in the Exodus tradition but omitted in this Psalm (see Exod 9:3-4).

and regards darkness as the most innocuous plague. Another possibility is that the psalmist sought to align the plagues with the creation tradition in Gen 1. Within this schema, the sending of darkness coincides with its removal in Genesis.⁶⁸

²⁹ הָפַךְ אֶת־מֵימֵיהֶם לְדָם וַיָּמֶת אֶת־דְּגָתָם

He turned their waters to blood and killed their fish

Since the psalmist's aim is to highlight YHWH's mighty deeds, he omits all intervening encounters between Moses and Pharaoh, and moves directly from the plague of darkness to the Nile's pollution without any account of the intermediate events. Just as God changed the hearts of the Egyptians to hate his people in v. 25, he now changes their water into blood. A comparison of vv. 25 and 29 reveals God's manipulation over man and creation to achieve his purposes. In addition to turning the waters to blood, the psalmist notes that YHWH also killed the fish, וימת את דגתם וְהַדָּגָה. Although the psalm reflects Exod 7:20–21, (וְהַדָּגָה אֲשֶׁר־בַּיְאֹר מֵתָה וַיִּבְאַשׁ הַיְאֹר וְלֹא־יָכְלוּ מִצְרַיִם לִשְׁתּוֹת מַיִם מִן־הַיְאֹר וַיְהִי הַדָּם בְּכָל־אֶרֶץ מִצְרָיִם, "And the fish which were in the Nile died, and the Nile stank and the Egyptians were not able to drink water from the Nile, and there was blood in all the land of Egypt"), it fails to mention the damage to the Egyptians' water supply. The psalmist's portrayal of the event here apparently softens the effect of the plague compared to the aforementioned Exodus account, as well as the account of the plague in Ps 78:44. The latter text emphasizes the effects to man, the interruption of the Egyptians' drinking supply (וַיַּהֲפֹךְ לְדָם יְאֹרֵיהֶם וְנֹזְלֵיהֶם בַּל־יִשְׁתָּיוּן, "And he changed their waters to blood, and their streams they could not drink").

³⁰ שָׁרַץ אַרְצָם צְפַרְדְּעִים בְּחַדְרֵי מַלְכֵיהֶם

*Their land multiplied with frogs, even in the chambers of their kings*⁶⁹

---

68. A fuller examination of the plagues appears in the section on allusions.

69. The plural of מלך is peculiar since there was only a single king (Pharaoh) during the plagues. Interpreting this as a plural of majesty is one way of alleviating this difficulty. In any event, the plural here creates a stronger link to v. 14 where God rebukes kings on behalf of the patriarchs.

Remember and Obey

After the rivers turned to blood, YHWH causes the land[70] of the Egyptians to teem with frogs: שרץ ארצם צפרדעים.[71] Previously the land, ארץ, represented the whole earth (vv. 7, 16), and the land of Canaan (v. 11). However, in his continuing development of land as a leitmotif, the psalmist uses the word ארץ here to indicate the land of the Egyptians, as he does in vv. 23 and 27; previously it represented the whole earth (vv. 7, 16), and the land of Canaan (v. 11). The unnatural teeming of frogs inconveniences the Egyptian kings as the frogs enter into their houses and rooms: בחדרי מלכיהם. The event recalled in Exod 8:3 [7:28] recalls a similar effect: וְשָׁרַץ הַיְאֹר צְפַרְדְּעִים וְעָלוּ וּבָאוּ בְּבֵיתֶךָ וּבַחֲדַר מִשְׁכָּבְךָ ("And the Nile teemed with frogs and they will go up and inter into your house and in your bedroom"). Once again, the psalmist's use of מלך recalls God rebuking kings for the sake of his promise in v. 14, and the control of the king in v. 20. As YHWH interacted with kings for the sake of the patriarchs, so too he admonishes them here for the sake of his people. As with the previous plague, the psalm here represents a mollified portrayal of events when compared with Psalm 78:45, which grants the frogs power to cause physical destruction, יְשַׁלַּח בָּהֶם עָרֹב וַיֹּאכְלֵם וּצְפַרְדֵּעַ וַתַּשְׁחִיתֵם ("he send against them swarms that consumed them, and frogs that destroyed them"). Notably, throughout this section, the author copiously employs the third-person plural suffix in most of the verses—"their waters" and "their fish" (v. 29), "their land", "their kings" (v. 30) etc. In doing so, he distinguishes between the land of the Egyptians and Goshen where the Israelites lived.

---

70. It is possible to read "their land" as the object of the verb "to teem," despite the fact that the feminine subject ארץ does not agree with the masculine verb שרץ, an interpretation followed by the Septuagint: ἐξῆρψεν ἡ γῆ αὐτῶν βατράχους (see also BDB 1056). In spite of this, it is probably best to read the verb שרץ as a causative, although no further biblical evidence exists for the reading. The reason for this interpretation is contextual. Throughout the plagues' narrative, God is the primary instigator and the one who directly executes each judgment; consequently, it would seem out of place to include a plague that God did not directly cause. One could theoretically re-point the root here as a *pi'el*, or accept that at some stage in its diachronic development, the verb may have possessed a causative meaning; see Dahood, *Psalms III*, 60–61.

71. With regard to this colon, one can detect a degree of alliteration as the psalmist repeats צ in each word.

³¹ אָמַר וַיָּבֹא עָרֹב כִּנִּים בְּכָל־גְּבוּלָם

He (YHWH) spoke and a swarm came, lice in all their border

The psalmist again demonstrates the power of YHWH's spoken word, the judgments of his mouth (v. 5), in his depiction of the fourth plague; he spoke, and there came forth swarms, (אמר ויבא ערב). Within the context of Ps 105, ערב need not be translated as "flies," but simply as "swarms," where the second colon further identifies the swarm content as lice, כנים, which enter into all the borders of Egypt (בכל גבולם). Thus, the psalmist recounts a single plague,⁷² unlike Exod 8:12, which recalls two separate incidents, וְהָיָה לְכִנָּם בְּכָל־אֶרֶץ מִצְרָיִם ("and there will be lice in all the land"). In the context of this psalm, a single plague allows for a seven-plague tradition, the number seven expressing completion.⁷³

The author's use of the phrase ויבא אמר ("he spoke and there came") is reminiscent of the creation story (see for example Gen 1:3). In both instances, God's spoken word produces results. Verse 31 recalls events in Exod 8:20 וַיָּבֹא עָרֹב כָּבֵד בֵּיתָה פַרְעֹה ("and a great swarm entered the house of Pharaoh"). In Exodus, as well as the present psalm, the swarms (ערב) are more of a nuisance than a serious health threat.⁷⁴

³² נָתַן גִּשְׁמֵיהֶם בָּרָד אֵשׁ לֶהָבוֹת בְּאַרְצָם

He made their rain [into] hail, a flaming fire in their land

After two plagues involving animal life, the psalmist now demonstrates God's manipulation over meteorological elements as he turns the

---

72. Loewenstamm, "The Number of Plagues," 34–38; and *Evolution* 185–86, also argues that the structure of "he spoke and they came," repeated in v. 34, constitutes a structural indication that this is a single plague, and further adduces that the psalmist applies at least two cola to each plague. Not all scholars adhere to this understanding; Margulis, "The Plagues," is opposed to a seven-plague tradition in Ps 105 along with any possibility that there could be an independent tradition underlying the psalm. Concerning the existence of an alternate tradition, Loewenstamm, *Evolution* 188, further suggests that the two seven-plague traditions (Pss 78 and 105) predate the account in Exodus.

73. Psalm 78 attests to this, moreover, other examples of seven representing completion and perfection appear in Gen 2:2–3, 7:2, 1 Kgs 6:38. See also Loewenstamm, *Evolution* 107, who further argues that seven is more preferable than ten for creating a climax.

74. Notably, in Ps 78:45, their function intensifies and they possess the ability to devour.

rain of the Egyptians into hail,[75] נתן גשמיהם ברד. As in the preceding plagues, the psalmist omits the physical damage inflicted on man and beast. Instead, he reinforces the notion of the plague as a demonstration of YHWH's power over creation, as opposed to a battle between YHWH and the Egyptians. Together with the hail, burning fire, (אש להבות) is sent against the Egyptians' land. Verse 32 recalls Exod 9:23, וַיְהוָה נָתַן קֹלֹת וּבָרָד וַתִּהֲלַךְ אֵשׁ אָרְצָה וַיַּמְטֵר יְהוָה בָּרָד עַל־אֶרֶץ מִצְרָיִם (and YHWH sent thunder and hail and fire went down to the earth, and YHWH rained hail on the land of Egypt), but adds להבות as a natural poetic accompaniment to אש (see Ps 83:14 [15], כְּאֵשׁ תִּבְעַר־יָעַר וּכְלֶהָבָה תְּלַהֵט הָרִים, "Like fire burning the forest, and like a flame setting the mountains on fire").[76]

וַיַּךְ גַּפְנָם וּתְאֵנָתָם וַיְשַׁבֵּר עֵץ גְּבוּלָם 33

He struck their vines[77] and figs, and shattered the trees of their territory

As our psalmist approaches the plagues' climax, he expands his description of each plague from one verse to two. To help express the totality of destruction, the psalmist includes a short list of crops destroyed. Both the Egyptian vines and figs were struck (ויך גפנם ותאנתם), in addition to every tree in their territory being shattered (וישבר עץ גבולם). The striking of the גפן (vines) is not mentioned in the Exodus account, but Ps 78:47 recounts the same plague recalling a destruction of the vines. Similarly absent from the Exodus account are figs (תאנתם); however, the two words often appear together to express the richness of a land, non-essential items or luxuries.[78] By mentioning these items first, one can see an increasing intensity of the plagues.

Repetition of שבר (shatter) recalls the famine initiated by God in v. 16, when every staff of bread was broken. This time, however, the disaster does not encompass the whole earth, but only the land of Egypt. Comparing this verse to Exod 9:25, וַיַּךְ הַבָּרָד בְּכָל־אֶרֶץ מִצְרַיִם אֵת כָּל־אֲשֶׁר בַּשָּׂדֶה מֵאָדָם וְעַד־בְּהֵמָה וְאֵת כָּל־עֵשֶׂב הַשָּׂדֶה הִכָּה הַבָּרָד וְאֶת־כָּל־עֵץ הַשָּׂדֶה שִׁבֵּר, ("Everything that was in the field from man to beast, and all the

---

75. For this meaning of נתן, see Isa 3:4 and Jer 9:11 [10].

76. See also Isa 47:14; Pss 29:7, 83:14 [15].

77. The words "vine," "fig," and "tree" should all be interpreted as nouns of species, or singular words representing plurals; see GKC §123.

78. See Deut 8:8; 1 Kgs 4:25 [5:5].

grass of the field the hail struck, and every tree of the field it shattered") highlights a significant difference: the psalmist avoids mentioning any destruction to livestock, an omission that tempers the damage done by the plague.

³⁴ אָמַר וַיָּבֹא אַרְבֶּה וְיֶלֶק וְאֵין מִסְפָּר

He spoke and locusts came, young locusts without number

As with the swarms of lice, God also commands[79] the locusts into action: he speaks and they come (אמר ויבא). The second colon expands the first, accentuating the number of locusts involved in the plague: וילק ואין מספר ("and young locust without number"). In contrast to Exod 10:14, לְפָנָיו לֹא־הָיָה כֵן אַרְבֶּה כָּמֹהוּ ("Previously there had never been so many locust") the psalmist uses the word ילק[80] as a poetic accompaniment for locusts, ארבה; the two often appear together in the context of judgment.[81] Ps 78:46 similarly employs a poetic compliment, חסיל, which Exodus fails to include. In contrast to v. 12 בהיותם מתי מספר ["when they were few in number"]), the repetition of מספר here denotes an uncountable multitude; it is a term that often accompanies the description of locusts, as in Jer 46:23, כָּרְתוּ יַעְרָהּ נְאֻם־יְהוָה כִּי לֹא יֵחָקֵר כִּי רַבּוּ מֵאַרְבֶּה וְאֵין לָהֶם מִסְפָּר ("They have cut down her forest," declares YHWH; "Surely it will no more be found, Even though 1they are now more numerous than locusts And are without number," see also Judg 6:5). The psalmist employs the expression to reflect the density of the locusts reported in Exod 10:15, וַיְכַס אֶת־עֵין כָּל־הָאָרֶץ וַתֶּחְשַׁךְ הָאָרֶץ, "For they covered the surface of the whole land, so that the land was darkened").

³⁵ וַיֹּאכַל כָּל־עֵשֶׂב בְּאַרְצָם וַיֹּאכַל פְּרִי אַדְמָתָם

It consumed all of the green things of their land, and it consumed all the produce of their land

As with the destruction caused by the hail and fire, the psalmist uses two verses to describe the plague of locusts; the first depicts the nature of the plague, and the second portrays the damage caused by the

---

79. See 2 Kgs 4:24; Ps 106:34; Esth 1:17.

80. The exact nature of these is uncertain; they are a type of locust or young locusts; see KB 2:413.

81. See Joel 1:4; 2:25.

plague. The locusts consume every green thing in their land, כל עשב בארצם, in addition to the produce of the earth, פרי אדמתם (see Deut 7:13 and Num 13:20 for this sense). An escalation in the destruction caused is apparent from the repetition[82] of אכל in both colons. The nature of the destruction also conveys a sense of increased severity in relation to the damage caused by the previous plague. Previously, the plagues destroyed only luxury produce, but now the psalm records a totality in the destruction of all the earth's produce. As a continuation of the ארץ (land) leitmotif in the psalm, it once again appears in this section referring to the land of Egypt. From a comparison with Exod 10:15, וַיֹּאכַל אֶת־כָּל־עֵשֶׂב הָאָרֶץ וְאֵת כָּל־פְּרִי הָעֵץ ("and they consumed all of the grass of the land and all the fruit of the trees") it would appear that the psalmist possessed a source similar to MT.

וַיַּךְ כָּל־בְּכוֹר בְּאַרְצָם רֵאשִׁית לְכָל־אוֹנָם 36

He struck every firstborn in their land, the first of all their strength

The final plague in the psalmist's sequence is the striking of the firstborn, ויך כל בכור, the first in his rendition that directly harms man. Up to this point, the previous six plagues have simply damaged crops and animals, causing a nuisance. Repetition of ויך ("and he struck") here recalls the beginning of v. 33 ויך גפנם ותאנתם ("and he struck their vines and their figs") but a comparison of the two verses reveals a sharp increase in intensity since human lives are damaged as opposed to plant life. The psalmist's rendition of the account certainly reflects Exod 12:29 (וַיהוָה הִכָּה כָל־בְּכוֹר בְּאֶרֶץ מִצְרַיִם, "YHWH struck every firstborn in the land of Egypt"); however, the phrase ראשית . . . און, referring to the firstborn (see Gen 49:3 and Deut 21:17), is absent from the Exodus tradition but appears in Ps 78:51, וַיַּךְ כָּל־בְּכוֹר בְּמִצְרָיִם רֵאשִׁית אוֹנִים בְּאָהֳלֵי־חָם ("And he struck all the firstborn of Egypt, the first strength among the tents of Ham"). The similarity could simply represent a logical word pair chosen by both psalmists; yet, it may raise the possibility of the author's dependence on a source other than Exodus, one shared by the author of Ps 78 (or even a version of Ps 78 itself).

The plagues' account finishes with three occurrences of כל (all/every) in the last two verses: כל עשב . . . כל בכור . . . כל אונם, which ex-

---

82. Watson, *Classical Hebrew Poetry*, 278–79, further explains the idea of initial repetition serving as a tool for intensification.

presses a totality of God's judgments against the Egyptians, accentuating the event's climax.[83] Within this fifth narrative, the threat to the promise comes in the form of the attempted eradication of the descendants of Abraham; God's intervention manifests itself through a series of seven plagues, which facilitate the release of his people from the Egyptians.

וַיּוֹצִיאֵם בְּכֶסֶף וְזָהָב וְאֵין בִּשְׁבָטָיו כּוֹשֵׁל [37]

And he brought them out with silver, and gold and not one among his tribes stumbled

The third and final recital from Israelite literary history begins with an account of Israel's journeys in the desert. Verse 37 concentrates on God's provision[84] for, and blessing of, the Israelites after the plague of the firstborn. He blesses them with silver and gold as they depart from Egypt (ויוציאם בכסף וזהב, "and he brought them out with silver and gold"). By alluding to Exod 12:41, (יָצְאוּ כָּל־צִבְאוֹת יְהוָה מֵאֶרֶץ מִצְרָיִם, "And all of the hosts of YHWH went out from the land of Egypt"), the psalmist's rendition emphasizes YHWH's work. Instead of using the simple *qal* form to depict their departure, the psalmist employs the causative *hipʿil*, emphasizing God brought them out. The account of their collection of the silver and gold (כסף וזהב)[85] with which the Israelites left Egypt, is unique among the selected psalms. It is employed in v. 37 to demonstrate God's abundant kindness towards his people. Although he is fulfilling his promise to Abraham, he does not simply provide them with the bare minimum, but endows them richly with material goods.

The Exodus rendition of Israel's flight from Egypt fails to mention that they left without weakness or stumbling, ואין בשבטיו כושל. Such a description of Israel's departure can also be found in the poetic passage of Isa 63:13, which depicts the same event (מוֹלִיכָם בַּתְּהֹמוֹת כַּסּוּס בַּמִּדְבָּר לֹא יִכָּשֵׁלוּ, "Who led them through the depths, like the horse in the wilderness, they did not stumble"). This indicates that the psalmist was either more familiar with Isa 63, or that the events recorded in Isaiah were simply more suitable to his work since they lend a degree of

---

83. Loewenstamm, *Evolution*, 82–86.

84. All traces of rebellion and murmuring disappear from our psalmist's rendition of events, as is discussed in the close reading of v. 40.

85. This phrase serves as a summary of all of the spoil with which Israel left Egypt (see Exod 11:2; 12:35); see Coats, "Despoiling the Egyptians," 452.

Remember and Obey

supernatural sustenance to the proceedings; YHWH not only led them, but also kept them from stumbling.

שָׂמַח מִצְרַיִם בְּצֵאתָם כִּי־נָפַל פַּחְדָּם עֲלֵיהֶם 38

Egypt were happy when they left because the fear of them [Israel] fell upon them [Egyptians]

In keeping with the overall positive of the psalm, Egypt's response to Israel's departure from their land is one of joy and happiness, שמח מצרים בצאתם. The Egyptians' emotional response finds no precise parallel in Exodus. Repetition of the root יצא ("to leave/exit") from the previous verse links the two verses, with v. 38 adding detail to the nature of the emancipation. For the second time in the psalm the word מצרים (Egypt) appears, which closes an inclusion that began in v. 23. Within this division, the psalm records all events that have transpired in Egypt, avoiding any mention of Egypt between vv. 23–38.

The second colon, כי נפל פחדם עליהם ("for the fear of them fell on them"), explains the reason for the Egyptians' happiness: relief from the fear of the Israelites' god that had fallen upon them (see 1 Sam 11:7; Esth 8:17). After being stricken with plagues, the Egyptians know that they would continue to suffer if the Israelites remain, and are glad to see them go. The psalmist's selection of this phrase probably reflects the influence of Exod 15:16, תִּפֹּל עֲלֵיהֶם אֵימָתָה וָפַחַד בִּגְדֹל זְרוֹעֲךָ יִדְּמוּ כָּאָבֶן עַד־יַעֲבֹר עַמְּךָ יְהוָה עַד־יַעֲבֹר עַם־זוּ קָנִיתָ ("terror and dread fall upon them; by the greatness of your arm they are motionless like a stone, until your people pass over, O LORD, until the people whom you have purchased pass over") which speaks of the fear that fell on the Israelites enemies when they traveled to Canaan. The psalmist, however, reapplies this phrase to broaden the scope of those who feared the work God did among the Israelites. In addition to the inhabitants of Canaan, the psalm includes the Egyptians. Egypt's happiness can be compared with Israel's joy, recorded in v. 3, ישמח לב מבקשי יהוה ("let the seekers of YHWH rejoice") which results from the great deeds God performed for them. Israel's joy does not stem from a fear of retribution. With v. 38 the reversal is complete. When Israel entered Egypt, vv. 23–25, they were the victims of the Egyptians, but now those who sought to oppress Abraham's descendants fear them.

פָּרַשׂ עָנָן לְמָסָךְ וְאֵשׁ לְהָאִיר לָיְלָה [39]

He spread out a cloud for protection and a fire to light the night

As part of YHWH's gracious treatment of the Israelites, he extends his mercies to his people in the form of protection and guidance. At first glance, this verse presents a reminder of events in Exod 13:21, וַיהוָה הֹלֵךְ לִפְנֵיהֶם יוֹמָם בְּעַמּוּד עָנָן לַנְחֹתָם הַדֶּרֶךְ ("And YHWH went before them daily in a pillar of cloud to lead them on the way"), when God sends a pillar of cloud by day to guide the Israelites on their journey. Contrasting this, however, is the phrase פרש . . . למסך (spread out . . . for protection), which implies a screen separating two entities, as with the curtains used in the Tabernacle (see Exod 38:18; 40:5). Such an understanding implies that God provided the Israelites with a similar degree of protection in sending the cloud. From this assumption, it is possible to read v. 39 as a reference to Exod 14:19–20, where the cloud that had originally provided guidance for the Israelites moved behind them, forming a protective screen between them and the pursuing Egyptians. Alternatively, the cloud functioning as a screen could also represent an alternate tradition in which God protected the Israelites from the heat of the sun during their desert journey. Such a tradition may indeed be reflected in Isa 4:5, וּבָרָא יְהוָה עַל כָּל־מְכוֹן הַר־צִיּוֹן וְעַל־מִקְרָאֶהָ עָנָן יוֹמָם וְעָשָׁן וְנֹגַהּ אֵשׁ לֶהָבָה לָיְלָה ("then YHWH will create over the whole area of Mount Zion and over her assemblies a cloud by day, even smoke, and the brightness of a flaming fire by night") in which a cloud constitutes an agent of protection. Additionally, Wis 10:17 attests to the existence of such a tradition, "he guided them in a marvellous way, and was unto them for a *cover* by day, and a light of stars in the night season" (italics the author's). Thus, here in the psalm the cloud is best viewed as a symbol of God's protection of Israel during their journey, thus also protecting the promise.

In addition to protection, God offers his people guidance for their journey via a pillar of fire to light the night, ואש להאיר לילה. The appearance of אש highlights a contrast in attitude between God's relationship with his people and his dealings with their adversaries. In v. 32 the fire came against the Egyptians as part of God's judgment against them, אש להבות בארצם ("a flaming fire in their land"); here, in v. 39 it represents an expression of his benevolence towards his people, caring for them while in the desert. Unlike the previous narratives, the present threat does not originate from people, but from the harsh desert environment.[86]

שָׁאַל וַיָּבֵא שְׂלָו וְלֶחֶם שָׁמַיִם יַשְׂבִּיעֵם [40]

They asked and he brought quail, with the bread of heaven he satisfied them

In addition to guidance and protection, God responds to Israel's request (שאלו)[87] for food. The psalmist's use of שאל notably contrasts its appearance in Ps 78:18. In the latter psalm, the Israelites test God with a request for food, וַיְנַסּוּ־אֵל בִּלְבָבָם לִשְׁאָל־אֹכֶל לְנַפְשָׁם ("They tested El in their hearts, requesting food for their appetites," see also Ps 106:15), whereas v. 40 refrains from any hint of rebellion. The Israelites simply turn to YHWH with a request and he meets their need. The author's choice of שאל additionally recalls vv. 3–4, which emphasize *seeking* YHWH, because שאל often appears together with דרש and בקש to convey the idea of seeking or searching (see Deut 13:14 [15]; Isa 65:1). By linking the verses, the author creates a bond between the wilderness generation and the psalmist's audience: Just as he answered the call of the desert generation when they sought him, so too he will answer the psalmist's generation when they seek him. Twice previously, the psalm employed בוא in the context of judgment falling on the Egyptians (see vv. 31, 34). Here, in contrast, it represents an expression of Israelite blessing, as God responds to their request.[88]

God's response to the Israelites' request is to send them meat, via quail שלו, and bread, לחם. Here the psalmist reflects events in Exod 16:8, בָּעֶרֶב בָּשָׂר לֶאֱכֹל וְלֶחֶם בַּבֹּקֶר לִשְׂבֹּעַ ("In the evening meat to eat, and bread in the morning to satisfy," see also Exod 16:4; Ps 78:24, 25). Unlike Exod 16, however, no additional restrictions appear concerning the manner in which the food is collected. Rather, God's provision is unconditional, freely bestowed according to his goodness. Additionally,

---

86. By this point in the proceedings, one would expect an explicit mention of the Reed Sea crossing, since it aptly demonstrates an act of God's intervention to save his people. This account, however, is strangely absent from the psalm. A possible rationale for the omission is that the psalmist sought to preserve a positive perspective, and the deaths of thousands of Egyptians would have ruined the effect.

87. This is probably a haplography; the scribe's failure to insert two *wāw*'s results in the third-person masculine singular perfect of שאל.

88. This constitutes another example of contrastive repetition, where the psalmist repeats a word to contrast two situations (see v. 32 for example, concerning the word אש).

the psalmist employs שבע as a *hipʿil*, as opposed to the *qal* in the Torah, emphasizing God's activity in the provision of food.

The psalm's previous mention of לחם in v. 16 was in association with the devastation caused by famine; here, it is the means by which YHWH sustains the life of Israel. The psalmist's phrase לחם שמים or "bread *of* heaven," reflects the tradition in Ps 78:24 (וַיַּמְטֵר עֲלֵיהֶם מָן לֶאֱכֹל וּדְגַן־שָׁמַיִם נָתַן לָמוֹ, "Then he rained on them manna to eat, the grain of heaven he gave them") more so than Exod 16:4, (וַיֹּאמֶר יְהוָה אֶל־מֹשֶׁה הִנְנִי מַמְטִיר לָכֶם לֶחֶם מִן־הַשָּׁמָיִם "Then YHWH said to Moses, 'behold I am raining down for you bread from heaven'"), meaning "bread *from* heaven."

פָּתַח צוּר וַיָּזוּבוּ מָיִם הָלְכוּ בַּצִּיּוֹת נָהָר 41

He opened a rock and water poured out, it ran in the dry places like a river

YHWH's response to Israel's request that begins in v. 40 continues here with the provision of water: God opens a rock, and water flows from it. Once again the occurrence of פתח ("he opened") appears in the context of deliverance. In v. 20, it is used to depict Joseph's release from prison, and here it speaks of Israel's deliverance from thirst in the desert. In both instances, God is directly responsible for the act, which is highlighted by Moses' absence from the proceedings.

In another instance of contrastive repetition, מים (water) here represents a life-giving entity to the Israelites, whereas in v. 29 it constitutes YHWH's punitive actions against the Egyptians. Although the event described here reflects similar situations recorded in Exod 17:1–7; Num 20:1–13; and Ps 78:15–20, the language employed by the psalmist resonates more with Isa 48:21, וְלֹא צָמְאוּ בָּחֳרָבוֹת הוֹלִיכָם מַיִם מִצּוּר הִזִּיל לָמוֹ וַיִּבְקַע־צוּר וַיָּזֻבוּ מָיִם ("They did not thirst when he led them through the dry places; he made water flow out of the rock for them; he split the rock and the water gushed forth"). The context of provision in the desert, as recorded in Isaiah, however, does not describe the exodus from Egypt, but from Babylon (Isa 48:20). This marks the second instance in which the psalmist relates his work to the later exodus.[89] The poetic phrase, הלכו בציות נהר,[90] ("it ran in the dry places like a river") portrays

---

89. See close reading for v. 1.

90. The form ציות being a poetic term; see Jer 2:6, 50:12; Hos 2:5.

Remember and Obey

God's benevolence through vivid imagery, suggesting water flowed into the desert like a river, providing an ample supply for the Israelites.

כִּי־זָכַר אֶת־דְּבַר קָדְשׁוֹ אֶת־אַבְרָהָם עַבְדּוֹ 42

Because he remembered his holy promise with Abraham his servant

Verse 42 represents an interjection in the psalmist's narration of events, as he turns to recall the promise originally mentioned in vv. 8–9. The verse stands out from its immediate context because of its lack of parallelism, either internally or with the surrounding verses. By deliberately deviating from the expected form, the psalmist draws attention to the verse's importance. At this point, the psalmist explains why God performed the deeds mentioned in the previous narratives: because he remembered his covenant with Abraham (כי זכר את דבר קדשו). YHWH's faithfulness to the Patriarchs and to Israel, as enumerated in the psalm, stems from his faithfulness in keeping the promise he initiated with Abraham. The Israelites have done nothing to deserve this treatment; they are merely recipients of his benevolence. Three words repeat themselves from vv. 8–9, זכר, דבר, and אברהם, (Abraham, promise, he remembered) linking the second and sixth stanzas. In repeating דבר, the psalm again recalls YHWH acting via the words of his mouth. Just as God's name is described as holy in v. 3, התהללו בשם קדשו ("praise his holy name") so too is his promise to Abraham, דבר קדשו את אברהם.

וַיּוֹצִא[91] עַמּוֹ בְשָׂשׂוֹן בְּרִנָּה אֶת־בְּחִירָיו 43

And he brought out his people with rejoicing, with shouts his chosen ones

After the interjection, the psalm resumes the narration of events. In the psalmist's rendition of the account, God brings Israel out of Egypt and through the desert with joy and with loud shouts of rejoicing. The word יוצא ("he brought out") creates an inclusion with v. 37 that surrounds events transpiring from the exodus to the end of the desert period. The title of the chosen ones, בחיריו, is introduced in v. 6, and the root also appears in v. 26, concerning Aaron's function as God's messenger, אהרן אשר בחר בו ("Aaron whom he chose"). Here, it is assigned once again to Israel, linking the opening section with the last. As with v. 15, and the structure of the fourth section, the psalmist employs chiasmus here for

---

91. This is an unusual pointing of the *hip'il*, there are additional occurrences in Deut 4:20; 2 Kgs 11:12; and Ps 78:16; the meaning of the verb is apparently unaffected.

emphasis (my people : joy :: shouts of joy : his chosen ones [עַמִּי : שָׂשׂוֹן :: רִנָּה : בְחִירָיו]). This verse apparently relates to the desert experience as recorded in Exodus, however, the wording is more reminiscent of Isa 51:11, וּבָאוּ צִיּוֹן בְּרִנָּה וְשִׂמְחַת עוֹלָם עַל־רֹאשָׁם שָׂשׂוֹן וְשִׂמְחָה יַשִּׂיגוּן ("And come to Zion with joyful shouting, and everlasting joy will be on their heads, rejoicing and gladness"), where the context again describes an exodus from Babylon.[92]

וַיִּתֵּן לָהֶם אַרְצוֹת גּוֹיִם וַעֲמַל לְאֻמִּים יִירָשׁוּ [44]

And he gave them the lands of the nations and the toil of the nations they [Israel] possessed

After a series of human and environmental threats and endangerments to the patriarchs and their descendants, YHWH finally fulfills the promise that was made in the second stanza. God promised the land to Abraham and his descendants in v. 11 (לך אתן את ארץ כנען), and now with similar words, he fulfills his promise: ויתן להם ארצות גוים ("and he gave them the lands of the nations"). Verse 44 refers to the land as ארצות גוים ("lands of the nations"), and recalls the patriarchal travels in v. 13, ויתהלכו מגוי אל גוי ("And they wandered from nation to nation"). The same land in which Israel's forefathers sojourned when they were small in number is given to their now numerous descendants as an inheritance.

The psalmist more deeply expresses YHWH's beneficence in the second colon, which declares that Israel possessed the toil of the nations, עמל לאמים.[93] All that the inhabitants of Canaan had worked for, their houses, crops, cities, etc., appears here as a gift bestowed to the descendants of Abraham as a possession. Rather than simply receiving the land of the Canaanites, the Israelites inherit all they had built on it. The sentiment here most clearly echoes Deut 6:10–11, which also recalls Israel's inheritance of property and goods for which they never worked. Just as the psalmist avoided accounts of desert murmurings, so too he omits the numerous battles occurring between the Israelites and the Canaanites before they fully possessed the land. In portraying Israel as the recipients of the Canaanites' hard work, the psalmist establishes

---

92. See close reading for v. 41.

93. This commonly appears with גוים, see Gen 25:23; Isa 34:1; Ps 2:1; 44:2 [3]; and Prov 14:34.

an instance of *measure for measure*:[94] Just as Israel were enslaved and labored hard for the benefit of their captors, they now receive the labor of others. The implicit question raised in the second stanza, as to whether YHWH can complete his promise amid adverse circumstances, is answered affirmatively here in the penultimate verse.

בַּעֲבוּר יִשְׁמְרוּ חֻקָּיו וְתוֹרֹתָיו יִנְצֹרוּ הַלְלוּ־יָהּ [45]

In order that they might keep his laws, and observe his instructions—Praise Yah

Following YHWH's faithfulness to his promise and his people, the psalmist now provides a rationale for God performing the mighty works mentioned in the psalm. He did it so that, בעבור (see 1 Sam 23:10; Mic 2:10; and Ps 106:32), they might keep his laws, (ישמרו חקיו). God's faithfulness carries direct implications for the recipients. All that YHWH did for the patriarchs and their descendants—protecting them from the malicious intentions of their enemies and manipulating creation for their preservation—was performed so that the descendants would respond in kind by obeying his laws.

Here חק carries a different meaning[95] than in v. 10: (ויעמידה ליעקב לחק, "he established it as an ordinance for Jacob"). The psalmist employs the word in reference to the Mosaic laws, whereas in v. 10 it describes God's unconditional promise to Abraham. Repetition here further links the second and sixth stanzas, but additionally implies that just as God was faithful to his promise, so Israel should be faithful to his covenant.

The second colon reiterates the sentiment of the first, ותורתיו ינצרו ("and observe his instructions"), but in reverse order, creating another instance of chiasmus within the verse for increased emphasis, accentuating Israel's responsibility in obedience.[96] Both words ישמרו and ינצרו mean "to keep," as in "to do,"[97] and the Law of Moses[98] regularly appears as their object. With the inclusion of the last verse, it is possible to rec-

---

94. For more on this concept, see Jacobs, מידה כנגד מידה.

95. The Septuagint recognizes this difference in meaning by translating the first instance of the word in v. 10 as προσταγμα (which is equivalent to משפט) and the second instance as δικαιωματα (which is usually associated with תורה).

96. See v. 43.

97. See Deut 33:9 and Prov 5:2.

98. Usually when חק appears with תורה, the inference is to the Law of Moses (Deut 4:8; 17:19; 30:10).

ognize a microcosm of the lawgiving at Sinai. YHWH first declares all he has done for Israel, and then specifies how they must respond to his mercy via obedience (see Exod 20:1-2). In the psalm, the proportion between God's acts of deliverance and response differ, but the structure is the same. First, the psalmist explicates all God has done for Israel in vv. 1–44, and then he states the obligation they must fulfill in v. 45. Closing the psalm is an imperative to praise YHWH, הללו יה,[99] which corresponds with the root הלל in the opening stanza (v. 3). Together, they create an inclusion for the entire work, ultimately classifying it as a work of praise.

MEANING

The final verse of Psalm 105 provides the clearest expression of its raison d'être: that Israel would keep YHWH's laws in response to his faithfulness in preserving his promise. The psalm was written to encourage its readers/listeners to obey God's laws. In reciting YHWH's faithfulness to them in the exodus, the psalmist highlights his audience's indebtedness to God, as well as the method of repayment via their obedience. Repetition of the word חק emphasizes this main theme as it represents both the promise (v. 10), signifying God's benevolence, and the law (v. 45), signifying how Israel is to repay him.

The idea of land, ארץ, repeated throughout the psalm, functions as a leitmotif and a constant reminder of the promise that was first mentioned in the second stanza. Although each individual section addresses a different period in Israelite literary history, they are all unified by at least one mention of "land." A recurring pattern of events in each narrative account—a threat to promise bearers, God's intervention, and deliverance of the promise bearers—constantly reinforces the idea of YHWH's faithfulness to his promise.

Along with the primary theme mentioned above—obedience on account of YHWH's benevolence to his people—the psalmist adopts additional sub-themes to teach and encourage his listeners. Two of the more prominent sub-themes are the intimate relationship between God and his people, and God's sovereignty over the whole earth. The

---

99. In the Septuagint, the phrase הללו יה appears at the beginning of the following psalm as opposed to the end of Psalm 105, a change corresponding with its placement of the same phrase from the end of Psalm 104 (MT) to the beginning of the present work.

Remember and Obey

former is expressed with a variety of words and lexical forms, including the third person suffix on עַם,[100] and the words בחר and עבד to describe individuals and the nation as God's chosen ones and servants.[101] Throughout the composition, YHWH's treatment of Israel is exclusively positive, compared to his treatment of the other nations, who are rebuked and reproved (vv. 14–15, 28–36). God's intimate relationship with his people as expressed in the psalm ultimately stems from his faithfulness to his promise. In initiating the promise to Abraham, God similarly creates a close and intimate relationship with his descendants too.

YHWH's sovereignty is conveyed in a variety of expressions. He calls a famine throughout the earth (v. 16); his judgments are known in all of the earth (v. 7); his authority and control are not restricted to his people, so he can rebuke kings (v. 14) and direct Pharaoh to release Joseph (v. 20). Finally, only YHWH possesses authority to apportion a land that is already inhabited to another nation as an inheritance. Complementing statements of his authority throughout the psalm are the constant reiterations of God acting via the word of his mouth.[102] From the beginning of the psalm to the end, these verbal judgments constitute a tool through which YHWH preserves the promise that he originally made to Abraham.

DATE

No explicit datable events people or places present themselves within Psalm 105 that situate it in any specific era in biblical history. However, its historiographic data allows one to determine its earliest date of origin because the psalm could not have been completed prior to the last literary-historical event cited. Events within the composition span from the patriarchs, with the mention of Abraham being the earliest, to the Israelites' entry into Canaan. Therefore, one can deduce with certainty that the psalm was written after Israel entered Canaan.

In regards to linguistic evidence, one should first note the lack of ABH in the composition; consequently, archaic origins for the psalm are unlikely. Concerning LBH, the phrase להעמיד ... ברית ("to establish

---

100. See vv. 24, 25, and 43 for example.
101. See vv. 6, 17, and 26 for example.
102. See close reading of vv. 5, 8, 11, 15, 16, 19, 27, 31, 34, and 42.

a covenant") in v. 10 is significant because the root עָמַד[103] ("to stand") in LBH adopts the meaning of קוּם ("to raise") in SBH. During the SBH era, the root קוּם bore the meaning of "establish" and "confirm." In later books, however, the root עָמַד adopts this meaning.[104] Thus, the presence of the phrase, לְהַעֲמִיד . . . בְּרִית, as opposed to לְהָקִים . . . שְׁבוּעָה/ בְּרִית in Gen 26:3[105] patently represents late language in our psalm.

With all of the primary evidence discussed, it is time now to consider the secondary evidence through two of the psalm's recurrent sub-themes. The first, the giving of land to Israel, features references to the exodus from Babylon to Judah. From this, it is possible to locate the psalm to the postexilic period, after such an exodus occurred.[106] Under this scenario, it would appear that the psalmist is recalling the second exodus as a re-enactment of the first, and an extension of YHWH's faithfulness to his promise to Abraham. Another notion present within the psalm, the ideal relationship between Israel and God, assists in narrowing down the date because it is *unlikely*[107] that a psalm with an idealistic theme was written during the exile when Israel was extremely conscious of their unfaithfulness to YHWH. Such evidence suggests a composition date either before or after the exile, but not during Israel's captivity in Babylon.

Another piece of evidence that should not be overlooked is the inclusion of the word נָבִיא (prophet) in v. 15. Scholars often consider this word a later addition to the text of Genesis. Consequently, it must be assumed that the psalmist recognized a relatively late rendition of the Genesis account.[108] In light of the evidence presented above, it is

---

103. Hurvitz, *A Linguistic Study*, 94–98, provides a more extensive survey of this phrase.

104. See 1 Chr 17:14; 2 Chr 9:8; Dan 11:14.

105. See also Lev 26:9.

106. Clifford, "Style and Purpose," 420–22, additionally argues that the motif of land was inspired by a time when the Israelites were without theirs; however, this evidence alone should not be considered conclusive with respect to the date.

107. "Unlikely" is emphasized because one could always argue the possibility that a positively themed psalm could be written during a nation trauma. However, during the exile, Laments such as Psalms 106 and 137 would be expected.

108. It is very difficult to be any more specific concerning exactly how late the word was added. Concerning its addition, Fretheim, *Genesis*, 482, argues that its use is anachronistic, which implies that it is temporally out of place and thus a later addition. Similarly, Westermann states, "The word prophet is not used here of Abraham in a technical but rather in a general sense; he is a 'man of God,' an intercessor, familiar to a

probably best to accept a postexilic date for Psalm 105, although not much else can be said at this point concerning its relative position within that era.

SOURCES

Table 2.1

Ps 105	Source	DH Source
Ps 105:23	Exod 1:1	P
Ps 105:23–24	Exod 1:7	P
Ps 105:25	Exod 14:5	JE
Ps 105:27	Exod 7:3	P
Ps 105:28	Exod 10:21	JE
Ps 105:29	Exod 7:20–21[109]	JE
Ps 105:30	Exod 7:28	JE
Ps 105:31	Exod 8:17 [13], 24 [20]	JE
Ps 105:32–33	Exod 9:25	JE
Ps 105:34	Exod 10:14	JE
Ps 105:35	Exod 10:15	JE
Ps 105:38	Exod 15:16	NS
Ps 105:40	Exod 16:4	JE
Ps 105:41	Isa 48:21	—
Ps 105:43	Isa 51:11	—

Table 2.1[110] shows that the primary source for Psalm 105's version of the exodus came from the book of Exodus.[111] Although the psalm never quotes from Leviticus, Numbers, or Deuteronomy, it would be imprudent to suggest the psalmist did not have these texts or their equivalent available to him. However, Leviticus and Deuteronomy have relatively little narrative material and so one can understand why the psalmist did not include them. Numbers would similarly be deemed unsuitable

---

later era; to speak or conceive of Abraham in such a way is very far removed from the patriarchal period" Westermann, *Genesis 12–36*, 324.

109. Though v. 20 is divided between JE and P, the part cited in the psalm belongs to JE.

110. See Appendix A for a more detailed comparison between the psalms' verses and the sources.

111. With the date established in the previous section, it is safe to assume that the psalm is later than the Torah and thus drew from it (i.e., texts reflecting its current form).

because its narrative accounts are predominantly negative and thus unsuitable for the psalm's overall purposes.

In addition to the Torah, the psalmist utilizes two locations in Isaiah to recount the wilderness tradition. The question of literary borrowing between Ps 105:41, 43 and Isa 48:21, 51:11 is difficult to gauge with certainty. Although Isaiah is included here as a source, there is also the possibility of either a common tradition underlying both, or Isaiah reusing the psalm.

Wording from at least three other psalms apparently influenced the psalmist's composition. The portrayal of the final plague in Ps 78:51 apparently influenced the psalmist's description of the same event in Ps 105:36, evidenced by both texts employing the phrase ראשית . . . אונם (first . . . their strength) as a poetic complement to בכור (firstborn). Additionally, Ps 105:40's description of manna as לחם שמים ("bread of heaven") may have originated from Ps 78:24–25's rendition of the same event.[112] Another more concrete connection exists between Ps 105:23, 27, and Ps 106:22, since the common phrase ארץ חם ("the Land of Ham") only occurs in these two places in the Bible.[113] All of the aforementioned cases probably represent instances of influence, whereby our psalmist borrowed phrases to form poetic complements without specifically alluding to the aforementioned texts. As a result, the following section does not investigate these texts further.[114]

Psalm 105 reveals signs of P, but predominantly reflects the JE tradition. The clearest example of the psalm's association with P stems from its emphasis on the power of YHWH's spoken word. Such an emphasis resonates well with P's account of the creation via God's spoken word.[115] The psalm additionally bears a connection with D; though no explicit citations appear from Deuteronomy, the weight of D's influence is nev-

---

112. See close reading for v. 40.

113. The very fact that this rare phrase occurs in juxtaposed psalms raises some interesting possibilities concerning the arrangement of these two works; see the section on Juxtaposition in chapter 3. Concerning the direction of borrowing between Psalms 105 and 106, the former represents the later work. Psalm 106 was written during the exile (see chapter 3) and Psalm 105 was written after the exile, as has been argued in the preceding section.

114. The association with Ps 106:22 however, will be addressed in the section on juxtaposition.

115. Another similarity concerns the inclination to exonerate the patriarchs of all sin; see Rofé, *Composition of the Pentateuch*, 42, for these characteristics of P.

ertheless present. The psalm's final verse is particularly telling because the phrase לשמור חק ("to keep an ordinance") is especially prominent in Deuteronomy.[116] Moreover, the Deuteronomic ideal of obedience to the Law being linked with residence in the land is also present in the psalm (see Deut 4:26 and 11:17, for example).[117]

In addition to the known sources, the close reading of Ps 105 reveals the possibility of an alternate tradition. In describing God leading the Israelites from Egypt, the psalm depicts him as stretching out a cloud for a screen (פרש ענן למסך). As discussed in the close reading for v. 39, this concept resonates more with an extra-biblical tradition concerning God's protection of Israel than it does with the Torah's version of desert events.[118]

Process of Selection

Psalm 105 draws upon five sub-motifs of the exodus: Israel in Egypt, the emancipation from Egypt, the giving of manna, provision of water, and the provision of meat. However, the psalm omits any reference to the deliverance at the sea. In view of the breadth of sources available to the psalmist, it is unlikely that he was unfamiliar with this tradition. Consequently, there must be another explanation for its omission. At this point, one can only assume that the psalmist did not seek to portray YHWH as being vindictive in any way. Thus, the destruction of the Egyptian army in the sea was not conducive to his overall plan. Further evidence of the psalmist's tendency to temper events appears in his depiction of the plagues, which are not as destructive to people as they are in the Exodus counterpart.

Another noticeable aspect of selection in Psalm 105 is the psalmist's omission of all negative aspects of the Israelites' desert sojourn. Although the psalm recalls the provision of water along with the giving of manna and meat, no recollection of the murmuring preceding these supplies of food are recorded. The conquest of Canaan is similarly portrayed in a trouble-free manner; no battles take place, but the land and the hard work of the Canaanite peoples were simply delivered to the

---

116. See 4:40, 5:1, 6:17, 7:11, and 17:19.

117. See Tucker, "Revisiting the Plagues," 407–8, for further Deuteronomic associations.

118. Due to doubts about the certainty of an alternate tradition here, this matter is discussed in the following chapter.

Israelites. As a result, the psalm has an overall euphoric feel from beginning to end, and paints a picture of constant harmony between Israel and YHWH throughout the desert journey. Examining these omissions in the overall plan of the psalm, it becomes clear that if the psalmist included negative events in his composition, the last verse would lose its impact. Inclusion of the rebellions in the desert would imply that the people would have already failed to keep his laws.

Also absent from the psalmist's retelling is the law-giving at Sinai, the instance in which God entered into a covenant together with Israel after he delivered them from Egypt. The psalmist's strict and uncompromising focus on the Abrahamic covenant provides us with an explanation for this omission. Inclusion of events at Sinai would have added some confusion between the two covenants, and the Sinaitic covenant, consequently, would draw attention away from the one God made with Abraham. Additionally, the inclusion of the lawgiving at Sinai would break the psalmist's plan to list a continuous series of events that epitomize YHWH's merciful deeds to Israel while maintaining his covenant.

ALLUSIONS

Israel in Egypt

Exodus 1:1 records the sons of Israel (בני ישראל) who came (הבאים) to Egypt (מצרימה), including Jacob (יעקב). Once there, they multiply greatly, becoming fruitful (פרו, 1:7), and very strong (ויעצמו במאד מאד, 1:7), and they fill the land. Their rapid multiplication soon makes them stronger than their enemies (עצום ממנו, 1:9), who subsequently conspire against them, enslaving them and attempting to destroy all their male children. Pharaoh's daughter saves one of these children, Moses (משה), and raises him in Pharaoh's household as an Egyptian. After killing an Egyptian in defense of a Hebrew, Moses is forced to flee to Midian where he settles down as a shepherd. YHWH calls Moses, sending him (משה . . . שלחני, 3:13) to deliver the Israelites from their captors, a calling he is initially reluctant to accept due to his lack of eloquence. God overcomes the problem by appointing his brother Aaron (אהרן) to accompany him as a spokesman. God sends both Aaron and Moses on their mission (see Exod 4:13–16). As part of his instructions in Exod 4:21, God tells Moses to return to Egypt with the signs (מפתים) he has put (שמתי) in his hand.

Remember and Obey

Ps 105:23 begins like Exodus, recalling Israel (ישראל) coming (ויבא) to live in Egypt (מצרים), and the children of Jacob living in the Land of Ham. Here, the psalmist opts to use an epithet for Egypt (ארץ חם, Land of Ham), which on one hand could simply reflect a poetic word pair, but could also represent a deliberately derogatory choice of phrase. Ps 105:24 then recalls how the Israelites became very (מאד) fruitful (ויפר) and stronger (ויעצמהו) than their oppressors. Unlike the source, however, Ps 105 does not simply record that the Israelites grew strong, but that YHWH *made* them stronger than their enemies. YHWH's dominance in all events constitutes a major theme in the psalm, and here it manifests itself by a change from simple forms in the source to causative forms in the psalm. Verse 25, הָפַךְ לִבָּם לִשְׂנֹא עַמּוֹ לְהִתְנַכֵּל בַּעֲבָדָיו ("He changed their heart to hate his people, and to conspire against his servants") apparently originates from the psalmist's imagination, but nevertheless reflects God's responsibility for hardening the heart of Pharaoh in Exod 4:21 (וַאֲנִי אֲחַזֵּק אֶת־לִבּוֹ וְלֹא יְשַׁלַּח אֶת־הָעָם, "And I will harden his heart and he will not release my people"),[119] which causes the ruler to keep the Israelites captive. However, the psalmist apparently applies God's treatment of Pharaoh to all of the Egyptians. Verses 26 enumerates how both Moses (משה) and Aaron (אהרן) are sent (שלח) by God, as well as the status ascribed to them as עבדו and בחר בו, neither of which appears in the source. In using these titles, the psalmist apparently seeks to associate Moses and Aaron with his audience in v. 6, where the same words describe his audience. As expected from the psalmist's rendition of events, negative instances, such as Moses' initial refusal to return to Egypt, play no role in the psalmist's composition.

---

119. See also 9:12.

From Bards to Biblical Exegetes

THE PLAGUES

The Plagues

Table 2.2

	Psalm 105		Exodus		Psalm 78	
1	חשך	28	דם	7:14–24	דם	44
2	דם	29	צפרדעים	7:25–8:15 [11]	ערב	45
3	צפרדעים	30	כנים	8:16–19 [12–15]	צפרדעים	45
4	ערב\כנים	31	ערב	8:20–32 [16–28]	ארבה	46
5	ברד	32–33	דבר	9:1–7	ברד	47
6	ארבה	34–35	שחין	9:8–12	דבר	48–50
7	מכת הבכור	36	ברד	9:13–35	מכות הבכור	51
8			ארבה	10:1–20		
9			חשך	10:21–23		
10			מכת הבכור	12:29–32		

The plagues' tradition in the current psalm differs significantly from the Exodus account (see Table 2.2). None of the earlier plagues and signs—the leprous hand, Moses' staff turning into a snake and crocodile—recorded in Exod 4:1–7 are recalled in the psalm. Instead, the psalmist concentrates on the ten plagues that strike the Egyptians, forcing them to submit and release the Israelites.

Moses turning the rivers and waters of Egypt to blood constitutes the first plague recalled in Exod 7:17–21. YHWH instructs him to meet Pharaoh in the morning with his staff and demand the Israelites' release. When Pharaoh refuses to comply, Moses strikes his staff on the water (מים) of the Nile turning it (ויהפכו) to blood (דם), causing the water to become undrinkable, and killing (מתה) the fish (הדגה). Psalm 105 positions the plague of blood as the second plague. Although it recalls the death of the fish, YHWH bears sole responsibility for their death, as opposed to the waters. The psalm omits any reference to Moses, Aaron, the staff of God, or the water being undrinkable, focusing exclusively on YHWH as the plague's instigator. Rather than causing any physical harm to the Egyptians, the plague is depicted more as a sign of God's power.

After the plague of blood, Exodus recalls the sending of frogs against the Egyptians (8:2–15 [7:27–8:11]). The frogs multiply (שרץ) coming out of the river, entering into houses and bedrooms (חדר משכבד), presenting themselves as a nuisance as they cover the whole of the land (ארץ). Psalm 105 deviates slightly from this portrayal by specifically mentioning that the frogs enter into the rooms of the kings, a detail not included in the source. It is possible, however, to see this alteration as a deliberate association to 105:14, לֹא־הִנִּיחַ אָדָם לְעָשְׁקָם וַיּוֹכַח עֲלֵיהֶם מְלָכִים ("He never permitted a man to oppress them, and reproved kings on their behalf"), which recalls God rebuking kings as an act of intervention on behalf of the patriarchs. In making this association, the psalmist highlights God protecting the people of Israel in the same way he protected their forefathers.

The third and fourth plagues in Exodus 8 (see Table 3.2), swarms and lice, appear together as the fourth plague in Psalm 105 (see Table 3.2). Exodus depicts the lice (כנים) being sent across the whole land of Egypt (בכל ארץ מצרים), affecting both man and beast. The swarms (ערב), sent after the lice, similarly cause a substantial amount of destruction across the land. By joining the two plagues together, the psalmist interprets the somewhat ambiguous word ערב (swarms) in v. 31[120] as a term that does not necessarily signify the precise nature of the individual constituent parts of the swarming body. Thus, by linking the two together the palmist explicates that the swarming body consisted of lice.

The following two plagues in Exodus, pestilence (9:1–7) and boils (9:8–12), are not mentioned at all in the psalm. The psalmist may have had concerns about the damage they inflicted in the source text. In Exodus, the pestilence destroys all of the cattle in Egypt in addition to the horses, donkeys and other flock animals. These same animals are also affected in the boils that follow and the hail after that, not to mention the death of the cattle's firstborn. In removing these plagues from the psalm, the psalmist alleviates a perceived difficulty in his source—how can the same animals be destroyed again and again by subsequent plagues—while reworking the text.[121]

---

120. See close reading for v. 31.

121. Concerning the omission of these two plagues, Tucker, "Revisiting the Plagues," 405–7, posits that because the mention of land does not appear at the conclu-

The sixth plague in Exodus, hail (see 9:13—10:11) ברד, strikes men, beasts, and plants, killing them; and among the destruction to the plant life, Exod 9:22 mentions that the hail destroys the grass of the field (עשב השדה). Along with the hail, Exod 9:23 reports of fire (אש) accompanying it, and together they destroy the grass of the field (עשב השדה) in 9:25 and break every tree of the field. Exodus 9:31 additionally mentions the flax and the barley being struck, while the wheat and the spelt survive because they were late crops. The psalm's reworking of events restricts itself to mentioning the destruction of plant life, but it too includes the appearance of fire (אש) in v. 32. Psalm 105, however, alters the identification of plants struck by this plague, and records fig trees and vines being affected along with the grass. Unlike the previous plague descriptions, the psalm dedicates two verses to this plague and additionally adopts the verb נתן to depict the sending of the plague, as opposed to המטיר in Exodus (see 9:18, 23), a change designed to recall the promise of land earlier recorded in 105:11. In the psalmist's portrayal of the hail, there is another example of him mollifying the events in his source not mentioning the danger to humankind recorded in the Exodus account.

Following the hail, both texts recall the sending of locusts (ארבה); Exod 10:1-20 recalls it as the eighth plague and Ps 105:34-35 as the sixth. In Exod 10:5, the locusts cover the land (וכסה את עין הארץ) and destroy the crops left by the hail. They enter the houses of the Egyptians, and Exod 10:6 describes the phenomenon as a unique event that none of the Egyptians' forefathers had witnessed since they dwelt in the land (אדמה). Exod 10:12, 15 depict the locust as consuming (ויאכל) everything green in the land (כל עשב הארץ). The source further states that an east wind is the source of the plague (10:13), and that no greenery (ירק, 10:15) remained after the plague ended. As the sixth plague in Ps 105, there is no mention in the recruiting or removal of the locusts; instead, they are summoned by God's word. For a poetic compliment to the word ארבה (locust) the psalmist adopts the segolate יֶלֶק ("young locust"), which recalls יֶרֶק, the similar sounding word for greenery in Exodus. The psalmist also repeats the phrase אמר ויבא to portray God sending the plague. By employing this expression, he recalls both the words of Exod 10:4, where God says he will bring (מביא) an abundance

---

sion of the plagues in Exodus, they were omitted from the psalm. His assumption here stems from the "land" leitmotif within the psalm.

of locusts on their territory, in addition to the calling of the swarms in v. 31. As with the previous plague, Psalm 105 dedicates two full verses to the locusts; the first announces the plague, and the second enumerates the destruction it wreaks.

The penultimate plague in Exodus is חשך, a pitch-blackness that covers the land of the Egyptians (10:21–23). As mentioned previously, Ps 105 relocates this event to the first position. The most probable explanation is the psalmist somehow deemed it a relatively innocuous plague, and consequently better suited to the first place in the sequence. It should also be noted that the removal of darkness appears as the first act of God in creation. Thus the psalmist may have deliberately aligned his rendition of the plagues to correspond, at least partially, with the creation story.[122]

In both texts, Exod 11:1—12:32 and Ps 105:2–36, the striking of the first-born (מכת הבכור) constitutes the final plague, which the Exodus account merges with the institution of Passover. The source reports that in the middle of the night YHWH struck (הכה) every firstborn male (כל בכור) in the land (ארץ) of Egypt. The psalmist recalls the event in words similar to the Exodus account, but adds the phrase ראשית לכל אונם ("first of all their strength") as a poetic compliment. When the psalmist selected this phrase, he was probably influenced by the same words describing the event in Ps 78:51, ראשית . . . אונים. In developing the association with the creation account, the striking of the firstborn corresponds with God's last creative act, the creation of man. Within this structure, the plagues' account in Exodus represents an undoing of creation. Instead of creating light God removes it, instead of creating man, he destroys him, instead of creating order for the world, he creates disorder, via unnatural meteorological phenomena and animal behavior.[123] The association with creation enhances and emphasizes the

---

122. With respect to the psalm as a whole, a further link to creation appears in the juxtaposition between Pss 104 and 105; see the section on Juxtaposition in this chapter. Tucker, "Revisiting the Plagues," 408–9, also suggests that darkness represents a sign of God's displeasure, and thus it was moved to the first position in order to set a tone highlighting God's anger for the remainder of the psalms.

123. Reinforcing the link with Genesis 1 is the order in which the plagues develop. From celestial entities, they continue to the water, then to the land and plants, and finally to man. Reflecting this progression is the development of creation in Genesis 1 (see Lee, "Genesis 1," esp. 259–60).

plagues' narrative by highlighting the extent to which God was willing to act on behalf of his people.

The Wilderness Wandering

Before leaving Egypt, Exod 11:2 and 12:35 records YHWH's instructions to the Israelites to request articles of gold and silver (כלי כסף וכלי זהב) from the Egyptians. They obey his command, plundering the Egyptians. Although Ps 105:37 recalls the event, the negative aspects are removed; instead the Israelites' receipt of gold and silver is depicted as an expression of benevolence from God to his people. The second part of Ps 105:37 departs from the Torah in favor to the poetry of Isaiah for a continued description of the initial desert period. Isaiah 63:7 begins recounting the great deeds of old that YHWH wrought on behalf of the Israelites and speaks of them turning against him, which incites him to fight against them (v. 10). God then remembers the days of old when he brought them through the Sea. He divided the waters through Moses, and led them through the sea like a horse through the desert. During this time, they did not stumble (לא יכשלו, v. 13). From this rendition of events, the psalmist only recalls the lack of stumbling (אין . . . כושל) among the tribes as they came into the desert. Furthermore, the context that frames these words in the psalm is purely positive. Although the psalm does not explicitly mention the sea crossing, the aforementioned allusion recalls the event.

Apparently recalling events in Exod 12:36, Ps 105:38 reflects the Israelites' departure from Egypt and the favorable disposition of the Egyptians. Exodus, however, neither explicitly recalls the Egyptians' happiness at the Israelites leaving, nor the fear that fell upon them. Both of these emotions are nevertheless understandable from the context since the Egyptians would have been glad at the sight of Israel leaving, and yet still fearful of God's wrath that had been leveled against them while the Israelites dwelled among them.

Following Exodus, Ps 105:39 records the Israelites' desert sojourn after their emancipation from Egypt. There are two notable omissions: the deliverance at the Reed Sea, and giving of the Law at Mount Sinai. After the Israelites leave Egypt, God leads them in the desert via a pillar of cloud (ענן) by day, and a pillar of fire (אש) to give them light (להאיר) at night, providing them with continual guidance (see Exod 13:21). Psalm 105's rendition of these events differs despite the mention of both the fire and cloud. For the psalmist, the cloud does not function as a guide. Instead, the psalmist depicts God spreading the cloud out like a screen, מסך, in v. 39, as opposed to a pillar, עמוד. This is an apparent allusion to Isa 4:5, which speaks of the future glory of Zion, a prophecy directly relevant to the psalmist's immediate situation. In Isaiah, both fire and cloud are depicted as forming a canopy over Zion. Their function, however, is not to guide, but to protect. The psalmist evidently relies on the notion of protection to express the care that YHWH exercises towards his people. In addition to leading them, he also preserves them from all harm.[124] This same idea of protection and the cloud as a shield is not entirely foreign to the Torah. It is possible to read מסך as a veiled allusion to the protection God provided at the Reed Sea. Just before the sea was split, Exodus recalls the cloud moving behind the Israelite camp and settling between them and the Egyptians forming a screen between the two camps, and creating a picture of YHWH protecting his people from the Egyptian army.

Soon after God delivers the Israelites from the sea in Exod 16, they begin complaining (v. 2) as they remember the fleshpots they enjoyed in Egypt. Moses brings the matter to God, who responds by promising to rain bread from heaven (לחם מן השמים, v. 4) upon them as part of a test to see if they would walk in his ways. He subsequently instructs them concerning its collection. God additionally promises them flesh (בשר, v. 8) to eat (לאכל, v. 8), enough for their satisfaction (לשבע, v. 8). YHWH reaffirms his promise of provision in v. 12 when he appears to the community, reiterating that he has heard their complaints, and that in the evening they will eat (תאכלו) meat (בשר) and in the morning they will be satisfied (תשבעו) with bread (לחם). According to God's word, later that evening quail (שלו, v. 13) came and covered the camp, and in the morning, together with the dew there was manna, which Moses declares as the bread (לחם, v. 15) that God provided for them to eat (לאכלה). In Ps 105, these events are recounted in a single verse, occurring immediately after the Israelites' depart from Egypt. As a result, the psalm avoids mention of Israelite complaining. Instead, he depicts them as simply requesting food, a petition that was soon answered by God. Such a change was necessary to develop the joyous nature of the psalm, omitting negative incidents involving God's people. Contextually

---

124. The idea of protection also surfaces in extra-biblical texts; see close reading of v. 39.

in line with this overall schema is the omission of the test linked with the provision of bread in Exodus.

After the provision of bread and meat in the Exodus itinerary, the Israelites proceed to Rephadim, where they complain again to Moses for water to drink (see Exod 17:5–6). He subsequently relays their complaints to God, who instructs him to take some of the elders and go (והלכת, Exod 17:5) to a rock (צור, v. 6) where God will be standing. Moses is then instructed to strike the rock (צור) whereupon water (מים, v. 6) would spring forth, from which the people could drink. Isaiah 48:20–21 also records YHWH's provision of water in the desert. This context, however, speaks of God's work among the exiles from Babylon, as they go forth from captivity back to their homeland. On their return, they are to declare and announce to the world that God has redeemed his servant Jacob (עבדו יעקב, v. 20), and that he led them (הוליכם, v. 21) through parched places; he made water (מים, v. 21) flow for them from a rock (צור, v. 21); he split the rock (צור, v. 21), and water (מים, v. 21) flowed out (ויזבו, v. 21). Although the psalmist was evidently aware of the Torah's rendition, he primarily depends on Isaiah's account. In selecting this record of events, the psalmist reflects a tradition temporally closer to his situation, and more importantly portrays his experience of the second exodus in light of the original exodus from Egypt. Psalm 105:1 similarly recalls the connection between two exodus accounts.[125]

A further association between the exodus from Egypt and that from Babylon appears with Ps 105:43's use of Isa 51:9–11. The latter recalls God's works of old, and calls for him to clothe himself with splendor as in the days of old when he defeated and dissected the dragon Rahab, and dried up the sea and the waters of the deep so his people could walk through. Isaiah calls for God to act in the same way to bring the ransomed of YHWH, those from Babylon, back to Zion with shouts of happiness (רנה, 51:11) and joy (ששון, 51:11). Psalm 105:43 depicts the happiness with which God brought his people through the desert and the shouting with which they entered the promised land with the same words. The allusion recalls the joy of the new exodus from Babylon, enumerated in Isaiah. With this third instance of melding old and new exodus traditions, it is apparent that the real joy the psalmist seeks to express in the psalm is not so much the promise of land to Abraham and its fulfillment in the days of Joshua, but the joy created from its fulfillment in the days of Judah's return from the Babylonian exile.

---

125. See close reading for this verse.

JUXTAPOSITION

Psalm 104–105

Psalm 104 constitutes a song praising YHWH for his work in creation. It begins in vv. 1–4 by extolling his majesty, and in doing so portrays the winds as his messengers and the fiery flames (אש) as his servants. Then it depicts YHWH's work in separating the dry land from the waters (vv. 5–11). The third stanza (vv. 12–18) continues by concentrating on YHWH's work in providing for the needs of all creation. He provides water that satisfies the earth (תשבע) and the trees (ישבעו) and supplies man with wine that cheers the heart (ישמח לבב). Verses 19–23 focus on the creation of the moon and sun, and the activities that occur in the day and night hours. When YHWH sends darkness (חשך) it becomes night and the beasts of the forest stir. The following verses (vv. 24–35) mention the multitude (אין מספר) of creatures he created, and all of whom are satisfied (ישבעון) by YHWH's provision. In the final verses of the psalm, the psalmist is moved to praising YHWH for creation. The psalmist says that he will sing to YHWH (אשירה ליהוה) as long as he lives, and make music (אזמרה) to him. He furthermore hopes that his meditation (שיחי) will be acceptable to YHWH, and rejoices in him (אשמח ביהוה).[126]

A degree of continuity appears in the positioning of Psalm 105 next to 104 because the former begins with a number of keywords found at the end of the latter. Psalm 105 begins with a call for the assembled community to speak out and declare YHWH's (יהוה, v. 1) deeds to the nations. In developing this notion, v. 2 calls for them to sing (שירו) to him, to make music (זמרו), and to meditate (שיחו) on all of his wonderful acts. The following verse additionally requests the seekers of YHWH (יהוה, v. 3) to rejoice (ישמח לב, v. 3). The link created in the repetition of these words and phrases develops the thematic continuity between the two works, moving from creation to the patriarchs, to Joseph and on to the exodus.

Additionally, a number of relatively rare words and phrases link the two works. The most prominent of these is אין מספר (without number), which Ps 104:25 employs to depict a multitude of creatures God created in the sea. Psalm 105:34 similarly relates the phrase to an act of God because he sent an innumerable multitude (אין מספר) of locusts

---

126. Cassuto, "Sequence and Arrangement," 5, discusses the phenomenon of common words linking the beginning of one text with the end of another text.

against Egypt. The phrase does not appear again in Book IV, and only twice in the remainder of the Psalter (40:12 [13] and 147:5). Another relatively rare word linking the two works is שבע, which serves as an expression of God's provision in both psalms. In Ps 104:13, 16, and 28 it is used to depict God supplying the needs of plants and animals in creation. In Ps 105:40, it similarly depicts God supplying needs, but this time for man, more specifically YHWH's people, the Israelites. Both psalms use חשך (darkness) in remarkably similar phrases to describe God's command of darkness, and its subsequent appearance. Psalm 104:20 recalls the phrase, תָּשֶׁת־חֹשֶׁךְ וִיהִי לָיְלָה ("You set darkness and it becomes night") to depict YHWH's creation of darkness as part of his formation of times and seasons; whereas, Ps 105:28 employs the phrase שָׁלַח חֹשֶׁךְ וַיֶּחְשִׁךְ ("he send darkness and it was dark") in a *less natural* occurrence, a break in the created order that causes darkness to fall upon the Egyptians.[127] Through the aforementioned association, a reading of the two psalms enforces the notion of darkness in Psalm 105 as being obedient to YHWH's command because Psalm 104 perceives it as one of his servants.

In light of the juxtaposition of Psalms 104 and 105, Psalm 105's tight association with creation deserves note. The close reading identifies numerous references to the power of YHWH's spoken word, which was used to enact his purposes (see for example vv. 11 and 16). Another potential relationship to creation concerns the psalm's rendition of the plagues. Darkness appears as the first of the plagues and the slaying of the firstborn appears as the last. Such sequencing reflects the creation tradition in Genesis 1, where God's first act is to dispel the darkness when he created the first light (Gen 1:3), and then at the end of creation he forms man. These associations with the creation story may have been recognized by an editor of the Psalter and influenced him when he decided to place Psalms 104 and 105 together.[128]

---

127. The relationship between Pss 105 and 106 is more developed than that between Psalms 104 and 105. The connections between the two are discussed in the following chapter, following an analysis of Psalm 106.

128. The two motifs of the creation and the exodus are frequently found together in the selected psalms, and the issue will be revisited again in the Conclusion.

3

Standing in the Gap

Psalm 106

The second of the selected works, Psalm 106, recounts numerous episodes of the Israelites' sojourn in the desert after their emancipation from Egypt. Like many of the other exodus psalms, events such as the crossing of the sea and the provision of food are recalled in Psalm 106. Contrary to the other exodus psalms, however, Psalm 106 recalls events in an entirely negative light as part of a confession of sin and a cry for deliverance from captivity. A unique feature of the psalm is that it evokes an instance of the Israelites sinning while they still dwelled in Egypt. The psalmist uses this recollection of Israel's sin in Egypt to further exemplify the nation's ingrained rebellious streak. The only other chapter in the MT that reflects such transgressions is Ezekiel (see 23:8, 19, 21).

STRUCTURE

Psalm 106 is best divided according to theme, although various lexical and poetic markers contribute to the clarification of the stanzas and strophes.

1. Introductory call to remember and recite YHWH's deeds (vv. 1–5)
2. Confession of sin from the exodus to the psalmist's present (vv. 6–46)
    A. YHWH's gracious deliverance at the Reed Sea and Israel's response (vv. 6–12)
    B. Israel forgets the deliverance and complains for food (vv. 13–15)

    C. Jealousy against YHWH's appointed leaders (vv. 16–18)
    D. Moses averts punishment from Israel for golden-calf idolatry (vv. 19–23)
    E. Israel's rejection of land and its ensuing punishment (vv. 24–27)
    F. Phinehas averts punishment from Israel for idolatry with Baal Peor (vv. 28–31)
    G. The Israelites cause Moses to sin (vv. 32–33)
    H. Increased sin as a result of mingling with the nations and its ensuing punishment (vv. 34–42)
    I. Cycle of sin and deliverance (vv. 43–46)
3. Plea for YHWH to deliver Israel from exile (v. 47)
4. Doxology (v. 48)

The introduction presents a number of key themes that recur throughout the psalm. The first two verses speak of YHWH's goodness, everlasting mercy, and heroic deeds. Following this, v. 3 introduces the idea of the righteous individual, which are represented in the psalm by Moses and Phinehas. Verses 4 and 5 find the psalmist isolated from the community, suggesting a discrepancy between his current standing and where he desires to be with respect to his relationship with God. The fact that he requests the benefits usually afforded the people of God implies he is not currently in a position to receive them. From a poetic standpoint, the root הלל envelops the introductory section.

The second stanza[1] opens with a confession of sin and subsequently recounts the act of salvation at the Reed Sea; it proceeds by recalling God's intervention for his people to save them from their enemies. Unlike the remaining incidents recorded in the psalm, this account includes an appropriate response to YHWH's intervention: Israel trusts in his word and temporarily sings his praise. As a background to this act of deliverance, the stanza recalls Israel's sins when they defy him at

---

1. Scholarly consensus generally agrees with this division; the only real point of contention arises with v. 6. Hoffman, יציאת מצריים, 132, includes it with the first stanza, whereas Allen, *Psalms 101–150*, 69, reads it as a much larger introductory stanza ranging from vv. 1–12. Additionally, Hacham, ספר תהלים, 281, understands v. 6 as an independent stanza. Concerning the remaining divisions, there is similar agreement; consequently, only the more radical divergences will be discussed.

the Reed Sea. This incident creates an important setting for the whole psalm because it shows that in spite of the people's sin and rebellion, YHWH is still willing to be merciful to them for his name's sake.

Section three records how YHWH's mercy was quickly forgotten, as those who were saved soon succumbed to wanton desires, leading them to test YHWH in the desert. Although the specific desires are not mentioned, the section recalls events in Num 16 when Israel craved meat to eat. From a literary standpoint, מדבר (desert) links this section with the previous one. Unlike the previous section, which records Israel's appropriate response to YHWH's display of power, the third stanza only records a pattern of sin and punishment.

Israelite rebellion is not directly targeted at God in the fourth stanza, but his appointed leadership. Similarly, not all the Israelite congregation are implicated, only the company of Dathan and Abiram, who envy Aaron's and Moses' leadership. Like the previous stanza, this one only includes an instance of sin and its ensuing punishment.

Stanza five, consisting of five verses, recounts Israel's idolatry in worshiping the image of a golden calf. As in the third stanza, the psalmist offers an explanation for the sinful behavior: because Israel forgot the deeds performed for them in Egypt. The root ישע links the two sections and explicitly refers to God *delivering* Israel from their enemies in v. 10. Unlike the previous two stanzas, punishment is averted because one righteous man, Moses, intercedes on the people's behalf, turning away God's wrath. However, the sequence of events differs from the last two sections and a pattern of "sin committed, punishment averted" emerges.

Four verses comprise the sixth stanza, two describe sin and two the resulting punishment. The crime here is Israel's failure to trust God; they did not believe he could bring them into the promised land and drive out its inhabitants. Reusing the verb האמין (see vv. 12 and 24), the psalm inserts a reference to the second section, especially v. 12, when the people trusted in YHWH's promise soon after experiencing deliverance. Like the first stanza, an inclusion delimits this section via the word ארץ (land, see vv. 24, 27), which plays an integral part in the people's sin and punishment. The sequence of events in this stanza is: sin committed; judgment decreed; the psalmist fails to mention the judgment's execution.

Similar to the fifth stanza, the seventh stanza recalls the worship of false gods. This time, however, the Israelites do not forge their own idol, but begin serving and worshiping the gods of the surrounding nations. Like the fifth stanza, this there is an extended sequence of sin, punishment, and punishment averted, but with the addition of a reward for the intercessor. Once again a righteous man stands in the gap; this time it is Phinehas; who, unlike Moses, receives a reward for his act. Both אכל (eat) and פרץ (breakthrough) link this stanza with the fifth, which recites Moses' act of intercession.

Almost by way of apology, the two verses in stanza eight recount the rebellion at the waters of Meribah. Although this short stanza depicts one of the many Israelite sins in the desert, it excuses Moses' sinful actions by placing the onus on the Israelites for the leader's rash behavior. Although the people sin, which leads Moses to sin, no explicit punishment is mentioned for either party.

Following the shortest stanza is section nine, which is the longest. The sin is described in far more detail than the previous transgressions (vv. 34–42), recounting a descent into depravity. The basis of the sin is the Israelites' failure to destroy the previous occupants of Canaan. This initial act of disobedience escalates and culminates with the Israelites sacrificing their sons to idols and demons, thus polluting the land. For the third time (see also stanza five and stanza seven), idolatry ensnares Israel. As punishment, YHWH delivers them into the hands of the nations, who rule and oppressed them. The familiar pattern of sin and punishment returns.

Instead of detailing another specific example of Israel's sin, the tenth stanza recalls a perpetual pattern reflecting both the events explicated in the psalm's main body, and the continued sequence of events after the Israelites conquered the land and dwelt therein. A distinct change enters into the penultimate section: No specific punishment is decreed or enacted by God. Instead, the psalmist portrays a general picture of Israel being humbled as a result of their punishment, which causes God to respond by delivering them from their own self-inflicted distress. The stanza concludes on a positive note, leading the reader to the psalm's climax in v. 47.

The final verse, v. 47,[2] constitutes a plea for help that is anchored on everything previously recounted in the psalm, thus establishing a variety of pertinent literary links with the psalm. The recurring theme in

---

2. See close reading of v. 48.

Standing in the Gap

almost every stanza is the sinful behavior of the Israelites, and because of this, the psalmist cannot request any assistance from God based on their behavior. Consequently, he establishes his plea on the basis of God's mercy.[3] Only at this stage in the psalm does it become clear why the psalmist singles himself out as a separate individual in the opening section. Throughout the psalm, the psalmist recalls the roles of Moses (see stanza five) and Phinehas (see stanza seven), individuals who were morally separate from the community and who were able to intercede on Israel's behalf. In this last section, the psalmist also assumes the role of an individual intercessor.

CLOSE READING

הַלְלוּיָהּ הוֹדוּ לַיהוָה כִּי־טוֹב כִּי לְעוֹלָם חַסְדּוֹ ¹

Praise Yah; proclaim thanks to YHWH for he is good, surely his mercy is everlasting

Although Psalm 106's opening verse should by no means be considered unique, since it frequently appears in psalms praising God (see Ps 118:1; 1 Chr 16:34), the overall context in which these verses are set, especially with regard to exodus psalms, differs significantly. Comparing Pss 106:1 and 136:1, the same verse appears introducing two appreciably disparate aspects of YHWH's everlasting kindness. The latter celebrates compassion that manumits his people from their foes and allots them land,

---

3. The two most divergent divisions from the structure proposed above come from Allen and Terrien. Allen, *Psalms 101–150*, 62–64, proposes four major divisions: vv. 1–12, 13–23, 24–31, and 32–47—with the last verse excluded because it is not organic to the psalm (see close reading for v. 48). This proposal however, is not radically different from the division presented in this chapter, but simply unites the smaller units into larger sections. The other variation proposed by Terrien, *The Psalms*, 726–33, adopts a five-strophe model where each strophe consists of three stanzas with the addition of a three-verse stanza as a prelude, and vv. 47, 48 as a postlude: prelude 1–3; strophe I, vv. 4–5, 6–7, 8–10; strophe II, vv. 11–13, 14–16, 17–18; strophe III, vv. 19–22, 23–24, 25–27; strophe IV, vv. 28–31, 32–33, 34–36; strophe V, vv. 37–38, 39–41, 42–46; postlude, vv. 47–48. Such a division, derived from the so-called "pattern and layout" of the psalm bears little sensitivity to the psalm's internal content and poetic markers. Uniting v. 13 with vv. 11–12, for example, creates a degree of tension because it unites negatively toned verses with a positive one. The Israelites' positive response marked in this stanza creates an ideal model depicting how they should have responded to their deliverance; an ideal they fail to attain throughout the remaining stanzas. Additionally, his division between vv. 41 and 42 ignores the inclusion created by the word יד ("hand," see the close reading for these verses).

primarily accentuating God's benevolence towards his people, Israel. YHWH's anger in Psalm 136 is generally leveled against other nations, Amorites and Egyptians, whereas here, it is turned towards his people.

As with Psalm 135, Psalm 106 opens and closes with הללו יה ("praise Yah"), which forms an inclusion and creates a framework of praise that should be remembered throughout the psalm. Even though retribution and punishment come from his hand as a result of disobedience, YHWH still deserves praise for curtailing the extent of all punitive actions. In the context of the psalm, the phrase כי טוב ("for he is good") constitutes a compelling testimony of the psalmist's hope and trust in God. In spite of the dire pattern painted in the psalm—Israel's inclination to rebel and God's punitive responses—the opening verse still exhorts the community to declare God's inherent goodness first.[4] YHWH's eternal grace, חסדו, never fully materializes in this psalm; rather, it is a declaration of his nature, recited in the hope that he will one day be faithful to that nature and deliver his people. Again, this contrasts with Psalm 135, where the congregation celebrates his past acts of mercy. The eternal nature of God's mercy finds expression within Psalm 106's main body as it surveys hundreds of years of Israelite literary history, from their emancipation in Egypt to the exile; for the psalmist such mercy will hopefully continue.

[2] מִי יְמַלֵּל גְּבוּרוֹת יְהוָה יַשְׁמִיעַ כָּל־תְּהִלָּתוֹ

Who can speak of the heroic deeds of YHWH, (and) declare his praiseworthy acts

The idea of declaration continues in v. 2. Verse 1 employs a plural imperative of the root ידה, which not only expresses thanksgiving but also "declaration" and "annunciation" (see close reading of Ps 105:1). Verse 2 similarly begins with an expression of declaration, ימלל (speak),[5] and

---

4. This becomes more pronounced when considering that the implication of כי טוב ("for he is good") is often כי טוב לנו ("for he is good to us"), according to Hacham, ספר תהלים, 281.

5. This is the standard Aramaic word for "speak" or "say," and may reflect the psalm's lateness. See Jastrow, *Dictionary*, 792.

poses a rhetorical[6] question: Who can tell, or speak of YHWH's might.[7] Through a relatively simple process of deduction, one may conclude that the psalmist speaks of himself in a sense, because he recounts YHWH's mighty deeds in the psalm's body. Both תהלה and גבורה ("praiseworthy acts" and "heroic deeds")—although the parallel pair is not attested elsewhere—represent puissant acts performed by God. The former may depict a king's accomplishments similar to the way God's deeds are expressed here, וְיֶתֶר דִּבְרֵי יֵהוּא וְכָל־אֲשֶׁר עָשָׂה וְכָל־גְּבוּרָתוֹ ("Now the remainder of the deeds of Yehu, and all that he did all his mighty acts," 2 Kgs 10:34; see also 13:12), the latter represents deeds that evoke a response of praise. In Ps 9:15, praise for YHWH stems from his ability to deliver, לְמַעַן אֲסַפְּרָה כָּל־תְּהִלָּתֶיךָ בְּשַׁעֲרֵי בַת־צִיּוֹן אָגִילָה בִּישׁוּעָתֶךָ ("So that I may tell of all your praiseworthy deeds, in the gates of the daughter of Zion I will rejoice in your salvation," see also Ps 78:4). Thus, in effecting the psalmist's redemption, God evokes the writer's praise.

אַשְׁרֵי שֹׁמְרֵי מִשְׁפָּט עֹשֵׂה צְדָקָה בְכָל־עֵת ³

Blessed is the man who keeps justice, and performs righteous deeds at all times

Although v. 3 does not attempt to answer directly the question posed in v. 2, the juxtaposition of the verses assumes one who keeps the law as being worthy to tell of God's deeds. The word אשרי means "fortunate," "happy," or more importantly "blessed," as Ps 32:1 suggests, אַשְׁרֵי נְשׂוּי־פֶּשַׁע כְּסוּי חֲטָאָה ("Blessed is he whose transgressions are forgiven, whose sin is covered"; see also 1 Kgs 10:8 for the queen of Sheba's description of Solomon's servants). Such terminology is usually reserved for Wisdom literature, e.g., Prov 3:13 (אַשְׁרֵי אָדָם מָצָא חָכְמָה וְאָדָם יָפִיק תְּבוּנָה, "Blessed is the man who finds wisdom and the man who gains understanding," see also Prov 8:34 and Job 5:17). Its presence in this psalm, however, should not be totally unexpected because similar didactic elements appear in Psalm 78. Additionally, the

---

6. Rhetorical questions, like the one posed in this psalm, usually anticipate an implicit negative answer, as in Joel 1:2; see Watson, *Classical Hebrew Poetry*, 341, and also Seybold, *Die Psalmen*, 422. With this understanding, it is possible to interpret the psalmist's statement as "Who can speak of his mighty acts now, at a time when we are in such despair?" Such an interpretation de-emphasizes the YHWH's heroic deeds and focuses more on Israel's sins.

7. For גבורה strictly in the sense of power or might, see Judg 5:31; Ps 21:13 [14]; Job 39:19.

wisdom theme guides the reader in reading the psalm, emphasizing that its message is valuable for instruction and should be learned.[8] The term שמרי משפט ("keeper of justice") is best understood as a description of one who obeys God's laws, a definition exemplified by Lev 18:5: וּשְׁמַרְתֶּם אֶת־חֻקֹּתַי וְאֶת־מִשְׁפָּטַי ("You will keep my laws and my judgements" cf. Ps 119:106), in which משפט represents "laws" and שמר equates to "obey." Echoes of this verse reverberate throughout the remainder of the psalm, which adduces concrete examples that convey the misery of those who fail to obey God's laws, and the rewards of those who obey. By repeating כל (all), the psalmist forges a literary nexus between vv. 2 and 3, with an association that develops the concept of deeds: v. 2 enumerates the deeds of God whereas v. 3 expounds the deeds of man. Comparisons between these deeds frequently appear throughout the present work.

זָכְרֵנִי יְהוָה בִּרְצוֹן עַמֶּךָ פָּקְדֵנִי בִּישׁוּעָתֶךָ [4]

Remember me O YHWH with the favor of your people; visit me with your deliverance

Here marks a turn in the composition as attention focuses on the psalmist (or speaker/reciter of the psalm). Verse four reflects his desire (רצון) to be remembered with the good will and favor YHWH affords his people.[9] Exegetes often interpret the personal element on the imperative זכרני ("remember me") as a copyist error and replace it with the first-person common plural ending (זכרנו, "remember us"),[10] but this alteration may indeed be unnecessary. The notion of a righteous individual interceding for a sinful people finds expression within the psalm's main body (cf. vv. 23 and 30). Moreover, juxtaposed elements in the psalm's opening reveal a certain innocence and righteousness of the speaker because he is the first person mentioned after, "Who can speak of his deeds" and "Blessed is the man who keeps his laws."

The psalmist's cry for God to remember does not represent a call for mental activity by YHWH, but a petition for his physical interven-

---

8. Concerning this didactic element in the psalm, Allen, *Psalms 101–150*, 66, notes, "The commendation formula of v. 3 reveals a didactic ethical function comparable with Psalm 105:45."

9. See Ps 5:12 [13] and especially Isa 61:2 where it involves vindication and comfort.

10. This change is reflected in certain Septuagint documents as μνήσθητι ἡμῶν, a reading Kraus, *Psalms 60–150*, 315, adopts.

tion. Such an entreaty for help and intervention involving the parallel pair זכר and פקד ("remember" and "visit") appears in Jer 15:15 when the prophet calls for God to intervene and judge his enemies (זָכְרֵנִי וּפָקְדֵנִי וְהִנָּקֶם לִי מֵרֹדְפַי, "Remember me and visit me and avenge me on those who pursue me"). Echoes of the psalmist's distress additionally come to the fore in the word ישועה, the root of which (ישע) commonly expresses a demand for deliverance through physical intervention in contexts of war and oppression (see Exod 14:13 and 1 Sam 14:45).

לִרְאוֹת בְּטוֹבַת בְּחִירֶיךָ לִשְׂמֹחַ בְּשִׂמְחַת גּוֹיֶךָ לְהִתְהַלֵּל עִם־נַחֲלָתֶךָ 5

To see the goodness of your chosen ones, to rejoice with the joy of your people, to rejoice with your inheritance

Verse 5 continues to develop the request for YHWH to remember the psalmist with good will. The infinitive construct together with the *lamed* prefix is a form often employed to modify a preceding verb,[11] in this instance פקדני ("visit me") in v. 4. Thus, v. 5 forms a continuation of the sentiment originally expressed in v. 4, "remember me . . . that I might see." Overall, the verse expresses the psalmist's continual yearning to experience the benefits afforded a chosen people, such as deliverance from enemies and the bestowal of land as an inheritance as recounted in Psalms 135 and 136. Emphasis on Israel's intimate relationship with YHWH finds expression in repeated statements נחלתך . . . גויך . . . בחיריך ("your inheritance . . . your people . . . your chosen ones"). Such an emphasis serves as a reminder to YHWH that they are still his special people, thus eliciting his compassion for them. Somewhat unexpectedly, however, the psalmist chooses a rare word, גוי, to designate the people's privileged status. On one hand, this may simply stem from a desire to avoid repetition,[12] since עם appears in the previous verse. On the other hand, גוי serves as a sullen reminder of the people's current status before God, they stand before him almost as though they had forfeited their unique status and were simply one of

---

11. See Gen 18:19; Exod 31:16; Deut 13:18 [19]; also JM §124°.

12. A similar usage of this word also occurs in Zeph 2:9, (ויתר גויי ינחלום, "and the remainder of my people shall possess them").

the *other* nations. Other occurrences of גוי within the psalm[13] enforce such an interpretation.[14]

Each expression depicting the select status of God's people corresponds with a term denoting joy and happiness. Within such a framework, התהלל adopts this meaning, as in Isa 41:16, וְאַתָּה תָּגִיל בַּיהוָה בִּקְדוֹשׁ יִשְׂרָאֵל תִּתְהַלָּל ("and you rejoice in YHWH, glory in the Holy One of Israel"), where it parallels גיל. Verse 5 closes the opening section with an inclusion created by טוב (good), a word embodying the initial stanza's disposition. It evades any recollection of Israel's sinful past, focusing on YHWH's goodness and omnipotence, and only obscure hints are provided with respect to the perceived gulf the psalmist recognizes between the nation (and himself) and their God.

חָטָאנוּ עִם־אֲבוֹתֵינוּ הֶעֱוִינוּ הִרְשָׁעְנוּ [6]

We have sinned with our fathers, we have committed iniquity, we have acted wickedly

The second section's opening verse witnesses a dramatic contrast to the opening stanza's optimism. Opposing the previous verse's tri-colon signifying the joys of intimacy with YHWH, stands another tri-colon denoting sin, transgression, and wickedness. Just as the repetition in v. 5 emphasizes[15] joy, here it inculcates the severity of Israel's transgressions. The three roots employed here to represent the people's transgressions, חטא, עוה,[16] and רשע, (iniquity, sin, and wicked) additionally appear in Jer 14:20 (יָדַעְנוּ יְהוָה רִשְׁעֵנוּ עֲוֹן אֲבוֹתֵינוּ כִּי חָטָאנוּ לָךְ, "Lord, we know our wickedness, and the iniquity of our fathers, for we have sinned against you"). The verse's wording has much in common with Solomon's prediction of Israel's sins and their turning back to God in 1 Kgs 8:47. These same words may have been adopted into part of a

---

13. See vv. 27, 35, 41, and 47.

14. Cody, "Chosen People," 6 classifies numerous instances in which the word גוי relates to the people of God. Amid his classification, he acknowledges instances in which the word is derogatively employed, citing Deut 32:28, Judg 2:20, and Isa 1:4 among others, but he fails to include this verse. Instead, he classifies Ps 106:5 as an instance of an alternative B-word for people. However, it seems too coincidental that within a psalm with such negative overtones, this ascription appears.

15. For a further example of a threefold emphatic repetition, see Isa 6:3, וְאָמַר קָדוֹשׁ קָדוֹשׁ קָדוֹשׁ יְהוָה צְבָאוֹת, "and he said 'holy, holy, holy is the Lord of hosts'").

16. The word עָוֹן ("commit iniquity") originates from the root עוה; see BDB 730–31.

standard lament formula designed to evoke Solomon's entreaty for God to see Israel's suffering and turn from his anger.[17]

Along with the repetition of the three words for transgression comes the tripartite deployment of first-person common plural suffixes. These suffixes conjoin the wrongdoings of the psalmist's community with those of their forefathers. No distinction appears between the sins of the two generations; both are combined and confessed together, and the contemporaneous generation stands as guilty as their forefathers. Such a picture contrasts with Psalm 95, which attempts to detach the desert generation's rebellious behavior from the community reciting the psalm at the temple.

אֲבוֹתֵינוּ בְמִצְרַיִם לֹא־הִשְׂכִּילוּ נִפְלְאוֹתֶיךָ לֹא זָכְרוּ אֶת־רֹב חֲסָדֶיךָ וַיַּמְרוּ עַל־יָם בְּיַם־סוּף 7

Our fathers in Egypt never learned from your mighty acts, they never remembered your great mercy, and they defied Elyon at Yam Suf

Moving from an abstract reference to Israel's transgressions, the psalmist proceeds to detail the misdeeds and acts of rebellion committed by "our fathers."[18] While in Egypt, the forefathers failed to השכילו, which is best understood as "learn" or "gain insight from,"[19] as witnessed in Neh 8:13, וּבַיּוֹם הַשֵּׁנִי נֶאֶסְפוּ רָאשֵׁי הָאָבוֹת לְכָל־הָעָם הַכֹּהֲנִים וְהַלְוִיִּם אֶל־עֶזְרָא הַסֹּפֵר וּלְהַשְׂכִּיל אֶל־דִּבְרֵי הַתּוֹרָה ("On the second day, the heads of the fathers' houses of all the peoples, the priests and the Levites gathered to Ezra the scribe to learn the words of Torah"), when the dwellers of Judah congregated *to learn* from the law.[20] The generation in Egypt never learned from the mighty deeds (נפלאות) YHWH enacted in Egypt. In

---

17. The powerful imagery of an individual confessing the sins of his generation together with that of his forefathers also appears in Dan 9:16.

18. Richardson, "Psalm 106," 193, incorrectly seeks to "complete" this verse into a double bi-cola by adding ימרדו ("they rebelled") after מצרים (Egypt); however such an alteration is unnecessary.

19. Kraus, *Psalms 60–150*, 319, interprets the verse as though the Israelites did not understand the significance of God's deeds. Although this perception is similar, it softens the verse's impact by implying the Israelites were unable, through no fault of their own, to understand the significance of the works wrought. The context of the psalm, however, suggests a stronger nuance; they understood, but simply refused to act accordingly.

20. See also Ps 2:10, where kings are advised *to learn* from discipline. The word is also common in Wisdom literature, a genre echoed in v. 2's rhetorical question, and the word אשרי (blessed) in v. 3.

all likelihood, the נפלאות, are used here to refer to the plagues since they are often described in this way (see v. 22 and Exod 3:20). Moreover, the plagues constitute the event that immediately precedes the sea crossing in Israelite literary history. Psalm 106's portrayal of plagues wrought against Egypt differs slightly from the other psalms discussed in this volume where they are employed to demonstrate YHWH's power over the enemy in defense of his people. On the other hand, the psalmist infers that the purpose of the plagues was to teach the Israelites to depend on YHWH.

The forefathers are chastised here for not remembering (זכרו) YHWH's merciful acts towards them. As with v. 4, "remember" connotes more than just mental recollection, but taking action that is appropriate to the memory. In paralleling the two terms השכיל and זכר, (learning and remembering) the verse links the two concepts of failing to learn and failing to remember. Both roots זכר and חסד (remember and mercy) link the present stanza with the opening one. YHWH's deeds in Egypt exemplify his everlasting mercy or חסד, and in the context of the current verse, the word portrays his power to liberate from oppression, as witnessed from the corresponding word, נפלאות ("mighty acts"). Moreover, verses such as Ps 33:18, הִנֵּה עֵין יְהוָה אֶל־יְרֵאָיו לַמְיַחֲלִים לְחַסְדּוֹ[21] ("Behold the eye of YHWH is on those who fear him, those who hope in his mercy") reveal a similar correspondence.[22]

The shortcomings mentioned in the previous two statements—never learning or remembering—are made more explicit in v. 7b; they defied (מרו)[23] God[24] at the Sea of Reeds. The reference here recalls events in Exod 14:12 when the Israelites were caught between the Sea

---

21. See also Ps 17:7; 109:26.

22. See also Richardson, "Psalm 106," 192, who, concerning חסד states, "normally provides deliverance from dire straits . . . God's *hesed* is delivering, protecting power."

23. A common word denoting rebellion, particularly in the context of God's relationship with Israel in the desert (see Deut 31:27; Ezek 20:13; Ps 78:17, 40).

24. Various explanations exist for עַל יָם. The Septuagint reads it as αναβαινοντες, as though the *vorlage* read "עֹלִים," resulting in a translation of "When they went up by the Sea of Reeds." Alternatively, Keil and Delitzsch, *Psalms*, 153, opt to preserve the reading claiming the preposition על alternates with ב elsewhere, citing Ezek 10:15 and Joel 4:8b. Perhaps the best reading, however, is עֶלְיוֹן (Elyon), signifying that the Israelites rebelled directly against YHWH at the Reed Sea. This corresponds with a similar verse in Ps 78:17, and complements the psalm's main theme of Israel rebelling against the Most High. See also Kraus, *Psalms 60–150*, 315; Brooke, "Psalms 105 and 106," 278; and Richardson, "Psalm 106," 194, who all reach the same conclusion by

and the Egyptian army and immediately began crying out against God[25] and complaining to Moses.[26]

וַיּוֹשִׁיעֵם לְמַעַן שְׁמוֹ לְהוֹדִיעַ אֶת־גְּבוּרָתוֹ 8

But he saved them for the sake of his name, in order to proclaim his heroic acts

As a response to the forgetfulness leading to rebellion at the Reed Sea, God still acts to deliver his people (ויושיעם). This work of redemption, however, is strictly founded upon his merciful nature and performed according to his eternal mercy (see v. 1). The fact that YHWH delivers his people for his namesake (למען שמו, see Ps 23:3; 25:11; 79:9), and not for the sake of their behavior, sustains a fundamental theme underlying the entire psalm: all requests are based on God's mercy and not Israel's behavior. The juxtaposition of vv. 7 and 8 contrast Israel's sin and God's mercy towards them. Numerous other devices employed by the psalmist, as explained below, similarly contrast these ideas.

Verse 8 closely associates acts of deliverance performed by God with the declarations of such acts: God extricated the Israelites so his deeds would be proclaimed. Exodus 7:5 echoes this notion on numerous occasions when it distinctly states that his acts of deliverance should lead to a knowledge of him, וְיָדְעוּ מִצְרַיִם כִּי־אֲנִי יְהוָה בִּנְטֹתִי אֶת־יָדִי עַל־מִצְרָיִם וְהוֹצֵאתִי אֶת־בְּנֵי־יִשְׂרָאֵל מִתּוֹכָם ("And the Egyptians will know that I am YHWH, when I stretch out my hand on Egypt and I bring out the sons of Israel from their midst"; see also Exod 14:4). The verse echoes v. 2, which begs the question: "Who can speak of [his] mighty acts?" Comparing the two verses suggests the community in which the psalmist lives earnestly seeks an act of deliverance. If God acts so his

---

reading עלים as deriving from the proper noun עלי, denoting God (the form is attested in a theophoric name in the Samaria Ostraca, with the addition of an enclitic *mem*).

25. Concerning Israelite rebellion in Egypt, however, another possibility presents itself in the form of an earlier tradition that suggests the Israelites may have participated in some form of idolatry, as Ezek 20:7–9 suggests. This option, however, seems less tenable because the point emphasized in v. 7 is that immediately after God had manifested his wonders—in this instance, the plagues—they failed to learn from them, and trust in him again to deliver them from the Egyptians. Allen, *Psalms 101–150*, 71, raises this possibility, although Loewenstamm, *Evolution*, 26, further suggests that Ezekiel's version consists of an exegetical adaptation of events and does not rely on a specific tradition.

26. RaDaK mentions the possibility that they were afraid to walk into the dry river bed once the sea had opened up; see Cohen, *Psalms*, 121.

deeds may be proclaimed, v. 8, and the psalmist enquires "Who can proclaim [his] mighty acts?" in v. 2, then it follows that none can proclaim them because none have experienced his acts of salvation.

וַיִּגְעַר בְּיַם־סוּף וַיֶּחֱרָב וַיּוֹלִיכֵם בַּתְּהֹמוֹת כַּמִּדְבָּר ⁹

He rebuked Yam Suf[27] and it dried up, then he led them through the deep like a desert

After the general description of God saving his people for the sake of his name is given in v. 8, the psalm proceeds to present a more detailed description of events. As in the previous two verses, the *waw* consecutive in this verse functions as it would in biblical narrative by progressing the plot. YHWH rebukes the sea, ויגער בים סוף ("He rebuked *Yam Suf*"), to rescue his people. The word גער, though often appearing in a human context meaning to "rebuke" or "tell off"[28] (see Gen 37:10, and a more extreme case in Ps 9:6), introduces a potentially mythical element, alluding to the instance during creation when God rebuked the primeval waters.[29] Similar traditions echo in biblical passages such as Nah 1:4, (גּוֹעֵר בַּיָּם וַיַּבְּשֵׁהוּ וְכָל־הַנְּהָרוֹת הֶחֱרִיב), "He rebukes the sea and dries it up, and all the rivers dry up"), portraying God's power over creation and its reaction to his wrath, and Ps 104:7, which specifically recounts events in creation. In Ps 106, the same image of power and domination manifests itself in YHWH's redemption of his people for his name's

---

27. The term "Yam Suf" appears interchangeably with "Sea of Reeds" or "Reed Sea" throughout the present study.

28. Concerning this, Hacham, ספר תהלים, 284 suggests the sea somehow refused to obey God's command and needed rebuking; Briggs, *The Book of Psalms*, 349, further asserts, "The sea is conceived as a servant, who had exceeded his authority and done what he ought not to have done." He further suggests this particular word was omitted from the prose accounts of the Torah because of its mythological associations.

29. Also adding to the mythological aspect is the appearance of תהום for "deep," which bears the obvious similarity to the name Tiamat, the water god defeated by Marduk in the Babylonian epic *Enuma Elish*. Richardson, "Psalm 106," 104, rightly asserts that תהום echoes the ancient Near Eastern myths, but more importantly notes the relationship between the two events, stating: "the historical account of liberation was enlarged by incorporating into it elements of the Creation myth." (For more on the mythological associations this word bears, see Norin, *Er Spaltete das Meer*, 58–62. Concerning this verse, Loewenstamm, *Evolution*, 251, further mentions that the victory here was over the sea itself, and that such an understanding is reflected in Ps 136:13–16. Additionally, Cassuto, *Biblical and Oriental Studies*, 83, 89, remarks that both תהום ("the deep") and גער ("to rebuke") were employed in an Israelite national epic recounting YHWH's victory over the sea.

Standing in the Gap

sake. With the repetition of ים סוף (*Yam Suf*, which is the Reed Sea), one is reminded of Israel's rebellion in v. 7, וַיַּמְרוּ עַל־יָם בְּיַם־סוּף ("They defied Elyon[30] at *Yam Suf*"), which introduces a touch of irony—after they defy him at the sea, God rebukes the water and not the rebellious people. Such irony hints towards God's compassion because it creates an example of the Israelites failing to receive what they deserve.

Of all the psalms containing quotes from the exodus tradition, only Ps 106 employs the verb החריב ("to be dried up") as a vivid portrayal of the sea drying up, thus creating an antithesis of the desert experience when God caused water to flow in arid places. Similar sentiments, however, are apparent in Isa 63:13, מוֹלִיכָם בַּתְּהֹמוֹת כַּסּוּס בַּמִּדְבָּר לֹא יִכָּשֵׁלוּ ("Who led them through the deep, like a horse in the wilderness they did not stumble"). Unlike the exodus account in the book of Exodus, Moses' role diminishes here, and events at the Reed Sea become solely the work of YHWH—as an act of mercy towards his people. Moses' reduced role accentuates the psalmist's desire to highlight YHWH's role. Later in the psalm, the psalmist recalls Moses' involvement in other events.[31]

וַיּוֹשִׁיעֵם מִיַּד שׂוֹנֵא וַיִּגְאָלֵם מִיַּד אוֹיֵב 10

And he saved them from the hand of the hater and he redeemed them from the hand of the enemy

Verse 10 continues enumerating events at the Sea of Reeds, detailing the deliverance from the Egyptians, as opposed to the sea in the previous verse. Repetition of ויושיעם ("he saved them"), found in v. 8, reminds the reader that the deed was not performed on account of the Israelites' obedience, but according to God's compassion, so his name might be proclaimed. In the context of this verse, both שונא (hater) and אויב (enemy) refer to the Egyptians even though they are not explicitly mentioned by name. Such an omission expands the possibility of God's salvation: he can save from any enemy, not just the Egyptians, but those oppressing the psalmist's contemporaneous generation.[32] The pure par-

---

30. See the close reading for this translation of the verse.

31. All of this contrasts with Cross, *Canaanite Myth*, 135, who states, "other psalms, most of them late, reflect precisely the prose tradition: Psalm 136:15; 66:6; 106:9."

32. They appear again in vv. 41–42.

allelism employed by the psalmist in v. 8 repeats and accentuates the redemption from Egypt, which constitutes a pivotal act in the psalm.

וַיְכַסּוּ־מַיִם צָרֵיהֶם אֶחָד מֵהֶם לֹא נוֹתָר [11]

And water covered their oppressors, and not one of them remained

More than just saving his people from the hand of their enemy, YHWH administers the *coup de grâce* by destroying the Egyptians in the midst of the sea. Verse 11 echoes Exod 14:28, which reports the same event in similar words, וַיָּשֻׁבוּ הַמַּיִם וַיְכַסּוּ אֶת־הָרֶכֶב וְאֶת־הַפָּרָשִׁים לְכֹל חֵיל פַּרְעֹה הַבָּאִים אַחֲרֵיהֶם בַּיָּם לֹא־נִשְׁאַר בָּהֶם עַד־אֶחָד ("And the waters returned and covered the chariots and horsemen; of all the soldiers of Pharaoh who came after them not even one of them was left"). Without expressly mentioning the Egyptians, the psalmist alludes to them here through the form מים צריהם which is lexically and phonologically similar to מצרים.[33] Further linking vv. 10–11, this same word, צר constitutes a third synonym for Egypt, although it usually bears a more general meaning of "enemy" or "adversary" (see Esth 7:6, where it parallels אויב [enemy]). The deliverance and destruction finds completion in the verse's final words, לא נותר ("did not remain"), stressing that the threat of an Egyptian attack was not just partially removed but entirely eliminated.

וַיַּאֲמִינוּ בִדְבָרָיו יָשִׁירוּ תְּהִלָּתוֹ [12]

Then they trusted in his promise and sang his praise

As a result of being saved from their enemies and witnessing God's hand at work for them, the Israelites correctly respond, in this instance, by believing him. In this verse, דבריו ("his promise") echoes the promise recorded in Exod 3:8, when God vows to intervene and deliver Israel and lead them to a spacious land, וָאֵרֵד לְהַצִּילוֹ מִיַּד מִצְרַיִם וּלְהַעֲלֹתוֹ מִן־הָאָרֶץ הַהִוא אֶל־אֶרֶץ טוֹבָה וּרְחָבָה ("And I will come down to save him from the hand of Egypt and bring him up from that land unto a good and spacious land"). Due to God delivering the Israelites from Egypt, they trusted in his promise (ויאמינו בדבריו) that he could and would bring them to a spacious land. Their response, singing (ישירו) his praises re-

---

33. A similar play on this sound occurs in Ps 105:24, where the similar sounding מצריו is employed, and also in Ps 78:42, which contains the phrase מני צר that once again recalls מצרים on account of the lexical similarity.

Standing in the Gap

calls the song of the sea in Exod 15:1, אָז יָשִׁיר־מֹשֶׁה וּבְנֵי יִשְׂרָאֵל אֶת־הַשִּׁירָה הַזֹּאת ("Then Moses and the sons of Israel sang this song"), following the similar sequence of events in Exodus. Perhaps more importantly, the reference here to singing YHWH's praises, or magnificent works (תהלתו), alludes back to v. 2 where the psalmist asks, "Who can tell of his magnificent deeds?" Consequently, v. 12 creates at least a partial answer to this question by claiming "those who have seen his mighty acts can tell of them."[34] This verse also contains the last of any positive and encouraging traits ascribed to Israel; thus, the psalm praises them for seeing his deeds and responding in accordance with what they saw, even if it was only for a short while.

13 מִהֲרוּ שָׁכְחוּ מַעֲשָׂיו לֹא־חִכּוּ לַעֲצָתוֹ

They quickly forgot his deeds (however) and never waited for his instructions

Verse 13 marks the beginning of a new section; after believing for a brief time in God's promises to them, Israel quickly forgets what he did for them. From this point on, the psalm adopts a negative tone in which the Israelites are unable to recover from a downward spiral of sin and rebellion. Within this verse, the author paraphrases and interprets events with his own words rather than quoting from a specific source. The hendiadys[35] מהרו שכחו ("quickly forgot") represents the time it took for the Israelites to rejoice at seeing God's hand at the Sea, to their first complaint at a time of need. Moreover, שכחו creates a semantic link with v. 7 (לא זכרו, "They never remembered"). The idea of forgetfulness leading to disobedience appears first in v. 7, and now in v. 13 the psalmist provides a practical example.

More than just implying "waiting," the phrase חכו ל also denotes "longing for" or "deeply desiring." Such a sentiment is apparent from Job 3:21, הַמְחַכִּים לַמָּוֶת וְאֵינֶנּוּ וַיַּחְפְּרֻהוּ מִמַּטְמוֹנִים ("Those longing for death, but there is none, and search for it more than hidden treasure"), which not only speaks of one who waits for death, but longs for its coming.[36] The psalmist's choice of עצה ("counsel/instructions") is open to a num-

---

34. See v. 47 for the development of this idea.

35. See also 1 Sam 25:42, Abigail *quickly* rises; and Ps 143:7, a call for God to answer *quickly*.

36. The selection of חכו ("they waited") here creates an instance of assonance with שכחו ("they forgot").

ber of interpretations³⁷ since it is not immediately clear to which עצה he refers. In the immediate context, it alludes to Israel's grumbling for food, rather than waiting for God to guide and instruct them, implying they requested sustenance too soon without waiting for YHWH to *advise* them. The Torah, however, never mentions such a sin. The word עצה may also be interpreted as law, גַּם־עֵדֹתֶיךָ שַׁעֲשֻׁעָי אַנְשֵׁי עֲצָתִי ("Also your testimonies are my delight, they are my counselors"; Ps 119:24); therefore it could be interpreted here as a veiled reference to the lawgiving at Sinai when the Israelites did not wait for Moses to return with the law but quickly forgot about him and disobeyed him by forging a calf idol. Such an interpretation is strengthened by the emphasis on the speed with which they sinned while at Mt. Sinai, סָרוּ מַהֵר מִן־הַדֶּרֶךְ אֲשֶׁר צִוִּיתִם עָשׂוּ לָהֶם עֵגֶל מַסֵּכָה ("They turned quickly from the way you commanded them, and made for themselves a calf image"; Exod 32:8).

וַיִּתְאַוּוּ תַאֲוָה בַּמִּדְבָּר וַיְנַסּוּ־אֵל בִּישִׁימוֹן ¹⁴

And they craved desires in the desert and tested El in the wasteland

Exemplifying how the people quickly forgot his deeds, the psalm now details a specific incident. Although the stem אוה does not necessarily imply an evil desire, as in Ps 132:14, here it does as the psalmist alludes to Num 11:4, referring to the mixed multitude that desired flesh to eat, וְהָאסַפְסֻף אֲשֶׁר בְּקִרְבּוֹ הִתְאַוּוּ תַּאֲוָה וַיָּשֻׁבוּ וַיִּבְכּוּ גַּם בְּנֵי יִשְׂרָאֵל וַיֹּאמְרוּ מִי יַאֲכִלֵנוּ בָּשָׂר ("And the riff-raff who were amongst them craved desires, and also the sons of Israel wept again, and they said, 'Who will feed us meat?'"). Numbers' context evidently indicates a selfish and wanton desire because the people's complaint is not based on need; they had already been provided with manna (11:6) and now desired a wider variety of food. To further the contrast between the people's rebellion in their wanton desire and God's merciful treatment of them, the psalmist repeats the word מדבר (desert), which appears in v. 9 where it expressly states that YHWH led them through the deep as though it were a desert.³⁸

37. For Keil and Delitzsch, *Psalms*, 154, it refers to "the plan with respect to the time and manner of the help"; along similar lines Allen, *Psalms 101–150*, 71, understands it as YHWH's intention to provide Israel with material needs. Quoting Isa 28:29, Hacham, ספר תהלים, 285, understands it as the next miraculous deed performed to solve a problem.

38. Moreover, the parallel between מדבר (desert) and ישימון (wasteland) appears in Psalm 107, and creates an interpretive link between the two; see section on juxtaposition in that chapter.

Standing in the Gap

In employing the stem נסה ("to try/test"), which the Torah never uses with respect to the sending of quail, the psalmist recalls numerous other instances in the Pentateuch in which the Israelites tried and tested YHWH in the desert. One such instance occurred at the waters of Meribah in Exod 17:2, וַיֹּאמֶר לָהֶם מֹשֶׁה מַה־תְּרִיבוּן עִמָּדִי מַה־תְּנַסּוּן אֶת־יְהוָה ("And Moses said to them, 'why do you quarrel with me, and why do you test YHWH'"; also recalled in Deut 6:16). Numbers 14:22 additionally recalls ten instances in which Israel tested God in the wilderness, וַיְנַסּוּ אֹתִי זֶה עֶשֶׂר פְּעָמִים וְלֹא שָׁמְעוּ בְּקוֹלִי ("and they tested me these ten times, and they never obeyed me"). Overall, the image created by recalling the word creates a negative picture of Israel's relationship with God.

וַיִּתֵּן לָהֶם שֶׁאֱלָתָם וַיְשַׁלַּח רָזוֹן בְּנַפְשָׁם 15

So he gave them their desire, and sent wasting in their gullet

As a result of Israel's wantonness in v. 14, the first colon indicates that YHWH grants them their request (שאלה; see 1 Sam 1:27; 1 Kgs 2:16). Although this exact word never appears in the Torah with respect to the provision of quail in the desert, Psalm 78 employs the verbal form לשאל ("to ask/request") in a similar context, וַיְנַסּוּ־אֵל בִּלְבָבָם לִשְׁאָל־אֹכֶל לְנַפְשָׁם ("They tested El in their hearts, requesting food for their appetites"; Ps 78:18, see also Ps 105:40).

Fundamentally, two possibilities exist for interpreting the second colon, and each alternative hinges on the understanding of רזון. If understood positively, one could read the verse as an expression of YHWH's mercy towards his people, understanding רוה as a theoretical root meaning "sated."[39] In this instance, disregarding Israel's lustful desires mentioned in the previous verse, God still sated them, or provided for their wants; thus, he never gave them what they deserved, but acted in accordance with his mercy. This understanding ultimately complies with the psalm's message, because the cry in v. 47 implores YHWH not to act in accordance with the people's behavior and what they deserve,

---

39. The Peshitta, Septuagint, and Vulgate, along with McCann, "Psalms," 1111, all interpret it this way; Briggs, *The Book of Psalms*, 350, who claims a copyist error that should be corrected to מזון, and Seybold, *Die Psalmen*, 421, both concur with a positive assessment of YHWH's actions here. Richardson, "Psalm 106," 195, also agrees with a positive context for the verse, but does so with a negative interpretation of רזון. He understands the word with a positive connotation of "wasting," and reads the ב in light of Ugaritic. His final conclusion being that God drove out the leanness from their throat (נפש), which is to say he removed their hunger.

105

but in accordance with his everlasting mercy. Alternatively, the word could be understood negatively as "wasting"[40] in light of Isa 10:16, לָכֵן יְשַׁלַּח הָאָדוֹן יְהוָה צְבָאוֹת בְּמִשְׁמַנָּיו רָזוֹן ("Therefore the Lord YHWH of hosts will send a wasting sickness among their fat ones"). Such a translation renders God's response as one of judgment, whereby he does not meet their desire but increases it.[41] The specific mention of נפש suggests "throat," i.e., an eating organ, which specifically associates the verse with Num 11:6, indicating that the previously unnamed desire was indeed food related.

Numbers 11 harmonizes the two potential views mentioned above. On one hand, the people were provided with their desires and YHWH sent quail to satisfy their request for dietary variation, וְנָתַן יְהוָה לָכֶם בָּשָׂר וַאֲכַלְתֶּם ("and he will give you flesh and you will eat," Num 11:18). On the other hand, an element of judgment presents itself in the proceedings as God punishes them through the very means by which their desires are met, עַד חֹדֶשׁ יָמִים עַד אֲשֶׁר־יֵצֵא מֵאַפְּכֶם וְהָיָה לָכֶם לְזָרָא ("For a month until it comes out of your mouths, and it will become loathsome to you," Num 11:20). In this instance, the form לזרא recalls the word רזון in the psalm via a similarity in form. A negative reading of the verse complies with the psalm's overall theme, and parallels later recorded incidents in which Israel's sins are recorded along with God's punitive response. Consequently, reading this verse as either a negative or positive statement contributes to the psalm's message.[42] In addition to the dual meaning mentioned above, one can detect a wordplay with רזון, stemming from its similarity with רצון, meaning "will," or "desire" (לַמְּדֵנִי לַעֲשׂוֹת רְצוֹנֶךָ כִּי־אַתָּה אֱלוֹהָי, "Teach me to do your will for you are my God," Ps 143:10). Such a reading cynically hints that God indeed gave them their desire.

---

40. Scholars such as Keil and Delitzsch, *Psalms*, 154—who argue that the ancient translations mentioned are wrong, and read that a wasting disease came upon them, quoting Num 11:33-35—and Kraus, *Psalms 60-150*, 319, support this negative slant to the verse.

41. Similarly, interpreting רזון as "ruin" in light of Prov 14:28 renders a negative light on the proceedings, connoting judgment upon the evil actions of the Israelites.

42. Here we see an example of deliberate ambiguity in the psalm; the psalmist selects a word, absent from his source, reflecting two meanings. See Raabe, "Deliberate Ambiguity," and Zakovitch, "אחת דבר אלהים," who report on this and similar phenomena.

Standing in the Gap

וַיְקַנְאוּ לְמֹשֶׁה בַּמַּחֲנֶה לְאַהֲרֹן קְדוֹשׁ יְהוָה 16

Then they envied Moses in the camp, and Aaron YHWH's holy one

Moving on from the sins of the entire congregation against God, v. 16 retells an instance involving the rebellion of a small group of individuals against those whom YHWH had placed in authority. From the psalmist's perspective, they essentially defy YHWH in rebelling against divinely appointed leadership.[43] The verse order in this account emphasizes those who were sinned against; only after Moses and Aaron are identified do we discover who the guilty individuals are. As with the other incidents recounted in the psalm, the people's sin against God functions as the dominating topic of this section. Unlike any other exodus psalm, only Psalm 106 recalls this specific rebellion against Moses and Aaron.

The specific sin mentioned in v. 16 is jealousy (ויקנאו); the rebels envied Moses and Aaron, as "Rachel was envious of her sister" in Gen 30:1 (וַתְּקַנֵּא רָחֵל בַּאֲחֹתָהּ; see also Prov 3:31).[44] The inclusion of Aaron as YHWH's "holy one" increases the severity of the sin. The crime is not just against Aaron, but also against God since he set Aaron apart for a task. Psalm 105:26 (and 77:20 [21]) recognizes both Moses[45] and Aaron as leaders[46] of Israel, but the specific mention of Aaron as קדוש יהוה ("The holy one of YHWH") is unique in historiographic psalms. However, such a reference can plausibly be construed as an influence from verses detailing the high priest's vestments, e.g., Exod 28:36;

---

43. Cf. Samuel's complaint that the people have rejected him, and God's response (1 Sam 8).

44. Certain problems arise with the preposition in this verb because the root קנא together with ל usually appears in a positive context, as in Joel 2:18; Ezek 39:25; and Zech 1:14. For this reason it may be wise to adopt the Septuagint's reading of παρώργισαν, the equivalent of הקניא or הכעיס ("to provoke" or "to anger"; see Deut 32:21; Judg 2:12; and Jer 8:19).

45. With the exception of Psalm 105, this is the only psalm that mentions Moses' role in the exodus. The only possible exception is Psalm 77, which includes Moses and Aaron in the last verse (in all likelihood, Ps 77:20 [21] represents a later addition).

46. Concerning this appearance of both leaders, Cross, *Canaanite Myth*, 197 n. 16, states, "In the J material in Numbers 20:1–13, Aaron is not associated with Moses; only in Priestly sections does Aaron appear, and even here in a secondary role." This observation implies a late date for the psalm because both leaders appear together, and Aaron's role is not secondary.

39:30⁴⁷). A further reference to Aaron's status as holy occurs in Num 16:5, (בֹּקֶר וְיֹדַע יְהוָה אֶת־אֲשֶׁר־לוֹ וְאֶת־הַקָּדוֹשׁ "In the morning YHWH will make known who belongs to him and who is holy"), when YHWH singles him out as the chosen priestly leader.

¹⁷ תִּפְתַּח־אֶרֶץ וַתִּבְלַע דָּתָן וַתְּכַס עַל־עֲדַת אֲבִירָם

And the earth opened and swallowed Dathan, and covered the congregation of Abiram

After a veiled reference in v. 16, in which the offenders find concealment within the third-person plural "they envied," v. 17 now reveals the identity of those involved and describes their fate. The verse names the culprits as Dathan and the "gathering of Abiram," reflecting Num 16, וַתִּפְתַּח הָאָרֶץ אֶת־פִּיהָ וַתִּבְלַע אֹתָם "and the earth opened its mouth and swallowed them," v. 32), and further in v. 33 וַתְּכַס עֲלֵיהֶם הָאָרֶץ וַיֹּאבְדוּ מִתּוֹךְ הַקָּהָל ("and the earth covered them, and they perished from the midst of the assembly"). Both instances report the same uprising and punitive action against a specific group of Israelites; however, the psalm stops short of implicating Korah, who finds inclusion among the list of perpetrators in Num 16:24.⁴⁸ Emphasis on the punishment appears in the use of verbs in this verse: the earth opened, and swallowed, and covered over. No option for intercession arises for those guilty of this rebellion.

---

47. Seybold, *Die Psalmen*, 423, and Briggs, *The Book of Psalms*, 351, adopt such a stance.

48. Such an omission, on one hand, may simply reflect an abbreviation of people involved based upon space constraints for the verse; on the other hand, this may be an instance in which the psalmist refrains from including Korah as a mark of respect for his descendants who went on to establish a prominent guild of singers; see Kraus, *Psalms 60–150*, 319, and Brooke, "Psalms 105 and 106," 278. Contrary to this opinion, however, is the possibility that the tradition in Numbers consists of more than one source. In one of these assumed traditions the main instigator of the rebellion was Korah, and in the other instance, Abiram and Dathan. Thus, at the time of writing the psalm, our psalmist only had the latter tradition available to him (of course such an idea counters any suggestion that the psalmist had a Torah similar to ours today (see Norin, *Er Spaltete das Meer*, 121–22). Although Liver, "Korah, Dothan and Abiram," rejects the sources to the tradition according to the Documentary Hypotheses, he nevertheless reads two sources in Numbers. The relationship between Numbers and Psalm 106 will be pursued further in the section on sources.

Standing in the Gap

¹⁸ וַתִּבְעַר־אֵשׁ בַּעֲדָתָם לֶהָבָה תְּלַהֵט רְשָׁעִים

Then fire burned against their congregation and a flame burnt up the wicked

An emphatic semantic chiasmus, תלהט : להבה :: אש : תבער (it burned : fire :: a flame : burned, (closes the section and highlights the continued judgment passed on those opposing divine leadership: fire burned against the congregation. Although only the word fire (אש) appears in Numbers, its associated word flame (להבה), frequently appears with it in poetic literature (see Hos 7:6; Joel 1:19). The repetition of congregation (עדה) from v. 17 creates a degree of continuity with the previous verse and links this act of judgment with the remaining followers of Dathan and Abiram (עדתם, "their congregation"). In the second colon, a flame burns against the wicked (רשעים) referring to the aforementioned congregation. The same word links v. 16 with v. 6, חָטָאנוּ עִם־אֲבוֹתֵינוּ הֶעֱוִינוּ הִרְשָׁעְנוּ ("we sinned with our fathers we have committed iniquity we have acted wickedly"), suggesting an appropriate punishment for the wicked. Thus, it is possible to interpret that those of the psalmist's generation also deserve to die for their wickedness. Verse 18 evidently recalls Num 16:35, which records the same incident, but additionally echoes Num 11:1–3, which records how fire from YHWH broke out against the Israelites for their complaining, וַיְהִי הָעָם כְּמִתְאֹנְנִים רַע בְּאָזְנֵי יְהוָה וַיִּשְׁמַע יְהוָה וַיִּחַר אַפּוֹ וַתִּבְעַר־בָּם אֵשׁ יְהוָה ("Now when the people complained bitterly in the hearing of YHWH, YHWH heard and became angry, and the fire of YHWH burned among them," v. 1). The latter incident reflects the psalm's context because it also includes instances of rebellion, God's judgment, and works of intercession by a prominent individual.

¹⁹ יַעֲשׂוּ־עֵגֶל בְּחֹרֵב וַיִּשְׁתַּחֲווּ לְמַסֵּכָה

They made a calf at Horeb, and bowed down to a cast idol

With v. 19, the psalm begins a new stanza recounting how the Israelites created an idol while at Mount Horeb.[49] In placing the account here, the psalmist reverses the ordering determined by Exodus and Numbers.[50]

---

49. This is the only mention of the event in the historical psalms, though Nehemiah quotes it in his confession (see Neh 9:18).

50. For a more complete examination of the changes in the order of events, see the section on sources in this chapter.

109

From Bards to Biblical Exegetes

Just like the other excerpts employed by the psalmist, this one concentrates on Israel's sin. The letters חרב here remind the reader of YHWH rebuking and drying up the sea in v. 9, ויגער בים סוף ויחרב ("And he rebuked Yam Suf and it dried up"), an allusion which illuminates God's acts of mercy and Israel's sinful response: he dries up the sea to save them, and they create a cast idol at Horeb as a response. After forging the idol they proceed to worship it (וישתחוו למסכה), as they did in Exod 32:8, סָרוּ מַהֵר מִן־הַדֶּרֶךְ אֲשֶׁר צִוִּיתִם עָשׂוּ לָהֶם עֵגֶל מַסֵּכָה וַיִּשְׁתַּחֲווּ־לוֹ ("They quickly turned from the way I commanded them, and made for themselves a calf image and worshipped it").[51]

²⁰ וַיָּמִירוּ אֶת־כְּבוֹדָם בְּתַבְנִית שׁוֹר אֹכֵל עֵשֶׂב

And they exchanged his glory for the image of a bull eating grass

The physical undertaking of creating and worshiping a calf idol in the previous verse here finds a *spiritual* interpretation. In the creation and worship of this idol, the Israelites effectively exchange the glory of God[52] for an idol, a repugnant representation of a calf. The phrase וימירו את כבודם ("They exchanged his glory") should not be understood so much as exchanging the "glory" or "honor" of God, but as Israel exchanging YHWH for another god, as understood from verses such as Jer 2:11, הַהֵימִיר גּוֹי אֱלֹהִים וְהֵמָּה לֹא אֱלֹהִים וְעַמִּי הֵמִיר כְּבוֹדוֹ בְּלוֹא יוֹעִיל ("Has a nation exchanged gods, which are not gods, but my people have exchanged their glory for that which is non beneficial") in which the two equivalent phrases, both depicting an exchange of gods, have been juxtaposed.[53] The very form of the word exchange (ימירו) also serves as a subtle reminder of v. 7 describing Israel's rebellion (ימרו) at the Sea of Reeds.

By mentioning תבנית (image), the psalmist recalls the law prohibiting the fashioning of images. Deuteronomy 4:16–18 specifically warns against such acts, פֶּן־תַּשְׁחִתוּן וַעֲשִׂיתֶם לָכֶם פֶּסֶל תְּמוּנַת כָּל־סָמֶל תַּבְנִית זָכָר אוֹ נְקֵבָה ("Lest you bow down and make for yourselves an idol, a likeness of

---

51. At this stage, however, Deut 9:16 is a strong candidate.

52. The *mêm* should be read as *wāw* here, reading כבודו ("his honor"), and should be understood as a *tiqqun sopherim*, in which a scribe altered the text to preserve God's honor; see Terrien, *The Psalms*, 731, and Allen, *Psalms 101–150*, 71–72, who follow the BHS; and Hacham, ספר תהלים, 287.

53. Although there is probably another *tiqqun sopherim* in this verse, כבודי<כבודו (see BHS), the concept of a nation exchanging God for something worthless is still apparent.

any image of a figure, male or female," v. 16). Rather than explicitly declaring the moral sin involved in transgressing the laws given at Horeb, the psalmist instead chooses to explain in manifest terms the crime's ludicrous nature. Israel was delivered by the mighty hand of an unseen God, and in response they worship and pay obeisance to an image of a beast (שור, bull)[54] eating grass. This is the only biblical evidence of the two words appearing in parallel, and the word choice enhances the Israelites' absurd act. Numerous medieval commentators[55] have already highlighted the disgusting appearance of cows as they masticate and regurgitate food. The aforementioned image creates a polarized picture of honor, contrasting the high honor of God with the base dishonor of a man-made idol.

שָׁכְחוּ אֵל מוֹשִׁיעָם עֹשֶׂה גְדֹלוֹת בְּמִצְרָיִם 21

They had forgotten El who saves them, who did great deeds in Egypt

The interpretation of the sin first mentioned in v. 19 continues in v. 21; in bowing down to the idol, the Israelites effectively forgot the God who saved them. Numerous allusions to earlier acts of God's mercy to Israel appear in v. 21 as well as the nation's previous rebellious acts against him. The proper noun El (אל), repeated from v. 14, reminds the reader of how the nation "tested El in the wasteland" (וַיְנַסּוּ־אֵל בִּישִׁימוֹן). Repetition of שכח (remember) and עשה (make/do) recalls a similar instance in v. 13 when Israel quickly forgot YHWH's deeds, מִהֲרוּ שָׁכְחוּ מַעֲשָׂיו ("They quickly forgot his deeds"). The present verse demonstrates that nothing has changed with respect to the Israelites' attitude; once again, they forget YHWH who accomplished mighty acts in Egypt. As already witnessed in v. 19, עשה ("to do/make") recalls the differences between YHWH's deeds and those of his people. A semantic chiasmus with v. 7, במצרים : שכחו :: לא זכרו : במצרים (In Egypt : they never remembered :: they forgot : in Egypt), further emphasizes the root of the problem: Israel's forgetfulness of God's works in Egypt. In mentioning the "God who saved them" (אל מושיעם), the psalm refers back to the time when God "delivered Israel from the hand of their haters," in v. 10

---

54. Kraus, *Psalms 60–150*, 320, suggests this choice of word may relate to sources in Ugaritic literature linking *tr* (= שור) to the god El, but this may simply be the author's choice for a suitable B-word, or an original reading of the psalmist's source.

55. See, for example, Rashi and RaDaK (Cohen, *Psalms*, 122–22).

(וַיּוֹשִׁיעֵם מִיַּד שׂוֹנֵא). Because Israel had forgotten this act of deliverance, they were led to commit idolatry with the calf idol.

נִפְלָאוֹת בְּאֶרֶץ חָם נוֹרָאוֹת עַל־יַם־סוּף [22]

Amazing deeds in the land of Ham, fearful works at Yam Suf

Verse 22 continues the tri-cola beginning in v. 21b that recalls YHWH's accomplishments at the Reed Sea: נפלאות בארץ חם, גדלות במצרים ("Great deeds in Egypt, amazing deeds in the land of Ham"), and נוראות על ים סוף ("fearful works at *Yam Suf*").[56] Each of the aforementioned parallel cola depicts a deed performed and the location in which it occurred. God's deliverance of Israel should have prompted them to recall his acts continually and to behave in accordance with their recollection. Instead, they forgot his accomplishments, which ultimately led to their disobedience and rebellion. The appearance of נפלאות ("amazing deeds") here refers back to v. 7, which brings to mind the mighty acts God performed while they were in Egypt. Just as his deeds for the people then should have been enough to prevent them from rebelling against him at the sea (v. 7), so too a memory of his acts now should have discouraged them from forging a calf idol. The sentiment of Exod 14:31, וַיַּרְא יִשְׂרָאֵל אֶת־הַיָּד הַגְּדֹלָה אֲשֶׁר עָשָׂה יְהוָה בְּמִצְרַיִם וַיִּירְאוּ הָעָם אֶת־יְהוָה וַיַּאֲמִינוּ בַּיהוָה וּבְמֹשֶׁה עַבְדּוֹ ("When Israel saw the great work that YHWH performed against Egypt, the people feared YHWH and believed in YHWH and in Moses his servant"), is reflected in vv. 21 and 22, which possess both lexical and contextual congruency. Unlike the people's response in Exodus, which should have been emulated, the Israelites in this psalm fail to act accordingly. The phrase ארץ חם ("Land of Ham") only ever occurs in the neighboring Psalm 105, where it similarly epitomizes Egypt.[57] With respect to this phrase, another possible point of influence stems from the historiographic Psalm 78, recalling the expression "the tents of Ham," וַיַּךְ כָּל־בְּכוֹר בְּמִצְרָיִם רֵאשִׁית אוֹנִים בְּאָהֳלֵי־חָם ("And he struck every firstborn in Egypt, the first strength

---

56. For more on נפלאות, נוראות, and גדולות ("mighty acts," "fearful works," and "great deeds") and the language of miracles, see Yaron, "הנסים במקרא," 26–34, and Zakovitch, *Concept of the Miracle*.

57. This placement of the otherwise unique phrase in juxtaposed psalms either implies one author had access to the other's work, or an arranger was influenced by the common phrase in juxtaposing the psalms. For more on this observation, see the section on juxtaposition in this chapter.

among the tents of Ham," 78:51). Ultimately, the phrase alludes to the designation of Egypt as the land of Ham in the table of nations in Gen 10:6, in addition to Noah's son, Ham.[58]

23 וַיֹּאמֶר לְהַשְׁמִידָם לוּלֵי מֹשֶׁה בְחִירוֹ עָמַד בַּפֶּרֶץ לְפָנָיו לְהָשִׁיב חֲמָתוֹ מֵהַשְׁחִית
He intended to destroy them were it not for Moses his chosen one, who stood in the gap before him to return his destroying anger

Verse 23 develops the plot from the preceding verse, after Israel forged the molten-calf idol. YHWH intended to destroy them, and would have done so were it not for the intervention of Moses. After the people have transgressed, the psalm narrates God's response—made conspicuous in the verse's unusual length, as with v. 7 depicting the rebellion. The verb אמר ("he said") is best rendered "consider" or "intend," rather than simply "to say"; in the same way David's men *considered* stoning him in 1 Sam 30:6, וַתֵּצֶר לְדָוִד מְאֹד כִּי־אָמְרוּ הָעָם לְסָקְלוֹ ("David was very distressed because the people considered stoning him"). Moses' description as God's "chosen one"—only found here in biblical literature—corresponds somewhat with the portrayal of Aaron as "the holy one of YHWH" (קדש יהוה) in v. 16. Moreover, it sheds light on v. 5, where the psalmist desires to see the goodness of YHWH's chosen ones (בחיריך) After reading v. 23, one can assume the chosen ones alluded to in v. 5 are those who, like Moses, enjoy such a relationship with YHWH, they could influence him to alter his action.

Events in this verse allude to the narrative of Exod 32:11–14 when Moses successfully interceded for Israel.[59] At no point, however, in Exodus does the phrase עמד בפרץ ("stand in the gap") appear. Literally, it means "to stand in the gap," but here it adopts a metaphorical meaning, referring to one who breaches the gap between man and God, thus averting a catastrophe. God similarly sought such an individual in Ezek 22:30, וָאֲבַקֵּשׁ מֵהֶם אִישׁ גֹּדֵר־גָּדֵר וְעֹמֵד בַּפֶּרֶץ לְפָנַי בְּעַד הָאָרֶץ ("I searched from among them a man who would build a wall and stand in the gap before me on behalf of the land"), and the psalmist's selection of vocabulary suggests he was influenced by Ezekiel's words since these are the only two places in biblical literature where the expression occurs

---

58. Selection of this rare phrase creates a wordplay with חמתו ("his anger") in the following verse (see Hacham, ספר תהלים, 134).

59. Another strong candidate, however, is Deuteronomy 9.

with this meaning. As with vv. 20–22, the psalmist does not content himself with simply recounting history, or Israelite historiography, but continues to interpret them theologically.

The infinitive construct form together with the *lamed* (להשיב) signifies intent as in "in order to return his destructive anger."[60] The word השחית ("to destroy") itself commonly expresses punitive measures taken by God with respect to judgment. In Exod 12:23, "and he will not permit the destroyer to enter your houses to strike" (וְלֹא יִתֵּן הַמַּשְׁחִית לָבֹא אֶל־בָּתֵּיכֶם לִנְגֹּף), it signifies the angel of YHWH coming to destroy the firstborn of Egypt as punishment for enslaving his people. Similarly it appears in Gen 6:13 depicting the flood against mankind induced by the intolerable sins multiplied on the earth (see also Gen 18:28, concerning the destruction of Sodom and Gomorrah). Unlike the first colon, which recounts God's plan to destroy Israel as recorded in Exodus 32–34, the second one bears more similarities with Deut 10:10, וַיִּשְׁמַע יְהוָה אֵלַי גַּם בַּפַּעַם הַהִוא לֹא־אָבָה יְהוָה הַשְׁחִיתֶךָ ("and YHWH listened to me that time also and YHWH was unwilling to destroy you") in terms of context and vocabulary. In contrast with the previous stanza, this one does not end in disaster, but the aversion of a catastrophe, thus exemplifying YHWH's great mercy originally mentioned in the opening verse.

וַיִּמְאֲסוּ בְּאֶרֶץ חֶמְדָּה לֹא־הֶאֱמִינוּ לִדְבָרוֹ [24]

Then they refused the desirable land and never trusted his promise

From the creation of a cast idol, the theme of disobedience continues, and the psalm now recounts Israel's behavior when they were first presented with the land God had promised to their forefathers. The word ימאסו ("They refused") signifies the people's refusal to enter the land and recalls passages in the Torah such as Num 14:31, "I will bring them in and they will know the land which you rejected" (וְהֵבֵיאתִי אֹתָם וְיָדְעוּ אֶת־הָאָרֶץ אֲשֶׁר מְאַסְתֶּם בָּהּ), but in this refusal, they are effectively despising[61] the gift offered by God. Nowhere in the Torah is Canaan described as a desirable land (ארץ חמדה), but it is nonetheless an apt phrase reflecting the essence of the expression "flowing with milk and honey" (see, for example, Exod 3:8 and Num 14:8). Only in the prophets does the adjective חמד portray the land God intended for Israel, e.g., וַיָּשִׂימוּ אֶרֶץ־חֶמְדָּה לְשַׁמָּה ("For they made the desirable land a waste," see

---

60. See JM §124i.

61. See Prov 3:11 and Job 42:6 for this emphasis of מאס.

Zech 7:14; see also Jer 3:19). Israel's rejection of a *desirable* land offered on the basis of kindness and undeserved favor highlights their heinous attitude.

The people's failure to respond correctly to YHWH's saving acts at the Reed Sea is brought to light by the repetition of האמינו לדברו ("they believed his promise"). In v. 12, the generation delivered from Egypt trusted in his word/promise, and as a result, they sang his praise. Starkly contrasting this behavior, they now fail to trust in his word and reject his offer. The exact interpretation of דברו ("his promise") is somewhat equivocal since it may refer to God's general promise of land,[62] or, more likely, God's promise to go before them in battle against the land's inhabitants. The latter notion recalls the words spoken in Deut 1:32, וּבַדָּבָר הַזֶּה אֵינְכֶם מַאֲמִינִם בַּיהוָה אֱלֹהֵיכֶם ("But in this matter you did not believe YHWH your God") reflecting the same situation.

25 וַיֵּרָגְנוּ בְאָהֳלֵיהֶם לֹא שָׁמְעוּ בְּקוֹל יְהוָה

And they murmured in their tents (and) never obeyed the voice of YHWH

The narrative continues in v. 25 enumerating the Israelites' murmurings and complaints, with words similar to Deut 1:27, וַתֵּרָגְנוּ בְאָהֳלֵיכֶם וַתֹּאמְרוּ בְּשִׂנְאַת יְהוָה אֹתָנוּ ("And you grumbled in your tents and said, 'because YHWH hates us'"), which contains the only occurrence of רגן in the Torah and reflects the same situation found in the psalm. Throughout the psalm, the psalmist employs לא to illuminate negative Israelite behavior; they never remembered (v. 7), never waited (v. 13), never trusted (v. 24), and now they never hearkened to his voice. Deuteronomy is particularly fond of the phrase שמע בקול יהוה ("Hearken/obey the voice of YHWH," see for example, 13:18 [19]; 21:18; 26:14; 27:10), where it frequently stresses more than just the physical aspect of hearing what God says, but obeying his orders. First Samuel 12:15 exemplifies this usage וְאִם־לֹא תִשְׁמְעוּ בְּקוֹל יְהוָה וּמְרִיתֶם אֶת־פִּי יְהוָה ("And if you will not hearken to the voice of YHWH, but rebel against the command of YHWH"), where "not listening" to his voice equates to rebellion. Thus, when the psalmist states that Israel did not *obey* God's voice, he emphasizes they defied YHWH and refused to conquer the land. The chiastic relationship ישמיע : יהוה :: יהוה : שמעו (make hear : YHWH ::

---

62. Kroll, *Psalms*, 312, maintains this opinion, relating it to the promise of land made to Abraham in Gen 15:18–21 and repeated to the people in Exod 23:31.

From Bards to Biblical Exegetes

YHWH : hearkened) creates a nexus with v. 2 suggesting only those who obey YHWH can declare his praise; and more specifically, because Israel did not hearken to his voice, they were not in a position to declare his praises.

וַיִּשָּׂא יָדוֹ לָהֶם לְהַפִּיל אוֹתָם בַּמִּדְבָּר 26

So he swore concerning them, to kill them in the desert

As in the previous stanza, v. 26 reports how God intended to judge Israel's defiance; he planned to destroy them. The extent of God's intent is expressed by the phrase נשא יד, which literally means "to raise the hand (in oath)," namely, to be firmly resolved to act in a specific way. In the same way God resolved to bestow Canaan to Abraham's descendants in Exod 6:8 (וְהֵבֵאתִי אֶתְכֶם אֶל־הָאָרֶץ אֲשֶׁר נָשָׂאתִי אֶת־יָדִי לָתֵת אֹתָהּ לְאַבְרָהָם, "And I will bring you unto the land which I swore to give to Abraham"), he now resolves to judge those who have refused the desirable land. The word להפיל here implies "to kill," as witnessed in 1 Sam 4:10, וַיִּפֹּל מִיִּשְׂרָאֵל שְׁלֹשִׁים אֶלֶף רַגְלִי ("and there fell from Israel one thousand foot soldiers"), which depicts the results of a war (see also 2 Sam 1:4 and 1 Kgs 22:20). Thus, the judgment he intended for them was death, to kill them in the desert.

וּלְהַפִּיל זַרְעָם בַּגּוֹיִם וּלְזָרוֹתָם בָּאֲרָצוֹת 27

And to scatter[63] their seed among the nations and to disperse them among foreign lands

The final verse in the stanza develops the portrayal of punishment that began in v. 26; the bodies of those who refused the desirable land will be scattered among the nations, and their seed will be dispersed among peoples. Spanning vv. 26–27, the three infinitive constructs demon-

---

63. Due to the similarity between the forms להפיל and להפיץ, it may be preferable to harmonize this word with Ezek 20:23; others such as Allen, *Psalms 101–150*, 65, Kraus, *Psalms 60–150*, 315, Richardson, "Psalm 106," 197, and Duhm, *Die Psalmen*, 248, concur with the textual adjustment, which is also reflected in the Peshitta. Although one can see how a copyist may have been mistakenly influenced by the reading of להפיל ("to kill," lit. "to make fall") in the previous verse, a second reading of להפיל in v. 27 would create a degree of continuity linking the punishment of the desert generation with that of the psalmist. The association between the exile and the dispersion of bodies in the desert led Hacham, ספר תהלים, 288, to suggest that the exile was decreed together with the punishment of the forefathers, but it was not made specific so as not to discourage the people at that time.

strate this continuity of thought. The parallelism at the end of this stanza accentuates the punishment, dwelling on and repeating God's punitive action: dispersal among the nations. Unlike the previous verse, which bears a strong resemblance to the Numbers' tradition, this one resonates more closely with Ezek 20:23, גַּם־אֲנִי נָשָׂאתִי אֶת־יָדִי לָהֶם בַּמִּדְבָּר לְהָפִיץ אֹתָם בַּגּוֹיִם וּלְזָרוֹת אוֹתָם בָּאֲרָצוֹת ("Also I swore to them in the desert to scatter them among the lands"). For the psalmist, this association links the condemnation of the desert generation with that of the psalmist's generation, and reveals an instance of YHWH's mercy. For their defiance, the desert generation were killed and buried in the desert; they had no chance of seeing the land God promised their forefathers. On the other hand, though the psalmist's generation also defied YHWH, yet they were not treated as severely as their forefathers, and still have the opportunity to repent and receive God's mercy. The interpretation of the desert generation's punishment here flies in the face of that recorded in the Torah. In Numbers, the punishment is specifically aimed at one generation, those who refused the land; the following generation was thus allowed to enter into Canaan.

וַיִּצָּמְדוּ לְבַעַל פְּעוֹר וַיֹּאכְלוּ זִבְחֵי מֵתִים 28

Then they joined themselves to Baal Peor and consumed the sacrifices of the dead

Verse 28 opens a new section describing Israel's idolatry, adding more variation to the ways in which they had defied YHWH: lustful desires (vv. 13–15), refusing divine leadership (vv. 16–18), worshiping the calf idol (vv. 19–23), refusing the desirable land (vv. 24–27), and now worship of foreign gods. In this verse, Israel is indicted for joining themselves יצמדו (see 2 Sam 20:8; Ps 50:19) to Baal Peor as in Num 25:3, וַיִּצָּמֶד יִשְׂרָאֵל לְבַעַל פְּעוֹר וַיִּחַר־אַף יְהוָה בְּיִשְׂרָאֵל ("So Israel was yoked to Baal Peor, and YHWH's anger burned against Israel"). The second colon has apparently received influence from Num 25:2, וַתִּקְרֶאןָ לָעָם לְזִבְחֵי אֱלֹהֵיהֶן וַיֹּאכַל הָעָם וַיִּשְׁתַּחֲווּ לֵאלֹהֵיהֶן ("And they invited the people to the sacrifice of their gods, and the people ate and bowed down to their gods"), which bears similar vocabulary. The use of זבחי מתים ("sacrifices of the dead") may simply be understood as a metaphor describing a deeply detestable act. Additionally, however, it suggests the gods worshipped were mere idols with no signs of physical life (see Ps 135:15–17), that is to say dead;⁶⁴ and just as Israel worshipped an inanimate idol in v. 20, they now sacrifice to dead inanimate gods.⁶⁵ The same phrase, זבחי מתים, forms a wordplay between a living God, as seen in Deut 5:26, כִּי מִי כָל־בָּשָׂר אֲשֶׁר שָׁמַע קוֹל אֱלֹהִים חַיִּים מְדַבֵּר מִתּוֹךְ־הָאֵשׁ, "For who among all flesh has heard the voice of the Living God speaking from the midst of the fire"), and dead idols/gods. This wordplay becomes more pronounced in light of the association created with אכל (eat/consume), linking this verse with v. 20 (בְּתַבְנִית שׁוֹר אֹכֵל עֵשֶׂב, "for the image of a bull eating grass"). In both instances the Israelites are exchanging something of worth and value with something worthless.

וַיַּכְעִיסוּ בְּמַעַלְלֵיהֶם וַתִּפְרָץ־בָּם מַגֵּפָה ²⁹

And they angered (him) with their deeds, and a plague broke out among them

As with other instances in biblical literature, Israel's idolatry stirs YHWH's anger, a result witnessed by Deut 32:16, יַקְנִאֻהוּ בְּזָרִים בְּתוֹעֵבֹת יַכְעִיסֻהוּ ("They made him jealous with strange gods, and with abominable things they angered him"; see also Judg 2:12 and 2 Kgs 17:17). Numerous words for "deeds," "works," or "actions" appear in the psalm; here the author chose מעלליהם, which contrasts God's merciful acts in v. 13. Verse 29 not only describes the anger caused by the act, but continues to elaborate upon the punishment, an outbreak of plague. Interestingly enough, however, the psalmist fails to associate explicitly the plague's outbreak with YHWH's punitive action: he does not indicate that it was YHWH who sent the plague. Such an association is only implied through the juxtaposition of the cola. The psalmist's decision

---

64. Similar versions of this conclusion are mentioned by both medieval scholars—such as Ibn Ezra (see Cohen, *Psalms*, 122)—and modern, such as Allen, *Psalms 101–150*, 72, who further associates the verse with the declaration in Deut 26:14 in which those who offer sacrifices must declare they have not offered them to the dead. Keil and Delitzsch, *Psalms*, 136, state, "The sacrificial feastings in which, according to Num. XXV. 2, they took part, are called eating the sacrifices of the dead because the idols are dead beings." Similarly Hacham, ספר תהלים, 289, asserts the sacrifices were made to gods who were themselves dead; see also Kraus, *Psalms 60–150*, 320, and Kroll, *Psalms*, 313.

65. Richardson, *Psalm 106*, 198, relates the "sacrifices of the dead" to funerary practices centering on communal meals at burial sites. A potentially ironic way of understanding the phrase is to relate it to the punishment of those who practiced such sacrifices. Because those who offered these sacrifices were subsequently killed, it is possible to interpret the act as sacrifices leading to death, hence sacrifices of the dead.

Standing in the Gap

to phrase the matter in this way reflects an anomaly in Num 25, which only states that the plague was stayed without a word concerning its origin. The word for plague, מגפה, only ever appears in the context of judgment in the Bible. Exodus 9:14 recalls the plagues wrought against Egypt, כִּי בַּפַּעַם הַזֹּאת אֲנִי שֹׁלֵחַ אֶת־כָּל־מַגֵּפֹתַי אֶל־לִבְּךָ ("Surely this time I will send all my plagues into your midst"); 2 Sam 24 recounts the plague sent against Israel due to the census arranged by David (see also 1 Sam 6:4 and Zech 14:12).

³⁰ וַיַּעֲמֹד פִּינְחָס וַיְפַלֵּל וַתֵּעָצַר הַמַּגֵּפָה

But Phinehas arose and interceded, and the plague was stopped

As with the fifth stanza, the seventh recounts an instance of human intervention diverting divine punishment. The verb עמד ("to stand") directly links this stanza with the fifth stanza, specifically v. 23, וַיֹּאמֶר לְהַשְׁמִידָם לוּלֵי מֹשֶׁה בְחִירוֹ עָמַד בַּפֶּרֶץ לְפָנָיו ("He intended to destroy them were it not for Moses his chosen one"), which depicts Moses standing in the gap to avert God's anger. This time, however, it is Phinehas who rises up to divert YHWH's destructive anger. The verse is reminiscent of Num 25:7, וַיַּרְא פִּינְחָס בֶּן־אֶלְעָזָר בֶּן־אַהֲרֹן הַכֹּהֵן וַיָּקָם מִתּוֹךְ הָעֵדָה ("And Phinehas the son of Eleazar the son of Aaron the priest saw, and rose up from among the congregation"), where קום ("rise up") equates[66] to עמד (stand) in v. 30. The verb פלל ("to intercede"), though absent from Numbers, should be viewed as the psalmist's interpretation of events that transpired. According to the psalm's context, this word bears a meaning of "intercede," i.e., to represent the people before God pleading for mercy.[67] Interpreting the word in this manner best describes Phinehas' actions since he stood on the people's behalf to avert God's anger. This interpretation additionally resonates with 1 Sam 2:25, אִם־יֶחֱטָא אִישׁ לְאִישׁ וּפִלְלוֹ אֱלֹהִים וְאִם לַיהוָה יֶחֱטָא־אִישׁ מִי יִתְפַּלֶּל־לוֹ ("If a man sins against a man, God can intercede, but if a man sins against YHWH, who will intercede for him"), where Eli explains to his sons that God can *intercede* when a man sins against another man, but if a

---

66. This correspondence between the two words reflects the diachronic change between SBH and LBH. The section on dating in this chapter revisits this issue; see Hurvitz, בין לשון ללשון, 173.

67. For this meaning, see BDB 813, and more recently Janowski, "Psalm CVI:28-31," 170.

man sins against God then nobody remains to *intercede*. Similarly, the word here represents the actions of one who stands to avert judgment.[68]

Just as this plague begins without a clear indication that God had initiated it, so too the psalmist's choice of a *nip'al* verb וַתֵּעָצַר ("and it was stopped"), disguising the subject, obscures the notion that God ultimately stopped the plague, leaving the reader with the impression Phinehas alone caused it to cease. Up to this point, God apparently adopts a secondary role, and Phinehas finds himself functioning as the main protagonist.

וַתֵּחָשֶׁב לוֹ לִצְדָקָה לְדֹר וָדֹר עַד־עוֹלָם 31

And it was considered to him as righteousness from generation to generation forever

Unlike the other verses in the psalm's main body, the closing verse of the seventh stanza does not recount Israel's sin, or their punishment, or an act of intercession. Instead, the psalmist relates to the reward ascribed to Phinehas, who averted YHWH's anger in the previous verse. Such treatment, somewhat surprisingly, is not ascribed to any other individual in the psalm. Verse 31 focuses on Num 25:12, when God rewards Phinehas for his zeal in spearing two individuals who committed a lewd act in the Tabernacle's vicinity (לָכֵן אֱמֹר הִנְנִי נֹתֵן לוֹ אֶת־בְּרִיתִי שָׁלוֹם, "Therefore say behold I give to him my covenant of peace"). Noticeably absent from Numbers is the word צדקה (righteousness); the verse simply states that God made a "covenant of peace" with Phinehas, and that his descendants would receive an everlasting priesthood (Num 25:13). To find a rationale for the author's selection of צדקה, we can turn to at least two, non-mutually exclusive solutions. First, selection of this spe-

---

68. The translation rendered here is not accepted by all; numerous commentators—such as Ibn Ezra, who reads it according to Job 31:28 (Cohen, *Psalms*, 125); RaDaK (Cohen, *Psalms*, 123), who reads it according to Exod 21:22; and the JPS and KJV translations—have chosen to interpret the word as "judge." The meaning of "intercede" is supported and ratified by Speiser, "The Creation Epic." In his article, he demonstrates that the root פלל carries the basic sense of "to judge," with the meaning "to assess," or "to estimate." However, he asserts that the *pi'el* of this stem often assumes the meaning "to mediate," quoting Psalm 106 as an example. Janowski, "Psalm CVI:28–31," similarly refutes a meaning of "to judge," supporting the sense of "intercession." Hoffman, יציאת מצריים, 135, rightfully suggests that the word can be interpreted as "pray," in line with Gen 48:11. Such a rendering in the psalm's context demonstrates that the prayers of a single righteous individual can avert an impending catastrophe for the nation.

cific word creates an internal association with v. 3, in which the psalmist declares, "Blessed is the man who does righteous works" (עשה צדקה). In associating the two verses, the psalmist exemplifies in v. 31 an abstract statement in v. 3, proving that the man who does righteousness is blessed (אשרי). Such a lesson encourages individuals, even those living among a sinful people, to perform acts of righteousness, because such men are rewarded. The second solution is that the psalm alludes to Gen 15:6, the only other location in biblical literature in which the phrase חשב . . . צדקה ("considered . . . righteousness") occurs. Abraham's willingness to obey God by following his command to relocate to a foreign land is expressed with these words: וְהֶאֱמִן בַּיהוָה וַיַּחְשְׁבֶהָ לּוֹ צְדָקָה ("And he believed in YHWH and he attributed to him as righteousness"). In applying this phrase, to Phinehas, the psalmist elevates his status, and the importance of his intercessory work is likened to Abraham's faith in obeying God's command.

וַיַּקְצִיפוּ עַל־מֵי מְרִיבָה וַיֵּרַע לְמֹשֶׁה בַּעֲבוּרָם 32

Then they angered (YHWH) at the waters of Meribah and it was bad for Moses on account of them

The eighth stanza opens with the psalmist recalling events at the waters of Meribah. Although the object of יקציפו, "to provoke," or "to anger" (see Ps 38:1 [2]), is not explicitly stated, we can, on one hand, assume YHWH is intended from the context, since the psalm previously recounted instances in which the Israelites provoked him to wrath (see v. 29, for example). Moreover, whenever the Torah employs the *hifil* of this verb, God is always the object, as in Deut 9:22, וּבְתַבְעֵרָה וּבְמַסָּה וּבְקִבְרֹת הַתַּאֲוָה מַקְצִפִים הֱיִיתֶם אֶת־יְהוָה ("And at Taverah and at Massah and at Qibrot Ta'avah you provoked YHWH," see also Deut 9:7, 8). On the other hand, it is possible to read Moses as the direct object; the Israelites provoke him, with negative consequences for him.[69]

By employing the phrase מי מריבה,[70] ("Waters of Meribah") the psalm associates this event with the crossing of the Reed Sea, especially v. 11 in which God delivers Israel from their enemies by causing the

69. It should be noted here that whenever the verb appears in Deuteronomy the direct object has been included, whereas the psalmist fails to identify it here, introducing a level of ambiguity.

70. This section recalls another instance in which the psalm reflects an order different than the Torah. Such instances will be explored further in the section on allusions.

water to cover them (ויכסו מים צריהם, "And the water covered their enemies"). The link between the two sections once again contrasts Israel's disobedience with YHWH's faithfulness. Almost as if to protect Moses, the psalmist, according to the second reading, places the weight of culpability on Israel; because they angered Moses, he was forced to sin.[71] The attempted preservation of Moses' reputation here conforms to the psalm's general tenor, which previously elevated the status of individuals who have interceded for Israel, as in v. 23.

33 כִּי־הִמְרוּ אֶת־רוּחוֹ וַיְבַטֵּא בִּשְׂפָתָיו

Because they embittered his spirit, he spoke rashly with his lips

Continuing with the incident at Meribah, v. 33 partially explicates Moses' sin,[72] but only after further emphasis falls on the people for causing him to behave as he did. המרו can be read here in at least two different ways, each contributing to the psalm's meaning. First, it can represent הִמְרוּ, the *hipʿil* of מרה, meaning "to rebel against," suggesting that Israel rebelled against Moses causing him to sin. This is reminiscent of Moses' words to Israel in Num 20:10, שִׁמְעוּ־נָא הַמֹּרִים הֲמִן־הַסֶּלַע הַזֶּה נוֹצִיא לָכֶם מָיִם ("Hear now O rebels, must we bring for you water from this rock") Additionally this word can be re-pointed to read as הֵמֵרוּ, meaning "to embitter,"[73] with Moses as the object, suggesting Israel embittered Moses' spirit, which is to say they made him angry, causing him to speak rashly. [74]According to the psalmist, Moses' transgression at Meribah was to speak rashly, or carelessly with his lips, and just like the Torah account, no explicit details are provided explaining

71. Concerning this subtle shift in blame, Briggs, *The Book of Psalms*, 352, writes, "The author thinks that Moses had to suffer not so much on account of what he had done, as for his association with guilty Israel."

72. Here two significant differences must be noted that will be addressed in the following sections. First, only "the waters of Meribah" are mentioned and not Massah, as in Exod 17:7; second, only Moses is mentioned here, but both he and Aaron incur the penalty of being denied entrance to the promised land (Num 20:12). The phrase מי מריבה ("waters of Meribah") recalls Aaron's involvement in this incident as recorded in Num 20:24. Similarly, it reminds the reader of Num 27:13, which speaks of God refusing Moses entry into the promised land because he failed to sanctify YHWH's name at the waters of Meribah.

73. This reading concurs with two medieval Hebrew mss, the Septuagint, and the Peshitta.

74. One could also interpret that the people embittered God's spirit by complaining for water, and this situation caused Moses to sin.

the precise nature of Moses' crime. The aforementioned link with Num 20:10, however, suggests that Moses verbal transgression took place when he spoke those words to Israel in the desert. With the exception of Ps 106:33, the phrase בטא בשפתים ("to speak rashly") only appears[75] in Lev 5:4, אוֹ נֶפֶשׁ כִּי תִשָּׁבַע לְבַטֵּא בִשְׂפָתַיִם לְהָרַע אוֹ לְהֵיטִיב ("or a person that rashly speaks an oath to do wicked or good"), which speaks of a man who thoughtlessly swears an oath, to do good or bad. Although no mention of an oath appears in the present verse, the idea of Moses speaking thoughtlessly is nevertheless present.

לֹא־הִשְׁמִידוּ אֶת־הָעַמִּים אֲשֶׁר אָמַר יְהוָה לָהֶם 34

They never destroyed the peoples that YHWH commanded them

The ninth stanza forms the longest record of Israelite rebellion against God. The main indictment appears in v. 34: they never destroyed the peoples of Canaan according to God's word. Here the psalmist echoes to Josh 9:24, כִּי הֻגֵּד הֻגַּד לַעֲבָדֶיךָ אֵת אֲשֶׁר צִוָּה יְהוָה אֱלֹהֶיךָ אֶת־מֹשֶׁה עַבְדּוֹ לָתֵת לָכֶם אֶת־כָּל־הָאָרֶץ וּלְהַשְׁמִיד אֶת־כָּל־יֹשְׁבֵי הָאָרֶץ מִפְּנֵיכֶם ("for it was surely told to your servants that which YHWH your God commanded Moses his servant, to give to you all the land and to destroy all of the dwellers of the land before you"). From this fundamental act of disobedience stem all the sins and punishments mentioned later in the section. The word השמיד ("to destroy") forms part of a chiastic structure, אמר :: השמידו : להשמידם : ויאמר (and he said : to destroy them :: they destroyed : he said), linking this verse with v. 23, and perhaps more importantly, this section with section five. The two uses of "to destroy" starkly contrast with each other. The former in v. 23 elaborates on YHWH's mercy, since he did not destroy the people as originally intended. However, v. 34 employs the word as a statement of disobedience. As with Esth 1:17 הַמֶּלֶךְ אֲחַשְׁוֵרוֹשׁ אָמַר לְהָבִיא אֶת־וַשְׁתִּי הַמַּלְכָּה לְפָנָיו וְלֹא־בָאָה, "King Ahashverosh commanded to bring Vashti the queen before him, but she never came"; see also Josh 11:9; 2 Kgs 4:24; 1 Chr 21:17), אמר should be interpreted in the present context as "command," signifying Israel rejected a direct command from God.

---

75. The individual word בטה does, however, appear in Prov 12:18 denoting one who babbles.

From Bards to Biblical Exegetes

³⁵ וַיִּתְעָרְבוּ בַגּוֹיִם וַיִּלְמְדוּ מַעֲשֵׂיהֶם

And they commingled with the nations and learned their ways

Disobedience mentioned in the previous verse leads to Israel's further involvement with the peoples they should have destroyed. Just as Israel joined themselves (צמד) with Baal Peor in v. 28, here they "commingled with the nations" (ויתערבו בגוים). It was indeed this very transgression that invoked Ezra's dismay after the exiles returned from Babylon, כִּי־נָשְׂאוּ מִבְּנֹתֵיהֶם לָהֶם וְלִבְנֵיהֶם וְהִתְעָרְבוּ זֶרַע הַקֹּדֶשׁ בְּעַמֵּי הָאֲרָצוֹת ("For they took wives for themselves from their daughters and for their sons, and intermingled the holy seed with the people of the land," 9:2). Although he specifically mentions the mixing of "holy seed," the sentiment remains the same: Israel should not have mingled with the surrounding nations.

As a consequence of Israel's assimilation with the surrounding nations, they learn their ways (וילמדו מעשיהם, "and they learned their deeds"), contradicting the direct warning against learning Canaanite customs in Deut 18:9, כִּי אַתָּה בָּא אֶל־הָאָרֶץ אֲשֶׁר־יְהוָה אֱלֹהֶיךָ נֹתֵן לָךְ לֹא־תִלְמַד לַעֲשׂוֹת כְּתוֹעֲבֹת הַגּוֹיִם הָהֵם ("When you come into the land YHWH your God is giving you, do not learn to do the abominable practices of the those nations"). Even the psalmist's specific choice of מעשיהם ("their deeds") recalls the notion of idolatry. Throughout the Bible this word frequently represents the images and idols forged by the work of men's hands. Deuteronomy 4:28 speaks of Israel's exiles being forced to serve other gods, which are the work of men's hands וַעֲבַדְתֶּם־שָׁם אֱלֹהִים מַעֲשֵׂה יְדֵי אָדָם ("There you will serve gods, the work of men's hands"). Jeremiah 10:3 similarly associates the two, and in Ps 135:15, the nation's idols are described as the works of their hands, עֲצַבֵּי הַגּוֹיִם כֶּסֶף וְזָהָב מַעֲשֵׂה יְדֵי אָדָם ("The idols of the nations are silver and gold, the work of men's hands"; see also Deut 27:15). The term מעשיהם ("their deeds") additionally serves as a reminder of v. 13, explicating how Israel quickly forgot God's deeds. The link between the verses highlights another catastrophic result of forgetfulness.

³⁶ וַיַּעַבְדוּ אֶת־עֲצַבֵּיהֶם וַיִּהְיוּ לָהֶם לְמוֹקֵשׁ

Moreover, they worshipped their idols, and they (the idols) became a snare for them

The decline continues in v. 36; as a result of commingling with the nations, the Israelites begin to serve their idols. Again in this verse they transgress the command against serving the gods of the other the nations, וְלֹא תַעֲבֹד אֶת־אֱלֹהֵיהֶם כִּי־מוֹקֵשׁ הוּא לָךְ ("do not serve their gods, for it will be a snare to you," Deut 7:16; see also Exod 23:33). The derogatory[76] term עצבים (idols)—since the nations never referred to their objects of worship in such a manner—heightens the absurd nature of Israel's turning from God, reminding us of v. 20 where they exchanged YHWH for the image of a ruminant eating grass. Unlike Psalm 135 where עצבים are the object of ridicule, depicted as worthless and reserved for other nations, here Israel turns to worship them.[77] Consequently, the idols become a מוקש (snare) to the people, an object causing trouble and grief, as Saul hoped his daughter Michal would be for David in 1 Sam 18:21, וַיֹּאמֶר שָׁאוּל אֶתְּנֶנָּה לּוֹ וּתְהִי־לוֹ לְמוֹקֵשׁ ("And Saul said, 'Let me give her to him, so she will be a snare to him'"). For the Israelites, the grief stems from the punishment detailed later in the section. Within the psalm's framework, this notion of trouble introduces a degree of irony: Israel turns away from YHWH, the God who has consistently delivered them from trouble (see vv. 8 and 10), to serve idols that bring trouble upon them.

וַיִּזְבְּחוּ אֶת־בְּנֵיהֶם וְאֶת־בְּנוֹתֵיהֶם לַשֵּׁדִים 37

They sacrificed their sons and their daughters to demons

As a result of serving idols, Israel is led to human sacrifice, offering up their sons and daughters to שדים (demons). Specific instances of human sacrifice, as perpetrated by Israel, are absent from the Torah as well as from Joshua and Judges,[78] which recount the early conquest and settle-

---

76. This word, always in plural, denotes an object made by human hands, and is always symbolic of idol worship; see Hos 4:17; 8:4, and Isa 10:11 where it parallels אליל. In the present verse, the context of idolatry is reminiscent of Israel's worship of the calf idol in vv. 19–20.

77. This word often appears in texts polemicizing the gods of the nations. Fabry, "פלל," 283, further notes that the psalm is not criticizing the existence of other gods, but their efficacy.

78. We usually hear of kings leading the nation in this barbaric act nearer the destruction of the first temple. Contrary to this, Thompson, "A Missing Hexateuchal Narrative," 35–51, suggests the practice was present during the era of judges and further suggests that Ps 106 reflects a lost tradition of child sacrifice from the period of the judges.

ment.⁷⁹ However, the injunction against such an act presents itself in Lev 18:21, וּמִזַּרְעֲךָ לֹא־תִתֵּן לְהַעֲבִיר לַמֹּלֶךְ ("And from your seed you will not offer to Molech"; see also 20:2–5; Deut 12:31). Only in the latter stages of Israel's history is it possible to witness instances of Israelites sacrificing their sons and daughters to another god, Molech, as in Jer 7:31, וּבָנוּ בָּמוֹת הַתֹּפֶת אֲשֶׁר בְּגֵיא בֶן־הִנֹּם לִשְׂרֹף אֶת־בְּנֵיהֶם וְאֶת־בְּנֹתֵיהֶם בָּאֵשׁ ("They built the high places of Tophet, which is in the valley of Hinnom, in order to burn their sons and their daughters in the fire," see also 32:35). Verse 37 further describes the recipients of the sacrifices as שדים.⁸⁰ This term only appears in two other places in biblical literature, and from the present context they are best understood as malicious spirits of some description. The word's appearance here recalls Deut 32:17, יִזְבְּחוּ לַשֵּׁדִים לֹא אֱלֹהַּ אֱלֹהִים לֹא יְדָעוּם ("And they sacrificed to demons and not God, gods they never knew"), a verse depicting sacrifices to demons, but not human sacrifice. Somewhat paradoxically, the introduction of שדים brings an amount of life to the previously identified idols (עצבים) which do not possess life. The idols' identification with demons thus creates a far worse picture of Israelite behavior.⁸¹

³⁸ וַיִּשְׁפְּכוּ דָם נָקִי דַּם־בְּנֵיהֶם וּבְנוֹתֵיהֶם אֲשֶׁר זִבְּחוּ לַעֲצַבֵּי כְנָעַן וַתֶּחֱנַף הָאָרֶץ בַּדָּמִים

And they shed innocent blood, the blood of their sons and their daughters, which they sacrificed to the idols of Canaan and polluted the land with bloodshed

The tight lexical association, brought about through the repetition of keywords, closely links vv. 37 and 38, as the latter continues enumerating Israel's acts of apostasy. The original sin of failing to destroy

---

79. The exception being Jephthah's rash oath to sacrifice the first thing he sees upon returning from a military victory (Judg 11:31), which constitutes the thoughtless act of an individual rather than a nation seeking to please the gods of the surrounding peoples.

80. This is either a loanword from Akkadian, *šēdu*, which describes a protective spirit (Greek δαιμονίοις; see also BDB 993, CAD [vol. 17, 256–59],); or originates from the Aramaic שדיא. It is difficult to know whether the psalmist properly understood the word, or whether he simply copied from his source. According to Briggs, *The Book of Psalms*, 353, these were originally the ancient gods of Canaan, and the original word simply meant "lords," used similarly as the divine title "Ba'alim" with no negative connotation. Soon, however, this title became associated with Baal, which was equivalent to "demon" in the mind of the psalmist.

81. See Hacham, ספר תהלים, 135, and Hoffman, יציאת מצריים, 135.

the Canaanites in v. 34 has led Israel to shed innocent blood, וישפכו
דם נקי (see also Jer 22:17), a crime YHWH specifically hates, שֵׁשׁ־הֵנָּה
שָׂנֵא יְהוָה . . . וְיָדַיִם שֹׁפְכוֹת דָּם־נָקִי ("Six things YHWH hates . . . and
hands that shed innocent blood," Prov 6:16–17). Jeremiah 19:4–5 particularly relates this crime to the Israelite acts of child sacrifice. The
triple repetition of דם (blood) further inculcates the crime's heinous
nature, as does the plural form דמים which often signifies murder, or
killing someone who does not deserve to die, as in the case of Cain,
וַיֹּאמֶר מֶה עָשִׂיתָ קוֹל דְּמֵי אָחִיךָ צֹעֲקִים אֵלַי מִן־הָאֲדָמָה ("And he said,
'what have you done? The voice of your brother's blood cries unto me
from the earth,'" Gen 4:10). The blood that was shed belonged to innocent individuals, the children of those performing the sacrifices,
דם בניהם ובנותיהם ("The blood of their sons and their daughters").[82] The
detestable picture painted in this verse is further illuminated by the
chiastic relationship formed between this verse and the previous one,
זבחו : בניהם ובנותיהם :: בניהם בנותיהם : יזבחו (they sacrificed : their sons
their daughters :: their sons their daughters : they sacrificed), emphasizing the sacrifice of one's own flesh and blood. In a return to the imagery
introduced in v. 36, the psalmist repeats the notion that the Israelites
sacrificed to lifeless idols (עצבים) of Canaan. Moreover, the duplication
of עצבים from v. 36 creates an inclusion in which the act of idolatry
is depicted.

The idea of the whole land being polluted, or defiled (ותחנף ארץ)
by bloodguilt is reflected particularly in Num 35:33, וְלֹא־תַחֲנִיפוּ אֶת־
הָאָרֶץ אֲשֶׁר אַתֶּם בָּהּ כִּי הַדָּם הוּא יַחֲנִיף אֶת־הָאָרֶץ וְלָאָרֶץ לֹא־יְכֻפַּר לַדָּם אֲשֶׁר
שֻׁפַּךְ־בָּהּ ("Do not pollute the land which you are in, for blood pollutes
the land, and there is no atonement for the land for blood which was
shed on it"). Although Numbers is not set in a context of human sacrifice, it is possible to surmise that because the crime is the same, namely
the defilement of the land with innocent blood, then so is the verdict;
there is no expiation except by the death of him who sheds it. Reading
this understanding into our psalm indicates the deserved punishment

---

82. Similarly, the plural דמים implies the guilt surrounding a person who takes an
innocent life, אִם־זָרְחָה הַשֶּׁמֶשׁ עָלָיו דָּמִים לוֹ שַׁלֵּם יְשַׁלֵּם אִם־אֵין לוֹ וְנִמְכַּר בִּגְנֵבָתוֹ ("If the sun
rises on him, there is bloodguilt on him, he must surely pay; if he has nothing, he shall
be sold for his theft," Exod 22:2; see also Lev 20:9), for which atonement must be made.
If not, the bloodguilt pollutes the land, as Deut 19:10 indicates, וְלֹא יִשָּׁפֵךְ דָּם נָקִי בְּקֶרֶב
אַרְצְךָ אֲשֶׁר יְהוָה אֱלֹהֶיךָ נֹתֵן לְךָ נַחֲלָה וְהָיָה עָלֶיךָ דָּמִים ("lest innocent blood is shed in you
land, which YHWH your God is giving you for an inheritance, and so bloodguilt will
be upon you"); this verse possibly influenced the psalmist's choice of words.

for Israel is death. Outside the Torah, only Jer 3:2 employs the term for "pollution of land" (חנף ארץ), setting it in the context of spiritual idolatry committed by Israel in the latter part of First Temple period, (וַתַּחֲנִיפִי אֶרֶץ בִּזְנוּתַיִךְ וּבְרָעָתֵךְ) ("and you have polluted the land with your harlotries and your wickedness").

וַיִּטְמְאוּ בְמַעֲשֵׂיהֶם וַיִּזְנוּ בְּמַעַלְלֵיהֶם ³⁹

And they were defiled in their acts, and spiritually adulterous in their deeds

An emphatic parallel structure in v. 39 highlights the corrupting nature of Israel's actions, ויטמאו במעשיהם ("And they defiled with their acts"). In v. 38, the psalmist stated that they defiled the land, (ותחנף ארץ), with innocent blood, now they themselves become ritually unclean⁸³ (see Lev 15:26) through their deeds. The second half of the verse continues to explain how the Israelites desecrated the land through spiritual adultery. The term זנה literally refers to the physical act of unfaithfulness involving a man and his wife (Prov 6:26), or a woman of loose morals (Gen 34:31; 38:15).⁸⁴ In this context, however, the term refers to a spiritual harlotry, portraying Israel's propensity to chase after foreign gods, thus proving unfaithful to YHWH.⁸⁵ The use of "spiritually adulterous," (זנה) together with "defiled," (טמא), in the context of spiritual idolatry is also attested in Hos 5:3, כִּי עַתָּה הִזְנֵיתָ אֶפְרַיִם נִטְמָא יִשְׂרָאֵל ("for now you have prostituted yourself Ephraim and Israel is defiled," see also Ezek 20:30⁸⁶). Israel's sinful deeds again find mention in v. 39 through the

---

83. McCann, *Psalms*, 1111, also refers to this as Levitical ritual impurity, relating it to the results of idolatry, as in Ezek 20:30–31 and Hos 5:3; 6:10.

84. The physical act of prostitution recalls the apostasy with Baal Peor, when the Israelites physically prostituted themselves, as recorded in Num 25:1, וַיֵּשֶׁב יִשְׂרָאֵל בַּשִּׁטִּים וַיָּחֶל הָעָם לִזְנוֹת אֶל־בְּנוֹת מוֹאָב ("And Israel remained in the Shittim and the people started to commit harlotry with the daughters of Moab").

85. For the sense of spiritual unfaithfulness, see Exod 34:15 and Jer 3:1. The word also has the sense of turning astray and subsequently being far from God, as Ps 73:27 indicates. The very notion of Israel whoring after other gods repeats throughout the psalm, since they did the same thing at Mount Horeb (vv. 19–23), and with Baal Peor (vv. 28–31).

86. The poignant imagery of Israel's unfaithfulness to God finds mention in various places in biblical literature (such as the Hosea verse mentioned above and Jer 2:20); however, such references and especially evident in the book of Ezekiel. Chapters 16 and 23 are particularly graphic concerning the spiritual unfaithfulness of both the northern and southern kingdoms.

repetition of two terms, "acts," (מעלליהם) and "deeds," (מעשיהם) also associated in Psalm 28:4, תֶּן־לָהֶם כְּפָעֳלָם וּכְרֹעַ מַעַלְלֵיהֶם כְּמַעֲשֵׂה יְדֵיהֶם ("Give them according to their works, and according to the wickedness of their acts according to the deeds of their hands"). By repeating the latter, the stanza creates an inclusion with v. 35 that encapsulates the acts of spiritual idolatry that defiled the land.

וַיִּחַר־אַף יְהוָה בְּעַמּוֹ וַיְתָעֵב אֶת־נַחֲלָתוֹ ⁴⁰

And YHWH burned with anger against his people and despised his inheritance

After the relatively long description of Israelite sin, v. 40 begins recording YHWH's response; he is angered with his people, וַיִּחַר־אַף יְהוָה בְּעַמּוֹ ("and YHWH burned with anger towards his people"). The phrase חרה אף, "to become angry" (see Gen 30:2; 1 Sam 20:30) frequently describes God's anger against Israel, וְעַתָּה הַנִּיחָה לִּי וְיִחַר־אַפִּי בָהֶם וַאֲכַלֵּם ("and now leave me so my anger may burn against them and consume them," Exod 32:10),⁸⁷ as indeed it does here. More importantly, a similar picture of God's anger being aroused by child sacrifice appears in 2 Kgs 23:26 אַךְ לֹא־שָׁב יְהוָה מֵחֲרוֹן אַפּוֹ הַגָּדוֹל אֲשֶׁר־חָרָה אַפּוֹ בִּיהוּדָה עַל כָּל־הַכְּעָסִים אֲשֶׁר הִכְעִיסוֹ מְנַשֶּׁה, "But YHWH did not turn from his great burning anger which burned against Judah because of all the provocations which Manasseh provoked him"), in which Manasseh's leading of Judah into detestable practices incurs God's wrath. In this verse, YHWH's anger causes him to utterly despise his inheritance (יתעב את נחלתו).⁸⁸ The same word, תעב, appears in 1 Kgs 21:26 to describe Ahab's abominable acts in chasing after idols,⁸⁹ וַיַּתְעֵב מְאֹד לָלֶכֶת אַחֲרֵי הַגִּלֻּלִים ("He committed many abominations, going after idols"). Almost ironically the psalmist employs the term "inheritance," (נחלה) to describe his people, a term which so often conveys the intimate relationship shared between Israel and YHWH, as witnessed in Ps 33:12, אַשְׁרֵי הַגּוֹי אֲשֶׁר־יְהוָה אֱלֹהָיו הָעָם בָּחַר לְנַחֲלָה לוֹ ("Blessed is the nation whose Lord is God, the people he chose for his possession";

---

87. See also Exod 4:14 in which God's anger is directed at Moses, and Num 11:1.

88. According to Briggs, *The Book of Psalms*, 353, this word together with the phrase חרה אף ("burning anger") are of Deuteronomic influence. Additionally, Richardson, *Psalm 106*, 144, notes that the former develops the latter a step further: חרה אף describes thoughts and feelings, whereas תעב depicts the subsequent action.

89. See also Ps 119:163 where it opposes אהב (love).

see also Isa 63:17 and Jer 10:16). The psalmist uses the term in a negative context to demonstrate the extent of YHWH's anger, revealing how far he has been driven, even to the point of hating his inheritance, his beloved people. Such imagery is reinforced when this verse is compared with v. 5, להתהלל עם נחלתך ("to rejoice with your inheritance"), where נחלה (inheritance) epitomizes enjoyment within the confines of a close relationship with God.⁹⁰

וַיִּתְּנֵם בְּיַד־גּוֹיִם וַיִּמְשְׁלוּ בָהֶם שֹׂנְאֵיהֶם ⁴¹

And he delivered them into the hand of the nations, and their haters ruled over them

As a result of his great anger against Israel, YHWH delivers them into the hands of the nations. His punishment characterizes the punitive action frequently recorded in Judges, וַיִּחַר־אַף יְהוָה בְּיִשְׂרָאֵל וַיִּתְּנֵם בְּיַד־שֹׁסִים ("And YHWH's anger burned against Israel, and he gave them into the hand of plunderers," 2:14; see also 3:8; 4:2; 6:1; 10:7). In light of the previous references to the sacrificing of children to idols, however, the psalmist also recalls events from the First Temple era. One such instance is recorded in 2 Kgs 17:20, וַיִּמְאַס יְהוָה בְּכָל־זֶרַע יִשְׂרָאֵל וַיְעַנֵּם וַיִּתְּנֵם בְּיַד־שֹׁסִים ("And YHWH rejected the seed of Israel and he subdued them, and gave them into the hand of plunderers"), to describe the northern kingdom's exile by Assyria. The word גוי in the present verse, together with its appearance in v. 35, creates an instance of "measure for measure"; the very people from whom the Israelites learned their religious practices become their oppressors. Similarly, the repetition of שנא (hate) together with יד (hand) forms an inclusion with v. 10. The connection between the verses returns Israel to where they began: suffering at the hand of their oppressors. Ironically, one can also see the same God who delivered Israel *from* the hand of their haters in v. 10 delivering them *back into* the hand of those who hate them.

וַיִּלְחָצוּם אוֹיְבֵיהֶם וַיִּכָּנְעוּ תַּחַת יָדָם ⁴²

And their enemies oppressed them and they (Israel) were subdued under their hand

---

90. Concerning this word, one can read two meanings: the inheritance can refer to both the land and the people (see Hacham, ספר תהלים, 29).

Standing in the Gap

Verse v. 42a intensifies v. 41b, stressing that Israel's enemies not only ruled over them, but oppressed them too, even as the Israelites were oppressed by the Egyptians as recorded in Exod 3:9, וְגַם־רָאִיתִי אֶת־הַלַּחַץ אֲשֶׁר מִצְרַיִם לֹחֲצִים אֹתָם ("I have also seen the oppression with which Egypt oppresses them"). This recalls the scene in the second stanza which recorded events that occurred in Egypt. The connection with v. 10 in the second stanza creates an instance of chiasmus, ידם : אויביהם :: אויב : יד (their hand : their enemy :: enemy : hand). As in v. 41, the irony of God delivering the Israelites *from* the hand of their oppressors to him only to deliver them *into* the hand of their enemies continues. Inclusion of the verb כנע, to "humble," "subdue," or "bring low"—as in 1 Sam 7:13 (וַיִּכָּנְעוּ הַפְּלִשְׁתִּים וְלֹא־יָסְפוּ עוֹד לָבוֹא בִּגְבוּל יִשְׂרָאֵל, "And the Philistines were subdued and never entered again the borders of Israel"), when the Philistines were subdued at the hands of Israel—creates a word-play with כנען (Canaan) in v. 38. Thus, the very people whose gods the Israelites served have now become their oppressors. The phrase כנע . . . תחת יד ("subdue . . . under the hand") occurs in two other places in biblical literature, and only one of these mentions Israel and an enemy, וַתִּכָּנַע מוֹאָב בַּיּוֹם הַהוּא תַּחַת יַד יִשְׂרָאֵל ("And Moab was subdued that day under the hand of Israel," Judg 3:30).[91] Unlike this context, however, Israel in v. 42 is subdued by their enemy, and not vice versa. Verse 42 closes the ninth and longest stanza, detailing the climax of Israel's sins, human sacrifice, and the zenith of their punishment, deliverance into the hands of their enemies. This reality is punctuated by the inclusion in vv. 41–42 formed by יד (hand), which encompasses the description of Israel's oppression at the hand of their enemies and those who rule over them. Unlike the incident with Baal Peor, however, nobody stands in the gap to intercede for the people and avert judgment.

פְּעָמִים רַבּוֹת יַצִּילֵם וְהֵמָּה יַמְרוּ בַעֲצָתָם וַיָּמֹכּוּ בַּעֲוֺנָם 43

Many times he saved them but they rebelled in their counsel, and they were debased in their iniquity

Without relating to specific instances in Israel's history, this new stanza summarizes the persistent pattern of sin and salvation characteristic of Israel's relationship to God throughout the history of their existence in

---

91. The other instance occurs in Job 40:12, enumerating how God brings down the proud.

the land.⁹² The many times (פעמים רבות) God delivered them recalls not only the sequence of sin and deliverance depicted in Judges, but also the monarchic era. Despite the many times he saved them, they continually rebelled by persistently walking in their own counsel. Unlike the beginning of the psalm, a degree of detachment is discernable as the psalmist now distinguishes between his community and his forefathers. The psalm employs the third-person plural pronoun המה, rather than the first-person common plural characteristics of v. 6 that included the psalmist and his generation together with the unrighteous forefathers. Repetition of מרו ("they rebelled") here recalls the rebellion encountered in vv. 7 and 33, at the Sea of Reeds and against Moses respectively, and expresses the continuity of rebellion from the deliverance at the sea through the era of Israel's kings (see Neh 9:26). Within the psalm's layout, rebellion marks both the beginning and end of the historical narration. Israel's rebellion through walking in their own counsel, mentioned here, recalls their failure to wait for God's counsel in v. 13 (לא חכו לעצתו, "they never waited for his instructions").

The psalmist employs וימכו ("he brought them low," from the root מכך), a rare word to describe the result of the Israelite rebellion and self-debasement; it is only found in two other places in the Bible.⁹³ Literally, it means "to bring low physically," as in Eccl 10:18, (בַּעֲצַלְתַּיִם יִמַּךְ הַמְּקָרֶה וּבְשִׁפְלוּת יָדַיִם יִדְלֹף הַבָּיִת, "Through laziness the beams sag, and through slackness the house leaks"), but the present context implies moral degradation. At least two meanings of עון are relevant to v. 43's context. On one hand, it refers to the people's sin and self degradation that incur God's wrath, as attested in v. 19. On the other hand, it may additionally be interpreted as the punishment brought about by their sin, as in Gen 4:13, וַיֹּאמֶר קַיִן אֶל־יְהוָה גָּדוֹל עֲוֹנִי מִנְּשֹׂא ("And Cain said to YHWH, 'My punishment is greater than I can bear'"), where Cain's *punishment* for iniquity is more than he can bear (see also 1 Sam 28:10; 2 Kgs 7:9).

⁴⁴ וַיַּרְא בַּצַּר לָהֶם בְּשָׁמְעוֹ אֶת־רִנָּתָם

---

92. Semantically הציל ("to rescue/save") creates a link within the psalm to הושיע ("to save/deliver") and recalls instances in which YHWH had accomplished this for his people, as in vv. 8, 10, and 21.

93. It should be noted that this word could constitute a corruption of the verb מוך, a word meaning "to be poor, destitute." If this is the case, then there would be another strong connection with priestly material because the root only appears in Lev 25:25, 35, 39, 47; and 27:8.

Standing in the Gap

But he saw their distress and heard their cry

The previous adverbial phrase, פעמים רבות ("many times"), continues to govern verse v. 44; thus, many times YHWH "saw their distress" (וַיַּרְא בַּצַּר). The verb ראה ("he saw") here does not just have the simple meaning "to see," but to look upon with compassion (see Gen 29:32; 1 Sam 1:11), and to notice with the intention of intervening and helping (see, וַיַּרְא אֱלֹהִים אֶת־בְּנֵי יִשְׂרָאֵל וַיֵּדַע אֱלֹהִים, "And God saw the sons of Israel and God took note of them," Exod 2:25). God sees Israel's suffering with the intention of delivering them. Often in biblical literature, as it does here, the root צרר connotes suffering at the hands of one's enemies, as seen in Num 10:9, תָבֹאוּ מִלְחָמָה בְּאַרְצְכֶם עַל־הַצַּר הַצֹּרֵר אֶתְכֶם ("you go to war in your land against the enemy who oppresses you" see also 1 Kgs 8:37 and Ps 143:12). Thus, in the present context God not only sees their distress, but also hears their call. The correspondence between seeing and hearing in this verse emphasizes YHWH's attentiveness to his people; moreover, the link with v. 25 via the word שמע contrasts with Israel's and YHWH's attitudes towards each other. God *sees* and *listens* to their cry of distress (רנתם), whereas they fail to *listen* to his advice. Such a contrast reflects his compassion; in spite of their behavior, he is faithful to them. As seen from Ps 105:43, the word רנה, can imply a shout of joy and rejoicing. However, here it expresses an entreaty, or cry of supplication to God, as Jer 7:16 indicates, וְאַתָּה אַל־תִּתְפַּלֵּל בְּעַד־הָעָם הַזֶּה וְאַל־תִּשָּׂא בַעֲדָם רִנָּה ("But you, do not pray for this people and do not raise up for them a cry," see also 1 Kgs 8:28; Ps 119:169).

וַיִּזְכֹּר לָהֶם בְּרִיתוֹ וַיִּנָּחֵם כְּרֹב (חַסְדּוֹ) [חֲסָדָיו] 45

And he remembered his covenant to them, and was merciful according to his great loving kindness

Verse 45 continues describing God's response to his people's dire situation: he remembers his covenant for their sake, i.e., for their benefit. The specific identification of the covenant alluded to here is unclear. Because, however, it is evident that the psalmist has been influenced in part by Priestly literature, one can surmise that the reference is to the lawgiving at Sinai, as seen in Lev 26:45, וְזָכַרְתִּי לָהֶם בְּרִית רִאשֹׁנִים אֲשֶׁר הוֹצֵאתִי־אֹתָם מֵאֶרֶץ מִצְרַיִם, "And I will remember for them the covenant of their fathers, whom I brought them out from the land of Egypt"), that specifically depicts a pact with the people who had just received their freedom.[94] Moreover, the contexts in which v. 45 and Lev 26:45 appear also correspond. In both instances it is after the Israelites have sinned and been punished through exile that YHWH remembers his covenant and preserves them in the land of their enemies (Lev 26:44). Together זכר ("he remembered") and רב חסד ("great loving kindness") remind the reader of v. 7, and raise another contrast between the people and YHWH. He remembers them according to his loving kindness, but they fail to remember his kindness. Usually in biblical literature, when God acts in remembrance of a covenant he relents from punishment, or intervenes to save his people (Gen 9:15; Exod 2:24; 6:5), and that is also the case here.

The second colon effectively repeats the sentiment of the first: YHWH's remembrance of Israel corresponds with the mercy he shows them, ינחם ("to relent, turn back from"; see Exod 32:12, and Ps 90:13 where it means "to have pity"). This behavior accords with his great loving kindness towards his people. Although this kindness is not specifically mentioned in the accounts recorded in the psalm's main body, it has been an omnipresent factor. God's actions are not based on Israelite behavior, which has been sinful and rebellious. Only because of his loving kindness, which is eternal (v. 1), the Israelites were not entirely destroyed by their enemies, or by YHWH himself.

וַיִּתֵּן אוֹתָם לְרַחֲמִים לִפְנֵי כָּל־שׁוֹבֵיהֶם [46]

He was merciful to them before their captors

In remembering his covenant, God responds compassionately towards his people in v. 46. Verse 41 saw the verb נתן used as an expression of punishment, but here it is reversed, signifying an expression of pity and mercy, (לרחמים . . . נתן, "he was merciful";[95] see Deut 13:18). More specifically, this phrase directly corresponds with 1 Kgs 8:50, וְסָלַחְתָּ לְעַמְּךָ אֲשֶׁר חָטְאוּ־לָךְ וּלְכָל־פִּשְׁעֵיהֶם אֲשֶׁר פָּשְׁעוּ־בָךְ וּנְתַתָּם לְרַחֲמִים לִפְנֵי שֹׁבֵיהֶם

---

94. Certain commentators raise other possibilities such as the Davidic covenant and the Abrahamic covenant; see Kraus, *Psalms 60–150*, 322; and Allen, *Psalms 101–150*, 73, in light of Exod 2:24. The consensus, however, for various reasons, remains with the Sinaitic covenant; see Ibn Ezra, (Cohen, *Psalms*, 123), and Richardson, "Psalm 106," 201.

95. The *lāmed* in this expression represents either an emphatic particle, or the second accusative object marker for נתן ("to give").

⁹⁶וְרִחֲמוּם ("and you will forgive your people who are against you, and all their transgressions which they transgressed against you, and you show compassion on them before their captors that they may have compassion on them"). Just as Solomon called for God to show mercy towards the Israelites after punishing them via exile, so too the psalmist states that God has indeed granted Solomon's petition, and has shown Israel mercy through the hand of their captors (שוביהם, see Gen 34:29; Ps 137:3). Further strengthening the association with Solomon's prayer are the confessional statements opening the historiographical narrative in v. 6. Additionally, Lev 26:44 is recalled by v. 46, whereby God declares that he will not abhor Israel in the land of their enemies.

The summary of Israel's cycle of rebellion and deliverance⁹⁷ in the tenth stanza ends on a positive note with v. 46. Contrasting with the close of stanzas five and seven, God's mercy is not directly invoked by a mediator, but appears simply as an expression of his own goodness. Verse 46 terminates the psalmist's historical recitation that began in v. 7, and the positive ending sets the stage for the psalm's closing verses.

⁴⁷ הוֹשִׁיעֵנוּ יְהוָה אֱלֹהֵינוּ וְקַבְּצֵנוּ מִן־הַגּוֹיִם לְהֹדוֹת לְשֵׁם קָדְשֶׁךָ לְהִשְׁתַּבֵּחַ בִּתְהִלָּתֶךָ

Save us YHWH our God, and gather us from the nations to proclaim your holy name, and to boast of your praiseworthy deeds

Without a doubt, the climax of Psalm 106 appears here in what is effectively the last verse. With a variety of lexical links to numerous incidents recited in the psalm, v. 47 launches from, and supplies meaning to, previous events. Unlike vv. 7–46, no literary-historical texts are recalled, and the psalmist entreats God's assistance.

The opening imperative cry by the psalmist, הושיענו, hearkens back to vv. 8 and 10, recalling the God who delivered his people from both the Egyptians and the Reed Sea. YHWH's proven ability to save in the past forms the cornerstone of the psalmist's hope. For the first time in the psalm, the psalmist appeals to YHWH's intimate relationship with his people by identifying the covenant name, יהוה, with the God of the

---

96. Even though the majority of Solomon's prayer in 1 Kings 8 is considered a later expansion, especially the section linked to the psalm, see DeVries, *1 Kings*, 121, and Mulder, *1 Kings*, 376, the literary connection still forces us to read these words in the context determined by Solomon.

97. As Kroll, *Psalms*, 314, and Allen, *Psalms 101–150*, 73, have already argued, the cycle described in vv. 43–45 was probably inspired by Judges.

people, אלהינו ("our God"). The plea is further detailed by the psalmist's imperative cry to gather them, קבצנו (see Gen 41:35, gathering food; Deut 13:16 [17], gathering spoil), from the nations.[98] Echoes of God gathering Israel from among the peoples in which he has scattered them appear in Deut 30:3, וְשָׁב יְהוָה אֱלֹהֶיךָ אֶת־שְׁבוּתְךָ וְרִחֲמֶךָ וְשָׁב וְקִבֶּצְךָ מִכָּל־הָעַמִּים אֲשֶׁר הֱפִיצְךָ יְהוָה אֱלֹהֶיךָ שָׁמָּה ("And YHWH your God will return you from your captivity and have compassion on you and gather you again from all the peoples which YHWH your God scattered you there"), and similar to that verse, the psalmist in the present context hopes that after Israel repents, God will gather them from the nations.

The reason the psalmist offers for YHWH to rescue his people is that they in turn may "proclaim thanks to his holy name," להדות לשם קדשך. The idea of proclaiming thanks to YHWH creates an inclusion for the whole psalm: להדות : יהוה :: ליהוה : הודו (to proclaim thanks : to YHWH :: YHWH : proclaim thanks).[99] In spite of the negative tone throughout the psalm's composition, both the beginning and the end contain the same statement of thanksgiving. God's name, שם, in the present verse recalls v. 8, (וַיּוֹשִׁיעֵם לְמַעַן שְׁמוֹ לְהוֹדִיעַ אֶת־גְּבוּרָתוֹ, "And he saved them for his namesake, to proclaim his heroic acts"), which in turn provides justification for any deliverance YHWH may procure: for his namesake, and not according to Israel's behavior. The *hitpael* of שבח, "to speak out" or "boast about," only occurs here in the Bible (excluding 1 Chr 16:35, which adopts verses from this psalm). In the present context it is associated with להדות, which also connotes speaking out and declaring.[100] Giving thanks and proclaiming the deeds of YHWH constitutes acts that the psalm identifies as the principle reason for God's heroic deeds on Israel's behalf—a principle seen in v. 8, where he saved them so that they could proclaim his deeds. With this understanding, what could be perceived as a degree of coercion appears on the part of the psalmist. If the declaration of God's mighty deeds is indeed contingent on his acts of deliverance, then for the people to declare once again his praises, he must act to save them. Repetition of תהלה ("praiseworthy deeds") also lends to this idea. Only after the Israelites were delivered

---

98. With respect to the nations among which the Israelites find themselves scattered, the greatest likelihood is that the psalmist is here referring to the Babylonian exile. We shall revisit this issue in the section on dating.

99. See the following verse for the question of whether v. 48 is organic.

100. See close reading for Ps 105:1.

Standing in the Gap

at the sea did they trust God and sing his praises (וַיַּאֲמִינוּ בִדְבָרָיו יָשִׁירוּ תְּהִלָּתוֹ, "Then they trusted in his promise and sang his praise," v. 12); similarly, God's deliverance is needed now so they can once again respond with praise.

בָּרוּךְ־יְהוָה אֱלֹהֵי יִשְׂרָאֵל מִן־הָעוֹלָם וְעַד הָעוֹלָם וְאָמַר כָּל־הָעָם אָמֵן הַלְלוּ־יָהּ ⁴⁸

Be blessed YHWH God of Israel from everlasting to everlasting; and all the people said "amen." Praise Yah

Verse 48 is not organic to Psalm 106, and was probably added at a later stage in the Psalter's composition. This is apparent from two observations. First, the close reading of Psalm 106 shows how the psalm progressed from praise, to recounting sin, to a petition for God to deliver the people on account of his namesake and merciful character. Consequently, v. 47 forms the psalm's natural climax with the request; therefore, v. 48 does not naturally fit in with this overall scheme. Second, the structure of v. 48 recalls a fixed formula used in ending the Psalter's first three books: Table 4.1 reveals the similarity:

Table 4.1

אָמֵן	Optional Blessing	Expression of Eternity	God	בָּרוּךְ	Psalm
אָמֵן וְאָמֵן		מֵהָעוֹלָם וְעַד הָעוֹלָם	יְהוָה אֱלֹהֵי יִשְׂרָאֵל	בָּרוּךְ	41:13 [14]
אָמֵן וְאָמֵן	וְיִמָּלֵא כְבוֹדוֹ אֶת־כֹּל הָאָרֶץ	לְעוֹלָם	שֵׁם כְּבוֹדוֹ	וּבָרוּךְ	72:19
אָמֵן וְאָמֵן		לְעוֹלָם	יְהוָה	בָּרוּךְ	89:52 [53]
אָמֵן	וְאָמַר כָּל־הָעָם	מִן־הָעוֹלָם וְעַד הָעוֹלָם	יְהוָה אֱלֹהֵי יִשְׂרָאֵל	בָּרוּךְ	106:48

The repetition of this pattern suggests a common hand, independent of the psalmist, inserted all four doxologies.[101]

---

101. This synopsis finds agreement among modern commentators such as Duhm, *Die Psalmen*, 249, Seybold, *Die Psalmen*, 418–19, and McCann, "Psalms," 1112. The fact that the doxology also appears in 1 Chr 16:36 indicates the divisions of the Psalter were already in place at the time of Chronicles' composition. Contrary to this school of thought, Weiser, *The Psalms*, 682–83, suggests the doxology is organic and that this factor influenced the arranger of the Psalter in placing Psalm 106 at the end of Book IV.

Notwithstanding this fact, a number of associations arise between the doxology and the psalm itself. The name YHWH creates both continuity with v. 47 (as does אלהים [God]) and a literary link with the psalm's opening. That God should be blessed from everlasting to everlasting corresponds with his eternal beneficence mentioned in the first verse: in as much as his kindness is eternal, he should eternally be praised for it. The final הללו יה ("praise Yah") creates an inclusion for the entire psalm, and in spite of a negative and mournful tone dominating throughout, encloses the entire composition with words of praise.

MEANING

As lucidly demonstrated in v. 47, Psalm 106 constitutes a confession of sin and cry for YHWH to assist the exiled community by delivering them from the hand of their captors, and returning them to their land. Feelings of detachment between YHWH and Israel are expressed in two ways throughout the psalm. First, the repetitive cycle of sin recounted from beginning to end, in addition to its gradual intensification, tangibly accentuates the feelings of abhorrence YHWH bears towards his people. Second, only scant references to the closeness and intimacy between God and his people appear, a theme commonly found in Exodus psalms. The structure contributes to the meaning since the first part of the confession, vv. 1–12, predominantly speaks of the good works YHWH performed on behalf of Israel. Against the background of his goodness, the remaining stanzas document Israel's rebellious response that fails to improve as the psalm progresses. Because the actions of the Israelites are utterly disdainful from beginning to end, the psalmist cannot base his plea for compassion on their behavior. Consequently, he constructs his request on the basis of YHWH's benevolent nature; because the psalmist knows that YHWH is a merciful God, he hopes that God will listen to his request.

An important, and yet easily overlooked, theme found in the psalm is the exalted role of certain individuals. This concept manifests itself in at least two ways: first, of all the historiographic psalms in the Psalter that refer to the exodus,[102] only Psalm 106 raises the status of individuals in Israelite literary history to being anything close to heroic. The prevailing image presented in exodus psalms is that of YHWH as the ultimate hero, who intercedes on behalf of his people to defend them

---

102. This includes Psalms 66, 77, 78, 81, 95, 105, 106, 114, 135, and 136.

against their enemies, usually appearing in the form of other nations. Psalm 77 briefly mentions Moses and Aaron as those who led Israel in the desert, but they adopt an instrumental role, and it is God who leads his people *through* them.[103] David is mentioned in Ps 78:70, but forms the object of God's actions: God takes him and makes him a shepherd for his people. At no point does David himself take the initiative to perform an act worthy of praise and reward. The patriarchs and Joseph are similarly recalled in Psalm 105, where they all function passively in a psalm recounting God's control of history in the execution of his promise. Psalm 106 alone portrays individuals, in this instance Moses and Phinehas, with the capability of acting on their own accord and performing noteworthy deeds. In presenting individuals in this light, the psalmist unites his personal situation with the literary history he has recited. As seen from the close reading of v. 4, although the psalm is community oriented, the psalmist singles himself out as a righteous individual in his prayer of intercession for the nation. In this respect he likens himself to Moses and Phinehas, aligning his current situation with theirs: Israel is under punishment due to their sin and needs someone to stand in the gap and intercede for them.

DATE

Concerning the date of Psalm 106, the most conspicuous evidence stems from the penultimate verse. Verse 47 constitutes a plea for help, that YHWH would save his people and, most importantly, gather them from the nations (וקבצנו מן הגוים).[104] Additionally, v. 27 suggests a context of exile because it mentions dispersal among the nations, a punishment that was not decreed for the refusal of the promised land. Since Psalm 106 is primarily a community oriented confession lamenting the exile, it is logical to assume with some degree of assurance that the psalm was composed while Israel was still in captivity. Furthermore, because there is no apparent distinction in the psalm between the northern and southern kingdoms, it is reasonable to assume that the entire nation was in exile. In view of these data, it is prudent to suggest the psalm was written during, or just after, the Babylonian exile.

103. Additionally, we must remember that in all likelihood this verse is a later gloss that does not appear in early translations of the Septuagint.

104. In light of events recorded in the psalm, it is most logical to assume the Babylonian exile.

From Bards to Biblical Exegetes

To further the assertion that the psalm constitutes a product of the exile, one can adduce additional linguistic and internal evidence. With respect to language, two words in the psalm reveal the probability of Aramaic influence on the psalmist. First מלל, a standard word in Aramaic for "speaking" that is much less common in Biblical Hebrew appears in v. 2.[105] Additionally, השתבח ("to boast") the *hitpael* of שבח is considered by some[106] to be an Aramaism.[107] Two other points for consideration are the use of עמד ("to stand") as a late synonym for קום in v. 30 and the plural form ארצות (lands) in v. 27.[108] Together, the evidence cited precludes any possibility of the psalm originating during the exile of the northern kingdom or any other period prior to the Babylonian exile.

Although most scholars agree[109] with this hypothesis, some prefer to adopt a more conservative stance. Weiser, *The Psalms*, 680, postulates that the psalm's date cannot be determined with any degree of certainty and that vv. 46–47 do not necessarily presuppose the exile. Additionally, Keil and Delitzsch, *Psalms*, 151, assert that the psalm is Davidic since part of it is put in the mouth of David by the chronicler in 1 Chronicles 16. None of the above theories, however, stands against the preponderant weight of evidence indicating a later date.

---

105. There are some doubts concerning this word because it appears in a Phoenician text: *wbl kn mtmll bymty ldnnyn* ("And there was no one speaking against the Dananians in those Days"). This would imply the word was known in a West Semitic context before the exile; see Dahood, *Psalms III*, 67.

106. See Allen, *Psalms 101–150*, 67.

107. At this point, I must stress that this evidence alone cannot confirm a late date, but should only be used to supplement more weighty evidence. Concerning the reliability of using Aramaic as an indicator of date, see Hurvitz, "Chronological Significance," 85.

108. Polzin mentions both of these (*Late Biblical Hebrew*, 148 and 127 respectively). Concerning the latter, he says: "Late language represented by Chronicles prefers plural forms of words used earlier primarily in the singular"; see also Hurvitz, בין לשון ללשון, 173.

109. See for example Kraus, *Psalms 60–150*, 317, Driver, *An Introduction*, 384–85, Hoffman, יציאת מצריים, 133, and McCann, *Psalms*, 1110.

Standing in the Gap

SOURCES

Table 4.2

Verse	Source	DH
Ps 106:9	Isa 63:13[110]	—
Ps 106:10	Isa 63:9	—
Ps 106:11	Exod 14:28	P
Ps 106:12	Exod 14:31—15:1	NS
Ps 106:14	Num 11:4	JE
Ps 106:17	Num 16:32–33	JE
Ps 106:18	Num 16:35 + 11:1	P + JE
Ps 106:19	*Exod 32:42*[111]; Deut 9:16	D
Ps 106:23	Deut 9:25 + Ezek 22:30	D
Ps 106:24	Deut 1:32	D
Ps 106:25	Deut 1:27	D
Ps 106:26	Num 14:29–30 + Ezek 20:23	P
Ps 106:27	Ezek 20:23	—
Ps 106:28	Num 25:3	JE
Ps 106:29	Num 25:8–9	P[112]

110. Verses 106:9 and 10 are tentatively addressed in the section on allusions because of the high level of uncertainty surrounding the direction of borrowing between the psalmist and Isaiah. There is the possibility of a common tradition, or Isaiah borrowing from the Psalm.

111. Italics are used here because the reference represents a less likely alternative.

112. Here a conflict arises between the views of Driver, *An Introduction*, 67, who argues for P, and Campbell and Campbell and O'Brien, *Sources of the Pentateuch*, 263, who argue a non-sourced tradition. The source is represented here as P because of the additional witnesses of Budd, *Numbers*, 277, and Eissfeldt, *The Old Testament*, 189.

Table 4.2 (cont.)

Verse	Source	DH
Ps 106:30	Num 25:7 + 17:15	P[113]+P
Ps 106:31	Gen 15:6[114]	JE
Ps 106:38	Num 35:33	P[115]

Table 4.2 presents the sources employed by the psalmist to recreate Exodus events.[116] In addition to the Torah, the psalmist was apparently influenced by Ezekiel, as seen from vv. 23, 26, and 27. Moreover, vv. 9 and 10 also suggest some access to Isaiah; however, the direction of borrowing concerning this assumed source is somewhat obscure. The keywords ויתאוו תאוה ("and they craved desires") undoubtedly link Ps 106:13–15 with Numbers 11, since they do not repeat elsewhere in biblical literature and refer to the same context.[117] Although two possibilities present themselves with respect to the source of Ps 106:19, Exod 32:4 and Deut 9:16, Deuteronomy is a more preferable option for the following reasons: first, חרב appears as the name for the mountain of God;[118] second, the idea of intercession forms a common theme be-

---

113. A similar conflict appears here. Driver, *An Introduction*, 63, argues P for Num 25:7, and Campbell and O'Brien, *Sources of the Pentateuch*, 263, claim a non-sourced tradition for the same verse. I have chosen to represent it as P, due to the support of Budd, *Numbers*, 277, and Eissfeldt, *The Old Testament*, 189.

114. A reference to Genesis has been included, although it possesses no relation to the exodus tradition, because it bears a special relevance to the psalmist's portrayal of the exodus. Because the Torah, or documents that were used in its compilation, are assumed to be in existence at the time of the exile, the highest probability is that the psalmist borrowed from Genesis.

115. In this instance, the verse is represented as P. Driver, *An Introduction*, 69, claims it is P, whereas Campbell and O'Brien, *Sources of the Pentateuch*, 263, argue a non-sourced tradition; however, both Budd, *Numbers*, 379, and Eissfeldt, *The Old Testament*, 189, concur with Driver.

116. See Appendix B for a more detailed comparison between the sources and the psalm verses.

117. Primarily due to the psalm's relative lateness, it is more probable that the psalmist had in his possession a text reflecting Num 16, on which he based vv. 16–18. In spite of the possibilities of the psalmist's rendition representing an alternate tradition, the present study treats the psalmist's version as an instance of interpretation in the following section.

118. This designation is the preferred choice of Deuteronomy in depicting the mountain. There is a remote possibility that the psalmist employed it simply to form a poetic association with 106:9, which uses the lexically similar form ויחרב ("and it dried up").

Standing in the Gap

tween the psalm and Deuteronomy; third, among the numerous words connecting the psalm to the Torah, only Ps 106:23 and Deut 9:19 employ the words השמיד (to destroy) and חמה (rage). In addition to these points of similarity, both texts finish the account with God's anger being stayed by the intercessional work of Moses. Exodus, on the other hand, concludes by describing the slaughter of three thousand Israelites at the hands of the Levites, who volunteer to perform God's instructions to slay those involved in the idolatry. With respect to Moses' act of intercession, the psalmist reinforces the image by further alluding to Ezek 22:30. The marker associating these two texts is the phrase עמד בפרץ ("to stand in the gap"), which only ever occurs in the context of intercession in these two locations. Concerning the direction of borrowing between the psalm and Ezekiel, nothing can be said with any certainty. Although Ezekiel is portrayed as the source here, the possibility also exists that Ezekiel read from the psalm, or a common tradition, oral or otherwise, served both authors. At least two markers link Psalm 106 with Deuteronomy 1: the words האמין and דבר ("believe" and "word," 1:32) and the description of the Israelites complaining in their tents, (רגן באהל, 1:27). Concerning the allusion to Ezek 20:23, the markers employed by the psalmist are: פוץ, גוים, זרה, נשא, יד, and ארצות ("scatter, nations, scatter, lift up, hand, and lands").[119] The psalmist's account of the incident at Meribah in which God provided water for the Israelites is most probably based on Num 20:1–12. This is more evident from the contextual congruence between the two texts than the presence of lexical markers. Only the passage in Numbers recalls the whole of the Israelite rebellion together with the transgression by Moses and Aaron. The phrase מי מריבה ("waters of Meribah") also appears in Deut 32:51[120] and Num 27:14, but both instances serve only as reminders of the event narrated in Num 20:1–12. Both passages fail to mention the people's involvement in the proceedings and concentrate on Moses' unfaithful act, thus providing a reason for why he did not enter the promised land. Exodus 17:1–7 presents itself as another potential source simply because it mentions the provision of water and the place name "Meribah";

---

119. It is interesting to note here the chiastic relationship between the psalm and the source. This lends credence to the idea that the psalmist purposefully alluded to the passage in Deuteronomy; for more concerning this phenomenon, see Saidel, "מקבילות," 149–88.

120. Deut 33:8 additionally mentions the location, but the context is specifically related to the testing of the Levites.

however, in this account, there is no record of Moses transgressing God's command in any way.

From the sources examined thus far, Psalm 106 presents the clearest examples of all sources from the Documentary Hypothesis being employed. In this instance, it would almost appear as though the psalmist had before him a copy of the Torah that resembled MT's Pentateuch. For the first time in this investigation, it is possible to witness direct quotes from D as a source, as opposed to influence from Deuteronomic redactors. Evidence of a priestly influence arises with the inclusion of Phinehas' act of zeal. The P account of the desert itinerary is built around four covenants, one of which is that between God and Phinehas.[121] The presence of all four sources in Psalm 106 further solidifies the probability that they had been combined before, or at least during the exile. Of particular interest, concerning sources, is the allusion from 106:12 to Exod 14:31—15:1. Most scholars agree that the song beginning at Exod 15:1 constitutes an entity separate from the traditional pentateuchal sources that was inserted into the Exodus narrative. Because, however, the psalm recognizes the narrative of Exod 14:31 in close association with the song, it would appear that at the time of the psalm's composition the insertion had already been made.

Process of Selection

From the psalmist's corpus, as outlined above, two prevalent themes have apparently dictated his selection: first, sin, with its respective punishment; second, intercession. The sins recalled are limited to Israel as a nation, and the shortcomings of the patriarchs and their respective families are exempt from any accusations. Similarly, the psalmist omitted, or at least marginalized, instances in which individuals have sinned. He fails to mention Aaron and Miriam's rebellion as recorded in Numbers 12, although it is strikingly similar to Dathan's rebellion, which is recalled. This avoidance may stem from the quantity of people involved. In Aaron and Miriam's case, it was only two individuals and therefore not classified as *corporate* sin, whereas with Dathan, one reads of a congregation (עדה) that participated in the rebellion.[122] Likewise,

---

121. Concerning this summary of P's desert account, see Rofé, *Composition of the Pentateuch*, 41.

122. Another possibility for this exemption is that the psalmist is predisposed to protecting the reputation of those he might conceive as divinely appointed leaders.

Standing in the Gap

the psalmist omits Num 15:32–40, which reports of an individual who is caught collecting firewood on the Sabbath, most likely because the incident only involved one individual. With the exception of these two incidents from the Torah, every major instance of Israel's rebellion in the desert is mentioned in the psalm in some way. Accompanying the transgressions, the psalmist often includes the punishments meted out in return.[123] Because of the psalmist's plan to focus on instances of rebellion it is only natural to expect an omission of the lawgiving at Sinai.

Although the number of instances in the Torah of one man interceding to save a nation is limited, the psalmist carefully selected words that allude to all occurrences in the desert. In spite of the psalmist only mentioning specifically two instances—Moses interceding after the golden calf incident (v. 23) and Phinehas staying the plague (v. 30)—other instances are recalled.[124]

ALLUSIONS

Deliverance from Egypt

Even though one cannot specifically pinpoint the psalmist's source for his recounting of Israel's departure from Egypt, one can still identify a process of interpretation and adjustment in his work.[125] The psalmist introduces the element of rebellion in his retelling of events, which was presumably interpreted from Exod 14:10–12, a text detailing how Israel complained against Moses and God when they were caught between

---

This inclination is apparent in his portrayal of Moses' rebellion at Meribah, in which the psalmist levels most of the blame at Israel, and not against Moses himself.

123. This is not, however, always in accordance with the Torah.

124. See the section on allusions to Baal Peor.

125. Due to the uncertainty surrounding the direction of borrowing, only tentative remarks on the associations between Psalm 106 and Isaiah 63 can be made. A number of similarities, both linguistic and contextual, associate the two texts. Isaiah 63:7–14 begins with a declaration in which the speaker proclaims YHWH's kindness, and the good things YHWH has done for his people. It also speaks of God delivering Israel, not because of their inherent goodness, but because of his love and mercy. Moreover, YHWH acting for his namesake לַעֲשׂוֹת לוֹ שֵׁם עוֹלָם ("to make for him an everlasting name," 63:12) forms an important part of the pericope. In light of God's mercy towards Israel, Isa 63 records their response, rebellion. All of these features are present in Psalm 106. Additionally, Isa 63:10 enumerates God's response to their rebellion, describing how he battled against them, and although different words appear in Psalm 106, the same idea is evident. Furthermore, Isa 63:13 recalls Moses' role in the exodus, and reports the desert journey with words similar to those in our psalm, מוֹלִיכָם בַּתְּהֹמוֹת

the sea and the Egyptian army. This addition of the rebellion at the sea makes the psalmist's account unique among other exodus quotes in the selected psalms. Elsewhere, when the event is remembered, it either magnifies the greatness of YHWH's might, or highlights his mercy towards Israel. Although both these elements are present in Psalm 106, they are offset by a recollection of Israelite sin. This addition of rebellion, of course, accommodates the psalmist's overall intention of depicting a rebellious people who have disobeyed YHWH from their birth as a nation to the exile.

Three times in vv. 10 and 11, epithets are given to the Egyptians—צרים, אויב, and, שונא (adversary, enemy, and hater)—and although it is clear from the context to whom these terms refer, the actual name "Egyptians" never appears. Although such an omission is slight, the author's primary intent may be to portray a victory by YHWH over *unnamed* enemies. In emphasizing this, the psalmist creates a more abstract situation in which YHWH delivers his people despite their sin. Such a scenario embodies the hope of the psalm: in spite of all their transgressions, YHWH will once again deliver Israel from their present enemies. Another conspicuous omission in the psalm is Moses' role in the deliverance at the sea. Elsewhere in the psalm he figures as an important character who averts the Israelites' destruction, and yet he is not included as God's *assistant*, one who led Israel though the sea. This omission highlights God's significant involvement in the proceedings and helps demonstrate that ultimately deliverance belongs to him alone.

כַּסּוּס בַּמִּדְבָּר לֹא יִכָּשֵׁלוּ ("who led them in the deep like a horse in the desert, they never stumbled").

In spite of the similarities between the two sections, two conspicuous differences also arise. First, in Isa 63:12, Moses is recalled as a leader, who led the Israelites through the sea with respect to the exodus. Although God clearly instigates events, he nevertheless elicits Moses' assistance in the task. In Psalm 106, Moses does not play any part in the sea crossing. It is God alone who divides the water and leads the people through. By contrasting the two usages of the sea crossing, the psalmist exalts the role of God and his mercy in the psalm. The psalmist additionally adds the destruction of the Egyptians to highlight God's care for his people, another aspect absent from Isaiah. Second, Isaiah only devotes a short space to the sins Israel committed against God and his response, and more time to portraying YHWH's work in deliverance and care for his people. Psalm 106, as we have already discussed, devotes most of its energies to enumerating Israel's sins.

Standing in the Gap

Cravings in the Desert

Numbers' rendition of events[126] begins with a group of people who presumably were not Israelites, אספסף ("riff-raff," "those who," "*tagged along*"),[127] that first felt gluttonous desires (התאוו תאוה, v. 4). Their cravings subsequently influence the Israelites to weep and complain because of the lack of variety in their diets. Upon hearing the complaints, Moses becomes distressed and God's anger is aroused. As a response, God promises to send meat for the Israelites to eat in such abundance that it will come out of their nostrils and become loathsome[128] to them (והיה לכם לזרא, v. 20). At this point in the narrative, the precise reason for God's anger is revealed: because the people were upset at having left Egypt. After promising the meat, a wind from YHWH brings in an abundance of quail (שלוים, v. 31) that falls around the Israelites' camp. While the Israelites were gathering it, however, a very severe plague strikes them.

Within the psalmist's reuse of his source he is careful to omit certain incidents and nuances for the sake of an improved compliance with his work, and also casts events in a purely negative light.[129] His reuse of Numbers 11 fails to include the riff-raff (אספסף) who are the instigators of the evil desires in the source, removing any excuse of a "third party" inciting the people to complain against YHWH and placing the full burden of guilt on Israel.

Although the psalmist undoubtedly alludes to the quail incident of Numbers 11, he omits the specific mention of the word "quail" (שלו). As

---

126. The account in Numbers 11 is interwoven with another, possibly more dominant, account of Moses and the division of his authority among the seventy elders. Within this tapestry, the quail narrative draws the user to compare the complaints of Moses with those of the Israelites; additionally, the story in the original context functions etiologically, providing the origin behind the place name Kibroth Hattaavah. For the psalmist, however, these matters are not important, and he selects only those aspects of the account that highlight an instance of Israel's sin and its ensuing punishment. These issues create a thread connecting all of the psalmist's selected sources.

127. See Budd, *Numbers*, 124, and close reading of v. 15.

128. BDB 266 defines the word thus, whereas the Septuagint uses the Greek χολεραν, referring to a violent stomach illness such as cholera or dysentery (see LSJ 1997).

129. The provision of meat in Numbers is not always employed in a negative light, Ps 105:40 views the incident as a positive manifestation of God's mercy in provision, as do later biblical interpreters such as Josephus, who interprets it as an example of provision, see *Antiquities* 3:4 (see Whiston, *The Works of Josephus*, 79).

a result ,the psalmist broadens the indictment against Israel to portray a general portrait of their wanton desires beyond meat and a variation in diet. Furthering the general portrayal, Ps 106:14, וַיְנַסּוּ־אֵל בִּישִׁימוֹן ("and they tested El in the wasteland"), employs the stem נסה (not mentioned in Numbers' rendition of events), which serves as a general reminder of Israel testing YHWH at the waters of Massah, מַה־תְּנַסּוּן אֶת־יְהוָה ("how you tested YHWH," Exod 17:2; see also the ten times the Israelites tested God in the wilderness in Num 14:22). The broader scope of desires incorporates the underlying cause of Israel's complaint in Numbers 11, which is not so much for a variation in their diet as it to return to captivity in Egypt (see Num 11:20). In doing so, they rejected the work YHWH did for them. Even from the source, the desire for meat seems somewhat artificial because a number of biblical passages report that the Israelites were relatively rich with respect to flocks and herds (e.g., Exod 12:38; 17:3).

In addition to the above, the psalmist effects further adjustments to his source. To heighten the Israelites' sin, he inserts v. 13, a verse explicitly mentioning the speed at which they forgot YHWH's deeds. This addition creates the sense of consecutive events, an image different from the Torah, which includes the bitter waters at Marah, the giving of manna, and the deliverance from the Amalekites. Additionally the psalmist adds that Israel never waited for God's instruction,[130] עצה, implying they acted too hastily, a sin not mentioned in the source. Such an addition, recalled again in v. 43, may constitute a word of encouragement to the psalmist's readers, encouraging them to be patient in waiting for God to deliver them from exile. In v. 15 the psalmist replaces the phrase וְהָיָה לָכֶם לְזָרָא ("and it became loathsome to you") in Num 11:20 with וַיְשַׁלַּח רָזוֹן בְּנַפְשָׁם ("and he sent wasting in their gullets").[131] It is quite possible this was done to alleviate a potential difficulty in the source, which employs the *hapax legomenon* זרא (loathsome). If this assumption is correct, then the psalmist would have replaced זרא with the word רזון (wasting); however, at least to the modern reader, such a

---

130. The idea of waiting for God's instruction and counsel, although not immediately clear from the source, is mentioned by Josephus in his rendition of events in Numbers, "and accordingly he exhorted them to continue quiet, and to consider that help would not come too late, though it come not immediately," *Antiquities* 3:4 (see Whiston, *The Works of Josephus*, 79).

131. Here, the possibility exists that the psalmist is playing on the graphical similarities between זרא (loathsome) and רזון (wasting).

motivation seems strange because the rephrasing involves a similarly ambiguous word.¹³²

Dathan's Rebellion

Numbers 16:2 reports that Korah, Dathan, and Abiram, together with other prominent men from the congregation, rose up (ויקמו) against Moses. Their accusation was that Moses had set himself and Aaron above the rest of the congregation. The issue at stake concerned who YHWH considered holy (הקדוש, v. 5), and whom the Lord had chosen. Moses is dismayed at the accusation, and devises a test to establish God's chosen one. The rebel group, together with Aaron, is to offer incense to God, who would thus select for himself, via the offerings, those he considered holy. The leaders of the rebellion remain in their tents when the suggestion is made (v. 12), and 250 of their representatives present themselves before YHWH. YHWH's anger is aroused and he instructs the congregation to separate themselves from the dwelling of the leaders; at this point, the text recalls Korah, Dathan, and Abiram as the primary instigators. God vents his anger upon them causing the ground to open up and consume them (ותפתח הארץ . . . ותבלע אתם, v. 32), before the earth covers them over (ותכס עליהם הארץ, v. 33) along with their property. At this point in the narrative, attention turns to the 250 representatives. Numbers 16:35 recalls that fire (אש) issued forth from YHWH and consumed them as they offered incense.

Psalm 106:16 recalls that a group of men were jealous of Moses and Aaron, and initially refers to Aaron as being holy (קדוש), which reflects the dispute in Num 16:5. The psalmist, however, chooses the word ויקנאו ("and they envied") to express the rebellion as opposed to ויקמו ("and they rose up") in Num 16:2. A possible motivation for this is that יקמו would produce an unwelcome association with Phinehas' righteous act in v. 30. He also rose up (ויעמד), but for a righteous purpose. Although the psalm specifically mentions the leaders Dathan and Abiram, the name Korah is omitted, contrasting the source that names him first among the rebel group. As mentioned in the close reading, the psalmist probably omitted this name to protect the later musical guild that went by the same name. Other signs exist suggesting the psalmist avoided defaming the name of prominent individuals support this

---

132. The close reading of this verse details the numerous possibilities for this word.

theory.¹³³ After recalling the fate of the leaders in v. 17—the earth opening up and swallowing them (תפתח ארץ ותבלע)—the psalm turns to the remainder of the faction (v. 18). Although it fails to mention the trial by censor specifically, it recalls the fire (אש) that came out from YHWH to consume the wicked congregation.

Refusal of Land

Deuteronomy 1:22–40 is set in the context of Moses recounting the history of the Israelites' forefathers just before they enter into Canaan. Moses recounts in their presence all that transpired in the first attempt at conquering the land. He reminds them of how they selected twelve men from each of the tribes for a reconnaissance mission, and how they returned with fruits and produce. The report concerning the land itself was positive, but the Israelites complained in their tents (ותרגנו באהליהם, v. 27) because they also heard that the indigenous population included some fearsome warriors. Moses challenges the Israelites by saying that in spite of all YHWH had done for them, they still had no faith in their God (ובדבר הזה אנכם מאמינם, v. 32). In the end, God hears their complaints (וישמע יהוה את קול דבריכם, v. 34) and vows that none of that generation will enter the land that he promised them, with the exception of Joshua and Caleb. As a punishment, YHWH decrees that they are to wander in the desert for forty years.

Within Psalm 106, selection of the word מאס (refused, in v. 24)—expressing the Israelites' rejection, and even despising, of the promised land—interprets¹³⁴ events recounted in Deuteronomy 1.¹³⁵ Humanly and rationally speaking, one can understand the response of the Israelites in the source. Twelve men were sent out to survey the land and brought back a report of what they saw, a good land that had

---

133. See section on the golden calf.

134. Both vv. 24 and 25 contain instances in which the psalmist juxtaposes a source with its interpretation. In v. 24 the Israelites refused the land (source) which stems from them not believing in his promise (interpretation, rationale for the refusal). Similarly, the complaint in the tents (source) equates to them not hearkening to his voice.

135. It is worth noting that the verses selected by the psalmist appear in the center of a concentric structure (see Christensen, *Deuteronomy 1:1–21:9, 29*) in Deuteronomy 1 that deals with the rejection of Canaan. Thus, it is likely that the psalmist specifically selected these verses to emphasize, even as the source does, this idea of punishment for the rejection of the promised land.

fearsome inhabitants. One naturally would expect a disconcerting response. This aspect of reality is ignored and even marginalized by the psalmist, who reduces the event to an act of unbelief by the Israelites. The further addition of the adjective חמדה (desirable)[136] goes some way to intensify the nature of the rejection: even when God strives to offer the Israelites a *pleasant* land, they refused to accept it and complain in their tents (וירגנו באהליהם, v. 25). The psalmist paints the picture of the whole Israelite community rejecting the promise of God and not trusting in his word (לא האמינו לדברו, v. 24), and in order to create this image he omits any mention of Joshua and Caleb, the two spies who returned with the same report but believed YHWH could accomplish what he promised. Contrasted with Deuteronomy, in which God hears the sound of the Israelites' complaints, the psalmist uses the same phrase to denote the Israelites' disobedience (לא שמעו בקול יהוה, "they never obeyed YHWH's voice," v. 25).

After recounting the desert generation's sin, the psalmist continues by merging two separate instances of punishment: wandering in the desert for forty years, which led to the death of the rebellious generation, is amalgamated with the Babylonian exile, the reality in which the psalmist's generation find themselves. The psalmist accomplishes this assimilation by alluding to Ezek 20:1–26 (esp. v. 23).[137] In this section, YHWH recounts instances of the Israelite forefathers' previous rebellions and rejections of God's laws while in Egypt. When the children of those delivered from Egypt similarly reject God's laws in the desert, YHWH first determines to destroy them, but then relents and instead swears (נשאתי את ידי להם, "I swore to them," v. 23) to them in the wilderness (במדמר, v. 23) that he would scatter (להפיץ, v. 23) them among the nations (בגוים, v. 23) and disperse them (ולזרות אותם, v. 23) throughout the lands (ארצות, v. 23) because of their failure to obey him. In the context of Ezekiel, this oath represents a declaration of the exile

---

136. This phrase may have formed an alternative designation for Canaan adopted at some time around the exile and after; it occurs in Jer 3:19 and Zech 7:14. Semantically, a wordplay could be in effect here: previously the Israelites were guilty of harboring wanton desires, and now they refuse a desirable land.

137. Similar words appear in Ezek 22:15 but these reflect a continuation of the thread originating from chapter 20, which speaks of the forthcoming exile. We should also note that like the psalmist, Ezekiel stands as an intercessor of sorts because he forms the mouthpiece for the people in 20:1–2 when they approach him to enquire God's will.

(of which the prophet himself is a victim) while Israel was still in the desert.[138]

In merging the exile and the desert generation's punishment, the psalmist describes for us his current situation, exile. Just as the desert generation were punished for not believing God's word, so too were subsequent generations, which led to exile of the psalmist and his contemporaries to Babylon. The amalgamation of the desert generation's punishment and the psalmist's generation's punishment (exile) corresponds with the psalmist's words in v. 6, in which he confesses the sins of the fathers together with those of his generation. Together they fall under the same judgment.

Golden Calf

In Deuteronomy 9, Moses reminds the Israelites of their own sin by recalling events at Horeb, when he ascended the mountain to receive the Law. While on the mountain, God tells Moses to return to the people because they have strayed and made a molten image (מסכה, v. 12). At this point, YHWH suggests destroying them (ואשמידם, v. 14) and building a new nation starting with Moses. Moses then descends from the mountain with the tablets of the covenant, and discovers for himself that the Israelites had indeed made for themselves a molten calf (עגל מסכה, v. 16). In his anger, Moses throws down the tablets, breaking them, and returns up the mountain to intercede for the people. In addition to God's anger against Israel, he also expresses his anger with Aaron, to the point that he was ready to destroy him (להשמידו, v. 20) had not Moses also interceded for him.

Like other accounts mentioned by the psalmist, his portrayal of the Israelites worshiping the image of the calf appears out of sequence with his presumed source. The psalm locates it after the congregation's expression of their wanton desires, and Dathan's rebellion, whereas the source in Numbers mentions it before these two events.

In the psalmist's account of the golden calf, no mention of the law explicitly appears; this is a little surprising because transgression of God's law is a primary theme in the psalm. Similarly unexpected is the omission of Aaron's negative involvement. In the source, it was

---

138. See Greenberg, *Ezekiel 1–20*, 368, and Eichrodt, *Ezekiel*, 269–70.

Aaron who managed the project of forging the idol, and Moses had to intercede to avert God's anger from him.[139]

The psalmist's reuse of Deuteronomy 9 is approximately restricted to the first and last verses of his account, vv. 19 and 23. In between these verses, the psalmist adds his own interpretation of the events. His additions primarily serve to heighten the seriousness of the Israelites' sin. Perhaps the most conspicuous comes with the addition of a polar expression that compares God's magnificence with the sight of a bull[140] eating grass. The psalmist's interpretation is furthered by his use of שכחו ("they forgot") in v. 21, recasting Israel's rebellion as an expression of their forgetting what God had done for them. The dramatic threefold repetition of YHWH's acts of deliverance at the Reed Sea, 106:21b–22, which links to v. 8 of the psalm, directly contrasts his mercy towards Israel with their response towards him, emphasizing the extent of their sin. By employing repetition, the psalmist heightens the severity of the transgressions and consequently the anger felt by God. Thus, in the reading of v. 23, the action of one man, who is able to turn aside such wrath, becomes so much more pronounced.

The overall context in which the golden calf incident is framed also differs between Deuteronomy and the psalm. Deuteronomy 9 is set just before Israel crosses over the Jordan into the promised land. At this point, Moses recounts all of Israel's rebellious and sinful behavior during their desert wanderings. In reciting those events, it is Moses' hope that the people will learn from their past and not repeat the same mistakes once they have crossed over into the promised land. Thus, the purpose is to remind the Israelites of their past to encourage improved behavior in the future. The psalmist, on the other hand, recalls this incident to confess the transgressions of the people—after Moses' hope

---

139. A degree of doubt arises concerning the omission mentioned here because the text in Deut 9:20 may constitute a later gloss to harmonize events with Exodus' rendition of the golden calf. Aaron appears strangely absent from the Deuteronomy pericope up until this point. Furthermore, Loewenstamm, *Evolution*, has shown that Deut 9:20 reveals signs of a later gloss because of the phrase בָּעֵת הַהִוא ("at that time") at the end. Notwithstanding such evidence, the probability still exists that Aaron was omitted because he is also conspicuously absent from the psalmist's rendition of events at the waters of Meribah.

140. The psalmist's description of this idol as a bull (שור) is also an addition to intensify the way we perceive Israel's sin and rebellion because it reflects aspects of Canaanite worship; see Phillips, *Deuteronomy*, 70.

of improved behavior failed—in the hope that YHWH will again be gracious unto them and bring them back from captivity.

In Ezek 22:30, God searches for one man to stand in the gap (עמד בפרץ), to intercede on behalf of Israel so that he could spare them. Unfortunately, in this instance, nobody was found and Judah was sent into exile. This situation contrasts with Ps 106:19–23. In the context of the psalm, the Israelites sin, but unlike Ezekiel's record, someone is found to mediate for them. By including the allusion to Ezekiel, the psalmist develops the idea of intercession, showing that without one man to intercede for the people, they suffer God's wrath; conversely, the intercessory actions of just one man are enough to turn God's anger from the nation. This theme is important to the psalmist since he ultimately casts himself in the position of that one man who intercedes for the people to divert God's punitive anger.[141]

Baal Peor

Numbers 25 reports how the Israelites, whilst staying in Shittim, prostituted themselves with Moabite women, who invited them to sacrifice to their gods (לזבחי אלהיהן, v. 2). The people responded by eating (ויאכל, v. 2) sacrificial meals and bowing to the Moabite gods. Israel thus joined themselves with Baal Peor (ויצמד . . . לבעל פעור, v. 3), an act which raised YHWH's anger against them. As a punitive measure, God instructs Moses to impale publicly all those who had prostituted themselves in this way. At this time, an Israelite man brought a Midianite woman over to the tabernacle in the sight of Moses and the Israelite community. When Phinehas (פינחס, v. 7) saw this, he arose (ויקם, v. 7) from the assembly, and taking a spear in his hand, he stabbed the man and the woman in the sight of all. At this point in Numbers, the author reports that a plague, presumably sent as punishment when the idolatry began, ceased (ותעצר המגפה, v. 8) although no explicit record of its outbreak was ever made. Because of his zealous actions, God makes a covenant of peace with Phinehas and his descendants (v. 13).

Although the points of association are strong, the psalmist has, just like other allusions in the psalm, chosen to omit from his source those issues that he deemed unimportant or contrary to his message. Phinehas' zeal (קנא) is emphasized in the source (see Num 25:11, 13),

---

141. See the close reading of further details on this topic.

Standing in the Gap

and although no reference to it appears in the psalm, it nevertheless constitutes an important part of Phinehas' character that reinforces his act of intercession. A possible motivation for this omission is that the psalmist wanted to avoid an internal negative association with the root קנא, which also appears in the recounting of Dathan's rebellion. Just as the psalmist chose words to create internal allusions through repetition, here he alters a word to avoid such an allusion.

The specific nature of the sin committed by the Israelites, and Phinehas' violent act that ended it, are details the psalmist has presumably omitted[142] because they ultimately were not important to his message. Avoiding mention of the above also means it was not incumbent upon the psalmist to explain exactly what occurred in Num 25:6.[143] Another important alteration concerns the nature of the covenant made with Phinehas. Numbers 25:12 refers to it as a covenant of peace, בריתי שלום.[144] The psalmist's decision to alter this phrase may have been dictated by the overall message of the psalm which opposes any notion of peace between God and Israel. In omitting the reference to the covenant of peace, the psalmist replaces the blessing with an allusion to Gen 15:6 that describes Abraham being attributed with righteousness (צדקה) for believing God's word. Thus, Phinehas is likened to a character who believed and trusted God's word. Consequently, he is individually characterized with the very trait the Israelites lacked in the psalm: believing, having faith, and trusting in God (see v. 24). By receiving the same blessing Abraham received, Phinehas' status is also elevated to

---

142. This is how Fishbane, *Biblical Interpretation*, 398, primarily interprets the act, but in the psalm's context, we should also consider the psalmist's principal themes, including that of intercession. Although he may indeed be alleviating the cruelness and harshness of Phinehas' actions, he is also interpreting the act according to a theme central to his psalm: one man acting on behalf of the people to stay God's wrath.

143. The precise nature of the act eliciting Phinehas' response is not altogether clear from the account in Numbers.

144. Noordtzij, *Numbers*, 242, calls this as an everlasting relationship of peace with God. Such a reward, however, is contradicted in the psalm since even the descendants of Phinehas would not be at peace with God. Some later interpreters see this covenant as a statement declaring that Phinehas would live forever. Support for this comes from Judg 20:28, in which Phinehas is still alive long after his contemporaries have died. Further support for this idea appears in *Num. Rab.* 21:3, and *Tg Ps.-J* Num 25:12–13.

that of Abraham, suggesting that God viewed both individuals in the same way.¹⁴⁵

The Numbers account of the idolatry with Baal Peor is somewhat unclear with respect to the plague. Although its end is recorded in Num 25:8, there is no record of when the plague began. This lacuna in the source is resolved by the psalmist because his account implies that the plague began after the Israelites joined themselves with Baal Peor.¹⁴⁶ Additionally, the psalmist's employment of the phrase "and the plague was stopped" (ותעצר המגפה, v. 30) alludes to Num 17:15. Although the phrase also appears in 2 Sam 24:21,¹⁴⁷ depicting an end to the plague caused by David ordering a census of the people, the similar context of Num 16:50 [17:15] suggests it influenced the psalmist. Numbers 17 speaks of a plague separate from the one instigated by the worship of Baal Peor. It describes an instance when Israel complained about the high number of God's people who died after Dathan's rebellion. This complaining angers YHWH and he sends a plague on the people as punishment. Reacting to this, Moses instructs Aaron to light a censer and bring it to the altar, an act which succeeds in halting the plague (והמגפה נעצרה, v. 15). The important point of association between this act and the psalm is the description of Aaron. After he succeeds in stopping the plague, he is depicted as standing between the living and the dead. Such a description reflects the essential notion of intercession: one man preventing a calamity upon a nation. This same theme is also critical to Psalm 106 because the psalmist sees himself in that role.¹⁴⁸

145. His elevation of Phinehas' status may indeed be further proof that the psalmist himself is a priest and a descendant of Phinehas.

146. An interesting act of interpretation occurs in v. 29, which may constitute an attempt by the psalmist to reflect the ambiguity in the source. The psalmist effectively makes two separate statements concerning the coming of the plague: first, that God was angered; second, that a plague broke out. Although it is implicit from the context, the psalmist does not explicitly state that God sent the plague as a result of his anger. Instead, one event is simple stated after the other.

147. One should not be too hasty in rejecting this passage as an allusion because it too contains the important idea of the effects one man's actions have on a larger community. Although the psalmist is primarily concerned with the positive effects, such as interceding to God on the people's behalf, the text in 2 Samuel provides an antithesis: the sinful effects of one man bringing destruction to a nation. The idea of an antithesis to heighten the positive example also occurs in Ps 106:23, which alludes to Ezekiel (see above, concerning the golden calf).

148. A glance at the psalm's overall context in relation to its source reveals other alterations. The primary purpose of Numbers 25 is to clarify the special position

Standing in the Gap

Waters of Meribah

Only two verses are devoted to describing the provision of water at Meribah, and like many of the other episodes recounted by the author, this one occurs out of sequence. The incident's placement, however, approximately corresponds with Deut 32:51, where it appears immediately prior to the Israelites entering into the promised land, as reflected in our psalm.

After Miriam's death in Num 20:1–13, the Israelites were without water and gathered against Moses (משה, v. 3) and Aaron (אהרן) complaining that they should have remained in Egypt because they now lacked water in the desert. Moses and Aaron then fall on their faces before God (vv. 6–8) who instructs them to order a rock to yield water. Moses subsequently takes Aaron's rod and angrily chastises the people before striking the rock with the staff, whereupon water gushes out. God then punishes Moses and Aaron for not affirming his sanctity before the people, the punishment being denial of entry into Canaan. These events reportedly transpire at the waters of Meribah (מי מריבה, v. 13).

From the psalmist's source, two notable alterations occur: the omission of Aaron's involvement in the affair, and a heightening of Israel's role. The omission of Aaron is partly understandable since he does not play an important part in the source. In many ways his role is that of a hapless victim caught up in events beyond his control. Numbers 20 recognizes Moses as the protagonist who acts and speaks, and yet Aaron is punished for what appears to be Moses' sin.[149] In mentioning the people's involvement, the psalmist adapts the source to the overall pattern and central message of the psalm—highlighting the Israelites' persistent rebellion. Primary emphasis on the people's sin mollifies the degree of accountability ascribed to Moses in the source. In Numbers, no question arises concerning Moses' and Aaron's culpability, irrespec-

---

of Phinehas' descendants within the circle of Aaronite priests, and to highlight the moral degradation of certain elements within Israelite leadership; see Num 25:4, and Noordtzij, *Numbers*, 240. The latter element contributes to the psalm's development because it demonstrates the depth at which the rebelliousness of the Israelites had reached, even to members of the leadership. The former element, however, is dropped in its entirety by the psalmist. Instead, he further adapts the narrative to exemplify how one man's righteous act can effectively save the entire nation from God's punitive wrath.

149. See Propp, "Massah and Meribah," 601.

tive of the people's actions. Moses failed to sanctify God's name in the presence of the Israelites (Num 27:14), and for this he is punished by being denied entrance into the promised land. The psalmist's rendition of events is somewhat apologetic with respect to Moses: because of the people's behavior, Moses is angered and sins on their account. Such an emphasis on the people driving Moses to sin has particular relevance to Ps 106:19–23; after Moses intercedes to turn God's fury away, they repay him by bringing wickedness upon him.[150]

Reordering

Concerning the psalmist's overall scheme for the arrangement of his selected material it is difficult to assert categorically that he had a single strategy in mind. It is clear, however, that he rearranged material to suit his specific purposes. While an all-encompassing strategy eludes us, motives that may have influenced the psalmist in his arrangement of the psalm may be suggested.[151] The order of events in both psalm and source are listed below.[152]

---

150. At this point, it is worth noting that Deut 1:34–37 may have influenced the author's work to some degree, and he may even have attempted to harmonize the two texts. Deuteronomy 1 forms part of a recital depicting Moses' refusal of entry into Canaan, and in v. 37 YHWH denies Moses entry to the land because of the Israelites' refusal to enter it at the first opportunity. Even though no reference appears here to מריבה (Meribah) it is relevant because Aaron is not mentioned, as in the psalm, and Moses' denial of entry into the land comes as a direct result of Israel's actions.

151. Now the possibility that the psalmist worked with a *vorlage* reflecting a different order from that which we have today must be acknowledged. Although this is possible, it is also a less likely scenario because of the relatively late date of the composition.

152. Events omitted from Psalm 106 are in italics.

Standing in the Gap

Psalm 106	Exodus(E)/Numbers(N)
1) Reed Sea Crossing	1) Reed Sea Crossing (E)
2) Egyptians' Destruction	2) Egyptians' Destruction
3) Song of the Sea	3) Song of the Sea
4) Desire for Quail	*Bitter Waters at Marah (E)*
5) Dathan's Revolt	*Manna (E)*
6) Golden Calf	*Massah/Meribah (E)*
7) Moses' Intercession	*Lawgiving (E/N)*
8) Rejection of Land	6) Golden Calf (E)
9) Baal Peor	4) Desire for Quail (N)
10) Meribah	*Aaron's Rebellion (N)*
	8) Rejection of Land (N)
	7) Moses' Intercession (N)
	5) Dathan's Revolt (N)
	10) Meribah (revisited?) (N)
	Bronze Serpent (N)
	Bilaam (N)
	9) Baal Peor (N)

On the whole, one can see that the psalmist pays some respect to the chronological ordering of events in his source. Beginning with the crossing of the Reed Sea, he portrays the desert period, and proceeds from there to the conquest and habitation of Canaan. This sequence of events reflects the Pentateuch and former prophets. His decision to place the quail incident before events at Sinai, may reflect two possible motivations. First, it could have been viewed together with the manna account and ordered as a pre-Sinai event according to Exodus. Supporting this view is the fact that quail are not specifically mentioned in the psalm, only "desires," which may encompass both the desire for meat and for bread. Second, the psalmist may have sought to order events from the least to the most severe. Thus, the quail incident was, in his view, the least serious. Because the desire for food is natural and understandable, he may have conceived it as being more excusable.[153]

The placement of Dathan's rebellion, which occurs much later in the source, before the events at Sinai, may also have been motivated by the psalmist's attempt to arrangement events according to severity. Since Dathan's rebellion involved a smaller section of the community

---

153. The possibility exists that based on the source, it was not the Israelites who instigated the complaints but the riff-raff (אספסף) who accompanied them from Egypt (Num 11:4).

159

and was only indirectly leveled against YHWH via his leadership, the instance of rebellion may have been deemed more trivial. Following Dathan's rebellion is the account of the golden calf. This represents a sin more severe than all of those preceding, possibly reflected in the psalmist's extra effort to remind the reader of the deliverance at the Sea together with the theological interpretation of the event in v. 20. Although this incident represents an escalation in the transgression's deplorability, it is ameliorated to some extent by the act of intercession that follows.

Moses' intercession should be read together with the promised land's rejection and Phinehas' act of intercession. Together, these events teach the reader about the importance of intercession. With the righteous acts of individuals, God's anger can be stayed despite the community's acts of idolatry, as in Moses and Phinehas' case. But without an intercessor, the people suffer under God's punishment. One reason for the placement of Phinehas' act so late in the proceedings is that it heightens the impact of his deeds. After sin has multiplied and become habitual for Israel, a place still exists for effective intercession. This theme would have been important to the psalmist, since he would have stood at a time much later in Israel's history, after the habitually rebellious behavior became more ingrained in Israelite society.

The account of Meribah is primarily employed by the psalmist as an apologetic for why Moses was denied entrance to Canaan even after his intervention to save the people. It additionally highlights Israel's ingratitude, since it reveals that after he had prevented their destruction, they repay him by provoking him to sin. With this account, the psalmist returns to a semblance of chronological ordering, since this was one of the last events occurring before Israel crossed the Jordan into Canaan. Following this incident the psalmist retells instances of child sacrifice. As the sins grew more abhorrent, so its effects broadened. Previously each man's sin defiled him, and him alone, and he was punished for it. In this later incident, however, the sin of the people affects both their innocent children in addition to the land, which becomes polluted. Consequently, the act of rebellion should certainly be considered worse than all of its predecessors, completing the picture of progressive severity.

Standing in the Gap

JUXTAPOSITION

Psalms 105–106

After a general introduction of praise (vv. 1–7) exhorting the audience to praise and remember YHWH's deeds, Psalm 105 establishes its primary theme: God's promise (דבר, v. 8) of land to Abraham and his descendants. It continues by recalling incidents from the patriarchs' lives and proceeds to enumerate events in Joseph's life. The psalm recalls how God sent (שלח, v. 17) a man before the patriarchs, who is further identified as Joseph. He is sold as a slave and bound as part of a process in which God tests him. After a designated period, God sends (שלח, v. 20) for the king, who releases (ויפתחהו, v. 20) Joseph and appoints him ruler over all he owned. After this, the psalm continues by recounting Jacob's sojourn to Egypt, the land of Ham (ארץ חם, v. 23) and the events leading to Israel's oppression and enslavement. In order to secure their emancipation, God sends (שלח, v. 26) Moses and Aaron, and through them he works signs against the Egyptians, the plagues. Among the plagues, it is specifically noted that God sent (שלח, v. 28) darkness, which did not rebel (לא מרו, v. 28) against his word, and a flaming fire (אש, v. 32). As a result of the plagues being unleashed against the land of Ham (ארץ חם, v. 27), YHWH secures the Israelites' freedom and leads them out into the wilderness with silver, gold, and much rejoicing. When they became hungry during their desert sojourn, they asked (שאל, v. 40) for food, and he provided them with meat, bread, and water as an expression of his kindness. At this point, the psalm recalls that God performed all of these deeds on behalf of Israel because he remembered his holy promise (דבר, v. 42) to Abraham. The psalm then reiterates the joy (רנה, v. 43) with which God delivered Israel, and proceeds to explain YHWH's desired response to his benevolence (see close reading on Ps 105:45). In each of the above contexts, the words cited appear in a positive light, i.e., YHWH assists the Israelites in some way, bringing about the fulfillment of his purposes.

Psalm 106 adopts a number of the aforementioned common words and reworks them into a wholly negative context concerning God's relationship with Israel. Following the introduction, Psalm 106 continues to recount Israel's sinful past as part of a national confession of sin. After recounting how God delivered them from the sea and Pharaoh's army, the psalm speaks of the Israelites' evil desires for food, contrasting the more polite request in Psalm 105. God answers their request (שאלתם, v. 15) and also sends (ישלח, v. 15) leanness to their soul as punishment. Subsequent to this, a group of Israelites, Dathan and his company, instigate a rebellion against Moses and Aaron. As a response to the insurrection, the rebel group is punished when the ground opens (תפתח, v. 17) and swallows Dathan, and a fire (אש, v. 18) is kindled in their company. Psalm 106 reports three other instances of sin: idol worship with a calf idol, the Israelites' refusal of the promised land, and a further instance of idolatry with Baal Peor. After this, Israel rebels (המרו, v. 33) against Moses at the waters of Meribah, causing him to speak rashly with his lips. The following section in the psalm details Israel's acts of child sacrifice soon after the conquest, and then the psalm summarizes their actions while they dwelt in the promised land. They rebelled (ימרו, v. 43) numerous times and were punished by YHWH, who permitted their enemies to oppress them. God, however, would hear their cry (רנתם, v. 44) and take pity on them.

In each instance above, keywords link Psalm 106 with Psalm 105, however, the apparent reversal from positive to negative[154] acts as a tool for highlighting the comparison between the two works. Psalm 105 portrays the work of a benevolent God who, from his own initiative, acts in mercy towards Israel so that they in turn would obey him. Contrasting this, Psalm 106 depicts Israel's response. They constantly rebel against him, failing to respond correctly to his kindness. As a result, YHWH is forced to punish them with the same measure with which he previously shows mercy to them.

The only two places in the Bible that use the phrase ארץ חם ("Land of Ham") are Pss 105:23, 27 and 106:22.[155] This fact alone certainly suggests that one psalmist was familiar with the work of the other. Moreover, the arranger of the Psalter may even have used this phrase as a reason to juxtapose the two works.[156] Irrespective of which psalm was

---

154. Here, the reversal is portrayed in terms of positive to negative because this reflects the order of the psalms as they appear in the Psalter. One could also view the change as being from negative to positive if one understands that Psalm 105 was written after Psalm 106 and the author of the former psalm sought to place a positive slant on the negative reporting of the desert events.

155. Notwithstanding the similar phrase in Psalm 78:51, אהלי חם ("the tents of Ham").

156. Keil and Delitzsch, *Psalms*, 21, have suggested this as a possible motive for juxtaposition.

Standing in the Gap

written first, a sequential reading of the two compositions with regard to this phrase is insightful. Psalm 105 first employs the phrase as part of a detailed description of God's work in redeeming the Israelites from slavery, a portrayal that includes the multiplication of Jacob's family, the Egyptians' change of heart and the plagues wrought against them. With this in mind, when the reader continues to read the same phrase in Psalm 106, he has a lucid and fuller picture of the magnificent deeds performed in the land of Ham (Ps 106:22). Psalm 106 does not specifically mention the plagues against Egypt, but via the link, ארץ חם, the psalm reminds the reader of the events. In a similar fashion, the phrase ארץ חם completes a lacuna in Psalm 105, which fails to recall the events of the Reed Sea, jumping from Israel's departure from Egypt to the desert wandering. Via ארץ חם, however, the reader is brought to Ps 106:22, which recalls the miracle.

In Psalm 105:8, דבר represents a promise that YHWH makes to Abraham and his descendants to give them the land of Canaan. This promise (דבר) is fulfilled in v. 42 when YHWH proves faithful and grants Israel the land of Canaan, in addition to the toil of the indigenous population. Contrasting this situation, in light of God's proven faithfulness to his promise (דבר) Israel fails to trust in him when the time first came for them to conquer the land (106:24).

The two prominent themes appearing in both psalms—deeds and remembrance—further augment the comparison mentioned above. Numerous synonyms appear in the two works reflecting these notions (as the close reading of both psalms reveals). Psalm 105 recounts how God remembers his promise by performing deeds to help save Abraham and his seed. YHWH acts by rebuking those who threaten the patriarchs, sending Pharaoh to release Joseph,[157] sending the plagues against Egypt to emancipate his people, feeding his people in the desert, and generously bestowing upon them the land of Canaan, which he had promised. Contrasting this, Psalm 106 disparagingly narrates how Israel does *not remember* God's deeds. Verse 7 states they did not remember the multitude of his mercies, v. 13 says they quickly forgot his deeds, and v. 21 describes how they forgot the God who saved them.[158]

---

157. This is a valid reading of the verse even though a few commentators and modern translations disagree; it better fits the psalm's theme of YHWH's omnipotence.

158. Synonyms for *wicked deeds* ubiquitously occur in Psalm 106: חטאנו ("we sinned," v. 6), העוינו ("we have committed iniquity," v. 6), ויתאוו ("they craved desires,"

Just as individual words are redeployed in inverted contexts, so are these two themes in Psalms 105 and 106.[159]

Following the aforementioned contrast, the juxtaposition of Pss 105 and 106 reinforces an important and established lesson from biblical tradition. It implores the listeners to remember God's deeds in history, because forgetting these deeds leads to dissolute behavior. Psalm 105 is primarily a call to remember God's works as an aid to obedience (see v. 45). Following this, Psalm 106 graphically describes the consequences of forgetting (106:13–14). Deuteronomy similarly reflects this lesson. Deuteronomy 8:15–18 enumerates various deeds God performed for the Israelites, v. 19 then directly associates forgetting God's acts for Israel in the past with committing sinful actions: walking after other gods.

In addition to the contrasts mentioned above, Psalm 106 constitutes a corrective compliment to Psalm 105. Reading Psalm 105 alone suggests the wilderness events occurred without any rebellious behavior and Israel was fully compliant and cooperative with God's purposes. Verse 40 suggests Israel never complained for food and water, but politely requested food to eat, and God stood ready to supply their needs.

---

v. 14), and ויטמאו במעשיהם ויזנו במעלליהם ("And they were defiled in their acts, and spiritually adulterous in their deeds," v. 39).

159. Contrast as a rationale for juxtaposition is by no means a rare phenomenon, and there are instances in biblical literature of events juxtaposed with the intention of emphasizing the deeds of an individual. For example, 1 Samuel 25 recounts the conflict between David and Nabal. David sends messengers to Nabal requesting a share of Nabal's profits claiming that in some part, he deserves it, because he and his men protected Nabal's shepherds. After Nabal declines David's request, David's action is swift; he gathers his men, puts on his sword and vows to kill Nabal, who offers no direct threat to David's life. Immediately after this account, we read the account of Saul's pursuit of David with the intention of taking his life. During this pursuit, David has the opportunity to kill Saul, but instead chooses to spare him. The juxtaposition of these two stories highlights David's behavior. In the first story, the author portrays him as a man who is quick to kill for a relatively negligible affair. The second account emphasizes David's remarkable restraint for YHWH's anointed. In another example, Gen 11:1–9 recounts the Mesopotamian's actions as they strive to make a name for themselves by disobeying God's command to go out into all of the earth (Gen 1:28, פְּרוּ וּרְבוּ וּמִלְאוּ אֶת־הָאָרֶץ וְכִבְשֻׁהָ, "be fruitful and multiply and fill the earth and subdue it"). Because of their disobedience, God instigates their dispersal throughout the world, and they fail to achieve their quest for fame. The following story describes Abraham obeying God's call to fill the earth; consequently, he receives the very thing the Mesopotamians tried to attain, a name. The juxtaposition of these stories emphasizes Abraham's obedience in contrast to the Mesopotamian's disobedience.

Standing in the Gap

By way of contrast, a sequential reading of Psalm 105 and Psalm 106 corrects any misconceived ideas, recounting numerous instances of rebellion (Ps 106:7, 33, 43). God did answer their request (complaint) for food, but sent them leanness with it (106:15); there was fire sent against Israel's enemies (105:32), but also against them (106:18). Via certain keywords appearing in both psalms, Psalm 106 responds to 105 sending a clear message that Israel's history during the Exodus was not a picture of total obedience.

Psalms 106–107

Psalm 107 is essentially a psalm of thanksgiving for various calamities—that an individual or community may undergo—in which God intervenes to deliver.[160] Although the psalm depicts numerous situations, one cannot claim indisputably that the psalmist intended to enumerate specific instances in Israelite literary history. The end of the psalm reveals a purpose beyond simply that of thanksgiving, as it exhorts the reader to learn from past events. The psalm begins (vv. 1–3) with a call to praise (הודו ליהוה כי טוב כי לעולם חסדו, "Proclaim thanks to YHWH for he is Good, surely his mercy is everlasting," v. 1) that is addressed to the redeemed of YHWH, and those he has gathered from the lands (ומארצות קבצם, v. 3).[161] Verses 4–10 then continues to speak of his provision of sustenance and how he led individuals in a desert (בישימון, v. 4), and provided their weary souls (נפשם, v. 5) with sustenance despite their rebellion. The idea in v. 9 of YHWH as one who satisfies the hungry soul (נפש) is adopted as an example of his wonderful works (נפלאות) that deserve praise. Verses 10–16 portray a deliverance from captivity that was induced through rebellion against his counsel (המרו . . . עצת עליון, v. 11). Similarly vv. 17–22 speak of an affliction that was brought on by God as punishment for sin in which the soul (נפשם, v. 18) of the afflicted abhorred all manner of food; while in their distress, however, he healed them. As a response to this, they are exhorted to offer sacrifices of thanksgiving (ויזבחו זבחי תודה, v. 22). Verses 23–33 recount a situation in which individuals are saved from a storm at sea, and during their distress, the psalm depicts the souls (נפשם, v. 26) of

---

160. See also Allen, *Psalms 101–150*, 88.

161. Verses 2 and 3 probably do not belong to the original work (see Allen, *Psalms 101–150*, 88), and may have been added with the specific purpose of strengthening the relationship between the psalms.

these individuals as melting. In order to deliver them, however, YHWH stills the sea and guides them back to land. Next comes a return to the desert as vv. 34–38 detail God's work over creation in transforming a desert into a habitable land by creating streams and pools of water. The final section returns to the theme of deliverance from domination by enemies, although the oppression was instigated by YHWH for disobedience. The concluding verse, as previously mentioned, consists of an admonition to learn from history, and the mercy YHWH had previously shown to man.

Although Psalms 106 and 107 start with exactly the same words (הודו ליהוה כי טוב כי לעולם חסדו, "Give thanks to YHWH for he is good, surely his mercy is everlasting"), the contexts in which they appear differ significantly. Psalm 106 constitutes a lament that recounts Israel's continuous rebellion against YHWH and his constant need to punish them for their actions. As a result of their behavior they are ultimately exiled to the land of their enemies and cry out to God for deliverance. Against this background, the psalmist encourages the readers in v. 1 to give thanks and declare praise to God for his everlasting compassion. For the psalmist, the mercy has not yet been affected; he hopes for that which is unseen, and exhorts Israel to give thanks on the basis of that hope. In Psalm 107 the hope has been realized and God's mercy has been manifest in deliverance. His eternal mercy is no longer a hope, but a realization and a reason to celebrate.[162]

Although Psalm 107 may indeed have originated as a psalm of general thanksgiving, used by individuals who had undergone crises of varying descriptions, its position after Psalm 106 renews its meaning. When read after Psalm 106, it is transformed from an abstract prayer of thanksgiving in a variety of scenarios, to a specific prayer of thanksgiving for the psalmist's request in Psalm 106 for God to deliver Israel from exile. Concerning this transformation, perhaps the most important phrase is מארצות קבצם ("gathered them from the lands," v. 3). The lands (ארצות) appear in Ps 106:27 in the same plural form as a description of lands throughout which YHWH scattered those of Ezekiel's generation. Furthermore, the psalmist's plea in Ps 106:47 is that God would

---

162. Here one should note that Psalm 106 closes with the hope that if YHWH delivers the Israelites, they would then declare his praises. This is realized in Psalm 107, which declares his praises, giving thanks for God's deliverance.

Standing in the Gap

gather (קבצנו) the people from the nations.¹⁶³ Thus Psalm 106 paints a picture of Israel scattered throughout the nations, and an individual's plea for their return. In Ps 107:3, YHWH has answered this plea, and has gathered the people from the four corners of the globe. Without this continuation in the form of Psalm 107 there is no closure to Psalm 106 because the question remains: "Was God faithful to the psalmist's prayer?"

The repeated references to mighty acts (נפלאות) in Psalm 107 develop the notion of mighty acts that appear in Psalm 106. Psalm 106 only speaks of those acts which God performed for Israel whilst they were in Egypt, (במצרים לא השכילו נפלאותיך, "in Egypt they never learned from your mighty acts," v. 7). On the other hand, Psalm 107 employs the same term to describe a range of instances in which God intervenes to deliver people from danger and distress. In this instance, the consecutive reading broadens and develops the notion of God acting in might, showing that his ability to deliver continues throughout the generations.

Similar to the distribution of the phrase "Land of Ham" (ארץ חם) in Psalms 105–106 is the word ישימון, signifying the desert. Of the four times it occurs in the Psalter, its only consecutive appearance is in Psalms 106 and 107.¹⁶⁴ In both psalms it represents a synonym for the desert and serves as a stage for corporate sin. Although the reference in Ps 107:4 is far from specific with regards to the incident being recalled, a consecutive reading of the psalms connects "those who wandered in the wilderness" with the desert generation of Psalm 106.

A change in attitude occurs among the Israelites between Psalms 106 and 107 with respect to the sacrifices (זבחים) offered. Those sacrifices the Israelites formerly made to the dead (זבחי מתים, 106:28) along with those of their sons and daughters to idols (ויזבחו, v. 37), are no longer remembered. Replacing these aberrations, Psalm 107 only recalls correct sacrifices, offerings of thanksgiving presented on account of YHWH's deeds (107:22).

---

163. Although no exact lexical correspondence exists, the word גאל ("to redeem") also creates an association with Psalm 106 because it frequently depicts YHWH's redemptive work among the exiles in Babylon, and his returning them back to their land (see Isa 48:20; 62:12; and Mic 4:10). Consequently, the term here could refer to those whom God had returned from the exile, including the psalmist.

164. The other occurrences are in Ps 68:8, and the historiographic Ps 78:40.

From Bards to Biblical Exegetes

The words מרה עצה (rebel and counsel) in Pss 106:43 and 107:11[165] also links the psalms, demonstrating that rebellion ultimately has its consequences. In Psalm 106, the Israelites are specifically indicted for repeatedly rebelling against God's counsel (ימרו בעצתם, v. 43), which ultimately leads to a descending spiral of sin and degradation. Psalm 107, however, is not specific concerning who rejected God's counsel, but in both instances, the ultimate result of rejecting YHWH's counsel is that the transgressors are soon humbled and brought low (see 107:12).

Psalms 105–107

A sequential reading of Psalms 105–107 represents a pattern often seen in Israel's literary history that is particularly common to the book of Judges: God's faithfulness—Israel's sinful response—God's punishment—God's subsequent deliverance. Psalm 105 depicts YHWH's faithfulness to his people in history and closes with a statement determining his requirements of them: to obey his commandments. Psalm 106 follows by recounting how the Israelites failed to uphold these requirements and the ensuing punishment by God. The psalm is essentially a confessional call to repentance that escalates in intensity until the penultimate verse. Continuing the pattern, Psalm 107 constitutes a song of thanksgiving, probably originally written for general-purpose thanksgiving but due to its proximity to Psalm 106, may also be read as a thanksgiving song for God relenting of his punishment and delivering Israel from the exile. Linking these three psalms and reflecting the aforementioned sequence of events is the word רנה ("shout of joy"). The joy in Ps 105:43 when the Israelites are brought from their captivity is transformed to cries of distress in Ps 106:44 as they suffer under the hand of their oppressors. Finally, in Ps 107:22 רנה is developed into a cry of thanksgiving in light of God's deliverance.

---

165. The only two places in the Bible where they occur together.

Excursus

The Book of Moses

Both Psalms 105 and 106 are positioned at the end of Book IV in the Psalter.[166] Even though the fourth book is most commonly associated with kingship, it may also be termed *The Book of Moses*[167] because Moses creates an inclusion for the collection. Both the opening and closing of this book explicitly mention his name. Psalm 90 bears the title, תְּפִלָּה לְמֹשֶׁה אִישׁ־הָאֱלֹהִים ("A prayer of Moses, the man of God," v. 1), and as already noted, Psalms 105 and 106 frequently refer to this biblical figure. Furthermore, of the eight times the name "Moses" appears in the Psalter, seven of them occur in Book IV. The only instance in which it appears outside this collection is in Ps 77:20 [21], which, as we have already seen probably represents a later addition.[168] Psalm 99:6 recalls Moses and Aaron as being among YHWH's priests, מֹשֶׁה וְאַהֲרֹן בְּכֹהֲנָיו ("Moses and Aaron were among his priests," Samuel is also mentioned at this point). The psalm further hints towards the desert itinerary in v. 7 by stating that God "spoke to them in a pillar of cloud" (יְדַבֵּר אֲלֵיהֶם בְּעַמּוּד עָנָן), recalling instances such as Exod 19:9 and 33:9. Moreover, the mention of Moses and Aaron obeying the laws YHWH gave them, שמרו עדתיו וחק נתן למו ("they kept his testimonies and the ordinances he gave them," Ps 99:7) also recalls the lawgiving at Sinai during Israel's desert journey. Furthering Book IV's relationship with Moses is Psalm

---

166. Berlin, "Psalms," 1403, suggests that this placement was erroneous, and that the book should have concluded with Psalm 107 because it too alludes (somewhat vaguely in my opinion) to the Exodus tradition. This view is not necessarily well founded because by enforcing the cut-off point at Psalm 106, the arranger unquestionably forges the inclusion with Psalm 90 that defines the book.

167. Concerning this collection, Wilson, "Shaping the Psalter," 75–76, states: "This introductory group of psalms hangs together around a common theme that I have chosen to call 'Mosaic' (because of the title of Psalm 90, the use of the old divine names "El Shadday" and "El Elyon," references to Moses and Aaron, the Exodus wanderings and other thematic correspondences) ." Additionally McCann, "Psalms," 1040, says, "Book IV can be characterized as a Moses book."

168. See close reading for Ps 106:16. The very fact that seven out of eight instances appear in Book IV furthers the assumption that Ps 77:20 [21] represents a later addition.

103:7. In this composition, the psalmist declares that God made his ways known to Moses (דְּרָכָיו לְמֹשֶׁה), and the children of Israel.

Additionally, concerning this group of psalms[169] we must note the concentration of Exodus psalms (95, 105, and 106), psalms recalling a period in which Moses plays a key role. The second half of Psalm 95, vv. 8–11, even though it does not specifically mention Moses, patently recalls the desert period, when Moses served as Israel's leader. Finally, with respect to the selected psalms, the only two places where Moses is recalled in Exodus events occur within Book IV of the Psalter.[170] From the evidence presented above, it would appear that the decision to place Pss 105 and 106 at the end of Book IV represents a deliberate choice by an editor to define the general character of the Psalter's fourth book. Rather than place these two compositions in any other location, the arranger placed them at the end, along with Psalm 90 at the beginning, to create a collection of psalms that remember and even exalt the role of Moses during the desert era.

With the establishment of the Mosaic character of Book IV arises the question: "What is a book of Moses doing within a book traditionally ascribed to David?" Two potential answers can be found to such a question, neither of which is mutually exclusive. First, as mentioned previously, the Book of Moses appears immediately after a psalm detailing the destruction of Jerusalem and the temple, which amounts to no less than a cancellation of the Davidic kingship and thus God's covenant with David. This composition, Psalm 89, comes at the end of a collection of psalms that frequently mention David in their titles. The development within the Psalter, as certain scholars have already noted, begins with a recollection of the Davidic covenant in the first three books, which then culminates at the end of Book III, Psalm 89, with the Davidic covenant ending. As a response to this, the editors of the Psalter would have then continued with the Book of Moses to point to a new way forward. Instead of lamenting the earthly kingship as exemplified in David, they found a resolution by hearkening back

---

169. As previously documented (see Wilson, "Shaping the Psalter," 75), the location of Book IV, especially with its primary themes of the wilderness tradition and the kingship of God (see Pss 93:1, 95:3, 96:10, 97:1, 98:6, and 99:1), serves as a response to the demise of the Davidic covenant and the Israelites' loss of land, themes documented in the close of Book III, Psalm 89.

170. As previously noted, though Psalm 77:20 [21] mentions Moses and Aaron, the verse more than likely constitutes a later addition to the psalm.

to the Mosaic model with God as Israel's king and leader. Thus, the concentration of desert themes and a strong recollection of Moses as Israel's leader serves to remind, and almost cry out for, the model of leadership found during the desert era. Within this model, God served as Israel's king, hence the high number of kingship psalms, with Moses as his prophet. The second answer concerns the division of the Psalter into five books, usually viewed as a relatively late phenomenon. Such a division, coupled with the fact that the Psalter is frequently attributed to David, typically associates the five books of David with the five books of Moses,[171] the Torah. The association of a book of Moses within the book of David could, therefore, be viewed as an attempt by later editors of the Psalter to further the association between the works of these two prominent biblical figures.[172]

---

171. See McCann, "Psalms," 659.

172. This notion accords with Kraus' earlier observation that Psalm 78 constitutes an attempt to merge the Davidic covenant with Israel's salvation history (Kraus, *Psalms 60–150*, 129).

4

YHWH's Supremacy

Psalm 135

Psalm 135 is a hymn of praise that boasts of YHWH's omnipotence, and provides examples of his great works in creation and the exodus. Moreover, the psalm contrasts God's ability with that of the nations' idols. The Exodus content within the psalm constitutes a relatively small percentage of the entire work and is linked together with the creation motif. The psalm's most outstanding characteristic is its eclectic nature, as every verse contains at least an echo of other biblical texts. In spite of this eclectic quality, the psalm still functions as a unified composition with a single purpose.

STRUCTURE

According to content and linguistic characteristics, Psalm 135 divides into five units of varying length, as follows:

1. Introduction and reason to praise YHWH (vv. 1–5)
2. YHWH's omnipotence in creation and history (vv. 6–12)
3. Praise intermission; YHWH vindicates his people (vv. 13–14)
4. Impotency of other nations' idols (vv. 15–18)
5. Exhortation of temple groups to praise YHWH (vv. 19–21)

The psalm's opening section consists of two strophes: the first, vv. 1–3, contains a general exhortation for a temple group to praise YHWH, and the second, vv. 4–5, provides a reason for his praise. Lexical indicators demarcate both strophes; the first three verses begin and end with the word שם, forming an inclusion; and vv. 4–5 both begin with the particle כי. Unifying the whole stanza is the concentrated repetition of the Lord's name and references to him. The section introduces three important themes that the psalm develops throughout its remaining verses: first, YHWH's name and reputation, and the acts he performs that establish that reputation; second, the close relationship between YHWH and his people, which is particularly reflected in the terms עבדי יהוה ("servants of YHWH," v. 1), אלהינו ("our God," v. 2), and אדנינו ("our lord," v. 5); third, the explicit mention of YHWH's selection of Israel as a precious possession in v. 4.[1]

The second stanza begins with a general statement, claiming YHWH does as he pleases in any location, and then moves to exemplify ways in which his desires are practically expressed. Movement from the general to the particular forms a guiding principle throughout the psalm. As an expression of this principle, the second stanza develops the first by expanding the idea of YHWH's reputation. Thus vv. 6–12 detail some of the deeds wrought that generated YHWH's fame. The first demonstration of his ability appears in v. 7, with his involvement in maintaining creation. Following this, the remainder of the stanza is dedicated to showing his interaction with his people: he delivers them from Egypt (vv. 8–9), strikes mighty kings on their behalf (vv. 10–11), and grants them land as an inheritance (v. 12).

As the shortest section, stanza three consists of a two-verse intermission of praise. The words שם (name, v. 13), יהוה (YHWH, vv. 13 and 14), and כי (because, v. 14) associate the section with the opening verses, which contain the same theme. This short section primarily develops the idea of God's relationship with his people, emphasizing that he vindicates them and is merciful to them.

Subject matter clearly distinguishes section three from section four,[2] which discusses the idols of the nations as introduced by v. 15. The fourth stanza corresponds with section two, since both tackle the question of a deity's ability; the fullness of God's potency is compared with the impotency of idols. Repetition of the word רוח ("spirit/wind," vv. 7 and 17) together with the root עשה ("to make/do," vv. 6–7, 15, and

---

1. With respect to this division, only Hacham recognizes the individual units 1–3 and 4–5 (ספר תהלים, 505). The consensus is to isolate 1–4 as the opening section; see, for example, Keil and Delitzsch, *Psalms*, 323–24; Allen, *Psalms 101–150*, 285–86; and Weiser, *The Psalms*, 787–90. After this division, a number of variations arise between the exact stanza demarcations.

2. None of the aforementioned scholars disagree with this division.

18) establish the links between these sections. The psalmist employs the root עשה to create an inclusion for the stanza. Additionally, he uses רוח together with עשה to demonstrate that a God who controls the *wind* by bringing it from storehouses and *creates* lightning for the rain, cannot compare with idols that have no *breath* and are *formed* by the hands of men. A further comparison appears in the portrayal of the worshippers of the respective gods. Those who worship YHWH are considered his treasured possession (v. 4), whereas those who trust in idols are as useless as they are (v. 18).

The closing section[3] addresses the congregation that first appeared in vv. 1–2, exhorting various temple groups to bless YHWH. The stanza reintroduces the imperative forms from the first stanza, along with the repetitions of YHWH's name, two factors solidifying the correspondence between the two stanzas. Other common attributes between the two sections are the repetition of בית (house), and a returned focus to those worshipping in the temple courts. The final words of the psalm repeat its opening words, הללו יה ("Praise Yah"), which forms an inclusion for the whole composition.

CLOSE READING

הַלְלוּ יָהּ הַלְלוּ אֶת־שֵׁם יְהוָה הַלְלוּ עַבְדֵי יְהוָה [1]

Praise Yah, praise the name of YHWH; (give) praise servants of YHWH

The psalm begins with a call to worship that resembles Psalm 105 in many respects. Particularly noticeable are the repeated imperatives and the divine name. Three repeated imperatives, הללו, form a prominent part of v. 1; the first two use synonyms for God (יה, Yah; and שם יהוה, "the name of YHWH") as the verb's object, and the last addresses the audience in the vocative. Each of the opening imperatives recognizes YHWH in some way: first in the abbreviated form יה, then his name שם יהוה, and finally as an identifier for the worshipping community עבדי יהוה. His name, שם, may be interpreted in this context as his character, a synonym for who he is. Psalm 122:4 demonstrates a similar use, שָׁם עָלוּ שְׁבָטִים שִׁבְטֵי־יָהּ עֵדוּת לְיִשְׂרָאֵל לְהֹדוֹת לְשֵׁם יְהוָה ("There the tribes go up, the tribes of Yah go up—an ordinance for Israel—to proclaim thanks to the name of YHWH"), where ascending to give thanks to his

---

3. All the aforementioned scholars agree with this division.

YHWH's Supremacy

name equates to thanking YHWH himself (see also Ps 54:8; 113:2; and 148:5). Alternatively, שם can be rendered "honor," (כבוד), portraying God's fame, which stems from his mighty acts. Psalm 102:16 reflects such an interpretation, וְיִירְאוּ גוֹיִם אֶת־שֵׁם יְהוָה וְכָל־מַלְכֵי הָאָרֶץ אֶת־כְּבוֹדֶךָ ("The nations will fear the name of YHWH, and all the kings of the earth your glory"). The nations that fear his name stand in awe of his deeds, a sentiment enumerated in the psalm's following verses (see also Gen 12:2; 2 Sam 8:13). At this juncture, the psalm only hints at the deeds that generate such a fearsome reputation, but later in the psalm explicit examples appear. Naturally, the two potential meanings of שם mentioned above are not mutually exclusive since one's personality, essence, and character, are often reflected in one's deeds, which subsequently generate a reputation.

Although biblical literature frequently identifies individuals as servants of YHWH (Moses in Deut 34:5, Joshua in Josh 24:29 and Judg 2:8, and David in Ps 18:1[4]), v. 1 evidently refers to a body of people who have aligned themselves with the God of Israel. This designation becomes clear in the psalm's final verses when it addresses the congregation again, and singles out numerous groups—the house of Israel, the house of Aaron, the house of Levi, and the fearers of YHWH—assembled at the temple to worship YHWH. In opening the psalm with these words, the psalmist draws our attention to Ps 113:1, הַלְלוּ יָהּ הַלְלוּ עַבְדֵי יְהוָה הַלְלוּ אֶת־שֵׁם יְהוָה ("Praise Yah, O servants of YHWH give praise, praise the name of YHWH"), where all of the same words appear, but in the present psalm the word order undergoes an inversion. The lexical similarities positively testify to an instance of borrowing. Although the direction of reuse is not clear at this stage, one author certainly has prior knowledge of the other's work.[5]

---

4. The designation also frequently appears in Psalm 105; see vv. 6, 17, 25, 26, and 42.

5. Beentjes, "Inverted Quotations," and Saidel, "מקבילות‎," have devoted time to researching the phenomenon of lexical inversions in biblical allusion. Beentjes, "Inverted Quotations," 521, quotes many examples of the phenomenon, but resists positing a concrete motivation for such a textual alteration; in spite of this, he does tentatively suggest that certain inversions reflect an author's desire to transform a negative instance into a positive one. Unfortunately, in the present context, this motivation is irrelevant. Saidel suggests this type of inversion occurs when an author deliberately signifies that he is alluding to a specific text. While this holds true for a select group

From Bards to Biblical Exegetes

שֶׁעֹמְדִים בְּבֵית יְהוָה בְּחַצְרוֹת בֵּית אֱלֹהֵינוּ ²

Those standing in the house of YHWH, in the courts of the house of our God

The second verse consists of a relative clause further detailing the location of those invited to praise YHWH: standing in the house of God, in the courts of the temple. The corresponding words אלהינו ("our God") and יהוה intimately identify YHWH as the God of those worshipping in the temple,[6] and the remainder of the psalm repeatedly emphasizes this close kinship. A general description of the worshippers' location appears in the first colon, בבית יהוה ("in house of YHWH"), and the second colon further details the precise location, בחצרות בית אלהינו ("in the courts of the house of our God") the same parallel pair, חצרות and בית[7] also occurs in Pss 84:10 [11] and 92:13 [14].[8] Though v. 2 mentions the name יהוה, it is not associated with the people, as with v. 1, but with a building. Until this point, every noun mentioned in the psalm has, in some way, been related to YHWH: his name, his servants, and his house.

---

of occurrences, it becomes problematic with Psalm 135 whereby other textual associations appear without inverted words.

The psalmist's alteration in word order reveals a deviation from the expected double imperative form: imperative—vocative—imperative—(continuation), as seen in Judg 5:12 and Jer 31:21; see also Watson, *Classical Hebrew Poetry*, 358–59. The deviation, placing the vocative after the second imperative, is best explained by the psalmist's need to adapt the first verse to the second verse, in which he employs a relative pronoun. Were the order not reversed, the relative pronoun would take the divine name as its antecedent, which would result in an unacceptable reading. Such an alteration reveals the author's conscious adaptation of his sources to suit his needs.

6. Two factors here point towards a possible period in which the psalm was written: the relative particle ש and the mention of an extant temple. The section on dating will further discuss these potential signs of lateness.

7. These words often appear together in biblical literature, see 2 Kgs 21:5; Jer 19:14, 26:2; and Ezek 8:16.

8. The relationship between these two colons illustrates Kugel's description of the fundamental mechanics of parallelism, which condenses into "A is so, and what's more, B", where "B" surpasses "A" in detail or intensity (see Kugel, *Biblical Poetry*, 1–59). Within the context of v. 2, "A" corresponds to the house of the Lord, and "B" equates to the more specific descriptor: the courts of the temple. This definition opposes scholars, such as Oesterley, *The Psalms*, 540, who suggest two separate congregations are being addressed, those in the courts and the ministering priests who stand inside the temple.

YHWH's Supremacy

הַלְלוּ־יָהּ כִּי־טוֹב יְהוָה זַמְּרוּ לִשְׁמוֹ כִּי נָעִים ³

Praise Yah, surely YHWH is good; make music to his name for it is pleasant

Continuing to exhort the audience to praise, v. 3 repeats הללו יה, and creates an inclusion with v. 1 that defines and closes the opening strophe. Further reinforcement of the section's demarcation occurs with the second appearance of שם. Both occurrences of כי in v. 3 can be understood causally, providing a rationale for praising and making music to YHWH, but they also serve as emphatic particles, placing a stronger emphasis on the act of worship itself.[9] At least two valid interpretations for this verse exist with respect to the subjects of טוב and נעים ("good" and "pleasant"). The first, and most popular among the modern commentators,[10] interprets these words as attributes to God, rendering the clause as "Praise God because *he* is *good* and make music to him for *his name* is *pleasant*." Alternatively one may read it as, "Praise YHWH for *it* is good, make music to his name for *it* is pleasant," where the act of praise and worship itself is intrinsically considered a good and pleasant activity. Such an understanding is similar to Ps 92:1 [2], טוֹב לְהֹדוֹת לַיהוָה וּלְזַמֵּר לְשִׁמְךָ עֶלְיוֹן ("It is good to give thanks to YHWH, to make music to your name Elyon"), where the act itself of giving thanks and making music to God is undoubtedly considered good because the following verses further emphasize this sentiment (see also Ps 54:6 [8]). Verses 1–3 introduce the main subject of the psalm, YHWH, emphasizing his character, as opposed to his works. The opening also introduces three elements that have an important function in the remainder of the psalm: God's people, his house, and his reputation.

כִּי־יַעֲקֹב בָּחַר לוֹ יָהּ יִשְׂרָאֵל לִסְגֻלָּתוֹ ⁴

For Yah has chosen Jacob for himself, Israel for his treasured possession

The second part of the first stanza (vv. 4–5) supplies more reasons for the praise of YHWH, and like the first section, the particle כי opens

---

9. Muilenberg, "The Particle כי," 147, details numerous functions for כי, and argues that an aspect of emphasis typically accompanies each occurrence. He also notes that כי often appears after an urgent imperative, as in this instance הללו יה ("Praise Yah"; see also Pss 6:4–5 [5–6]; 12:1 [2]; 25:16; and 69:17 [18]).

10. See, for example, Hacham, ספר תהלים, 505, Duhm, *Die Psalmen*, 282, and Briggs, *The Book of Psalms*, 479; each of whom denies any alternate reading.

the statement. In the present verse, the particle serves both causally and emphatically (surely), stressing the selection of Israel; additionally, it opens a new strophe within the stanza (as in Amos 5:12 and Ps 5:5)[11] that focuses on the reason for the praise. The synonymous word pair ישראל // יעקב (Israel // Jacob) frequently appears in Isaiah (29:23; 41:8; 42:24; 44:1, 5, 21, 23), in addition to other historiographic psalms such as 78:5, וַיָּקֶם עֵדוּת בְּיַעֲקֹב וְתוֹרָה שָׂם בְּיִשְׂרָאֵל ("He established an ordinance for Jacob, and a law he placed on Israel"; see also 81:5; 105:10, 23; and 114:1). By specifically recalling the name of Jacob,[12] the selection process receives added attention. Esau and Jacob were twins, and simply because God exercised his prerogative of selection, Jacob was loved, as demonstrated by Mal 1:2, הֲלוֹא־אָח עֵשָׂו לְיַעֲקֹב נְאֻם־יְהוָה וָאֹהַב אֶת־יַעֲקֹב ("Was not Esau a brother to Jacob, says YHWH, but I have loved Jacob").[13] The psalm provides no information concerning why Israel was selected, or what was expected of them; the psalmist only concerns himself with the fact that they were chosen. Referring to the selection, the term סגלתו ("his treasured possession") indicates a special possession, or treasure,[14] just like precious metals such as silver and gold, as Eccl 2:8 states, כָּנַסְתִּי לִי גַּם־כֶּסֶף וְזָהָב וּסְגֻלַּת מְלָכִים וְהַמְּדִינוֹת ("I gathered for myself also silver and gold, and treasures of kings and provinces"; see also 1 Chr 29:3). However, this word also recalls the moment during the exodus when God selected for himself[15] a people from among the nations, כִּי עַם קָדוֹשׁ אַתָּה לַיהוָה אֱלֹהֶיךָ בְּךָ בָּחַר יְהוָה אֱלֹהֶיךָ

---

11. See Muilenberg, "The Particle כִּי," 157.

12. Goulder, *The Psalms of the Return*, 286, further suggests this name stems from the old northern psalms; the Dan psalms (46 and 84), and the Bethel Psalms 75, 76, 77, and 81.

13. See also Rom 9:10–15, where the selection of Jacob over Esau exemplifies God's sovereign freedom of choice, as opposed to works.

14. Concerning this word, Weinfeld, *Deuteronomy*, 226 n.2, draws attention to an Ugaritic text in which a vassal is referred to as "*sglt*" by his sovereign. The word apparently belonged to treaty and covenant terminology and describes the special relationship between a sovereign and vassal. According to Weinfeld, the basic meaning is to set aside a property for good (as in the case of the psalm) or evil intentions. Greenberg further attests to this word being related to the Akkadian root *skl*, which denotes private savings acquired over time, which later in the Bible came to mean "a dear personal possession, a 'treasure' only in the sense of that which is treasured or cherished" (Greenberg, "Hebrew segulta," 277).

15. Another potential way of reading this verse is from Israel's perspective, "that Jacob selected YHWH for himself, and YHWH selected Israel for his treasured possession," thus reflecting a bi-directional selection process.

YHWH's Supremacy

לִהְיוֹת לוֹ לְעַם סְגֻלָּה מִכֹּל הָעַמִּים אֲשֶׁר עַל־פְּנֵי הָאֲדָמָה) ("For you are a holy people to YHWH your God, YHWH your God chose you to be for him a *treasured people* of all the peoples who are on the face of the earth," Deut 7:6; see also Deut 14:2 and Exod 19:5).[16] Notably, before Psalm 135 enumerates any of YHWH's saving deeds, or acts in creation, it recalls his selection of Israel as a special people. It is possible to interpret this placement in at least two ways: one, the psalmist considers Israel's selection as YHWH's most important act in history, and thus he positioned this event first;[17] two, v. 4 pre-empts the ensuing verses: God chose Israel through the historical deeds soon to be enumerated.

כִּי אֲנִי יָדַעְתִּי כִּי־גָדוֹל יְהוָה וַאֲדֹנֵינוּ מִכָּל־אֱלֹהִים 5

For I know that YHWH is great; and our God (is greater) than all gods

Verse 5, like v. 4, declares YHWH's greatness, but it is not the selection of Israel that the psalmist lauds, but God's supremacy above all other gods and deities. The opening כי clause in the verse further proclaims God's greatness, linking it to the previous verse; however, the particle loses its causal meaning and bears an almost exclusively emphatic meaning.[18] Partially unexpected is the first-person singular declaration opening v. 5, which has led certain scholars[19] to amend the text; the preservation of this form, however, solidifies an association with Exod 18:11,[20] when Moses' father-in-law personally declares God's greatness after hearing about all he has done for Israel, עַתָּה יָדַעְתִּי כִּי־גָדוֹל יְהוָה מִכָּל־הָאֱלֹהִים ("Now I know that YHWH is greater than all gods"). The connection recalls the word שם in vv. 1 and 3, where they were translated as "reputation." Although he did not

---

16. Psalm 135 employs this word in a context radically different from those found in the Torah. These differences are detailed later in this chapter.

17. Kroll further argues, "In the minds of the Israelites the foremost reason for praising Jehovah was the election of the Jewish people as the chosen nation of God"; Kroll, *Psalms*, 399–400.

18. See Gersiel, "פרק קלה," 241.

19. Duhm, *Die Psalmen*, 282, for example, claims a copyist has erred here, and כי אני ידעתי כי ("for I know that") should read דעו כי ("know that") or הודו לו ("give thanks to him"), both of which are tempting alternatives.

20. It is interesting to note that both this verse and 2 Chr 2:5 [4] appear in contexts involving non-Israelites.

witness the deeds first hand, Jethro's declaration of God's greatness is based on YHWH's reputation. Similarly, the psalmist had not witnessed firsthand the deeds he is about to enumerate, but because he has heard of them, he can declare YHWH's supremacy.

The first-person plural suffix on אדנינו corresponds with אלהינו in v. 2, and together they further express the intimate relationship between YHWH and his people. Thus, even though a personal declaration appears in the verse's opening clause, the final words recognize the community's relationship to God. With respect to the names of God, v. 5 employs אלהים (God) with a different meaning than v. 2, not referring to YHWH who is called אדנינו (our lord), but referring to other gods. It is possible to understand the present verse as embodying the message of the entire psalm: YHWH is greater than all other gods. His greatness is demonstrated in history, as the ensuing verses exemplify, and also in the characterization of the other gods, to whom he is compared. Similar proclamations of YHWH's status above all other gods are echoed throughout the Bible, such as Hiram's declaration in 2 Chr 2:5 [4], כִּי־גָדוֹל אֱלֹהֵינוּ מִכָּל־הָאֱלֹהִים, ("for greater is our God than all other gods") after Solomon requested wood from him for building the temple. Likewise, Ps 95:3 proclaims his kingship over all other gods, כִּי אֵל גָּדוֹל יְהוָה וּמֶלֶךְ גָּדוֹל עַל־כָּל־אֱלֹהִים ("for YHWH is a great God, and a great king above all gods"; see also Ps 96:4).

כֹּל אֲשֶׁר־חָפֵץ יְהוָה עָשָׂה בַּשָּׁמַיִם וּבָאָרֶץ בַּיַּמִּים וְכָל־תְּהֹמוֹת [6]

Everything that YHWH desires he does, in heaven on the earth in the seas and all the depths

"God accomplishes anything he desires, in any place" is the fundamental claim of v. 6 and the message of the second stanza, which also demonstrates such a claim. In biblical literature, the two verbs חפץ and עשה[21] express an earthly sovereign's power to act as he pleases, as 1 Kgs 9:1 demonstrates, וַיְהִי כְּכַלּוֹת שְׁלֹמֹה לִבְנוֹת אֶת־בֵּית־יְהוָה וְאֶת־בֵּית הַמֶּלֶךְ וְאֵת כָּל־חֵשֶׁק שְׁלֹמֹה אֲשֶׁר חָפֵץ לַעֲשׂוֹת ("Now when Solomon finished building the house of YHWH and the king's house and every wish that

---

21. The somewhat unexpected perfect, *qatal*, form bears a present meaning here (as in Gen 14:22 and Amos 5:21); see also Chisholm, *From Exegesis to Exposition*, 95 n.70. Also, concerning this form, JM (365) notes, "In some poetic texts celebrating the greatness of God, the use of the tenses, of *qatal* especially, is very peculiar." Similarly, Driver, *A Treatise*, 15–16, also recognizes a present use of *qatal*.

YHWH's Supremacy

Solomon desired to do"), suggesting Solomon accomplished whatever he desired (see also Eccl 8:2–3). The two words, expressing a degree of omnipotence, similarly appear as a self description of God in Isa 46:10, אֹמֵר עֲצָתִי תָקוּם וְכָל־חֶפְצִי אֶעֱשֶׂה ("saying, 'my counsel will be established, and all that I desire I will do'"). In the present context, the sphere in which God has dominion is expressed by the words עשה, שמים, and ארץ ("to do," "heaven," and "earth" respectively).[22] However, these words additionally recall YHWH's activities in creation,[23] as in Exod 31:17, כִּי־שֵׁשֶׁת יָמִים עָשָׂה יְהוָה אֶת־הַשָּׁמַיִם וְאֶת־הָאָרֶץ וּבַיּוֹם הַשְּׁבִיעִי שָׁבַת וַיִּנָּפַשׁ ("for in six days YHWH made the heavens and the earth, and on the seventh day he was refreshed"). By alluding to the creation, the psalmist attributes certain rights to YHWH: he has authority to exercise his will in heaven and earth, *because* he created them. Although תהמות evidently contains mythical[24] connotations and allusions, the context here suggests a concrete meaning depicting the deep depths of the sea—as Jonah 2:5 [6] attests, אֲפָפוּנִי מַיִם עַד־נֶפֶשׁ תְּהוֹם יְסֹבְבֵנִי סוּף חָבוּשׁ לְרֹאשִׁי, where the waters engulfed him ("Waters surrounded me up to my neck, the deep encompassed me, sea weed wrapped round my head"; see also Amos 7:4 and Ezek 31:4).

Verse 6 enumerates the geographical limits of YHWH's rule in descending order: the heavens, the highest place, moving down to the earth, into the sea and finally down to the depths. Such a detailed merism[25] encompasses everything lying between heaven and the depths. On the whole, the present verse recalls Ps 115:3, וֵאלֹהֵינוּ בַשָּׁמָיִם כֹּל

---

22. Duhm, *Die Psalmen*, 282, suggests this verse is a later addition, "*denn v. 6 (=115 3ᵇ) ist von fremder Hand beigeschrieben* [then v. 6 (=115 3ᵇ) is written by a strange hand]," but this is unlikely because the ideas contained within form an important part of the psalm's message. God's ownership rights to the world stem from his creation of it, and therefore they justify his apportioning land as he pleases.

23. See Norin, *Er Spaltete das Meer*, 121, who specifically links this verse with the creation account of Genesis 1. At this point, it should be noted that there is another instance of the creation motif in an exodus psalm. This relationship between the two motifs is further explored in the concluding section, following the analysis of Psalm 136.

24. The mythical allusion relates to God's primordial battle with the sea (monster)—as alluded to in Hab 3:10, Isa 51:9, Ps 104:6–7 and also Kraus, *Psalms 60–150*, 493—and his victory over it.

25. A totality expressed in an abbreviated form. Such lists are not necessarily limited to two elements; see Watson, *Classical Hebrew Poetry*, 322–23. This psalm employs a more detailed list; more often, only the words "heaven" and "earth" summarize all that exists between them (Isa 44:24; 48:13; Jer 4:28).

אֲשֶׁר־חָפֵץ עָשָׂה ("but our God is in heaven and everything he desires he does"), which also devotes a significant number of verses to polemicizing the idols of the nations. The contexts in which this phrase appear, however, differs in both psalms. Psalm 115:3 employs these words to introduce the denunciation of idols, whereas the same phrase in our psalm precedes literary-historical examples of God acting as he pleases in heaven and earth.²⁶

מַעֲלֶה נְשִׂאִים מִקְצֵה הָאָרֶץ בְּרָקִים לַמָּטָר עָשָׂה מוֹצֵא־רוּחַ מֵאוֹצְרוֹתָיו ⁷

Raising clouds from the ends of the earth, making lightning for the rain, and bringing the wind from his storehouses

As an example of YHWH executing his will in the physical heavens, v. 7 depicts how he raises clouds from the ends of the earth, (מעלה נשאים מקצה הארץ), and makes lightning for the rain, (ברקים למטר עשה). Despite the fact that YHWH's name is not mentioned in this verse, the participle²⁷ מעלה (raising) still refers to him as its subject. Within the context of v. 7, נשאים are best understood as clouds or vapors that rise up from the earth,²⁸ as in Prov 25:14, נְשִׂיאִים וְרוּחַ וְגֶשֶׁם אָיִן אִישׁ מִתְהַלֵּל בְּמַתַּת־שָׁקֶר ("Like clouds and wind without rain is a man who boasts of his gifts falsely." NASB), which also contains references to rain and other storm elements (cf. Jer 10:13). Together with כל in the previous verse, קצה or "extremity," stresses totality, the total area of his jurisdiction (see Pss 19:6 [7]; 61:2 [3]). Reinforcing the picture of omnipotence is the idea of storehouses for the elements²⁹—in this case the wind—

---

26. A number of other significant differences exist, but these will be discussed later in the chapter.

27. This participle also emphasizes God's continual role in creation, constantly raising clouds, thus portraying him as a constant sustainer of the world. Driver, consequently, describes its usage as a "*continuous manifestation*" (Driver, *A Treatise*, 165).

28. See also the Septuagint, which translates νεφέλη as "clouds"; and the Targums, which read ענניו. Gersiel, "פרק קלה," 242, thus understands the verse as depicting the movements of the clouds across the sky; he also notes the association this imagery shares with Baal mythology.

29. Keil and Delitzsch evidently detect this imagery when they state, "What is intended is the fullness of divine power" (Keil and Delitzsch, *Psalms*, 325). Cf. Deut 28:12, which depicts the rain being kept in a storehouse; Job 38:22, which speaks of the snow and hail in storehouses; and Ps 33:7, which similarly implies a storehouse for the sea.

that only God has access to, and from which he brings them, מוֹצֵא רוּחַ מֵאוֹצְרוֹתָיו ("bringing wind from his storehouses").³⁰

The chiastic arrangement עשה : ארץ :: ארץ : עשה (he does : land :: land : he does) unites vv. 6 and 7 and expresses YHWH's dominance over creation; he created the world and does as he pleases in it. Furthering the notion of dominance is the image of YHWH conjuring up a storm with rain (מטר) and lightning (ברקים), elements that additionally recall theophanies, including instances when YHWH appears in judgment with visible displays of power.³¹ Psalm 77:19[18], קוֹל רַעַמְךָ בַּגַּלְגַּל הֵאִירוּ בְרָקִים תֵּבֵל רָגְזָה וַתִּרְעַשׁ הָאָרֶץ ("The sound of your thunder was in the whirlwind; the lightning lit up the world and the earth trembled and shook"), recounts how the earth quakes at God's thunder and lightning; Ps 97:4 presents a similar picture, הֵאִירוּ בְרָקָיו תֵּבֵל רָאֲתָה וַתָּחֵל הָאָרֶץ ("His lightning lit up the world, the earth saw and trembled"), with the earth trembling before his lightning bolts.³² The image of God appearing in judgment continues into the following verses that reveal how YHWH judged the kings and peoples of the world in addition to his own people. From v. 7 a lucid association with Jer 10:13 emerges, וַיַּעֲלֶה נְשִׂאִים מִקְצֵה (אֶרֶץ) [הָאָרֶץ] בְּרָקִים לַמָּטָר עָשָׂה וַיּוֹצֵא מֵאֹצְרֹתָיו רוּחַ ("He raised clouds from the ends of the earth, making lightning for the rain, and brought the wind from his storehouses"³³), whose context similarly contains a denouncement of foreign idols. Although the lexical similarity is clear, unlike the association in v. 1, the word order is perfectly preserved.

---

30. This defective form, for מוֹצִיא, probably stems from the source text's influence, which in this instance is Jer 10:13, וַיּוֹצֵא; see Keil and Delitzsch, *Psalms*, 325. Allen, *Psalms 101–150*, 286, however, suggests that a desired assonance with the form מֵאוֹצְרוֹתָיו (from his storehouses) may also have motivated the psalmist. This would not be out of character for the psalmist because later in the psalm he similarly utilizes epistrophe (end repetition).

31. These storm elements, in addition to their allusion to ancient Israelite literature, recall earlier Canaanite works. Loewenstamm claims, "All of these elements certainly originate in the traditions surrounding Hadad, the Canaanite god of thunder, lightning and rain" (Loewenstamm, *Evolution*, 247). For Weiser, *The Psalms*, 790, however, this storm imagery primarily alludes to a hypothetical autumnal festival, for which supplications for winter rains form a crucial part.

32. The words ברק and מטר also appear in contexts depicting God's work in Creation, as Jer 10:13 and 51:16 suggest.

33. These same words are also recorded in Jer 51:16.

שֶׁהִכָּה בְּכוֹרֵי מִצְרָיִם מֵאָדָם עַד־בְּהֵמָה ⁸

Who struck the firstborn of Egypt, from man to beast

Moving on from YHWH's involvement in creation, the following verses focus on his intervention in history. The psalm also progresses from a general description of YHWH working on a day-to-day basis, to a specific example of his magnificent deeds in Israelite literary history. Further emphasizing the break in section is the change in verb form: from a participle מעלה portraying continual involvement with creation, to the perfect הכה ("he struck") relating to a specific instance in history. Extending the emphasis on totality[34] in the present verse is the phrase עד בהמה ("to beast"). Usually, whenever the destruction of the firstborn appears, only the human firstborn are referenced (see 105:36 and 136:10). Psalm 135, however, unique among the selected psalms, additionally recalls the destruction of animals, adding an emphasis on the magnitude of destruction, which corresponds with the totality of YHWH's rule, as expressed in the previous verse via the extended merismus.

Thematically, the previous section recalls a picture of YHWH's appearing in judgment, here in v. 8, that judgment is directed toward the Egyptians. The present verse evidently recalls the smiting of the Egyptians' firstborn, as recorded in Exod 12:12, וְהִכֵּיתִי כָל־בְּכוֹר בְּאֶרֶץ מִצְרַיִם מֵאָדָם וְעַד־בְּהֵמָה ("And he struck every firstborn in the land of Egypt from man to beast"). The association to this specific location in Exodus is particularly pertinent because it describes a judgment against the Egyptians and their gods,[35] וּבְכָל־אֱלֹהֵי מִצְרַיִם אֶעֱשֶׂה שְׁפָטִים אֲנִי יְהוָה ("And on all the gods of Egypt I will execute judgments, I am YHWH"), which corresponds with the latter portion of this psalm that further characterizes the gods of the nations. Although the striking of the firstborn often appears in the selected psalms (see 105:36 and 136:10), here

---

34. Cf. vv. 6 and 7 with respect to the word כל, and the extended merismus in v. 6.

35. The very notion of God judging the gods of Egypt during the plagues is reflected in a midrash on Exod 12:29: "What could possibly be the sin of the cattle? Rather this was to prevent the Egyptians from saying, 'Our god brought this punishment upon us. How mighty is our god who has thus prevailed. How mighty is our god who was not affected by this punishment.'" (See Hammer, *The Classic Midrash*, 58.) In this instance, the gods of the Egyptians are the cattle, and they are judged because they too fall victim to the plague of the firstborn.

it is positioned as though it were the first plague. By positioning it thus, the psalmist apparently stresses its significance.³⁶

⁹ שָׁלַח אֹתוֹת וּמֹפְתִים בְּתוֹכֵכִי מִצְרָיִם בְּפַרְעֹה וּבְכָל־עֲבָדָיו

(And) sent signs and portents in the midst of Egypt, against Pharaoh and all his servants

God's judgment on the Egyptians continues in v. 9. Only now, however, *after* the psalmist recalls the killing of the firstborn, do we hear of the other mighty acts and signs (אתות ומופתים) God wrought against Egypt—referring to the plagues. A peculiarity concerning the plagues' quote as it appears here concerns שלח, the verb describing the sending of the plagues. More often than not, biblical literature employs the verb נתן ("he gave") as in Neh 9:10 and Deut 6:22, or שׂים ("to put") as in Pss 78:43 and 105:27, שָׂמוּ־בָם דִּבְרֵי אֹתוֹתָיו וּמֹפְתִים בְּאֶרֶץ חָם ("They executed against them his mighty works, and mighty acts in the land of Ham"). By employing שלח ("to send") here in this context, the psalmist recalls Ps 105:28, [דְּבָרוֹ] (דְּבָרָיו) שָׁלַח חֹשֶׁךְ וַיַּחְשִׁךְ וְלֹא־מָרוּ אֶת ("He sent darkness and it was dark, and they never rebelled against his word"), which depicts God sending darkness against the Egyptians and its subsequent obedience.³⁷ Both אות ("signs," "mighty act") and מופת ("wonders," "mighty deeds") frequently appear together with a specific reference to the plagues wrought on Egypt during Israel's deliverance. In addition to Pharaoh being struck by plagues, so are all of his servants (ובכל עבדיו). Repetition of the phrase עבדיו draws attention to v. 1, which calls upon the servants of YHWH to praise him. In comparing the destinies of the two groups of servants, we see that YHWH's servants are afforded the pleasure of standing in his courts and praising him, which, as we saw, can be construed as a pleasurable experience, whereas the servants of Pharaoh are plagued.

---

36. The specific mention of the firstborn's slaying is particularly relevant to this psalm because it unambiguously displays the work of God's hand. Loewenstamm recognizes the uniqueness and directness of this plague when he claims: "The narrative is shrouded with mystery in order to enhance its power ... there is no natural affliction imaginable which would kill all its victims in a moment and all of whose victims would be the firstborn" (Loewenstamm, *Evolution*, 101).

37. Additionally, the previous depiction of storm elements could be seen as a recollection of the plague of hail in Exod 9:13–34.

10 שֶׁהִכָּה גּוֹיִם רַבִּים וְהָרַג מְלָכִים עֲצוּמִים

Who struck great nations and killed powerful kings

This verse continues the recollection of God's past intervention in history. The reappearance of the relative particle שׁ, similar to v. 8, relates to YHWH in v. 5. Moving from God's work in delivering the Israelites from slavery in Egypt, however, v. 10 recalls YHWH's acts that initiated the process of Israel inheriting Canaan. As a reminder of v. 8, when God struck the firstborn of Egypt, שֶׁהִכָּה בְכוֹרֵי מִצְרָיִם מֵאָדָם עַד־בְּהֵמָה ("who struck the firstborn of Egypt, from man to beast"), the psalmist repeats the phrase שהכה ("who struck") here. Just as he went before Israel striking down the firstborn of Egypt to deliver his people, here he strikes strong nations (see Dan 8:24) or numerous nations (as Prov 7:26 implies). Repetition of the root נכה ("to strike") further links the two incidents as though they occurred at the same time, notwithstanding the numerous events transpiring in the desert between the aforementioned acts of God. The word pair הרג // נכה similarly appears in Jer 18:21, יִהְיוּ הֲרֻגֵי מָוֶת בַּחוּרֵיהֶם מֻכֵּי־חֶרֶב בַּמִּלְחָמָה ("Let their men be slain to death, their young men struck down by the sword in battle"), expressing the prophet's desired outcome for those who conspire to kill him. Concerning the parallel pair גוי // מלך, it could be understood here as a type of merismus that exemplifies a totality of peoples, those struck by YHWH. Such a nuance to the parallel is discernable in Ps 72:11, יַעַבְדוּהוּ כָל־מְלָכִים כָּל־גּוֹיִם יַעַבְדוּהוּ ("And they will bow to him, all kings, and all nations will serve him").[38]

The near exact quotation from Ps 136:17–18,[39] reflected in the present verse, overwhelmingly suggests an association with the neighboring psalm as opposed to a location in the Torah or the Prophets.[40] YHWH advancing before Israel and personally smiting the inhabit-

---

38. Notwithstanding this verse, the expected word order for this word pair is גוי followed by מלך (see Gen 17:6; Isa 41:2; and Ps 102:15 [16]), where the reference to "king" represents an intensification of "nation," in accordance to Kugel's definition of parallelism (see Kugel, *Biblical Poetry*, 1–59).

39. At this juncture in 4QPsⁿ—see Flint, "Three Psalms from Qumran," 42–43—a merge occurs between Psalm 135 and the corresponding passage in Psalm 136; this merger, however, is not reflected in the other Qumran rendition of Psalm 135, 11QPs^a.

40. Of course, two options exist concerning the direction of borrowing, and this issue will be further detailed later in the chapter. Scholars, such as Allen, *Psalms 101–150*, 291, automatically assume Psalm 135 borrows from Ps 136.

YHWH's Supremacy

ants of Canaan forms only a single perspective of the conquest events. Joshua 12:7, וְאֵלֶּה מַלְכֵי הָאָרֶץ אֲשֶׁר הִכָּה יְהוֹשֻׁעַ וּבְנֵי יִשְׂרָאֵל בְּעֵבֶר הַיַּרְדֵּן ("And these are the kings of the land whom Joshua and the sons of Israel struck on the other side of the Jordan") credits victory to Israel, and Josh 10:20 names Joshua and the Israelites as being responsible for slaying the five kings. However, because, YHWH constitutes the principle figure in the present psalm, and his reputation is being flaunted, the psalmist has chosen to portray YHWH as the destroyer of kings and nations, without any human intermediaries.

לְסִיחוֹן מֶלֶךְ הָאֱמֹרִי וּלְעוֹג מֶלֶךְ הַבָּשָׁן וּלְכֹל מַמְלְכוֹת כְּנָעַן [11]

Sihon king of the Amorites and Og king of Bashan and all the kingdoms of Canaan

Further details of the kings and peoples slain by God appear in v. 11, which reveals their identities as Sihon, king of the Amorites, and Og, king of Bashan,[41] and all the kingdoms of Canaan—contrasting Ps 136, which only mentions the kings and fails to recall the conquest of lands west of the Jordan. In a noticeable opposition to v. 10's two verbs, v. 11 contains no verbs, but only lists the victims of those who fought with YHWH. A peculiarity arises here, however, whereby only the kings east[42] of the Jordan are mentioned specifically by name, and the remaining kings who dwelt west of the Jordan are merely referred to as ממלכות כנען ("kingdoms of Canaan").[43]

---

41. The description of Og as a powerful or mighty king (מלכים עצומים, v. 10) is reflected in a Dead Sea Scrolls tradition in 4Q373 1[a+b], 2, which claims that he had a sword like a Cedar and a shield like a tower; see Martínez and Tigchelaar, 2:738–39).

42. Concerning the sole mention of the kings from east of the Jordan, Goulder, *The Psalms of the Return*, 217, hypothesizes that the psalm was written during the early exile, a theory conveniently fitting his overall notions concerning the compilation of Book IV of the Psalter and Nehemiah. Thus, he claims the recollection of the exodus mirrors the release from Babylon, and the references to Og and Sihon look forward to a time in which the Transjordan will once again belong to Israel. A possible explanation for this lack of detail concerning the precise naming of the west Jordanian kings is that the psalmist only had before him the five books of the Torah, and thus could not refer to events occurring in Joshua. Such an opinion is maintained by Loewenstamm, *Evolution*, 40.

43. Passages such as Jer 1:10, 18:7, and Zeph 3:8 witness the free interchange of ממלכה and גוי.

From Bards to Biblical Exegetes

וְנָתַן אַרְצָם נַחֲלָה נַחֲלָה לְיִשְׂרָאֵל עַמּוֹ 12

Then he gave their land as an inheritance, an inheritance to Israel his people

As the final verse of the stanza, v. 12 further states that God—who created and maintains the world, acts as he pleases in it, and intervenes in history—chose to bestow the land of the conquered kings to his special people as an inheritance. Similar to Ps 136:21–22, the deployment of the terraced pattern in this verse emphasizes the importance of the statement being made. The phrase לתת ארץ נחלה is particularly common in Deuteronomy where it appears under similar circumstances (see 4:38; 15:4; 19:10; 24:4; 25:19; 26:1; and 29:8 [7]). Similarly, in Psalm 135's context, נחלה signifies a possession, usually property, that is inherited, or passed from one party to another—typically from a father to his children as in Num 27:8, אִישׁ כִּי־יָמוּת וּבֵן אֵין לוֹ וְהַעֲבַרְתֶּם אֶת־נַחֲלָתוֹ לְבִתּוֹ ("a man who dies and does not have a son, you will move his inheritance to his daughter"). However, the same word also often describes the special relationship between God and his people, where they are recalled as his inheritance, אַשְׁרֵי הַגּוֹי אֲשֶׁר־יְהוָה אֱלֹהָיו הָעָם בָּחַר לְנַחֲלָה לוֹ, ("Blessed in the nation whose God is YHWH, the people whom he chose for his inheritance," Ps 33:12; see also Ps 28:9). Such an allusion corresponds with the various other words and phrases in the psalm that express this intimate relationship, such as סגלתו (v. 4) and עמו (v. 12). YHWH's ability to act as he pleases in the whole world, כל אשר חפץ יהוה עשה . . . בארץ ("All YHWH desires he does . . . on the earth," v. 6), is demonstrated here as he allots a portion of land (ארץ) to his people for an inheritance.

The picture presented in this stanza resonates with the psalm's overall theme. YHWH is depicted as the one who fights Israel's battles and grants them land, without any involvement of human intermediaries. Although such a portrayal contrasts the accounts in Joshua and Judges in which the Israelites fight numerous battles and their relationship to God is less than perfect, it agrees with the picture presented in Psalm 105 where Israel enjoys a close and positive relationship with YHWH, who fights for them and grants them an inheritance of land. Reference to עמו ("his people") here creates a comparison with v. 10. The latter portrays those people, גוים, who were struck down by YHWH, along with their mighty kings, whereas the former presents a people who are loved by, and have an intimate relationship with, the same God.

YHWH's Supremacy

יְהוָה שִׁמְךָ לְעוֹלָם יְהוָה זִכְרְךָ לְדֹר־וָדֹר ¹³

YHWH your name is eternal, YHWH your memory (is) for all generations

From YHWH's interventions in history, the psalm now returns to the theme of praise; with a reminder of the key elements from section one: the name of YHWH, יהוה, and his reputation שם. An important temporal shift also accompanies the change in stanza. Until this point, the psalmist has predominantly relied on perfect verbs—such as בחר ("he chose," v. 4), ידעתי ("I know," v. 5), חפץ ("he desired," v. 6), הכה ("he struck," v. 8), and שלח ("he sent," v. 9)—to express both past and present actions. The current section, in contrast, employs imperfect verbs to express the present-future: God's *eternal* name and his memory for *future* generations. The corresponding phrases לדר ודר ("for generation and generation") and עולם (forever) frequently occur together[44] in biblical literature (see Pss 33:11 and 85:6), as do שם and זכר (see Job 18:17; Isa 26:8), to depict the reputation and memory of one's past actions. For example, in Prov 10:7, זֵכֶר צַדִּיק לִבְרָכָה וְשֵׁם רְשָׁעִים יִרְקָב ("The memory of the righteous is a blessing, but the name of the wicked rots"), the remembrance of a man's deeds constitutes a blessing. Similarly within the context of Psalm 135, the deeds previously recorded create the memory which should be remembered for future generations. The psalmist uses the wording of the present verse to magnify YHWH's fearful reputation, and in doing so, he additionally recalls God's words concerning himself in Exod 3:15, זֶה־שְּׁמִי לְעֹלָם וְזֶה זִכְרִי לְדֹר דֹּר ("This is my name forever, and this is my memorial for all generations"; cf. Ps 102:12 [13]). The distant parallelism between v. 13 and v. 3, שמד : יהוה // לשמו : יהוה (YHWH : to his name // YHWH : your name) creates a link between the current section and the first section. Additionally cementing this link between the sections is the fact that both verses constitute words of praise directed to YHWH.

כִּי־יָדִין יְהוָה עַמּוֹ וְעַל־עֲבָדָיו יִתְנֶחָם ¹⁴

Surely YHWH vindicates his people, and is merciful to his servants

Verse 14 provides a reason for the exclamation of praise in the previous verse, although a causal rendering of כי in this verse comes secondary

---

44. It is noticeably common in Leviticus, describing perpetual ordinances for future generations (6:11 [18]; 7:36; 10:9; and 23:14, 21).

to its function as an asseverative particle emphasizing YHWH's gracious actions towards his people. Although דין often contains the sense "to judge"—that is to apportion good to those who do good and punish those who do evil,[45]—it often carries a sense of implied innocence, in which the petitioner, certain of his righteous position, requests that God punishes his enemies or removes him from his distress. Thus, a better interpretation of דין here is "to vindicate." First Samuel 24:15 [16] records David's words to Saul after David spared his life, וְהָיָה יְהוָה לְדַיָּן וְשָׁפַט בֵּינִי וּבֵינֶךָ ("May YHWH be judge, and judge between me and you"). David's innocence is assumed and the result of the vindication is his rescue (see also Ps 54:1 [3]). With this understanding, the psalmist casts[46] an interpretive light on the preceding events. Instances in which God has intervened in history to save the Israelites and punish their enemies presumes their innocence, and ignores occurrences in which this same people have disobeyed and angered him.[47] The imperfect form ידין should not be considered as expressive of the future, suggesting God *will* vindicate his people from an unnamed catastrophe, but as an ongoing action,[48] whereby the psalmist recognizes YHWH's constant vindication of his people, beginning with the interventions previously mentioned and continuing into the time of the psalmist. The appearance of עבדיו recalls v. 9, and again draws a comparison between servants: those of Pharaoh (and presumably the gods of the Egyptians) are punished with the plagues, even judged—וְהִכֵּיתִי כָל־בְּכוֹר בְּאֶרֶץ־מִצְרַיִם מֵאָדָם וְעַד־בְּהֵמָה וּבְכָל־אֱלֹהֵי מִצְרַיִם אֶעֱשֶׂה שְׁפָטִים אֲנִי יְהוָה ("And I will strike all of the firstborn in the land of Egypt, from man to beast, and against all the gods of Egypt I will execute judgment," Exod 12:12—whereas the servants of YHWH are not only vindicated but comforted, as YHWH grants them deliverance from their enemies and

---

45. As in the case of Ps 9:8 [9], וְהוּא יִשְׁפֹּט־תֵּבֵל בְּצֶדֶק יָדִין לְאֻמִּים בְּמֵישָׁרִים ("He judges the earth righteously, and judges the nations uprightly").

46. The word כי may also conclude a parable or section, or give meaning to an oracle; see Muilenberg, "The Particle כי," 146. In v. 14, it does not give meaning to an oracle, but closes the section and provides a reason for the previous historical events.

47. On numerous instances during their desert journey, Israel grumbled about their hardships, and rebelled against God. Exodus 15:24 reports grumbling at the waters of Meribah, Exodus 32 recounts the golden-calf idolatry, and Numbers 14 tells of the community's rebellion at the report of the spies. Psalms 105, 114, and 136 similarly refrain from reporting negative instances from Israel's past.

48. Gibson, *Hebrew Grammar*, 75–76, elaborates upon such a deployment of the imperfect.

YHWH's Supremacy

brings them to a place of rest (Gen 27:42, 37:35). The notion of God being gracious to one party and venting his anger on another has led, in certain contexts, to the interpretation of יתנחם as "to vent one's anger" (see Ezek 5:13, which portrays God's anger with Israel: וְכָלָה אַפִּי וַהֲנִחוֹתִי חֲמָתִי בָּם וְהִנֶּחָמְתִּי,[49] "My anger will be spent, and I will rest my rage on them, and I will vent my anger"). As with v. 7, the degree of replication between the verse as it appears in the psalm and another location in biblical literature is precise, without any lexical differences, כִּי־יָדִין יְהוָה עַמּוֹ וְעַל־עֲבָדָיו יִתְנֶחָם (Deut 32:36).

עֲצַבֵּי הַגּוֹיִם כֶּסֶף וְזָהָב מַעֲשֵׂה יְדֵי אָדָם [15]

The idols of the nations are silver and gold, the work of men's hands

The fourth stanza moves the reader's attention from YHWH and his servants to the gods of the nations, and highlights the inabilities of these gods by contrasting them with YHWH's activities in creation and history. The gods of the nations are depicted as idols, עצבים, that have been constructed with silver and gold. Such materials commonly appear in polemical descriptions of gods, such as Hos 13:2, וְעַתָּה יוֹסִפוּ לַחֲטֹא וַיַּעֲשׂוּ לָהֶם מַסֵּכָה מִכַּסְפָּם כִּתְבוּנָם עֲצַבִּים מַעֲשֵׂה חָרָשִׁים כֻּלֹּה ("And now they sin more and more, and make for themselves molten images, Idols skillfully made from their silver, all of them the work of craftsmen," NASB; see also Deut 4:28). Although silver and gold may be indicative of riches and God's blessing (Gen 24:35; 1 Kgs 10:21), when they appear in the contexts of other gods they become symbols of inadequacy. Repetition of גוים (nations) in this verse draws one's attention to those who were struck in v. 10, suggesting the nations who formed these gods from silver and gold were not subsequently delivered by them. Such a depiction reveals a subordination of these other gods to YHWH. If God defeated the nations, and their gods could not save them, then he is more superior. A further comparison is induced via the root עשה ("to make/do"), contrasting gods *formed* by the hands of men (מעשה ידי אדם) and the God who *makes* lightning for the rain as in v. 7, בְּרָקִים לַמָּטָר עָשָׂה.[50]

---

49. In this context, one could also render it as "revenge"; see Gen 27:42 where Esau comforts himself with thoughts of revenge.

50. When reading this verse, it is difficult not to think of the instance in which Israel attempted to forge their own god from gold (Exod 32:23–25).

פֶּה־לָהֶם וְלֹא יְדַבֵּרוּ עֵינַיִם לָהֶם וְלֹא יִרְאוּ ¹⁶

Mouths[51] *they have but do not speak; eyes they have but do not see*

Verses 16–17 further demean the foreign gods via a series of clauses that on one hand, compares them with created beings, but on the other hand, denigrates them to a status below such creatures. In this verse, they are ascribed mouths, פה להם, but lack the ability to speak ולא ידברו. The further description of having eyes and not seeing suggests these idols are foolish. God's indictment of Israel in Jer 5:21, שִׁמְעוּ־נָא זֹאת עַם סָכָל וְאֵין לֵב עֵינַיִם לָהֶם וְלֹא יִרְאוּ אָזְנַיִם לָהֶם וְלֹא יִשְׁמָעוּ ("Now hear this, O foolish and senseless people, Who have eyes but do not see; Who have ears but do not hear" NASB), demonstrates this association, where the foolish people have unseeing eyes and deaf ears.[52]

אָזְנַיִם לָהֶם וְלֹא יַאֲזִינוּ אַף אֵין־יֶשׁ־רוּחַ בְּפִיהֶם ¹⁷

Ears they have but do not hear; and there is no breath in their mouths

The derision of foreign gods continues here in v. 17 as the psalmist further depicts the idols as having ears but being unable to hear, (אזנים להם ולא יאזינו). Although the author employs repetition in vv. 16 and 17 (להם ולא, "they have but do not"), the fourth[53] and final colon breaks this rhythm to create an emphatic denial of the idols' capabilities. The somewhat peculiar phrase, אף אין יש (literally, "a nose there is not, there is"), introduces the second colon in v. 17, and carries with it a variety of nuances.[54] Regardless of its various interpretations, the basic

---

51. Though the Hebrew פה is singular, here the intention is plural. JM states: "Almost any noun may be used as a noun of species or of category—the generic use—and then it is equivalent to a plural" (JM 498). In Ps 135:16, it may be understood that all of these idols have a mouth of some description.

52. It is possible to detect a degree of irony between vv. 9 and 16. The psalm depicts the idols as being unable to see here, and v. 9 portrays God as working signs and portents, acts intended to be seen (see close reading of v. 9).

53. Zakovitch, "הדגם הספרות," discusses important aspects of the three-plus-one literary pattern, where three represents a mathematical superlative and four was thus viewed as surpassing it.

54. Many commentators simply interpret יש as a pleonastic element which should be discarded, e.g., Kraus, *Psalms 60–150*, 491; Briggs, *The Book of Psalms*, 480, who claims the whole verse is an addition; Dahood, *Psalms III*, 262, who also relates it to the Ugaritic emphatic phrase *bl iṯ bn lh*, "surely he has no son"; Weiser, *The Psalms*, 788, and the BHS also suggests deleting יש. An alternative solution is to correct the

YHWH's Supremacy

understanding is the same: these idols do not possess breath, and do not breathe. Although אף primarily functions as a particle of emphasis ("even") it also recalls the Hebrew word for "nose," which suits the context depicting other facial organs.[55] The emphatic nature of the final statement is stressed by the word רוח (wind/breath/spirit), which, as opposed to the other facial entities, is critical for human existence. It is possible to live without the ability to speak, see, or hear; but without breath, one dies (cf. Gen 7:22 and Job 27:3, where אף and רוח represent life). By mentioning the breath of one's mouth, רוח בפיהם, the psalmist recalls God's work in creation, where YHWH forms the heavens by the breath of his mouth, as reflected in Ps 33:6, בִּדְבַר יְהוָה שָׁמַיִם נַעֲשׂוּ וּבְרוּחַ פִּיו כָּל־צְבָאָם ("By the word of YHWH the heavens were made and by the breath of his mouth all their hosts"). Such an allusion compels a comparison between YHWH, who created the heavens by the breath of his mouth, and the false gods, who do not possess breath for their own lives.[56] Additionally, repetition of רוח further recalls v. 7, and compares God—who brings the *wind* from its storehouses, thus exhibiting dominance over this element—and the idols, which do not even have breath within their bodies to sustain life.

---

verse according to the *assumed* source, Ps 115:6, להם ולא יריחון ("they have but do not smell"). Attractive as this may be, it also excessively stifles the psalmist's creative ability. Talmon, "Double Readings," 172–73, presents another possibility, suggesting an intentional double meaning with synonymous particles juxtaposed in the middle of a sentence. Within such a rubric, two meanings are upheld: one that explicitly denies the idols any breath אף אין רוח בפיהם ("but there is not a breath in their mouth"); and the other that poses a rhetorical question presupposing a negative answer, אף יש רוח בפיהם ("but is there any breath in their mouth?").

55. Most modern commentators accept both of these possible renderings; see Seybold, *Die Psalmen*, 503, and Gersiel, "פרק קלה," 241. Hacham, ספר תהלים, 609, however, interprets it as a particle of emphasis where it carries a meaning stronger than גם.

56. Although this description of the other gods is somewhat sarcastic and demeaning, highlighting their uselessness and impotency, one should still be aware of the fact that the psalmist recognizes a need to mock them in such a way. Ironically, although these gods were ineffectual, there must have been a propensity in the psalmist's community to serve and worship such idols; otherwise, such a denouncement would be irrelevant. Concerning the need to denounce other gods, Oesterley claims this section reflects an advanced stage of monotheism, one that surpasses merely stating YHWH's dominance over other gods, and explicitly identifies these gods as ineffectual idols. He also suggests this castigation of foreign idols came at a time when Israelites were being seduced by Hellenism, claiming, "this denunciation against idols may well have had a greater significance than appears at first in view of the fact that Hellenism had a great fascination for many Jews" (Oesterley, *The Psalms*, 541).

In v. 17, פה creates an inclusion enveloping vv. 16–17, which depict the facial features of the nation's idols and derides their impotency. The attribution of facial organs to these idols contrasts the lack of such anthropomorphisms employed in the description of YHWH. Yet even without such physical attributes, he accomplishes works far beyond the capability of his counterparts. A similar description of idols occurs in Ps 115:5–6, where much of the same vocabulary appears. However, the contexts of the two psalms differ significantly, with our psalmist recalling fewer elements. Psalm 135 only includes facial features in its depiction of the idols, whereas Psalm 115 continues to detail arms, legs, and throat.[57]

¹⁸ כְּמוֹהֶם יִהְיוּ עֹשֵׂיהֶם כֹּל אֲשֶׁר־בֹּטֵחַ בָּהֶם

Their makers will be like them, and all those who trust in them

In v. 18, attention turns from the idols to those who worship them; just as the idols are described as ineffective and foolish, so too are those who trust in them. Here, the psalm's continued association with Psalm 115 is evident, particularly in regards to v. 8: כְּמוֹהֶם יִהְיוּ עֹשֵׂיהֶם כֹּל אֲשֶׁר־בֹּטֵחַ בָּהֶם ("Their makers will be like them, and all who trust in them"); and the omission of the "arms" and "legs" becomes more pronounced. Just as the word עשה ("to make/do") created an earlier inclusion in vv. 6–7, so too it demarcates the open and close of the stanza, and forms part of a chiastic arrangement with v. 6, כל אשר : עשיהם :: עשה :: כל אשר (All who : their makers :: make : all who), thus linking the second and fourth stanzas. Moreover, the root closely associates those who worship the idols, כמוהם יהיו עשיהם ("Their makers will be like them"), with the idols themselves, מעשה ידי אדם ("The work of the hands of man"). A similar association between people and their object of worship is expressed in v. 14. Compared to v. 18, however, the relationship in v. 14 is positive, as the people (Israel) who worship the deity (YHWH) are vindicated by him.

---

57. There is a clear instance of literary borrowing here, even if the direction of borrowing cannot be determined at this stage in the analysis.

YHWH's Supremacy

בֵּית יִשְׂרָאֵל בָּרֲכוּ אֶת־יְהוָה בֵּית אַהֲרֹן בָּרֲכוּ אֶת־יְהוָה ¹⁹

House of Israel bless YHWH; House of Aaron bless YHWH

The final stanza constitutes an exhortation to various temple groups to praise YHWH, and like the previous section, bears a strong resemblance to Psalm 115.[58] The language of this section reflects similar character-

---

58. The tight relationship between Psalm 115 and Psalm 135 deserves a slightly more detailed examination because of all the similarities we have witnessed thus far. It is this writer's opinion that Psalm 135 constitutes the latter of the two works primarily because of the nature of its composition. Up to this point, it has been made evident that every verse bears a close relationship with other biblical texts, and because the psalm is probably very late (as it shall be demonstrated in the section on dating), it is most logical to assume that the psalm has borrowed from all of the texts reflected therein.

Psalm 115 is a community lament in which the community faces an enemy who taunts them and their trust in YHWH. The first verse of the psalm directs the reader to God and his grace and truth. Following this, v. 2 unexpectedly switches focus to an enemy's mocking cry against Israel, sarcastically asking "Where is your God?" The direct reply to this quotation is that he is in heaven (v. 3) and does as he pleases. The response continues in vv. 4–8 as the psalm denounces the gods of the nations as idols with the appearance of men but without life. Also relating to the mocking in the second verse, vv. 9–11 instruct the community on the appropriate response to such taunts: trust in YHWH because he is their help and strength. Verses 12–14 recall YHWH's faithfulness to Israel in the past (v. 12) and this sparks hope for the future, that he will bless them once again; this hope is related to the taunt in v. 2 since a future blessing implies a future deliverance. Verses 15 and 16 return to focus on YHWH and his exaltedness, declaring heaven belongs to him, recalling v. 3. Another reminder of the threat posed by the nations in v. 2 materializes in v. 17. The fact that the dead cannot praise YHWH applies an amount of indirect pressure on him to deliver them from the threat of the enemy: if he fails, he receives no praise. Finally, v. 18 closes the psalm with a note of praise, in which the congregation agrees to continue praising God forever. Whether this stems from a certainty that God will deliver or a note of fatality—that come what may, for good or ill, they will continue to praise him—is unclear.

The first two verses of Psalm 115 form a critical part of the psalm's plot because they effectively introduce the danger and the threat to the community. Psalm 135, however, ignores these verses because it is essentially a psalm of praise. Notwithstanding this fact, one can still discern in Psalm 135 a response to the chants from the enemy calling out "Where is your God?" (v. 2) Instead of responding with the claim that he is in heaven, however, and that the people should trust in him, Psalm 135 responds by asserting that YHWH *can* act, and has previously succeeded in delivering them. Furthermore, this psalm continues to claim that the nations who inquire "Where is your god?" do not actually serve gods at all, but only idols made with human hands and incapable of basic human abilities. The fact that God dwells in Jerusalem (v. 21) also improves Psalm 115's response to the enemy's mocking. Psalm 135 asserts that he is not in heaven, but with the people in Jerusalem (v. 21), far closer to his people than Psalm 115 implies. Additionally, Psalm 135 stresses that although YHWH dwells in

istics to that in the opening section: plural imperatives from a speaker to those congregated at the temple, and repetition of the divine name. The reference to the house of Israel, בית ישראל, here in v.19 addresses all Israelites (as in Ezek 12:27, and Amos 5:25) who are gathered at the temple. From this general reference, the psalm moves to the house of Aaron, בית אהרן, which in all likelihood refers to a specific group of individuals. Such a group appears in 1 Chr 15:4, וַיֶּאֱסֹף דָּוִיד אֶת־בְּנֵי אַהֲרֹן וְאֶת־הַלְוִיִּם ("And David gathered the sons of Aaron and the Levites"), where David gathers together the sons of Aaron. The phrase בני אהרן ("sons of Aaron") in Chronicles corresponds with בית אהרן in 135:19, and verses such as Ezek 37:16 attest to the freedom at which בני and בית are interchangeable. First Chronicles 15:4 further attests to the sons of Aaron and Levi.

בֵּית הַלֵּוִי בָּרֲכוּ אֶת־יְהוָה יִרְאֵי יְהוָה בָּרֲכוּ אֶת־יְהוָה [20]

House of Levi bless YHWH; Fearers of YHWH bless YHWH

Verse 20 continues with the blessing formula that began in the previous verse and also identifies another two groups of worshipers: the house of Levi (בית לוי); and the fearers of YHWH (יראי יהוה). The house of Levi refers to another subgroup that functioned within the temple. Nehemiah 10:40 [39], כִּי אֶל־הַלְּשָׁכוֹת יָבִיאוּ בְנֵי־יִשְׂרָאֵל וּבְנֵי הַלֵּוִי אֶת־תְּרוּמַת הַדָּגָן הַתִּירוֹשׁ וְהַיִּצְהָר ("For the sons of Israel and the sons of Levi will bring to the chambers the offering of the grain, the new wine, and the oil"), mentions the same group of individuals, although it employs the slightly different but interchangeable word בן. The final colon in v. 20, in some respects, continues the repetition that began in v. 19 by mentioning a temple group, but this rhythm is broken with the identification of the fearers of YHWH, יראי יהוה, as opposed to the expression X-בית. Another break in repetition stems from the name of the specific group, יראי יהוה—a term frequently appearing in the Psalms 15:4; 25:12; 128:1; 4—which fails to recall Israel or his descendants, but all who fear

---

Jerusalem, his jurisdiction, and the area in which he rules exceeds this: the heavens, earth, seas, and depths—everywhere!

Finally, it is possible to describe the relationship between the two psalms as a "before and after" scenario. Before YHWH intervenes to save his people, they are threatened and mocked; as a result, the people are encouraged to trust in God. After God has intervened and delivered them from the hand of their enemies (Psalm 135), Israel praises God, the tables are turned and Israel mocks the gods of the nations.

YHWH. The designation may refer to a group of worshippers that were not physical descendants of Jacob, but nevertheless worshipped and served YHWH. On the other hand, the phrase יראי יהוה may equally refer to all the faithful amidst Israel (see Mal 3:16 and Ps 22:23 [24]) who have attended the temple service. The break in rhythm presents another example of the three-plus-one literary pattern.

בָּרוּךְ יְהוָה מִצִּיּוֹן שֹׁכֵן יְרוּשָׁלָ͏ִם הַלְלוּ־יָהּ [21]

Be blessed YHWH in[59] Zion, who dwells in Jerusalem, Praise Yah

After the psalm exhorts the worshippers to bless YHWH, it now addresses God, expressing the expectation that the congregation's praise is acceptable to him. In the psalms, the formula ברוך יהוה ("be blessed O YHWH") usually depicts the response to a specific deed.[60] Within this stanza, no such reasoning is immediately apparent, unless we assume gratitude is expressed simply because he dwells in Zion. A glance, however, at the entire context of the psalm, which recounts God fighting for his people (vv. 8–11), and the bestowing of land to them (v. 12), creates a good reason to praise God. Although Zion[61] evidently refers to Jerusalem (2 Sam 5:6–7; 1 Kgs 8:1; 2 Kgs 19:21), it more importantly signifies the place from which YHWH rules and reigns, and the place from which he goes out to deliver his people (Amos 1:2; Ps 14:7; and 20:1 [2]). The idea of YHWH delivering Israel is similarly echoed in the psalm, via deliverance from Egypt, and defeat of Canaanite kings. Almost in total contrast to the entire psalm—where God is never ascribed human attributes and unlike the idols in the previous sections—here YHWH is ascribed with an earthly dwelling place, שכן ירושלם ("dwells in Jerusalem").[62] The psalm's final two words dupli-

---

59. Here the מ has been interpreted as a ב as this provides a better reading. This interchange is a known phenomenon caused by graphic similarity; see Tov, *Textual Criticism*, 244–49.

60. He hears the voice of supplications (28:6), shows his mercy (31:21 [22]), accepts prayer (66:20), supports his people (68:19 [20]), gives power and strength to his people (68:35 [36]), teaches statutes (119:12), and trains hands for war (144:1).

61. Zion is particularly prominent in the Songs of Ascent (125:1; 126:1; 128:5; 129:5; 132:13; 133:3; and 134:3); although this collection does not include Psalm 135, the mention of Zion may have motivated an editor to juxtapose the two.

62. The fact that God's dwelling appears after recollections of his going out to battle and defeating kings and nations—effectively fighting for Israel—reflects an ancient pattern in which God returns to his dwelling place to reign after defeating his enemies.

cate the opening words, הללו יה ("Praise Yah"), and create an inclusion for the whole psalm. For all that he has done for his people, and for his greatness in comparison with the idols of the nations, the only fitting response is to praise him. The last stanza with its various references to the groups within the temple similarly returns to the place where the psalm began, the house of YHWH, via repetition of the word בית (house).

MEANING

Psalm 135 primarily consists of a hymn celebrating YHWH's omnipotence, superiority over idols, and selection of Israel. The first verse of the second stanza speaks of his control over creation, with particular emphasis on meteorological elements, and the remainder of the stanza is devoted to his domination over human enemies, where he personally fights against them. His supremacy is particularly evident in the last verse of the stanza where he bestows land to his people as an inheritance (נחלה). Such an expression implies that the land he bestowed first belonged to him, and that he then granted it to Israel. This fact, together with the allusions to creation, suggests YHWH possesses ownership rights of all that was created. The fourth stanza recalls the impotency of the idols, which, when compared with God's deeds, further emphasizes his greatness.

In addition to magnifying YHWH's greatness, the psalm polemicizes the gods of the nations. Not only does it portray them as merely the work of men's hands (v. 15), but as impotent, having facial features but being unable to use them (vv. 16–18). The precise context of such polemical language can only be assumed at this stage, but one can surmise that such words were written to discourage worshipping such idols, at a time when religious syncretism may have been on the rise. As an implicit response to rejecting such idols, the Israelites are encouraged to choose YHWH instead.

The Baal Cycle employs this pattern, whereby Baal builds a dwelling place after defeating Yam and Judge River, see Parker, *Ugaritic Narrative Poetry*, 131–34; similarly in Enuma Elish, Marduk defeats Tiamat, creates the world with her remains and soon after declares: "A house I shall build, let it be the abode of my pleasure," Foster, "Enuma Elish," 400. This psalm recalls God defeating his enemies and then dwelling in his residence, Zion. Psalm 68 recalls a similar pattern; see Klingbeil, *Yahweh*, 130–35.

YHWH's Supremacy

Another important point the psalm stresses is the closeness of YHWH's relationship with Israel. Short phrases throughout the psalm often express this intimacy: Israel was elected because God chose them (v. 4), and they are his treasured possession (v. 4). Both of these phrases appear before his works in creation and history are mentioned, suggesting a more pronounced emphasis on the act of selection. Additionally, Israel relates to YHWH as "our God" (אלהינו, v. 5); he bestows land to them as an inheritance (v. 12); and he vindicates and is merciful to them (v.14). Such an emphasis on YHWH's intimacy with his people ultimately serves as an encouragement for them to cling to him and reject the nations' idols.

DATE

As with the previous psalms, we shall examine the primary evidence for the determination of Psalm 135's date first. Linguistically, the psalm offers a relatively rich yield of data concerning its origins. In v. 2, the psalm employs the relative particle ש together with the active participle עמדים (standing). Because the form "ש+participle"[63] does not appear in First Temple literature, a corpus preferring the alternative form "ה+participle," this construction may be accepted as a sign of lateness.[64] Additionally, the *weqatal* forms, והרג and ונתן in v. 12, used to indicate a past-completed act ("he killed" and "he gave"),[65] reflect an Aramaic[66]

---

63. For more details on the distribution and linguistic equivalence of this construction, see Hurvitz, בין לשון ללשון, 156.

64. The presence of the relative particle ש suggests lateness; see Eccl 1:11; Ezra 8:20; 1 Chr 5:20, 27:27. Scholars such as Allen, *Psalms 101–150*, 288, adduce the particle alone as evidence for lateness, but when considered together with the participle it constitutes more solid proof.

65. See Allen, *Psalms 101–150*, 288. With respect to this claim, he presumably appeals to the fact that the majority of instances in which this construction occurs, *wāw* plus perfect, appear in later writings; see also Driver, *A Treatise*, §130.

66. Concerning the appearance of Aramaisms in the text, it should be emphasized that the mere presence of an isolated Aramaic form is not enough to claim the entire text is late; see Hurvitz, "Chronological Significance," whose work has since been reinforced by Rendsburg, "Hurvitz Redux," who has refuted a number of claims to lateness on the bases of Aramaic. The very presence of Aramaic features may only be indicative of a text written in a dialectal variant, IH. Notwithstanding the aforementioned observations, two points concerning the dating of Psalm 135 should be noted. First, this psalm is less likely to have been written under the influence of Israelian authors because it does not fall into the corpus of IH, as defined in Rendsburg's comprehensive listing (Rendsburg, "A Comprehensive Guide," 8, 224). This observation raises the

influence that is often considered late.⁶⁷ The psalm's final stanza recalls the temple group known as בית לוי ("house of Levi"), which constitutes a group peculiar to later literature, as Ezek 40:46; 1 Chr 23:24; and 24:20 indicate; moreover, corresponding texts in Samuel and Kings fail to mention such a group.⁶⁸ Further linguistic evidence may also be cited that suggests a postexilic dating, such as the phrase בית אלהינו ("the house of our God," v. 2), which predominantly⁶⁹ surfaces in postexilic literature, including Ezra 8:17, 25, 30, 33; 9:9; and Neh 10:32–39 [33–40] (passim; 13:4).⁷⁰ Additional indications are the preposition ל introducing a verb's direct object⁷¹—as in v. 11 where לעוג and לסיחון form the two direct objects of the verb הרג; the phrase כל אשר חפץ עשה⁷² ("everything he desires he does"); and the reference to the house of Aaron, בית אהרן ("the house of Aaron," v. 19).⁷³ Another general indication of Psalm 135's date presents itself in v. 2, which addresses those standing in the house of YHWH. Such a statement recognizes a functional extant temple; therefore, it is unreasonable to assume the psalm was written during the exile (ca. 587 BCE until the rebuilding of the Second Temple, ca. 515 BCE).⁷⁴ Further evidence concerning the date appears in v. 11, which virtually mimics Ps 136:19–20. Because the association cannot reasonably be viewed as coincidental,⁷⁵ one must assume an instance of borrowing. When, however, the nature of the additional material that appears in Ps 135:11—ולבל ממלכות כנען ("and

chances of any Aramaisms appearing in this psalm stemming from the influence of the postexilic era. Second, a concentration of Aramaic forms together with the other LBH forms strengthens the notion of the Aramaisms reflecting a late influence and thus significantly increases the possibility of the psalm's lateness.

67. Driver, *A Treatise*, §131, notes that this feature derives from heavy Aramaic influences during a later period.

68. Cf. 2 Kgs 11:18 and 2 Chr 23:7.

69. This excludes its appearances in the Psalter.

70. For the SBH linguistic equivalent of בית אלהים, cp. Exod 23:19 and Neh 10:36 [37]. See also Hurvitz, בין לשון לשון, 174.

71. This phenomenon most probably derives from the influence of Aramaic on LBH; see GKC §117, and more recently Hurvitz, בין לשון לשון, 174.

72. Hurvitz, *A Linguistic Study*, has demonstrated that this is a LBH variant of a legal formula known in SBH and Aramaic.

73. See Day, "Pre-Exilic Psalms."

74. For this date, see Bright, *A History of Israel*, 372; and Meyers, "Temple," 363.

75. See the following section for further support of borrowing between the two psalms.

to all the kingdoms of Canaan")—is considered, the likelihood arises that Psalm 135 borrowed from Psalm 136. This scenario is more likely because a later author would have been more troubled by the representation of the conquest as consisting only of the Transjordan. Thus, he would have sought to correct the earlier work to reflect his situation more accurately. Due to the preponderance of evidence presented above, a postexilic date for the psalm should be accepted as a working hypothesis.[76] Confirming this assumption, the majority of scholarly opinion opts for a postexilic origin for Psalm 135.[77]

SOURCES

Table 4.1

Psalm 135	Source	DH
Ps 135:4	Deut 7:6, 14:2	D
Ps 135:8	Exod 12:12	P
Ps 135:9	Deut 34:11	D
Ps 135:10	Ps 136:17–18	—
Ps 135:11	Ps 136:19–20	—
Ps 135:12	Ps 136:21–22	—

76. Norin, *Er Spaltete das Meer*, 156, additionally adduces what he considers an "un-classical use" of the phrase אין ישׁ; he explicitly states, "*äusserst unklassische weise benutzt*," ["An extremely un-classical example used"] but fails to supply further evidence of why it is "un-classical."

77. Most scholars either explicitly claim the psalm's postexilic date, without citing evidence, or implicitly agree with this assumption. Kraus, without adducing evidence, states: "Even Psalm 135, which is to be dated in a very late time" (Kraus, *Psalms 60–150*, 492). Similarly, Schaefer claims: "Jerusalem and the temple have been rebuilt and are functioning" (Schaefer, *Psalms*, 317–19). Additionally, Seybold, *Introducing the Psalms*, 504, without explicit justification, assumes a postexilic date for the psalm. It is possible to adduce additional evidence from slightly older sources such as Driver, *An Introduction*, 384–85. He mentions Professor Cheyne's work, *Origin of the Psalter*, which further places the psalm in the Maccabean period; and Briggs, *The Book of Psalms*, 478, who claims that the psalm cannot be earlier than the Greek period, although this assessment should be treated with caution due to his propensity to date all psalms to the Greek period unless overwhelming evidence suggests otherwise. Other authors, such as Hoffman, יציאת מצריים, 111; and McCann, "Psalms," 1218–21, acquiesce on the issue of dating, and only Weiser suggests the possibility of pre-exilic origins, stating, "Just as in the case of Psalm 115 so here the possibility of pre-exilic origin has to be seriously considered," Weiser, *The Psalms*, 789.

Table 4.1 list the psalmist's sources for his exodus citations. No doubts arise concerning the associations between Psalms 135 and 136. A degree of uncertainty, however, is apparent concerning Ps 135:4's sources,[78] where at least three associations can be identified via the key word סגלה ("treasured possession"): Exod 19:5; Deut 7:6; and 14:2, all of which have a similar context to the psalm. The additional word בחר ("to choose"), however, excludes Exod 19:5, which narrows down the association to the two Deuteronomy texts. Because these two texts are nearly identical, no further effort will be made to isolate them, and the following section addresses them both. The lexical congruity between Psalm 135 and Exod 18:11 removes all doubt concerning the association between these two texts.

There are four possible sources for Ps 135:8—Exod 12:12, 29; Num 33:4; and Ps 136:10. Exodus 12:29 and Num 33:4 should be excluded because they omit the additional detail of מאדם עד בהמה ("from man to beast"), which appears in the psalm. Although Psalm 135 depends on Psalm 136 elsewhere (see below), we should similarly disregard the latter psalm because it too omits the aforementioned phrase. Consequently, the most probable source is Exod 12:12, because it includes the added detail of the destruction of man and beast. Numerous possibilities arise for v. 9's associations. Exodus 8:21 [17] presents a reasonable possibility since it also includes the root שלח ("to send") when describing the sending of plagues. With respect to lexical congruencies concerning the remaining words, Neh 9:10, וַתִּתֵּן אֹתֹת וּמֹפְתִים בְּפַרְעֹה וּבְכָל־עֲבָדָיו ("You performed signs and wonders against Pharaoh and all his servants"), and Deut 6:22, וַיִּתֵּן יְהוָה אוֹתֹת וּמֹפְתִים גְּדֹלִים וְרָעִים בְּמִצְרַיִם בְּפַרְעֹה וּבְכָל־בֵּיתוֹ לְעֵינֵינוּ ("And YHWH performed great and terrible signs and wonders before our eyes against Egypt, Pharaoh and all his household"), also present themselves as viable possibilities, despite the fact that both adopt the root נתן to portray the sending of the plagues. Notwithstanding these possibilities, Deut 34:11, לְכָל־הָאֹתוֹת וְהַמּוֹפְתִים אֲשֶׁר שְׁלָחוֹ יְהוָה לַעֲשׂוֹת בְּאֶרֶץ מִצְרָיִם לְפַרְעֹה וּלְכָל־עֲבָדָיו וּלְכָל־אַרְצוֹ ("for all the signs and wonders which YHWH sent him to perform in the land of Egypt against Pharaoh, all his servants, and all his land") stands as the best association for v. 9, because it includes the root שלח to depict

---

78. See Appendix C for a closer comparison between the psalm's verses and those of the sources.

YHWH's Supremacy

"sending"[79] in addition to numerous lexical matches for the remaining words. Only D and P, two Documentary Hypothesis sources are reflected in Psalm 135's citations from the Pentateuch. Due to the lateness of the composition, however, it would be unwise to even suggest that the author was unaware of the other traditions.

Psalm 135:2 contains specific lexical similarities with Ps 134:1 via the phrase עבדי יהוה עמדים בבית יהוה ("servants of YHWH standing in the house of YHWH"); additionally, Ps 135:21, ברוך יהוה מציון ("Be blessed YHWH from Zion") bears a recognizable similarity to Ps 134:3, יברכך יהוה מציון ("may YHWH bless you from Zion"). Together, these links create an undeniable association between the two works. Concerning the direction of borrowing, it is more probable that Psalm 135 appropriated material from Psalm 134, and not the other way around because of the change in phrase הָעֹמְדִים in Ps 134:1 to שֶׁעֹמְדִים in Ps 135:2, both of which can be rendered "who stand," Ps 134:1 represents a later linguistic equivalent.[80]

With regards to the borrowing between Psalms 135 and 136, one must turn to the nature of Psalm 135 for help in establishing who borrowed from whom. Due to the intensive eclectic nature of the psalm,[81] it is most reasonable to assume that Psalm 136 constitutes the source for Psalm 135. If, as shown above, Psalm 135 has evidently appropriated a significant quantity of material from Exodus, Deuteronomy, and Psalm 134, then in continuing to compose his collage of biblical texts it is only reasonable to assume he additionally borrowed from Psalm 136.[82] Furthermore, a diachronic adaptation appears between the two psalms. Psalm 136, the earlier composition, employs the earlier *wayy-*

---

79. Another difference is that Moses forms the object of the root in Deuteronomy. For more details on this association, see the following section.

80. See the section on dating concerning these. Although Ps 135:2 does not contain exodus material, demonstrating that it reuses material from Psalm 134 lends weight to Psalm 135's overall eclectic nature, evidence that is required later in establishing the relationship between Psalms 135 and 136.

81. See close reading; especially on vv. 5, 7, and 14.

82. Admittedly, this constitutes the most tenuous evidence. Coupled, however, with the claim by certain scholars that Psalm 135 originates from a *very* late stage in the postexilic era, see Allen, *Psalms 101–150*, 288; and Kraus, *Psalms 60–150*, 492, there is enough reason to eliminate the possibility of three psalms reusing Psalm 135.

iqtol form וַיַּהֲרֹג in v. 18 to represent a past completed act, whereas the later equivalent *weqatal* form,[83] וְהָרַג, appears in Ps 135:10.

Process of Selection

From the sources established above, one may argue that the psalmist, when composing the psalm, most probably worked with texts reflecting Exodus, Deuteronomy, and Psalm 136 to retell the exodus. It would appear from his selection of events that he had very little interest in the desert itinerary, and thus all events transpiring therein have been omitted. Due to the psalm's overall tenor, it is easy to see why the psalmist omitted the idolatry narratives—such accounts conflict with the positive nature of the relationship between God and Israel depicted in the psalm. Moreover, such instances conflict with the psalmist's intent of portraying idols strictly as the possession of other nations. Almost as an inclusion of the exodus, he chose to enumerate those instances of YHWH's fighting for his people that occurred at the beginning of the exodus, in Egypt, and at the end, during the Transjordan battles.

With the psalmist's intent on demonstrating YHWH's goodness towards his people, it is somewhat surprising that he failed to include any mention of the provision narratives, or the battle with the Amalekites, since these too reflect YHWH fighting for his people. Concerning the provision of bread, water, and meat in the wilderness, it is possible that they may have been omitted because each one is associated with an instance of Israelite murmuring. Similarly, with respect to the battle against Amalek, the psalmist may have viewed it as a narrative portraying Israel's punishment for doubting God's presence among them. Thus, he would have deemed it incompatible with the psalm's overall tenor.

In addition to the smiting of kings, the psalmist has selected one other incident from the exodus, YHWH's selection of Israel as a special people. Of all the selected psalms, this constitutes the most explicit reference to the selection of Israel. Rather than including any of the conditional aspects that accompanied the status of "God's people," the psalmist opted only to include God's selection of Israel. By combining the act of selection with a denunciation of idols in vv. 15–18, the psalmist provides further encouragement to his generation to choose

---

83. Both forms rendered, "he killed."

YHWH's Supremacy

YHWH as their God: not only are the idols of the nations impotent, but YHWH, who is omnipotent, has initiated an interest in Israel.

ALLUSIONS

Israel's Selection

The previous sections establish that Ps 135:4 either reuses Deut 7:6 or 14:2. Clear lexical similarities exist between the psalm and these two Deuteronomy passages, as they inarguably refer to the same event: the selection of Israel. Regardless of the exact source text in Deuteronomy, the psalmist has reframed and manipulated the source's conditional aspect. Deuteronomy 7:6 and 14:2 recall Israel's selection as a treasured possession as a reason and motivation for obedience. The former relates to God commanding Israel to destroy all of the nations they are about to dispossess along with their altars and wooden images, and not to intermarry with them. This they should do because they are a chosen (בחר) people and a special possession (סגלה) to YHWH. For the same reason, YHWH instructs the Israelites not to shave the front of their heads for the dead in Deut 14:23. Opposing this conditional notion, Psalm 135 only adopts the idea of selection as a reason to praise YHWH, suppressing all notions of obedience. The psalm's context focuses on the closeness and intimacy of the relationship between Israel and YHWH[84] as a reason for praise and celebration, thus any conditional aspects of that relationship are deemed unimportant and consequently omitted.

Plagues against Egypt

The similarities between the psalm and source are striking in this instance. Each of the words, or roots, in Ps 135:8 also appears in the source text, Exod 12:12. Additionally, their contexts are identical: both depict the plague against the firstborn of the Egyptians. The selection of this particular verse as a source represents a rare instance in which the plague against the firstborn is conceived as a judgment against the gods of Egypt. Exodus' attention to this detail is reflected in Psalm 135, which speaks of the impotency of the other gods and YHWH's supremacy over them. Another important detail adopted from the source text

---

84. Peppered throughout the psalm, as previously mentioned, are numerous phrases emphasizing the close and intimate relationship between God and his people: vv. 2 (לסגלתו), 5 (אדנינו), 12, and 14 (עמו).

205

is the inclusion of the phrase מאדם ועד בהמה ("from man to beast"). The addition of this phrase contributes to the psalmist's abundant deployment of words and phrases emphasizing totality,[85] e.g., כל (vv. 5, 6, 9, 11, 18), and the extended merismus depicting YHWH's reign in v. 6.

With regard to the psalmist borrowing this verse, the primary alteration to the source is contextual: the striking of the firstborn is the last of the plagues mentioned in the psalmist's source, but this same plague appears first in the psalm. One potential reason for reversing the sequence would be to cast the first nine plagues in light of the final plague. The plague against the firstborn represents an undeniable forthright assault by YHWH himself[86] against the Egyptians. Unlike the other plagues, no *human* intermediaries (e.g., Moses and Aaron), or creatures (e.g., locust and flies etc) participate. By first mentioning the plague of the firstborn and then recounting the remainder of the plagues, omitting specific details concerning how they came about, the psalmist creates the impression that YHWH directly inflicted Egypt with each plague. Due to the lateness of the psalm, one can be sure that the psalmist was cognizant of the original ordering of the plagues and adapted the source to suit to his composition. Even if he were only familiar with a plagues' tradition such as that in Psalm 78 or 105, the aforementioned adjustment would still be apparent in his work.

Unlike the previous example, the quote from Deut 34:10-11 does not belong to a plagues' narrative, but from a passage describing Moses' death. After he dies, Israel mourns for him for thirty days in the plains of Moab. Then Deuteronomy states that there has never arisen a prophet like him through whom YHWH had worked such portents and mighty acts, וְלֹא־קָם נָבִיא עוֹד בְּיִשְׂרָאֵל כְּמֹשֶׁה . . . לְכָל־הָאֹתוֹת וְהַמּוֹפְתִים אֲשֶׁר שְׁלָחוֹ יְהוָה לַעֲשׂוֹת בְּאֶרֶץ מִצְרָיִם לְפַרְעֹה וּלְכָל־עֲבָדָיו וּלְכָל־אַרְצוֹ ("No other prophet arose in Israel like Moses . . . for all the signs and magnificent deeds which YHWH sent him to perform in the land of Egypt against Pharaoh, all his servants, and all his land"). In comparing the source's wording and Ps 135:9, one of the first noticeable divergences appears in the object of the verb שלח. Within the context of Psalm 135, YHWH directly *sends* the plagues against the Egyptians; whereas, the source depicts Moses being *sent* bearing YHWH's judgments, thus bringing the plagues against the Egyptians. At first glance, it seems strange that

---

85. As an expression of totality, מאדם ועד בהמה also appears in Jer 50:3.
86. See close reading of v. 8 for Loewenstamm's comments on the final plague.

the psalmist would draw our attention to this verse because the psalm's message primarily concentrates on YHWH and the deeds of power he performed to deliver the people he loves, thus removing any mention of intermediaries from the psalm. The very fact that the psalmist quotes from this particular location, however, indicates a vague desire to recall Moses' role, albeit indirectly, in the enacting of the exodus, since the source does not focus on God's deeds, but elevates Moses' role in the Exodus.

Transjordan Conquest

With regards to the Transjordan conquest, the psalmist effects numerous subtle, but meaningful, adjustments while importing his source into its new context. Psalm 135:10 replaces מלכים גדולים ("mighty kings") in the source (Ps 136:17), with גוים רבים ("many nations"), an alteration producing two decisive effects. First, it creates a link within Psalm 135 between the nations whom YHWH struck and those who fashion idols with their own hands and serve them, עֲצַבֵּי הַגּוֹיִם כֶּסֶף וְזָהָב מַעֲשֵׂה יְדֵי אָדָם ("The idols of the nations are silver and gold, the work of men's hands," v. 15). From this association, one can infer that the nations' idols lacked any capability to deliver them from YHWH's hand, thus emphasizing his supremacy. Second, the word רבים decidedly suggests a multitude of nations struck, as opposed to only the Amorites, as suggested in the source. This alteration complies with the psalmist's intent on widening his source's scope to include the conquest of the entire land of Canaan, and not just the Transjordan.[87]

Apparently with a similar motivation to the previous example, Ps 135:11 adds the phrase ולכל ממלכות כנען ("and to all the kingdoms of Canaan"), which reflects the psalmist's changing perspective towards the conquest and giving of land. Rather than simply stopping at the defeat of the Transjordan kings, Psalm 135 continues by referring to the conquest during Joshua's lifetime. Psalm 136's motivation for exclusively recording events found in the Torah may be tied to the Psalm's his-

---

87. The semantic differences between עצומים (mighty) in Ps 135:10 and אדירים (powerful/majestic) in the source, Ps 136:18, are indeed small. The selection of עצומים, however, in this instance may reflect the psalmist's desire to remain true to the biblical wording. The latter word is never used to describe either the kings or the nations conquered by Israel. On the other hand, instances such as Deut 4:38; 7:1; and 9:1 attest to the former word.

torical reality. It may reflect an era in which the Torah alone was highly circulated and considered divinely inspired.[88] Such a reality may have changed when Psalm 135 was written, and to reflect this alteration, the psalmist sought to broaden the perspective of his source concerning the conquest. Yet in spite of this change, still only two kings are specifically mentioned by name.[89]

JUXTAPOSITION

Psalm 134-135

Psalm 134 opens with an exhortation to bless YHWH, בָּרֲכוּ אֶת־יְהוָה, that is directed towards an unspecified group standing in the temple praising him, עַבְדֵי יְהוָה הָעֹמְדִים בְּבֵית־יְהוָה ("Servants of YHWH who stand in the house of YHWH," v. 1). The second verse continues with this theme supplying them with more details on how they should praise: with arms extended. Finally, it invites a blessing from God upon those worshipping, יְבָרֶכְךָ יְהוָה מִצִּיּוֹן ("May YHWH bless you from Zion"), and remembers YHWH as maker of heaven and earth, (עֹשֵׂה שָׁמַיִם וָאָרֶץ).

Opening in a similar fashion, Ps 135 addresses a group identified as YHWH's servants who stand in his house, עַבְדֵי יְהוָה שֶׁעֹמְדִים בְּבֵית יְהוָה ("servants of YHWH who stand in the house of YHWH," vv. 1–2). After recalling Israel's selection as a treasured people, it then recounts YHWH's ability to do as he pleases in heaven and earth, עָשָׂה בַּשָּׁמַיִם וּבָאָרֶץ ("he does in heaven and on earth," v. 6). A demonstration of these abilities is enumerated as the psalm portrays his work in history on behalf of his people. After a brief intermission of praise (vv. 13–14), the psalm proceeds to denounce the impotency of idols and then exhorts various temple groups to bless YHWH. The final

---

88. Of course, the question of canonization, the process in which the Bible was written, assembled, and updated, cannot be dealt with in this space. Consequently, the mention of the canon here refers to a period when the books of the Torah, more or less reflecting MT, were considered a single unified collection viewed by many as being God inspired, and closed with respect to adding and subtracting material; for more on the complexities of canonization see Anderson, "Canonical and Non-Canonical," and Gamble, "Canon."

89. Loewenstamm, *Evolution*, 40, tentatively suggests here that the psalmist only had the Torah available to him and consequently mentions the only two Canaanite kings recalled therein.

YHWH's Supremacy

words of the psalm constitute a call for God to be blessed in[90] Zion בָּרוּךְ יְהוָה מִצִּיּוֹן ("be blessed YHWH from Zion," v. 21).

The number of lexical correspondences demonstrated above cannot result from mere coincidence, and so must stem from one psalmist borrowing from another, and from the dating evidence, we can be sure Psalm 135 appropriated material from Psalm 134.[91] From a contextual standpoint, the comparison above demonstrates that the author of Psalm 135 not only borrowed a significant portion of material from Psalm 134, but carefully selected elements from the opening and close of his source. With the exception of the phrase ברכו את יהוה ("bless YHWH"), the opening words of Psalm 134 appear in the opening of Psalm 135; and respectively, closing words found in Psalm 134 corresponds with closing words in Psalm 135. Such an arrangement reflects the psalmist's awareness of his source's structure.

Psalm 135 develops Psalm 134, detailing an otherwise abstract psalm. The latter simply exhorts those standing in the courts to bless YHWH, without supplying a rationale for doing so. Psalm 135 recognizes this theme and develops it by specifying reasons for praising YHWH: selecting Israel as a treasured people (v. 4), sustaining the created order (v. 7), delivering his people from their enemies (vv. 8–11), and giving his people the land of their enemies (v. 12). Also complementing Psalm 134 is Psalm 135's deployment of the root ברך (to bless) in its last verse. Psalm 134 employs it to express a blessing from YHWH to the people, ("may they be blessed"), presumably in response to worshipping in v. 2. This act is reversed in Ps 135:21, whereby the worshippers are requested to bless/praise him in response for all he has done for them.[92]

---

90. Concerning the interpretation of the preposition, see the close reading for this verse.

91. Cf. the shared vocabulary between Psalms 136 and 137, in which few common words appear.

92. The following chapter addresses the relationships between Psalms 135 and 136, after it surveys Psalm 136.

5

A Love Never Ending

Psalm 136

As the last of the selected psalms, Psalm 136 is closely related to its predecessor in the Psalter, Psalm 135. The present work is a relatively short liturgical hymn that devotes thirteen of its twenty-six verses to the exodus motif. Together with the exodus, it includes a relatively detailed portrayal of creation. The psalm's most outstanding feature is its refrain, כי לעולם חסדו ("for his steadfast love is eternal"), which highlights the nature of God's steadfast love. This refrain was, in all likelihood, responsorial, i.e., the congregation chanted the words in response to a congregational leader. A possibility exists that the psalm existed in an earlier form without the refrain. Although no conclusive proof can be offered for this theory, two pieces of evidence support the idea. First, Psalm 135 reuses a number of verses from the psalm, as we have already seen, and in doing so it does not repeat the refrain. This is slightly peculiar because Psalm 135 frequently recites from its sources word-for-word, without omitting phrases. Second, the terraced parallelism appears to be abruptly interrupted by the refrain in vv. 21–22.[1]

STRUCTURE

The majority of commentators agree upon the rudimentary structure of Psalm 136; however, the more precise divisions between each section and the rationale behind the numerous divisions generates a plethora of solutions. For the purposes of this study the psalm has been primarily divided according to theme and the recurring pattern of "general

---

1. See close reading for these verses below.

A Love Never Ending

to specific"—repetition has also influenced this decision in certain instances. The psalm can thus be divided as follows:

1. Introductory praise lauding YHWH's supremacy (vv. 1–3)
2. Praise for YHWH's work in creation (vv. 4–9)
3. Praise for YHWH's work in the exodus (vv. 10–22)
    A. Deliverance from Egypt (vv. 10–15)
    B. Defeat of Transjordan Kings (vv. 16–22)
4. Praise summary for YHWH's deliverance of Israel and provision to creation (vv. 23–26)

The opening three verses undoubtedly identify themselves as the introductory stanza by their repetition of the phrase הודו ל ("give thanks to"), and their use of parallelism.[2] Within this section, the psalm's primary theme is established: giving thanks to God because of his steadfast love. YHWH's omnipotence over all earthly and heavenly rulers is also explicitly established at the beginning of the composition. The second stanza also presents no problems in recognition, with creation emerging as the stanza's main topic. Additionally, the absence of הודו at the start of the verses and the references to YHWH via the active participle decidedly indicate a break from the opening section. Within this section, the first instance of the "general to particular" pattern emerges; v. 4 states the general, "he performs great magnificent deeds," and the stanza's remainder adds specific detail by recalling his magnificent deeds in creating the world.

The third section, which includes vv. 10–22, outlines Israel's history from their departure from Egypt, when Egypt's firstborn were struck, to their entrance into Canaan, when they defeated the two Transjordan kings. Temporally, this division distinguishes itself from the remainder of the psalm: the events occurring within it transpire long after the world's creation. Further division of this stanza into strophes, however, presents a few complexities. Verse 16[3] has been excluded from the first

---

2. See close reading.

3. Many scholars, perhaps wisely, refrained from further dividing the stanza into strophes and have preserved vv. 10–22 as a composite unit describing the entire exodus from Egypt; see Dahood, *Psalms III*, 265; McCann, *Psalms*, 1224, and Hacham, ספר תהלים, 530. For those scholars who have attempted to divide this stanza further into strophes both Kraus, *Psalms 60–150*, 496–99; and Allen, *Psalms 101–150*, 292–93,

strophe in this stanza because of its incongruence with the "general to particular" pattern described above. The strophe opens with a general statement of God striking the Egyptians, which is subsequently detailed in its ensuing verses; he smote them via their firstborn and also by means of the Reed Sea. The second strophe in the stanza follows from this incident, beginning with the general statement of how God led Israel in the desert in v. 16, and subsequently recounts his conquest of the Transjordan, and the granting of them to Israel as an inheritance.[4] The repetition of ישראל (Israel) creates a degree of continuity between the two strophes.

The psalm's final stanza, vv. 23–26, serves as a summary of the previously recorded events. With respect to Israel, God remembered them while they were in their low estate in Egypt and delivered them from their enemies. The reference to YHWH's provision of food to all flesh links the last stanza with the second, which similarly recalls YHWH's relationship with creation in general. While the final stanza's delimitation is simple enough to identify, the specific time frame to which it refers presents more of a challenge. Some scholars, the present author included, understand it as a recapitulation of God's benevolence during the wilderness wanderings.[5] Others view it as an association between God's steadfast love in the remote past and his love for the contemporaneous generation.[6] The last verse of the stanza, and psalm, recalls the opening section via the phrase הודו ל ("give thanks to") which appears at the beginning of vv. 1–3.

---

have opted to include this verse in the first strophe of the stanza, they both understand it as summarizing the contents of the first strophe.

4. The duration of Moses' leadership of Israel augments this conception of the wilderness period. He led them until the crossing of the Jordan, that is, after the defeat of Sihon and Og.

5. See Allen, *Psalms 101–150*, 299.

6. McCann, *Psalms*, 1224, additionally suggests that these verses refer to the return of Israel from the Babylonian exile.

A Love Never Ending

CLOSE READING

הוֹדוּ לַיהוָה כִּי־טוֹב כִּי לְעוֹלָם חַסְדּוֹ ¹

Proclaim thanks to YHWH for he is good, for his steadfast love is eternal

Like Psalms 105 and 135, Psalm 136 opens with an exhortation to proclaim thanks to YHWH.[7] The parallelism in the first three verses implores the reader to thank God on account of his steadfast love. Verse 1 contains the only explicit mention of God's name in the entire psalm; from this point onwards, the psalm refers to him either implicitly as the subject of a participle, or by means of an epithet. YHWH's חסד, his steadfast love, undeserved favor, and grace manifesting itself in acts of benevolence,[8] constitutes the psalm's primary theme. Not only does the psalm constantly repeat this motif in the refrain, כי לעולם חסדו ("for his steadfast love is eternal"), but it articulates the motif in its main section (vv. 4–25) since each act mentioned expresses his steadfast love. Within the context of v. 1, one can read the refrain as an explanation of כי טוב ("for he is good"): YHWH is good primarily because his steadfast love never ends.[9] The entire first verse constitutes a set formula for the praise of God that is well attested in Second Temple literature (see 1 Chr 16:34; Ps 106:1; and a condensed form in 2 Chr 5:13, 7:3; and Ezra 3:11).

הוֹדוּ לֵאלֹהֵי הָאֱלֹהִים כִּי לְעוֹלָם חַסְדּוֹ ²

Proclaim thanks to the God of gods, for his steadfast love is eternal

Repetition of הודו ל ("Proclaim/Give thanks to") and parallelism with v. 2 further reiterates the call to declare God's never-ending love. In this instance, however, the psalm employs אלהי האלהים ("God of gods")—a superlative form similar to the title Song of Songs—to identify YHWH, instead of the divine name. The appearance of אלהי האלהים here represents a degree of progression because it ascribes further characteristics to YHWH: He is the God of gods, more superior in nature and deed than all other gods. In the present verse, the psalmist states this char-

---

7. See close reading for Ps 105:1.

8. The concept of חסד usually implies a benevolent action as opposed to a mere feeling. In Ps 13:5 [6], trusting in God's grace equates to rejoicing in his salvation—a physical act of deliverance. Similar associations may be found in Ps 77:7–11 [8–12].

9. The second כי can also be read as a particle of emphasis, resulting in the reading, "*surely* his love endures forever," as in Isa 7:9; see also GKC §159ee.

acteristic of YHWH, and in the psalm's remaining verses, he further enumerates YHWH's supremacy by detailing acts unique to him.

הוֹדוּ לַאֲדֹנֵי הָאֲדֹנִים כִּי לְעוֹלָם חַסְדּוֹ ³

Proclaim thanks to the Lord of lords, for his steadfast love is eternal

Verse 3 continues the repetition of the imperative phrase הודו ל ("Proclaim/Give thanks to") and the reason for praise (כי לעלם חסדו), and like v. 2, refers to YHWH with a superlative, אדני האדנים ("Lord of lords"). It is possible to view this term as a merismus with the previous verse: "God of gods" portrays the ruler of the heavens and all heavenly beings, whereas "Lord of lords" depicts his sovereignty over earthly rulers. YHWH's domination of earthly rulers is further enumerated in vv. 15, 17, and 18 of the psalm. Together, vv. 2–3 recall Deut 10:17,[10] כִּי יְהוָה אֱלֹהֵיכֶם הוּא אֱלֹהֵי הָאֱלֹהִים וַאֲדֹנֵי הָאֲדֹנִים ("For YHWH your God is God of gods and Lord of lords") which exists in a context recounting God's steadfast love to Israel through his selection of them as a chose people.

Within Psalm 136's opening three verses, there are two important features that characterize the entire psalm. First, the psalm's primary subject, YHWH, is firmly established, in addition to the specific qualities that render him worthy of praise; second, the "general to particular" literary pattern is established. The pattern first manifests itself with regards to the divine name/reputation (general), followed by a recitation of the deeds that describe that name/reputation.

לְעֹשֵׂה נִפְלָאוֹת גְּדֹלוֹת לְבַדּוֹ כִּי לְעוֹלָם חַסְדּוֹ ⁴

To the one who performs great magnificent deeds alone, for his steadfast love is eternal

After a relatively short introduction of praise, the psalm begins enumerating specific aspects of YHWH's mercy and steadfast love. This enumeration is first accomplished in general terms in v. 4, with more details added as the psalm continues. Although the initial הודו ("proclaim thanks") is absent from the present verses, it is implicitly understood from the *lāmed* + participle construction. Thus, v. 4 may read, "give thanks to the one who performs." The two words נפלאות ("amazing works") and גדולות ("great," often understood as a noun equating to

---

10. See Gen 40:1; 42:10; Judg 3:25; and Neh 3:5.

"great works") commonly represent God's supernatural deeds of power, too difficult for man to achieve on his own. More specifically, as demonstrated in earlier psalms (105, 106, and 135), these nouns frequently describe God's acts of deliverance during the exodus. Psalm 106:22, for example, states, נִפְלָאוֹת בְּאֶרֶץ חָם נוֹרָאוֹת עַל־יַם־סוּף ("Amazing works in the Land of Ham, fearful deeds at *Yam Suf*"; see also Pss 77:11 [12]; 78:4, 32). By employing such terminology at this point in the psalm, the psalmist hints at the ensuing content. As a continuation of God's uniqueness and exalted position—originally witnessed in vv. 2–3 where YHWH is proclaimed "God of gods" and "Lord of lords"—the psalm clarifies here that YHWH alone accomplishes great deeds. This adverbial qualifier, לבדו, extends to every exploit delineated within the psalm: YHWH alone performs them.

לְעֹשֵׂה הַשָּׁמַיִם בִּתְבוּנָה כִּי לְעוֹלָם חַסְדּוֹ ⁵

To the one who makes heaven with understanding, for his steadfast love is eternal

Verses 5 and 6 expound on v. 4 by describing God's נפלאות ("amazing works") in the creation of heaven and earth. Repetition of the verb עשה ("to make") from the previous verse associates the great deeds YHWH performs with the creation of heaven. The Bible frequently recalls God's work in creating heaven; Exod 20:11 states כִּי שֵׁשֶׁת־יָמִים עָשָׂה יְהוָה אֶת־הַשָּׁמַיִם וְאֶת־הָאָרֶץ ("For in six days YHWH made the heavens and the earth"), and Ps 33:6 similarly echoes this sentiment, בִּדְבַר יְהוָה שָׁמַיִם נַעֲשׂוּ וּבְרוּחַ פִּיו כָּל־צְבָאָם ("By the word of YHWH the heavens were made and by the breath of his mouth all their hosts"). The addition of בתבונה ("with wisdom"), however, finds no witnesses in the Torah, but is reflected in wisdom literature and the Prophets. Proverbs 3:19 suggests יְהוָה בְּחָכְמָה יָסַד־אָרֶץ כּוֹנֵן שָׁמַיִם בִּתְבוּנָה ("YHWH with wisdom founded the earth and established the heavens with *understanding*"), and Jer 10:12 paints a similar picture. The addition of בתבונה [11] ("with

---

11. The addition of this word also presents certain problems for the reading of the Psalm. If one understands the *bêt* as that of accompaniment (see Dahood, *Psalms III*, 266, and also Psalm 104:24), then it would suggest that someone/something else was present with God at creation. This suggestion conflicts with the previous verse that emphasizes God alone does great deeds. The notion of wisdom accompanying God during creation is additionally reflected in the Tgs. traditions of Genesis; see McNamara, *Targum Neofiti 1: Genesis*, 52.

wisdom") adds another dimension to God's creative works, so that wisdom complements his unequalled power.

לְרֹקַע הָאָרֶץ עַל־הַמָּיִם כִּי לְעוֹלָם חַסְדּוֹ ⁶

To the one who stretches the land on the waters, for his steadfast love is eternal

Further explicating God's work in creation, v. 6 focuses on the creation of land. The "*lāmed* + participle" construction appears again as YHWH is depicted as "stretching out" or "spreading out" (see 2 Sam 22:43 and Isa 40:19) the land over the earth. This description hints at the creation narrative in Genesis 1 via the root רקע ("to stretch out"). The noun form רקיע in Genesis represents the firmament used to separate upper and lower waters, וַיֹּאמֶר אֱלֹהִים יְהִי רָקִיעַ בְּתוֹךְ הַמָּיִם וִיהִי מַבְדִּיל בֵּין מַיִם לָמָיִם ("And God said, 'Let there be a *firmament* in the midst of the waters and let it separate the waters,'" Gen 1:6),[12] whereas in the present verse, the verb form portrays God spreading the earth over the water. Together, vv. 6 and 7 create a merismus formed by the words "heaven" and "earth," essentially implying that God also created everything in between. The ensuing three verses further detail this general picture.

לְעֹשֵׂה אוֹרִים גְּדֹלִים כִּי לְעוֹלָם חַסְדּוֹ ⁷

To the maker of great lights, for his steadfast love is eternal

This stanza continues with God's creation activities by specifying created elements in the heavens. Once again, the general allusion to Genesis is clear (see, for example, Gen 1:15: וְהָיוּ לִמְאוֹרֹת בִּרְקִיעַ הַשָּׁמַיִם לְהָאִיר עַל־הָאָרֶץ וַיְהִי־כֵן, "And may they be lights in the firmament of heaven to light the world, and it was thus"); however, a difference in spelling suggests the wording originated from another source. Genesis 1:16 fails to recall the specific phrase אוֹרִים גְדֹלִים ("great lights") and uses הַמְּאֹרֹת הַגְּדֹלִים (Gen) to refer to the creation of the sun. Notwithstanding this difference, גְדֹלִים (great) in the psalm recalls the great deeds mentioned in v. 4, לְעֹשֵׂה נִפְלָאוֹת גְּדֹלוֹת לְבַדּוֹ ("To the one who performs great mag-

---

12. The verb רקע usually has the meaning of spreading something out over another object (see Exod 39:3 and Num 16:39 [17:4]), and although Job 37:18 recalls God spreading out the sky with this verb, only Isa 44:24 sees God specifically stretching out the earth as an expression denoting power and ability (אָנֹכִי יְהוָה עֹשֶׂה כֹּל נֹטֶה שָׁמַיִם לְבַדִּי רֹקַע הָאָרֶץ, "I am YHWH who made everything, stretching out the heavens alone, *spreading out* the earth").

A Love Never Ending

nificent deeds alone"), thus directly associating YHWH's magnificent deeds with the earth's creation, and more specifically the creation of light. Further augmenting this association is the repetition of the root עשה, ("he did/made") which also occurs in v. 4. At this point, with respect to the light God created during creation, it is not clear to which light the psalmist is alluding: the light of Gen 1:3, (וַיֹּאמֶר אֱלֹהִים יְהִי אוֹר וַיְהִי־אוֹר, "And God said, 'let there be light', and there was light"), or the greater and lesser lights created on the fourth day, as recorded in Gen 1:14–18. The second view is more favorable since the psalmist continues to mention the sun and moon.

אֶת־הַשֶּׁמֶשׁ לְמֶמְשֶׁלֶת בַּיּוֹם כִּי לְעוֹלָם חַסְדּוֹ [8]

The sun to rule in the day, for his steadfast love is eternal

Continuing the depiction of heavenly lights, v. 8 details the sun's creation. The particle את, which identifies the verse as an accusative clause for the verb עשה, ("he did/made") links this verse with the preceding one. The psalmist continues developing and detailing the aforementioned great light in v. 7. To achieve this, he again recalls Gen 1:16, which depicts a greater light created to rule the day, וַיַּעַשׂ אֱלֹהִים אֶת־שְׁנֵי הַמְּאֹרֹת הַגְּדֹלִים אֶת־הַמָּאוֹר הַגָּדֹל לְמֶמְשֶׁלֶת הַיּוֹם ("And God made the two great lights, the greater light to dominate the day"). Strangely, however, the Genesis account does not explicitly mention the sun, only a reference to the "greater light." By specifically mentioning the sun, the psalmist excludes any possibility of a reference to the first light created by God in Gen 1:3.[13]

אֶת־הַיָּרֵחַ וְכוֹכָבִים לְמֶמְשְׁלוֹת בַּלָּיְלָה כִּי לְעוֹלָם חַסְדּוֹ [9]

The moon and stars to rule in the night, for his steadfast love is eternal

A further description of YHWH creating heavenly bodies appears in v. 9, and like v. 8, the present verse represents a continuation of v. 7, linked via the particle את. Here, a similar process of explication occurs whereby the psalm once again recalls the lesser light mentioned in

---

13. The creation account, as it appears here, reflects the different social circumstances between the psalmist and the author of his source. The Genesis account was probably written at a time when the author sought to avoid the specific mention of the sun, so as not to recall the sun god Shamash; see Milgrom, "Hidden Light." Such a constraint does not concern our psalmist, who felt at liberty to specify by name both the sun and moon.

Gen 1:16, וְאֶת־הַמָּאוֹר הַקָּטֹן לְמֶמְשֶׁלֶת הַלַּיְלָה וְאֵת הַכּוֹכָבִים ("And the lesser light to dominate the night and the stars"), which relates the light to the moon and stars even though the word "moon" (ירח) does not appear in Genesis. Evidently, the three verses of this stanza allude to select aspects of creation, omitting the creation of plants, animals, and man. This raises two important questions: Why does the author only mention these aspects of creation despite preserving the order of the Genesis account, and how does this affect the psalm's interpretation? Perhaps the best answer to this question arises through the examination of those aspects of creation upon which he focuses: the heavens, earth, and lights. Each of these entities can be considered eternal and never ending. The same sun that arose yesterday will arise today, tomorrow, and in the days after that. Similarly, the stars, the moon, the heavens and the earth also represent eternal entities. These contrast with other elements of creation that eventually die, e.g., fish in the sea, plants, animals, and man. Taking this fact into consideration, it's possible that the psalmist only included eternal and constant elements of creation because these properly reflect the enduring constancy of YHWH's steadfast love, as discussed above. Additionally, one must note that other psalmists associate creation with God's grace. Psalm 33:5–6 states, אֹהֵב צְדָקָה וּמִשְׁפָּט חֶסֶד יְהוָה מָלְאָה הָאָרֶץ בִּדְבַר יְהוָה שָׁמַיִם נַעֲשׂוּ וּבְרוּחַ פִּיו כָּל־צְבָאָם ("he loves righteousness and justice, YHWH's loving kindness fills the earth. By the word of YHWH the heavens were made, and by the breath of his mouth all their hosts."), clearly linking his steadfast love with the creation of the heavens by his word, and their hosts, by the breath of his mouth.

לְמַכֵּה מִצְרַיִם בִּבְכוֹרֵיהֶם כִּי לְעוֹלָם חַסְדּוֹ [10]

To the one who struck Egypt with their firstborn, for his steadfast love is eternal

After describing YHWH's work in creation, v. 10 opens a new section by introducing his mighty deeds that brought about Israel's emancipation from Egypt. The verse begins by recalling the exodus with the striking of the Egyptians' firstborn. Even though an obvious break exists with regard to subject matter, from creation to exodus, a degree of continuity is evident. Verse 9 depicts a scene from creation with respect to the night sky, and Exod 12:29 describes the smiting of the Egyptians' firstborn, with a similar reference to darkness, וַיְהִי בַּחֲצִי הַלַּיְלָה וַיהוָה

הִכָּה כָל־בְּכוֹר בְּאֶרֶץ מִצְרָיִם ("And it happened, in the middle of the night YHWH struck all of the firstborn in the land of Egypt"). Biblical literature often depicts the plague on the firstborn in words similar to those used in v. 10, e.g., Exod 12:12, וְהִכֵּיתִי כָל־בְּכוֹר בְּאֶרֶץ מִצְרַיִם ("And I will strike all the *firstborn* in the land of *Egypt*"), and the Psalms, וַיַּךְ כָּל־בְּכוֹר בְּמִצְרָיִם ("And he *struck* all the *firstborn* in *Egypt*," Ps 78:51; see also Num 8:17; 33:4; Pss 105:36; 135:8). Despite the fact that many Egyptians died when the angel of death passed through their midst, the psalm still includes this event as an example of God's loving kindness, thus raising the question: How can slaughtering hundreds of Egyptians be considered an act of steadfast love?[14] At this stage, it is best to conclude that the psalmist is confining the bounds of his composition primarily to portray YHWH's steadfast love to Israel alone.

וַיּוֹצֵא יִשְׂרָאֵל מִתּוֹכָם כִּי לְעוֹלָם חַסְדּוֹ [11]

And brought Israel from their midst, for his steadfast love is eternal

After God struck the Egyptians, Israel could depart from their midst. A rare instance of the *wāw* consecutive in v. 11 continues the thought of the previous verse, and uniting the two. The added emphasis of מתוכם ("from their midst") highlights the Egyptians' helplessness as Israel departed; although Israel was among them, the Egyptians were powerless to prevent Israel from leaving in light of YHWH's power.[15] Additionally, מתוכם recalls the sentiment of Deut 4:34, portraying YHWH extracting one nation, Israel, out from the midst of another הֲנִסָּה אֱלֹהִים לָבוֹא לָקַחַת לוֹ גוֹי מִקֶּרֶב גּוֹי בְּמַסֹּת בְּאֹתֹת וּבְמוֹפְתִים ("Has God attempted to enter and take one nation for himself from the midst of a nation with trials, signs and acts of power").

---

14. Ibn Ezra notes at this point that grace is indeed revealed to Israel because they were spared from this judgment, and because God took vengeance on their enemies. See Cohen, *Psalms*, 210; Radak similarly perceives this as an act of grace (see Cohen, *Psalms: Part II*, 211).

15. This sentiment is also echoed by Ibn Ezra with regards to the following verse לא כעבדים הבורחים מפני אדוניהם ("Not as slaves escaping from their masters"), which implies that Israel departed in the strength and boldness which YHWH empowered them and not as frightened slaves who needed to flee in secret. See Cohen, *Psalms*, 210.

בְּיָד חֲזָקָה וּבִזְרוֹעַ נְטוּיָה כִּי לְעוֹלָם חַסְדּוֹ ¹²

With a strong hand and an outstretched arm, for his steadfast love is eternal

Verse 12 shifts the psalm's focus from Israel's deliverance to God's work in effecting it, detailing the way in which redemption occurred: "with a strong hand and outstretched arm" (ביד חזקה ובזרוע נטויה). This phrase constitutes an anthropomorphism[16] that exclusively describes God acting on behalf of Israel to deliver them. Particularly descriptive of YHWH wielding his power in deliverance is the expression זרוע נטויה ("outstretched arm"), echoed in the Song of the Sea and Exod, 15:12 נָטִיתָ יְמִינְךָ תִּבְלָעֵמוֹ אָרֶץ ("You *stretched* out your right *arm* and the earth swallowed them"; see also Exod 7:5). Throughout this stanza, none of Israel's leaders are recalled—although Moses and Aaron, in the Exodus rendition of events, stretch (נטה) out their arms to help bring about the deliverance from Egypt (see 7:19, 8:5 [1], 9:22, 10:12)—it is God alone who acts according to his loving kindness.

לְגֹזֵר יַם־סוּף לִגְזָרִים כִּי לְעוֹלָם חַסְדּוֹ ¹³

To the one who split Yam Suf into pieces, for his steadfast love is eternal

A change in scene, from the midst of Egypt to the Reed Sea, marks a change in strophe. Once again the *lāmed* + participle construction subtly recalls YHWH as the primary instigator of events. Although the allusion directs us to the splitting of the sea, the Torah never recalls the phrase גזר . . . גזרים ("cut . . . pieces") with respect to the Reed Sea. At this point, one would expect to see the word בקע (split) as in Exod 14:16, וְאַתָּה הָרֵם אֶת־מַטְּךָ וּנְטֵה אֶת־יָדְךָ עַל־הַיָּם וּבְקָעֵהוּ ("And you, lift your staff and stretch out your hand over the sea, and split it").[17] The

---

16. It is well attested in Deuteronomy; see, for example, 5:15; 7:19; and 11:2.

17. Although the word גזרים is absent from biblical creation traditions, its association to mythological tradition has long been recognized; see Kraus, *Psalms 60–150*, 499. The psalmist might have selected this word because of its connection to earlier traditions that depict God's battle with the sea monster at the earth's creation (see Isa 27:1; 51:9–10; Ps 89:8–9 [9–10]; and Job 26:12). Fishbane, *Text and Texture*, 13–15, further explores the primordial battle motif in the Hebrew Bible, in which the enemy is given numerous names such as Yam, Rahab, and Tanin. This imagery resonates with the psalm because it associates the current section with the creation motif, recalled in the previous stanza, and demonstrates God's supreme command over all he created.

psalmist's use of the plural noun גזרים[18] ("pieces") reflects a covert representation of the exodus in Gen 15:17. Genesis 15 recalls Abraham's sacrifice to God. After Abraham arranges the pieces of the sacrifice into two lines, YHWH, in the form of a flaming torch, passes between the pieces. The picture of the flaming torch passing between the pieces of sacrifice that Abraham offers anticipates the manner in which YHWH would lead the Israelites through the sea (in a pillar of fire by night and a cloud by day; see Exod 13:21).[19]

וְהֶעֱבִיר יִשְׂרָאֵל בְּתוֹכוֹ כִּי לְעוֹלָם חַסְדּוֹ [14]

And brought Israel from its midst, for his steadfast love is eternal

After splitting the sea, YHWH led the Israelites safely through it, וְהֶעֱבִיר יִשְׂרָאֵל בְּתוֹכוֹ ("And he brought Israel from its midst," v. 14). This corresponds with Israel going out from the midst of Egypt;[20] in v. 11, the repetition of תוך and ישראל reinforce the association. God first brought the Israelites from the midst of the Egyptians, וַיּוֹצֵא יִשְׂרָאֵל מִתּוֹכָם ("and brought Israel from their midst"), and now he brings them out from the midst of the sea. A similar account appears in Ps 78:13, בָּקַע יָם וַיַּעֲבִירֵם וַיַּצֶּב־מַיִם כְּמוֹ־נֵד ("He split the sea and brought them through, and stood the water up like a heap").

וְנִעֵר פַּרְעֹה וְחֵילוֹ בְיַם־סוּף כִּי לְעוֹלָם חַסְדּוֹ [15]

And overturned Pharaoh and his soldiers into Yam Suf, for his steadfast love is eternal

It was not enough for God to deliver Israel from Egypt and open the sea for them to pass through, as a *coup de grâce* he hurls Pharaoh and his army into the sea. The wording in the present verse specifically relates to events recorded in Exod 14:27, וַיְנַעֵר יְהוָה אֶת־מִצְרַיִם בְּתוֹךְ הַיָּם ("and YHWH overturned the Egyptians into the sea"), the only other location in biblical literature where נער appears as a *pi'el* in relation to the exodus. Beside this present verse, Ps 135:9 features the only other specific mention of Pharaoh within the context of the sea-crossing. For Psalm

---

18. Dahood's rendering as a dual form is thus feasible (*Psalms III*, 266).

19. See Zakovitch, *And You Shall Tell Your Son*, 60.

20. Ibn Ezra similarly understands this as an act of grace because the waters did not collapse on Israel, and they were able to walk safely in its midst; see Cohen, *Psalms*, 210.

136, the reference alludes back to v. 3 and the declaration of God being "Lord of lords," a fact echoed here in a practical example of YHWH's domination over a human lord. As with v. 10, God's eternal steadfast love here should be viewed in light of its expression strictly towards Israel. The second mention of ים סוף creates an inclusion with v. 13 that closes the strophe and envelops a description of events transpiring at the Sea of Reeds. This inclusion bears some similarity to Ps 105:23, 38, where the word מצרים (Egypt) also demarks events occurring within that geographical location.[21] With the end of this strophe, the picture of God's steadfast love specifically towards Israel receives further emphasis.

לְמוֹלִיךְ עַמּוֹ בַּמִּדְבָּר כִּי לְעוֹלָם חַסְדּוֹ [16]

To the one who led his people in the desert, for his steadfast love is eternal

The theme of God's leading continues in this new section, but the location changes from the sea to the desert. Verse 16 represents a general introduction to ensuing events, reflecting the psalmist's tendency to develop stanzas from "general to particular."[22] God leading Israel through the desert, as recorded here, best reflects Deut 8:15, הַמּוֹלִיכֲךָ בַּמִּדְבָּר הַגָּדֹל וְהַנּוֹרָא ("The one who leads you in the great and fearsome desert") and the phrase ויוליכם . . . מדבר ("and he led them . . . desert") additionally echoes in Ps 106:9. At this point, it is noticeable that the psalmist omits all events transpiring in the wilderness. No mention appears of Israel's complaining and rebellion that often characterizes this period. Similarly, the psalmist refrains from mentioning the more positive events during this period, such as the provision of water, meat, and bread.

לְמַכֵּה מְלָכִים גְּדֹלִים כִּי לְעוֹלָם חַסְדּוֹ [17]

To the one who strikes great kings, for his steadfast love is eternal

After recounting YHWH's work in leading Israel through the desert, the psalmist brusquely moves to the Transjordan battle accounts. From the start of v. 17, the psalmist draws the reader's attention to v. 10 and the smiting of the Egyptians, לְמַכֵּה מִצְרַיִם בִּבְכוֹרֵיהֶם ("to the one who struck Egypt with their firstborn"). Just as God struck the Egyptians

---

21. See close reading for v. 38.
22. See the discussion on the structure later in this chapter.

A Love Never Ending

and Pharaoh, he now strikes other great kings. This verse also reminds the reader of YHWH's גדלות ("great deeds") mentioned in the opening stanza, the striking of mighty kings being one of those deeds by which God expresses his loving kindness, לְעֹשֵׂה נִפְלָאוֹת גְּדֹלוֹת לְבַדּוֹ ("To the one who performs great magnificent deeds alone," v. 4).

וַיַּהֲרֹג מְלָכִים אַדִּירִים כִּי לְעוֹלָם חַסְדּוֹ [18]

And killed mighty kings, for his steadfast love is eternal

Through the repetition and parallelism in vv. 17–18, the psalmist emphasizes God's superiority over kings and his ability to destroy them. The parallel word pair[23] הרג ("He killed") and נכה ("He struck") forcefully accentuates the fate of the great kings. Once again, the global view of God's loving kindness is restricted, as the benevolence towards his people leads to the destruction of others. The psalm glorifies the kings' status through the modifiers גדולים (great) and אדירים (mighty), terms absent from the Pentateuch's description of the Transjordan kings indicated in vv. 19–20 below. By elevating their status, the psalmist exalts YHWH's standing; however great and mighty they were, YHWH is greater because he overcame them. Furthermore, the psalm heightens the depiction of God's ability in battle by failing to mention any human elements from his source. Moses, Aaron, and the Israelites are absent from the psalmist's rendition of events, and the psalm recalls the situation as though YHWH alone fought and killed mighty kings. This situation contrasts with Num 21:24–25, which recounts Israel working alone to secure a military victory over a Transjordan king.

לְסִיחוֹן מֶלֶךְ הָאֱמֹרִי כִּי לְעוֹלָם חַסְדּוֹ [19]

Sihon king of the Amorites, for his steadfast love is eternal

Following the general reference to great and majestic kings in v. 18, the present verse begins revealing their identities, the first being Sihon, king of the Amorites. In the psalmist's rendition of events, he was directly killed by God. The *lāmed* at the beginning of the verse here functions as a direct-object indicator, in a similar fashion to 2 Sam 3:30, וְיוֹאָב וַאֲבִישַׁי אָחִיו הָרְגוּ לְאַבְנֵר ("And Joab and Abishai his brother killed

---

23. See close reading for Ps 135:10.

Abner," see also Job 5:2).[24] Here, the psalm recalls events recounted in Num 21:23–24, when the Israelites defeated Sihon and took his land, ("Now וַיֶּאֱסֹף סִיחֹן אֶת־כָּל־עַמּוֹ וַיֵּצֵא לִקְרַאת יִשְׂרָאֵל . . . וַיַּכֵּהוּ יִשְׂרָאֵל לְפִי־חָרֶב Sihon had gathered all his people and went out against Israel . . . but Israel struck him with the edge of the sword," see also Deut 2:24–37).

וּלְעוֹג מֶלֶךְ הַבָּשָׁן כִּי לְעוֹלָם חַסְדּוֹ [20]

And Og king of Bashan, for his steadfast love is eternal

In addition to YHWH smiting Sihon, as recalled in the previous verse, he treats Og, the king of Bashan, in the same way. The psalmist in vv. 19–20 recalls events in Num 21:33–35, וַיֵּצֵא עוֹג מֶלֶךְ־הַבָּשָׁן לִקְרָאתָם הוּא וְכָל־עַמּוֹ לַמִּלְחָמָה אֶדְרֶעִי . . . וַיַּכּוּ אֹתוֹ וְאֶת־בָּנָיו וְאֶת־כָּל־עַמּוֹ ("and Og king of Bashan went out against them, him and all his people to battle at Edrei . . . and they [Israel] struck him and his sons and all his people," see also Deut 3:1–7). The fourfold repetition of מלך (king), appearing twice in the plural and twice in the singular, tightly unites vv. 17–20. This preoccupation with earthly kings and leaders—also witnessed in the specific mention of Pharaoh's destruction, as opposed to the destruction of the Egyptians—reflects an important issue the psalmist sought to address when writing the psalm: YHWH's dominance over earthly leaders. Together, Israel's battles against Og and Sihon represent the initial battles for the possession of Canaan. With respect to the other selected psalms, and indeed other historiographic psalms, only Psalm 135 mentions these two Canaanite kings.[25]

וְנָתַן אַרְצָם לְנַחֲלָה כִּי לְעוֹלָם חַסְדּוֹ [21]

And gave their land as an inheritance, for his steadfast love is eternal

As a climax to defeating the two aforementioned kings, YHWH redistributes their land as an inheritance. Repetition of ארץ (land) from v. 6, לְרֹקַע הָאָרֶץ עַל־הַמָּיִם ("to the one who stretches the land on the waters"),

---

24. It could be understood as an explicative *lāmed*, and thus interpreted as "namely" (see Jer 1:18; Exod 27:19; and also KB 2:508); or as a *lāmed* of emphasis, see 1 Chr 28:21, and KB 2:510. For understanding it as direct object marker, see the section on dating.

25. The fact that only two kings are mentioned may result from the psalmist's limited sources; he may have only had access to Torah manuscripts. Loewenstamm, *Evolution*, 40, argues that didactic texts employing early history primarily depend on the Torah.

A Love Never Ending

links God's function as creator of the earth to his role in apportioning it to his people. Thus, his actions are justified: because he created the land he can bestow it as he sees fit. Although the wording of v. 21 commonly appears in Deuteronomy,[26] the association with Deut 4:34–38 is particularly noticeable, לְהוֹרִישׁ גּוֹיִם גְּדֹלִים וַעֲצֻמִים מִמְּךָ מִפָּנֶיךָ לַהֲבִיאֲךָ לָתֶת־לְךָ אֶת־אַרְצָם נַחֲלָה כַּיּוֹם הַזֶּה ("To dispossess nations greater and mightier than you from before you, to bring you in, to give you their land as a possession, as it is this day," v. 38). Both instances portray God as the subject, and both describe the means by which he delivers Canaanite lands to Israel. From a reading of v. 21, the psalmist creates the illusion that only the lands of Og and Sihon were conquered and given to the Israelites, because the remaining conquest activities are omitted.[27]

נַחֲלָה לְיִשְׂרָאֵל עַבְדּוֹ כִּי לְעוֹלָם חַסְדּוֹ [22]

An inheritance to Israel his servant, for his steadfast love is eternal

Continuing from v. 21, the current verse identifies Israel as the object of God's giving. The emphatic repetition of נחלה (inheritance) creates a terrace pattern with the previous verse and reinforces the idea that God gave the land of the aforementioned kings to Israel as an inheritance,[28] a notion the psalmist may have sought to emphasize to his community. The word ישראל (Israel) recalls v. 11, וַיּוֹצֵא יִשְׂרָאֵל מִתּוֹכָם ("And he brought *Israel* from their midst"), and creates an inclusion surrounding events from God bringing his people out of one land to settling them into another. Additionally, the two intimate terms עמו ("his people," v. 16) and עבדו ("his servant") combined with third-person suffixes, form an inclusion around the present stanza. Together, vv. 21 and 22 create a climax for the stanza, and divert attention from the destruction of great kings to the resulting action: God's granting of the dead kings' land to his people. Two stylistic alterations individualize these verses: the terraced pattern, as opposed to regular parallelism;[29] and the change in

---

26. See close reading for Ps 135:12.
27. Cf. Ps 135:11.
28. See KB 2:687 for this nuance of the definition.
29. From the various functions of terraced parallelism prescribed by Watson, *Classical Hebrew Poetry*, 208–12, he suggests that the psalmist here employs the device to create tension (ibid., 209). "Regular" refers to A : B :: A : B parallelism as opposed to the A : B :: B : C pattern here.

verb form at the start of v. 21; up until this point the psalm has almost exclusively employed the active participle as opposed to the perfect.

שֶׁבְּשִׁפְלֵנוּ זָכַר לָנוּ כִּי לְעוֹלָם חַסְדּוֹ [23]

That in our lowly position he remembered us, for his steadfast love is eternal

Verse 23 opens a new section in the psalm that primarily summarizes the events narrated thus far.[30] Whilst Israel was in a low estate, YHWH remembered them. Placement of the phrase שבשפלנו ("that in our lowly position") first in v. 23, creates an instance of *casus pendens*[31] emphasizing the peoples' suffering. The relative particle ש has YHWH as its antecedent, since he is the primary subject in the psalm; it is he who remembered Israel in their low esteem. YHWH's ability to remember those in a low estate is reflected in Ps 138:6, כִּי־רָם יְהוָה וְשָׁפָל יִרְאֶה וְגָבֹהַּ מִמֶּרְחָק יְיֵדָע ("For YHWH is exalted and he sees the humble but the proud he knows from afar").[32] Like the other selected psalms, God's remembrance, זכר, represents here a positive action, and an expression of his faithfulness, as witnessed in Ps 105:8 concerning the maintenance of his promise to Abraham, זָכַר לְעוֹלָם בְּרִיתוֹ דָּבָר צִוָּה לְאֶלֶף דּוֹר ("He remembers forever his covenant, the promise he determined for a thousand generations"[33]).

וַיִּפְרְקֵנוּ מִצָּרֵינוּ כִּי לְעוֹלָם חַסְדּוֹ [24]

And set us free from our oppressors, for his steadfast love is eternal

Explicating[34] the previous verse, v. 24 enumerates exactly how God remembered Israel in their lowly position: he freed them, ויפרקנו, from

---

30. Not all agree with this assessment; Keil and Delitzsch, *Psalms*, 330, relate these words to the congregations own experience. Radak (see Cohen, *Psalms*, 211) understand זכר לנו ("he remembered us") as a reference to the Babylonian exile (as does Hamari, ibid., 209), which, in effect, describes a contemporaneous act of salvation for the psalmist. Others, such as Allen, *Psalms 101–150*, 299, see this statement as a summary of all God's deeds towards Israel's forefathers that have been recited in the psalm.

31. A change in syntax for emphasis where the main verb's position is moved from initial to secondary; see JM, §156.

32. See also Eccl 10:6, the only other instance in the Bible where it opposes מרומים ("exalted places"); *BDB*, 1050, along with KB 4:1632, also define a similar meaning.

33. See also Ps 78:38–39, and 106:45.

34. This constitutes a legitimate function of the *wāw* consecutive; see JM §118j.

their oppressors. Although the basic meaning of the root פרק is "to remove" or "to take away" as in Gen 27:40, it also bears the meaning of "to deliver" in certain texts such as Lam 5:8.[35] The deliverance reflects the use of the "general to specific" principle where the general remembrance (v. 23) materializes into a more specific deliverance. In the immediate context, מצרינו ("from our oppressors") represents a general reference to the enemies of the psalmist's generation, and of Israel's enemies as a whole. The graphical similarity of מצרינו to מצרים ("Egypt," v. 10), however, also creates a word play[36] recalling YHWH acting on behalf of his people to deliver them from Egypt.

נֹתֵן לֶחֶם לְכָל־בָּשָׂר כִּי לְעוֹלָם חַסְדּוֹ 25

He provides food to all creatures, for his steadfast love is eternal

Up until this point in the psalm, we have noted how God's steadfast love was expressed specifically to Israel in kindness, and to the other nations—the kings particularly—in defeat and destruction. Now, as if to correct any misconceptions that YHWH only relates harshly to other nations, the psalm recalls his provision to all men. The broadening perspective here, relating to all mankind, associates v. 25 with the second stanza that addressed specific acts of creation. In both instances, all mankind are affected as opposed to just Israel. Although v. 25 begins with an active participle, נתן (providing), it lacks the *lāmed* preposition that accompanied this form in earlier verses (e.g., vv. 4, 5, 6, 7, and 13). The verb itself, נתן, recalls v. 21, which records YHWH bestowing land to Israel, וְנָתַן אַרְצָם לְנַחֲלָה ("and he gave their land for a possession"). YHWH is remembered in the present verse for his steadfast love and provision to all flesh (כל בשר), which can be interpreted either as all men (Isa 49:26, 66:23; Job 34:15), or as all creatures, man and beast (Gen 8:17 and 9:11).[37] Almost by way of compensation, the psalmist

---

35. See KB 3:973–74.

36. A similar play on these forms appears in Ps 105:24, וַיֶּפֶר אֶת־עַמּוֹ מְאֹד וַיַּעֲצִמֵהוּ מִצָּרָיו ("And he multiplied his people greatly and made them stronger than his oppressors"); see chapter 2 for the close reading of this verse.

37. A notable contrast arises when comparing v. 25 with the remainder of the psalm. To be sure, the notion of God as a provider of food often accompanies his portrayal as the divine judge, apportioning punishments and rewards according to peoples' actions. This is apparent from passages such as Deut 10:18, עֹשֶׂה מִשְׁפַּט יָתוֹם וְאַלְמָנָה וְאֹהֵב גֵּר לָתֶת לוֹ לֶחֶם וְשִׂמְלָה ("serving judgment for the orphan and widow, and loving the stranger giving him food and clothing"), that directly associate the

now refers to God's ability to provide food. Within the psalm's immediate context, it is possible to read this as an allusion to YHWH's miraculous provision of bread and meat to the Israelites during their desert sojourn.[38]

הוֹדוּ לְאֵל הַשָּׁמָיִם כִּי לְעוֹלָם חַסְדּוֹ [26]

Proclaim thanks to El of the heavens, for his steadfast love is eternal

With respect to sentence structure, the last verse recalls the opening stanza via the phrase הודו ל ("proclaim thanks to"), which appeared in vv. 1–3. Repetition of this formula creates an inclusion with the opening, re-emphasizing the psalm's primary purpose: giving thanks to YHWH for his steadfast love. The psalmist's depiction of YHWH as אל השמים ("God of the heavens")[39] constitutes an apt description of the second stanza because it primarily recalls his activity in creating the heavenly bodies. The phrase also echoes other texts where God is remembered as the creator of heaven, such as Isa 42:5, כֹּה־אָמַר הָאֵל יְהוָה בּוֹרֵא הַשָּׁמַיִם ("Thus says God, YHWH who created the heavens"), which in turn hints towards deeds wrought during creation like those mentioned in vv. 5–9.

---

provision of food with judgment, and Ps 146:7, עֹשֶׂה מִשְׁפָּט לָעֲשׁוּקִים נֹתֵן לֶחֶם לָרְעֵבִים יְהוָה מַתִּיר אֲסוּרִים ("Working justice to the oppressed and giving bread to the hungry, YHWH frees the prisoners"), which similarly associates the two ideas. Taking this into consideration, Psalm 136 implies that those kings and nations struck by YHWH were somehow punished for transgressions they committed, as opposed to being innocently struck as part of YHWH's display of steadfast love towards Israel.

38. A further degree of compensation becomes evident if we accept the reference of "all flesh" as a recollection of all creatures created on the fifth and sixth days of creation. In light of this assumption, the psalmist returns to remind the reader of the rest of YHWH's works in creation (in addition to the previously mentioned heavenly bodies).

39. Andrews, "Yahweh," reveals three important facts about the term אל השמים: first, it was originally employed by the Persians to describe the highest authority in any given pantheon, and they used it to refer to the God of Israel; second, it was a title exclusively adopted for use in international communications; third, within national circles, the local name for the deity was used. With this information, one can see that the employment of this phrase complies with the more international stance the psalm asserts at its conclusion, mentioning the provision of food to all flesh.

MEANING

The perpetual repetition of כי לעולם חסדו ("For his loving kindness is eternal") inculcates the principal purpose of Psalm 136, a celebratory hymn of thanksgiving that rejoices in YHWH's eternal grace. Although no one would doubt the psalm's primary purpose, a need still arises to qualify the specific aspects of God's grace the psalm celebrates. The composition dedicates most of its verses, vv. 10–22, to the exodus tradition. Although Israel is the obvious recipient of God's grace within this pericope, the same cannot be said for the kings and peoples mentioned. Pharaoh and the Egyptians are struck (vv. 10, 15) by God, and he also strikes and kills both Sihon and Og (vv. 17–20). Due consideration should also be given to vv. 21–22 that assert the lands of the aforementioned individuals were bestowed to Israel as an inheritance. In view of these facts one must reconsider, or at least modify one's initial assessment of the psalm's purpose. Psalm 136 is a hymn of thanksgiving celebrating God's grace, but more specifically, it encourages its listeners to praise YHWH for his loving kindness that was directly aimed towards his people, with particular regard to the deliverance from Egypt and the bestowal of land as an inheritance.

Whether the psalmist intended to or not, a number of other themes arise from the composition in addition to the main purpose described above. One such theme concerns the establishment of God's relationship with creation, and more specifically with man. Compared with the other psalms discussed in this volume, only Psalm 136 independently speaks of God's generic relationship with mankind. In v. 25, the psalm depicts God as a provider for all creation. Although other historiographic psalms include the participation of other nations, they are stereotypically portrayed as aggressors to Israel. Contrasting this, Psalm 136 mentions a notably positive relationship between God and all mankind. Although it only consists of a single verse, it acknowledges the idea of YHWH as the God who is merciful to all nations. And yet, when we compare the number of verses detailing his grace to Israel with the verses dedicated to his steadfast love towards the nations, the grace shown to his people is obviously far greater.[40]

---

40. Whether intentional or not, the exclusive mention of the Transjordan suggests that Israel, irrespective of its size at the time of writing, had a legitimate claim to these territories.

DATE

Perhaps the most conclusive primary evidence for dating Psalm 136 stems from its choice of אל השמים ("God of the heavens") as an epithet for God, and ש as a relative particle. The close reading of v. 26 has already demonstrated the relative lateness of the former expression.[41] It originated in the Persian period and entered Israelite vocabulary after the exile. Although both ABH and SBH[42] attest to isolated instances of the particle ש without the particle in Psalm 135, it only appears within early texts influenced by the northern dialect. Taking into consideration this caveat, all appearances of the particle occur in relatively late texts: exilic or postexilic.[43] Consequently, one should assume that the psalm is either late, or possesses northern origins. Supporting the possibility of a late date is the psalm's use of the preposition ל as a direct object marker for the verb הרג, and the use of the *wāw + qatal* form וְנָתַן to indicate a past completed act in v. 21.[44]

Secondary evidence concerning Psalm 136's lateness stems from various scholars. Hoffman[45] argues for the late use of the verb רקע, even though it also appears in earlier texts such as Exod 39:3. Notwithstanding the later appearances of this word, plausible evidence for lateness arises when it is coupled with ארץ as the verb's object—depicting God spreading out the earth at creation. This combination is unique to the psalm as well as to Isa 42:5 and 44:24. Thus, one *could* argue that the two authors were influenced by phraseology prominent in the exilic/postexilic period. Certain scholars also view the interpretation of פרק ("to redeem" or "to rescue") as an example of Aramaic usage,[46] and consequently assume

---

41. Andrews, "Yahweh," 52, states, "The origin of the title, therefore, should be sought in the diplomatic terminology of the Persian administration." He also demonstrates that its distribution is unique to LBH (ibid., 45–49). Berlin, "Psalms," 1434, similarly deems it late, but for different reasons. She argues that it originated at a time when "God was not imagined as localized at the temple."

42. See, for example, Judg 5:7 and 2 Kgs 6:11.

43. As in Ezra 8:20; 1 Chr 5:20, 27:27; and Eccl 1:11.

44. For more information on these forms, see the dating of Ps 135.

45. See יציאת מצריים, 111–12.

46. The distribution of this root with the meaning of "deliver" certainly raises suspicion because it only appears in one other late text, עֲבָדִים מָשְׁלוּ בָנוּ פֹּרֵק אֵין מִיָּדָם ("Servants rule over us and there is none to deliver from their hand," Lam 5:8). The Aramaic usage of this word as "to redeem" is particularly pertinent in the Tgs, where it frequently describes the exodus, and God *redeeming* Israel from Egypt (see, *Tg. Neof.*

A Love Never Ending

direct influence from exilic or postexilic circumstances. Additionally, Keil and Delitzsch assert that שפל constitutes late vocabulary, although the distribution of the noun form—only in Eccl 10:6—casts some doubt on this assumption. The fact that Psalm 136 reflects a liturgical[47] composition also lends some weight to a late dating,[48] although it is not entirely dependable because liturgies may have been compiled before the exile. Evidence that should also be considered is the phrase כי לעולם חסדו ("for his loving kindness is everlasting") whose distribution raises suspicion of its lateness: Chronicles (x6), Ezra (x1), Pss 118 (x1), 106 (x1), and 107 (x1), and Jeremiah. With the exception of Jeremiah, all of the above texts date to either the exilic or postexilic periods.

The primary evidence discussed above, and the majority of secondary evidence, suggests a postexilic composition date for Psalm 136. The primary evidence alone suffices to determine a late date, and the secondary evidence further solidifies that position. Thus, it could be argued that Psalm 136 originates from between the late exilic and early postexilic era. On the whole,[49] biblical scholars agree on a late dating of

---

Deut 5:15; 26:8; Exod 6:6; 13:13; and Lev 25:25). In addition to the Aramaic usage, evidence also emerges from the Dead Sea Scrolls that reinforces the late understanding of פרק with a meaning of "to deliver," as in the phrase וילך בשבי וישלח לבן ויפרקהו ("and he went into captivity, and Laban sent and redeemed him," 4Q215 1–3, 2); see Martinez and Tigchelaar, *The Dead Sea Scrolls*, 1:454. Among biblical scholars, Keil and Delitzsch, *Psalms*, 330, attest to its lateness, claiming it is "the customary Aramaic word for redemption"; Allen, *Psalms 101–150*, 295 similarly agrees with this assessment. Together, the evidence presented here suggests that the vocabulary belongs to LBH.

47. Numerous scholars adduce this evidence as a conclusive sign of lateness; see for example Driver, *An Introduction*, 384–85; Fohrer, *Introduction*, 292; and Hoffman, יציאת מצריים, 111–12.

48. Mowinckel, *Psalms*, 2:85, asserts a late date, stating, "It may be due to later developments that Hymns occasionally give a more graphic and epic description of one of Yahweh's great works . . . or one of his qualities." Such a statement accords with the focus of Psalm 136 where a single aspect of God's steadfast love is celebrated. Gunkel also determines the psalm's lateness on intuitive grounds, claiming it uses "current models," and "lacks a rigid order," *Introduction to Psalms*, 64. Similarly, Berlin, "Psalms," 1434, argues for a date in the late exile stating, "These verses [23, 24] bespeak the exilic condition, the probable time of this psalm's composition."

49. The one notable exception is Norin, *Er Spaltete das Meer*, 145–47, who predominantly relies on the psalmist's use of sources, and his lack of adherence to fixed pentateuchal traditions to arrive at a pre-exilic date. He states: "Zudem deutet der durchweg positive Grundton des Psalms darauf hin, dass er schwerlich nach der Zerstörung Jerusalems entstanden sein kann." (Moreover, the thoroughly positive tone of the psalm infers that it can hardly have originated after the destruction of

SOURCES

The pentateuchal sources for Ps 136:11, 12, 19–20, and 21–22 all appear to be taken from Deut 4:34; 2:24—3:3; and 4:38 respectively. The phrase ביד חזקה ובזרוע נטויה ("with a strong hand and an outstretched arm") in Ps 136:12 frequently appears in Deuteronomy within portrayals of the exodus from Egypt, depicting the way in which God delivered Israel.[50] Additionally, the phrase appears in other literature influenced by Deuteronomy such as Jer 21:5 and 2 Chr 6:32. In the latter two books, however, the authors do not use the phrase in the same context as Deuteronomy (the exodus); instead they use it to depict a general portrayal of YHWH displaying his might. The words describing God leading his people through the desert in Ps 136:16, למוליך עמו במדבר ("to the one who led his people through the desert"), are well attested in Deuteronomy (see 8:2, 15, and 29:5 [4]), but entirely foreign to Numbers and Exodus within the same context.[51] Both Deuteronomy 2 and Numbers 21 recount the Israelites' battles against Og and Sihon. However, because the Deuteronomy account alone associates both battles as part of God's plan for land distribution, the likelihood remains that Deuteronomy inspired the psalmist's words. The previously listed Deuteronomic associations also concur with this assumption. With respect to the giving of land, the phrase לתת ארץ נחלה ("to give land as an inheritance") completes the Deuteronomic picture, appearing widely in Deuteronomy (e.g., 4:21, 4:38, 15:4, 19:14, and 24:4) and in Deuteronomic literature as fixed terminology for God bestowing Canaan as an inheritance to Israel.

Jerusalem). Norin's analysis, however, does not properly consider the appearance of LBH within the psalm, and this fact affects his final decision.

50. See Deut 5:15, 7:19, and 11:2; see also Childs, "Deuteronomic Formulae," which positively identifies this phrase with Deuteronomists. Appendix D compares the verses in the psalm and those in the sources.

51. Although the likelihood exists that these words were influenced by Deuteronomy, some doubts remain because of the general nature of the words, they are less confined to Exodus contexts.

A Love Never Ending

Further isolation of the psalmist's sources from Deuteronomy present more of a challenge because many of the phrases mentioned above appear in a variety of Deuteronomic texts. However, two texts from Deuteronomy, can be isolated with some certainty. The first is Deut 2:24—3:7, which details the Israelites defeating Sihon and Og.[52] The aforementioned verses constitute their only appearance in Deuteronomy. The second text is Deut 4:32–38, which contains a number of additional connections to our psalm. Psalm 136:12 contains the phrase ביד חזקה ובזרוע נטויה ("with a strong hand and an outstretched arm"), which also occurs in Deut 4:34, אוֹ הֲנִסָּה אֱלֹהִים לָבוֹא לָקַחַת לוֹ גוֹי מִקֶּרֶב גּוֹי בְּמַסֹּת בְּאֹתֹת וּבְמוֹפְתִים וּבְמִלְחָמָה וּבְיָד חֲזָקָה וּבִזְרוֹעַ נְטוּיָה ("or did God attempt to enter and take for himself a nation from amidst a nation by signs and wonders and by war *with a strong hand and an outstretched arm*"). Deuteronomy 4:34 also contains the idea of God taking one nation out of another, לָבוֹא לָקַחַת לוֹ גוֹי מִקֶּרֶב גּוֹי ("to enter and to take for himself a nation from the midst of a nation"), which is the same notion expressed in Ps 136:11 with the phrase וַיּוֹצֵא יִשְׂרָאֵל מִתּוֹכָם ("And he brought Israel from their midst"). Moreover, the idea of giving land to Israel as an inheritance is recorded in similar words in Deut 4:38, לְהוֹרִישׁ גּוֹיִם גְּדֹלִים וַעֲצֻמִים מִמְּךָ מִפָּנֶיךָ לַהֲבִיאֲךָ לָתֶת־לְךָ אֶת־אַרְצָם נַחֲלָה כַּיּוֹם הַזֶּה ("To dispossess greater and mightier nations than you from your presence, to bring you in and to give to you their land as a possession as it is this day"). Solidifying the above associations are two ideas that appear in both texts. The first is the recollection of YHWH's uniqueness with respect to his power and works. In Deut 4:35, it is expressed as כִּי יְהוָה הוּא הָאֱלֹהִים אֵין עוֹד מִלְבַדּוֹ ("For YHWH is God, there is no other besides him"), and in the psalm, the same idea is reflected in v. 4, לְעֹשֵׂה נִפְלָאוֹת גְּדֹלוֹת לְבַדּוֹ ("To the one who performs wonders and great deeds alone"). The second idea is the apparent importance of heaven. In Deut 4:36, heaven is the location from which God spoke to the people when he gave them the law, מִן־הַשָּׁמַיִם הִשְׁמִיעֲךָ אֶת־קֹלוֹ ("From heaven he made you hear his voice"), and Psalm 136 primarily recalls YHWH's creation of the heavens (see vv. 5–9), and portrays him as the God of the heavens (v. 26). In light of the above associations, Deut 4:32–38 comprises the most probable source for the psalm.

---

52. At this point, Deut 1:4 should not be considered because it only refers to the incident in passing, and does not detail the battle or subsequent land distribution.

Contrasting the clearly Deuteronomic quotes mentioned above, only one specific quote from Exodus can be identified with any degree of certainty.⁵³ Exodus 14:27 depicts God "overturning" (נער) the Egyptians into the sea, וַיְנַעֵר יְהוָה אֶת־מִצְרַיִם בְּתוֹךְ הַיָּם ("And YHWH *overturned* Egypt into the sea"). The *pi'el* of נער (overturning) appears three times in the Bible and only twice concerning the exodus: Ps 136:15 and Exod 14:27.⁵⁴ The verse in Exodus is traditionally split between the P (v. 27a) and JE (v. 27b) traditions; however, the sentence containing the verb נער appears in the second half of the verse, which is ascribed to JE. This fact alone, however, does not necessarily suggest that the psalmist bore no knowledge of Exod 14:27a. Overall, more so than any of the other selected psalms, Psalm 136 clearly receives most of its influences from a single source, Deuteronomy.

Process of Selection

As established earlier, the psalmist who composed Psalm 136 was primarily interested in creating a work for recital that recalled YHWH's acts of steadfast love towards his people. Consequently, it is relatively easy to see why certain incidents were selected from the exodus tradition to help enforce his message. The deliverance from Egypt and the sea, together with YHWH fighting against Og and Sihon in order to give their land to his people all reveal YHWH's steadfast love towards Israel. With this in mind, it is largely understandable why the psalmist omitted events concerning Israel's sojourn in the desert, since this period bears the hallmark of murmuring against God, and rebellion. Notwithstanding the overall tenor of the desert sojourn, two incidents from this period surprisingly have been omitted: the provision stories (of water, bread, and meat), and the battle with Amalek. The former may have been overlooked because of the negative images accompanying the acts, most notably the murmurings against God occurred in each account. Another reason why the psalmist may have omitted them is that YHWH's role as a warrior is absent from these accounts, yet common in the selections included by the psalmist. The omission of the Amalekite battle presents more of a mystery because it recalls an instance in which God fought for Israel. Two possible explanations

---

53. A legitimate claim that Ps 136:11 borrows from Exod 12:31 or 12:51 is plausible, but far from certain.

54. The other occurrence appears in Neh 5:13.

A Love Never Ending

for its omissions are: one, the psalmist may simply not have had access to this tradition; two, the negative association connected with the account—that Israel's battle with the Amalekites arose because Israel questioned the presence of God in their midst[55]—proved too much of a deterrent to the psalmist.

ALLUSIONS

Transjordan Conquest

Psalm 136's reuse of the Sihon and Og traditions presents an example of a biblical interpretation of an interpretation. YHWH's role in the Transjordan battles differs significantly between Deuteronomy 2–3 and Numbers 21. The Deuteronomic Sihon and Og narratives reuse[56] the Numbers 21 account with various alterations and additions, and Psalm 136 subsequently reuses this adapted account. Before continuing this examination, a few words must be said concerning Judges 11, which contains an account remarkably similar to our psalm.[57] Although Judges 11 contains an early rendition of the Transjordan conquest tradition, our psalmist probably did not depend on Judges because only Sihon is mentioned there, as opposed to Sihon and Og in Psalm 136, and also because our source analysis positively revealed Psalm 136's heavy dependence on Deuteronomy.

Just like Numbers 21, Deuteronomy recalls the Israelites' journey by the Sea of Reeds and their request for passage through the land of Edom and Seir. At this point Deuteronomy details the death of the last of Israel's former fighting men, those who failed to conquer Canaan on the first attempt. Additionally the Deuteronomic author excludes the battle with the Canaanite king of Arad. After skirting around Moab and Edom, both accounts retell the battles against Sihon and Og. Notwithstanding these similarities, Deuteronomy casts new light

---

55. See Rashi (Katzenelenbogen, ספר שמות, 215) and Zakovitch, מבוא לפרשנות פנים-מקראית, 37–38.

56. Concerning the lateness of the Sihon tradition in Deuteronomy in relation to Numbers, see Weinfeld, *Deuteronomy 1–11*, 173–78, and Clements, *The Book of Deuteronomy*, 307. The picture concerning the Og tradition is, however, slightly more obscure, see Weinfeld, *Deuteronomy 1–11*, 181.

57. Another similar account not included is the historical record found in Neh 9. This too records the story of Og and Sihon but was probably written after Psalm 136 and so cannot be considered a source.

on the situation. The battle with Sihon in Numbers appears incidental when compared with its Deuteronomy counterpart. Numbers recounts Israel's request for passage through Sihon's territory, and as a response he confronts them in battle. Deuteronomy, on the other hand, casts God as initiating the battle with Sihon, as part of the larger program of conquering and inheriting the land. The act of land-giving also features more prominently in Deuteronomy than Numbers, which recalls Israel's inheritance of this land as an offshoot of defeating Sihon's army. Moreover, we should note that Deuteronomy fails to mention the Israelites' sins, including the complaints against Moses (see Num 21:5), and even suggests that Israel was somehow purged of their sins after the last of the rebellious generation died. Overall one could summarize by saying that for the author of Deuteronomy, God is more active in the battles of the Transjordan, and that these conflicts mark the programmatic onset of Israel inheriting the land (see Deut 2:24).

Psalm 136, like Deut 2–3, intensely focuses on God's involvement in the battles for the Transjordan and the bestowing of land to Israel. The conception of God initiating the battle with both kings, however, evolves much further in the psalm. Instead of merely initiating the battle, God personally fights and defeats these kings. The interpretation between Deuteronomy and Numbers saw the introduction of God's role in the battle against Sihon, but here in the psalm, God's role is amplified again, and the role of men eliminated altogether. Additionally, the context in which the Transjordan battles are featured significantly differs in the two accounts. For the author of Deuteronomy, the defeat heralds the commencement of God's plan to give Israel the land of Canaan, and begins the Deuteronomic history, along with Joshua and Samuel, which continue to portray how the land was conquered. Contrasting this, Psalm 136 redeploys the same narrative towards the end of a sequence of events; indeed, one could say it constitutes the climax of God's benevolence to Israel.

Deliverance at the Sea

In Exodus, after Egypt pursues the Israelites into the *Yam Suf* seabed, YHWH instructs Moses to extend his arm over the sea so that the waters would return back over the Egyptians, their chariots, and their horsemen. After Moses obeys this command, the pursuing Egyptians attempt to flee from the water, but God then intervenes by hurling (וינער, 14:27)

them into the sea. The waters then return, and Pharaoh's horsemen, chariots, and soldiers are subsequently covered by the sea. Concerning the psalm's rendition of the incident, two differences are particularly notable. First, the psalm entirely removes Moses' role from the events, and it only remembers YHWH fighting on behalf of the Israelites. Second, the immediate context of Exodus seems more concerned with portraying a battle between YHWH and the Egyptians in general. In Exod 14:26, the waters return upon the Egyptians, at daybreak when the sea returns it was the Egyptians who fled and who were hurled into the sea by God. Pharaoh is mentioned, but only as a qualifier to the army, it was his army. Psalm 136:15 seems to raise Pharaoh's profile, placing him first in the list of those God hurled into the sea. By effecting this adjustment, the psalmist adapts the source to his purposes by portraying an earthly king battling against YHWH. Such a picture resonates with the later depictions of Og and Sihon, another two earthly kings, defeated by YHWH.

The Exodus

In Deut 4:25–28, Moses instructs the Israelites on how they should respond after they settle in the land, rebel against YHWH by committing idolatry, and are exiled by their enemies. If they seek God, obey him, and return to him, then he will remember the covenant he made with their fathers. While in captivity, they must inquire of the past, to the great things YHWH did for them in Egypt (מצרים, v. 34), taking for himself one nation out of another (גוי מקרב גוי) with trials and wonders and a mighty hand and outstretched arm (ביד חזקה ובזרוע נטויה). Moses explains that all this was done so that they might know YHWH alone is God. Deuteronomy 4:37–38 further states that because YHWH loved Israel's forefathers, he brought them out (ויוצאך) of Egypt to dispossess great nations (גוים גדולים) and gave the Israelites their land as an inheritance (לתת לך את ארצם נחלה).

In recounting the exodus from Egypt, Psalm 136 first recalls the plagues (v. 10) and then describes YHWH extracting his people from amongst the Egyptians (ויוצא ישראל מתוכם, v. 11), which was done with a mighty hand and outstretched arm (ביד חזקה ובזרוע נטויה, v. 12). The psalm proceeds to recall briefly the defeat of Pharaoh at the sea, and YHWH's guidance of Israel through the wilderness. God's work in the conquest is remembered as being against great (גדלים, v. 17) kings, as opposed to great nations, a change in line with depicting God's omnipotence over earthly rulers. After striking them, he bestows their land to his people for an inheritance (ונתן ארצם לנחלה . . . לישראל עבדו, vv. 21–22). Overall, Psalm 136 sits in a context of praise and appreciation for what God accomplished for his people, and how he has been gracious to them. The psalmist fails to recall Israel's idolatry that led to exile, as witnessed in Deuteronomy.

JUXTAPOSITION

Psalm 135–136

Psalm 135 begins with a call for all those standing in the temple to praise YHWH (vv. 1–3) for his goodness. The reasons given for his praise are that he selected Israel for a special possession, and that he is greater than all other gods (אלהים, v. 5). The following verses then boast of his ability to do (עשה, v. 6) anything he desires in any place: in heaven (שמים, v. 6) on earth (ובארץ, v. 6), in the seas (בימים, v. 6) or the depths. Verses 7–12 then cite examples of YHWH acting in creation and in the exodus. As a climax to his acts in the exodus, he strikes two kings and bestows their land to Israel. The following two verses (vv. 13–14) constitute an interjection of praise that lauds YHWH's eternal name and memory (זכרך, v. 13) because he vindicates his people. Verses 15–18 describe the idols of the nations and ultimately denounce them and those who worship and depend on them. The final three verses constitute an exhortation to bless YHWH that is addressed to various temple groups.

Both lexical and contextual similarities associate Psalm 135 with Psalm 136. Both psalms not only include historiographic material, but also address the same approximate era in Israel's literary history, the exodus. More specifically, they both contain allusions to creation, the conflict with the Egyptians, and the giving of land. Each psalm employs the "giving of land" motif as the final act of God's intervention in history, and they both neglect detailing any desert events, including the lawgiving at Sinai. With respect to the framework in which each song is presented, both are broadly set within a context of praise, responding to what YHWH has done for his people. Psalm 136 manifests this through the overt repetition of הודו ("give thanks") in vv. 1–3, implicitly echoed throughout the psalm, whereas Ps 135:19, 20 exhort various temple groups to bless YHWH on account of his previously recited works in history.

A consecutive reading of the two psalms reveals a broadening of perspective in relation to YHWH's attitude towards, and relationship with, his people and the nations. Psalm 135 restricts itself, exclusively recounting the positive aspects of YHWH's relationships to Israel, he chose them to be his people (v. 4), and continually intervenes in history to save them from their enemies (vv. 8–11). Contrasting this view, the remainder of mankind, the nations (גוים), are either portrayed as enemies of YHWH and his people, or idol worshippers. Psalm 136 expands such an outlook because it not only recognizes the intimacy of God's relationship with Israel, but additionally establishes YHWH relating positively to the rest of mankind (Ps 136:25).

The portrayal of *other gods* in Psalm 135 affects how the same notion is understood in Ps 136:2–3. Psalm 135:5 recalls the phrase כִּי־גָדוֹל יְהוָה וַאֲדֹנֵינוּ מִכָּל־אֱלֹהִים ("for great is YHWH, and our God [is greater] than all gods") but later on, the psalm details this expression by clarifying that these are not gods, אלהים, at all, but idols, עצבי הגוים ("idols of the nations," v. 15). Consequently, when one reads הוֹדוּ לֵאלֹהֵי הָאֱלֹהִים ("give thanks to the God of gods") in Ps 136:2–3, there is no need to admit the existence of other gods or deities because their real identities were explicated in the previous psalm: mere idols and the works of men's hands.

The words ארץ (land), שמים (heavens), and עשה ("he made") reveal two different aspects of creation in the two psalms, and a combination of the two ideas broadens our overall perspective on the nature of the earth's formation. Often it is considered a single event occurring at the dawn of time (see Gen 1:1) as Ps 136:5–6 indicates. Repetition of the above words in Ps 135:7, מַעֲלֶה נְשִׂאִים מִקְצֵה הָאָרֶץ בְּרָקִים לַמָּטָר עָשָׂה מוֹצֵא־רוּחַ מֵאוֹצְרוֹתָיו ("Raising the clouds from the ends of the earth, making lightening for the rain, and bringing the wind from his storehouses"), however, reveals that creation is also an ongoing process continually sustained by YHWH: he maintains that which he created, keeps the clouds moving and creates lightning for rain. Additionally, the notion of YHWH's ability to act as he pleases undergoes an expansion with respect to the word ים (sea). Psalm 135:6 mentions the sea as part of the domain in which he operates, an idea furthered in Ps 136:13–14. The latter verses demonstrate YHWH acting as he pleases in regard to the sea: he splits it in order to bring his people through on dry land, and transforms it into a weapon to destroy his enemies. Thus an abstract idea in one psalm is exemplified in its neighbor.[58]

Psalm 136–137

Words common to both Psalms 136 and 137 are prevalent in the Psalter and consequently fail to yield any plausible linguistic justification for the juxtaposition of the two psalms. Even though this fact negates any possibility of arrangement via lexical similarity, it is profitable to the global search for juxtaposition strategies. The fact that lexical similarity is not consistently employed as a strategy for positioning psalms in the Psalter provides us with a valuable benchmark for gauging common words between psalms. It is only when comparing the relationships of other historiographic psalms with this picture that we can fully appreciate the way in which the editors of the Psalter were influenced by common vocabulary in the arrangement of compositions. The relationship between Psalms 136 and 137 thus serves as an example of psalms that have not been positioned according to lexical similarity. In simple terms, this is an example of the proverbial "exception that proves the rule."

Although an analysis of lexical similarities fails to provide a satisfactory rationale for the juxtaposition of Psalms 136–137, their contents suggest a more convincing explanation for sequencing. The placement of Psalms 136 and 137 reflects an editor's desire to juxtapose two familiar themes: God's historical deeds of deliverance (encompassing his supremacy and ownership of all creation), and a cry for deliverance. Psalm 136, as witnessed in the close reading, lucidly depicts God's acts of power in addition to his rights over creation. Complementing this, Psalm 137 consists of a cry for help by a people undergoing oppression (vv. 1–3), and a call for God to take vengeance upon Israel's enemies (vv. 7–9). Psalm 89 reveals the same pattern. God's deeds are first recounted: he ruled the swelling of the sea (v. 10), crushed Rahab and scattered the enemy (v. 11), and owns all creation (v. 12). Building on

---

58. The idea of exemplifying an abstract notion with a concrete example constitutes one of the defining points of *Midrash*; see Sarason, "Midrash," 155–56. In addition to the lexical associations mentioned above, Ps 135:10–12 appropriates material from Ps 136:17–21. The section on allusions in the previous chapter has already addressed this matter.

A Love Never Ending

this foundation, the psalm continues by portraying the oppressed state of those reciting the psalm and, more importantly, cries for help pleading: "how long will you hide your face" (v. 47). A similar juxtaposition of ideas emerges in Psalm 44, which begins with Israel remembering the deeds God had performed in days of old (v. 2), and how he planted their fathers in the land and drove out the previous inhabitants (v. 3). Verse 10 describes YHWH as forsaking the community and delivering them to their enemies. Later, v. 26 depicts them prostrate in the dust, and the following verse explicitly enumerates their cry for help. This sequencing is reversed in Psalm 77. God's works of deliverance in the past appear at the end of the psalm, but they still constitute the basis from which the psalmist can find solace from his distress, which is enumerated in the first half of the composition.[59]

---

59. See also Psalms 40 and 106 for similar examples of this type of juxtaposition.

6

Conclusions

With the examination of the selected psalms complete, it is necessary to return now to the questions posed at the beginning of the study concerning the psalmists' use of the exodus motif and the editors' placement of the selected compositions. The first of the following four sections addresses the questions concerning the sources employed by the psalmists, their nature, and their arrangement. The second section explores various characteristics of the psalmists and editors' work on the sources. Afterwards the wider issues regarding the psalmists' use of, and interaction with, the exodus motif are considered.

Before beginning with the discussion of sources, a few words need to be said concerning the diachronic order of the psalms in this study. With the date established for each of the selected psalms, it is possible to order them as follows: 106, 136, 105, and 135; with Psalm 106 representing the earliest composition and Psalm 135 the latest. Psalm 106 appears earliest because it was written early during the exile, and Psalm 105 postdates Psalm 136 because the former relies on relatively late traditions. Additionally, the author of Psalm 105 apparently utilized a text that contained evidence of a late emendation.[1] Furthermore, chapter 4 lucidly demonstrates Psalm 135's extremely late origins. The aforementioned ordering potentially indicates an emerging trend between the purposes of the psalms and the dates in which they were composed. Psalmists writing later in the postexilic era apparently employed the exodus primarily for purposes of praise and worship, as reflected in Psalms 136, 105, and 135; whereas, authors tended to emphasize more negative aspects of the tradition—employing the motif to reprimand

---

1. See close reading for Ps 105:15, particularly the section on sources for this composition.

Conclusions

and warn their audiences about the consequences of disobedience—in earlier psalms, such as Psalm 106.[2]

THE PSALMISTS' SOURCES

Biblical Sources

Regarding the exodus tradition, most of the selected psalms' material originated from the Torah, with Exodus and Numbers constituting the primary data pool. In certain instances, the psalmists turned to Deuteronomy,[3] and on even fewer occasions, they employed texts from Leviticus. For the most part, the legal material in the Torah was not relevant to the psalmists' needs. As for the literary genres quoted from the Torah, no specific preferences concerning poetic or narrative material are evident. Poetic traditions from Deuteronomy 32 and Exodus 15 appear as important to the psalmists as prose traditions from Exodus 1–14, 16–21, and Numbers 11–14, 16, 20–21, and 25. In isolated situations, psalmists took advantage of biblical traditions outside of the Torah to recount exodus events. Psalm 135:10–12 relies on the neighboring Ps 136:17–22 for recounting the defeat of the Transjordan kings Og and Sihon. In light of Psalm 135's lateness, one cannot say with certainty why the psalmist failed to utilize the Torah for data concerning these events. One possible reason is that he deliberately sought to link his work with its neighbor, and achieved the association by reusing a section of its text.[4] Despite a relatively strict dependence on the Torah for the majority of the exodus period, Psalm 105 turns to the poetry of Isaiah, particularly Isaiah 48 and 51, to recount the exodus from Egypt. Such a deviation mirrors the psalmist's postexilic context in which the return to the land of Israel from Babylon aptly reflects the original entrance into Canaan. Instead of recalling the journey from Egypt to the promised land, the psalmist opted to recount the journey via allusions to Isa 51:9–11, which depicts the exodus from Babylon. For the same

---

2. Though not included in the present study, early psalms such as Psalms 78, 81, and 95, support this theory because they all employ the exodus motif as a warning. Moreover, the postexilic composition Psalm 114 employs it for praise.

3. See for example Ps 135:14 (Deut 32:36) and Ps 136:2–3 (Deut 10:17).

4. He may thus have sought this association to correct a position held by Psalm 136; see below. Furthermore, the literary associations with the preceding composition, Psalm 134, strengthen the probability.

reason, the "water from the rock" tradition in Ps 105:41 recalls Isa 48:21 more than the Torah traditions recounting the same events.[5]

In addition to Pentateuchal sources, the examination of the selected psalms uncovered numerous occasions in which the psalmists apparently adopted *alternate traditions*: a plagues' tradition in Ps 105:28–36,[6] a tradition of divine shelter provided by a cloud in the desert (Psalm 105:39); human sacrifice during the initial conquest period (106:37–38); and possibly a rebellion at the Reed Sea (106:7).[7] Unfortunately, precisely defining the nature of such traditions proves overwhelmingly problematic; they could either constitute written accounts in the psalmists' corpus that are no longer available, or, more likely, oral traditions that were never committed to writing. It is apparent, however, that the earliest psalm, 106, more readily adopts such accounts; whereas, the later psalms generally avoid them. This observation suggests that psalms containing a high degree of quotations from texts closely resembling MT more likely originate from a later era than those frequently employing alternate traditions. A heuristic such as this cannot be adduced as primary evidence when engaged in dating psalms, but should be considered valuable secondary evidence.

To varying degrees, each of the selected psalms alludes to biblical traditions other than the exodus. The two later psalms, Psalms 135 and 105, reflect this tendency. Psalm 105 frequently alludes to Genesis because of its concern with the promise of land to the patriarchs, and God's preservation of that promise through subsequent generations. Psalm 135, on the other hand, alludes to an extensive range of texts throughout the composition, most notably Psalms 134 and 136:17–22. Additionally, on two different occasions, the author of Psalm 106 adopts texts from Ezekiel 20 and 22, to strengthen the notion of intercession (22:30), and to link God's denying Israel access to Canaan during the exodus with the psalmist's present exilic reality (20:23).

---

5. Psalm 106:9 also apparently uses Isa 63:9–13 for its rendition of the wilderness tradition.

6. Here there is some doubt because the alterations in the psalm may stem from a reworking of the Exodus tradition. (see also Psalm 78:44–51)

7. Although it is not related to the exodus tradition wisdom's role in creation (Ps 136:5) should also be considered.

Conclusions

The Documentary Hypothesis

Due to the limited scope of the present study, it is difficult to assert any firm conclusions concerning the proposed sources to the Pentateuch as they appear in the selected psalms. The primary limitations stem from the study's focus on the exodus motif, as opposed to other Pentateuchal traditions found within the selected works. Consequently, more source data could be uncovered relating to other Torah traditions excluded from the present study, e.g., creation and the patriarchal narratives. In spite of the aforementioned limitations, however, at least one tentative conclusion can be drawn from Psalm 106. The data from Psalm 106 suggests the sources of the proposed Documentary Hypothesis were already considered a unified and continuous text at the time of the exile when the psalm was composed. Clear evidence of P appeared in the psalm along with JE and D. Moreover, concerning the interlaced nature of sources in Psalm 106, one can conclude the Song of the Sea was already merged with the exodus narrative by the time of the exile. Psalm 106's blending of the two literary units supports this deduction.

The Arrangement of the Source Material

Examination of the selected psalms reveals that the various writers were not particularly concerned with preserving the order in which events occurred. For the psalmists, the greater concern apparently lay in the desired impact of their message. Perhaps the clearest example of this phenomenon occurs in Ps 135:4–9, which recalls the selection of Israel (v. 4) before the plagues (vv. 8–9). Because the psalm is relatively late, it is logical to assume that the psalmist knew that the selection of Israel chronologically occurs *after* the plagues were first wrought to deliver the Israelites from Egypt. Thus, even though the psalmist knew the ordering of events, he altered this sequencing to achieve a particular desired impact. Further evidence of reordering appears in Psalm 105. The psalm's date and its reliance on the Torah for the patriarchal narratives not only suggest that the psalmist knew the order of the plagues in Exodus, but that he deliberately chose to reorder them in his work. In this instance, the desired impact may have been to position the plagues with respect to their severity. Consequently, the author placed darkness first because he deemed it less severe than the other plagues. Similarly, the plagues of blood, frogs, and lice were not detrimental to the Egyptians' health and were thus positioned early in the sequence. The hail and locust appear next because they destroy the crops, thus bearing a more direct and adverse affect on man by causing starvation. The degree of escalation concerning these judgments also surfaces in the psalmist's choice to represent these plagues with two verses instead of one, as with the earlier plagues. The final level of escalation appears in the striking of the firstborn, the only plague to cause physical harm to the Egyptians, according to the psalmist.

Another possible motivation for reordering the plagues may have been the order of creation. Consequently, the psalmist would have moved darkness to the first position to resonate with God removing darkness by creating light as the first act in creation. Similarly, the last act in the plagues, the smiting of the firstborn, would correspond with God's final work in creation, man. Thus, the plagues essentially function as an undoing of the created order. In both of the scenarios mentioned above, the author's source tradition was altered. Numerous instances of reordering also arise within Psalm 106's rendition of rebellions during the wilderness period. It is possible to understand this rearrangement in terms of escalating severity. Thus, the least severe rebellion of wanton desires occurs first, and the possible sign of its triviality is reflected in the obscure nature of the ensuing punishment. Although it still constitutes an act of rebellion, it pales in comparison to the detestable acts of child sacrifice recalled at the end of the psalm.[8]

ASPECTS OF INTERPRETATION

The present study has revealed that a variety of circumstances and motivations inspired the psalmists and the editors of the Psalter to alter the meaning of their source traditions. The psalmists utilized sources consisting of verses and texts from the Bible, whereas the Psalter's editors

---

8. A few doubts arise concerning Psalm 106 because it is not certain that the traditions in the psalmist's possession reflected those in MT; consequently, he may have inserted the material in the order of his source. The concept of a book as we know it today, a bound collection of accounts arranged in historical order, is not necessarily what the biblical psalmists would have had at their disposal; see Barton, "Intertextuality." The psalmist may simply have possessed an unbound collection of traditions lacking any chronological order. Consequently, the order in which they occur in the psalm may indeed reflect the order in which the psalmist had them. Notwithstanding this, the previously quoted examples clearly reveal instances in which the psalmist ordered events to resonate with his purposes.

Conclusions

used the completed psalms as source texts. The more salient examples of alterations in meaning are discussed below. Before addressing the changes effected by the psalmists, however, it should be noted that the psalmists also adduced their source material to strengthen and reinforce specific points in their compositions.⁹ The most outstanding examples appear in Psalm 106, where the theme of intercession is particularly high on the psalmist's agenda. As part of that program, he includes multiple allusions to instances in which a lone individual represents Israel before God and successfully intercedes on their behalf, turning away YHWH's anger. One instance of this phenomenon occurs in v. 23, where Moses successfully staves off God's wrath after Israel worships a golden calf. This allusion primarily recalls the Torah's rendition of events. In order to strengthen the idea of intercession, however, the author adopts the term עמד בפרץ ("to stand in the gap") from Ezek 22:30, where God seeks an intercessor to stand in the gap for the nation. In this instance, the psalmist recalls both texts to strengthen the importance of intercession within the psalm. Another instance, again reinforcing the idea of intercession, appears with Psalm 106's use of the phrase ותעצר המגפה ("and the plague was stopped") in v. 30. As seen from the close reading in chapter 3, this phrase alludes to two instances of intercession to enrich a single event in his composition. First, it recalls the act of Phinehas, who stopped the plague through his actions in Numbers 25. Second, the same words recall Aaron's intercession on Israel's behalf to halt a plague that broke out as a result of Korah's revolt in Num 17:15.¹⁰

---

9. This is, perhaps, the most well known function of biblical allusion; see Watson, *Classical Hebrew Poetry*, 302–3.

10. The degree to which the various psalmists preserved the wording from their sources varies significantly—assuming, of course, that the text forming the source closely reflects MT. Psalm 135 presents the strictest examples of word-form and word-order preservation. Psalm 135:7's use of Jer 10:13 virtually preserves every single word from the source. A similarly precise replication of sources appears in v. 14, which recalls Deut 32:36 (see also Ps 105:1's use of Isa 12:4). Psalm 135:1 also replicates all of the words from the source (Ps 113:1), but the psalmist slightly alters the word order. At the opposite end of the spectrum, we find instances in which scant lexical replication exists, if any at all, between the source and the psalm. Psalm 105:12–15 refers to instances within the patriarchs' lives when they faced mortal danger. Although no doubts arise concerning the allusion, only a few lexical markers appear that allude to a wide range of texts. For the most part, the psalmists' preservation of words from their sources falls between the two aforementioned extremes, and even though they generally sought to preserve key lexical items in their sources, they felt at liberty to adjust them as various needs arose.

From Bards to Biblical Exegetes

Removal of Derogatory Information

Often psalmists felt compelled either to remove or at least modify source data that they deemed derogatory or excessively disparaging towards individuals, groups, or the general tenor of a composition. Psalm 105 refrains from recalling any hint of rebellion during the desert-wandering period. The picture presented by the psalmist consists of a journey from Egypt to Canaan in which Israel only experiences joy and celebration, and never grumbles or complains at any stage. It was necessary for the psalmist to present such a picture of Israel because at the end of the psalm, the condition for God's kindness towards them becomes clear: they are to obey his laws. Had the psalmist introduced rebellion into the psalm during the desert wandering period, the impact of its *raison d'être* would have been severely compromised.[11] In Psalm 106, Aaron is not mentioned in the rebellion at Meribah (vv. 32–33),[12] and although Israel's esteemed leader, Moses, falls under condemnation, the psalmist is tangibly sympathetic to his cause. In the source, both Aaron and Moses are condemned for dishonoring YHWH's name when they perform his instructions in bringing water from a rock. For this, YHWH punishes both by forbidding them entrance into the promised land. In Psalm 106's rendition, Israel shares in the burden of guilt since they *cause* Moses to sin, thus removing a degree of responsibility from him. Also in Ps 106:16–18 is an instance in which the psalmist omitted Korah from the list of perpetrators in Dathan's rebellion. As noted in chapter 3, such a move was probably undertaken to protect the ecclesiastical Second Temple school that bears his name (see Pss 47:1, 48:1, and 49:1).

The Torah records YHWH's covenant with Israel as a conditional agreement; only when Israel complies with his statutes are they eligible to receive the blessings it affords, including the privilege of being called a "treasured possession" among all peoples. The psalmist apparently views the conditional nature of this promise negatively with regards

---

11. See the section in chapter 2 that discusses the process of selection.

12. Other alternatives exist for interpreting the omission of Aaron from this event. The psalmist may only be including Moses because he was the one who spoke to the Israelites (Num 20:10), and the psalm specifically alludes to the fact that the crime was verbal. Additionally, one could argue that the psalmist is exercising a degree of harmonization whereby texts such as Deut 1:37 and 3:26, which reflect Moses being punished on behalf of the people, have influenced his wording. In light of Psalm 106's respect for Phinehas and the priestly Korahite school, however, it is more reasonable to suggest that the psalmist deliberately omitted Aaron from this incident.

to the purposes of Psalm 135; in v. 4, which alludes to Deut 7:6, he exclusively recalls the positive covenantal aspects: that Israel *is* God's treasured possession. The relationship between Israel and YHWH, in contrast to the nations and their idols, constitutes a key theme in Psalm 135, and thus to introduce a potential weakness in the God–Israel relationship (Israel's unfaithfulness to YHWH's ordinances) would mollify the impact of the psalmist's message. Another avoidance of negative data arises from the contextual change found in Ps 135:14. This verse originally belonged to a disparaging text in Deut 32:37 that derided Israel for its unfaithfulness to God, and lauded his faithfulness towards them irrespective of their religious infidelity. From such a negative background, the psalmist adopted a single verse and relocated it to fit a context in which God unconditionally vindicates his people and avenges their enemies.[13]

Exalting the Role of God

The psalmists also effected additions and alterations designed to exalt further the role YHWH adopts[14] in the source texts. One method employed by the psalmists to achieve this is to modify a *simple* verb form in the source to a *causative* form in the psalm. An example of this arises in Psalm 105's portrayal of Israel's rapid growth while in Egypt. The source, Exod 1:7, recalls a simple multiplication that occurs naturally, without YHWH's direct intervention, פָּרוּ וַיִּשְׁרְצוּ וַיִּרְבּוּ וַיַּעַצְמוּ; Ps 105:24, however, specifies that God actively multiplied them (וַיֶּפֶר) and strengthened their numbers (וַיַּעֲצִמֵהוּ). In performing this change, the psalmist adapted the source to the framework of the psalm, reflecting YHWH's omnipotence in every event, whether good or bad. YHWH is responsible for summoning the king to release Joseph from prison

---

13. Although it does not form part of the exodus tradition, we can add Psalm 105's recitation of the Joseph narrative to these examples. The psalmist employs a passive form (נמכר, "was sold") in Ps 105:17's recollection of Joseph's brothers selling him to a group of Midianite/Ishmaelite traders (see close reading for this verse). In doing so, the psalmist masked the identity of those who sold Joseph—his brothers. Within the psalm's context, Israel and the patriarchs are all viewed positively, and an instance such as the sale of one's own brother into slavery would disparage the nation's founding fathers; consequently, the psalmist adapted the material before him to comply with the psalm's tenor.

14. For a detailed discussion of this topic, see Seeligman, "גבורות האדם."

(105:20), but also accountable for calling a famine on the land (v. 16), and causing the Egyptians to hate his people (v. 25).

The identity of Israel's leader throughout the desert era is also the subject of alteration. In the Torah, this role usually involves a combination of YHWH, Moses, and Aaron; however, YHWH alone assumes the task in the selected psalms, as Pss 105:37; 106:9; 136:11–12, 14, and 16 demonstrate. In a similar vein, battles that are fought and won by the Israelites and YHWH together in the source texts are recast, with the psalmist portraying them as though YHWH alone went forth to defeat Israel's enemies, as with the destruction of Og and Sihon recorded in Ps 136:19–20.[15]

Addressing Perceived Discrepancies in the Sources

At certain junctures during their recitation of exodus events, the psalmists apparently sought to address potential difficulties in their sources, and in doing so influenced its reading. Psalm 135:11's rendering of Ps 136:19–20 adds two words of clarification to the source. The latter psalm only recounts God's work in conquering the Transjordan, bestowing them to his people as an inheritance. By way of correction, when the same text appears in Psalm 135, it contains an addition confirming that *all* of the lands of Canaan, both east and west of the Jordan, were conquered and bestowed to Israel as an inheritance. This addition arose because the author of Psalm 136 apparently limited himself to working with the Pentateuch. As a result of this limitation, he only reports on events up until the end of his source material, the Transjordan conquest. The author of Psalm 135, who drew upon a wider range of sources, was able to expand this picture and include a reference to other Canaanite lands. In another example, we see a degree of ambiguity arising in Numbers concerning the eruption of a plague stemming from Israel's idolatry with Baal Peor. The end of the plague is recorded in Num 25:8, but no record exists of its beginning. Psalm 106:29 addresses

---

15. In addition to God's role being highlighted, there are occasions in which the role of men is similarly exalted. Psalm 105:26 refers to Aaron as being the chosen one of God (בחר), a title he never explicitly receives in the Torah sources. Psalm 106:16 similarly portrays Aaron as the holy one of YHWH (קדוש יהוה). In the same psalm, Phinehas' act of intercession (vv. 28–31) is attributed to him as righteousness, where the specific designation of an act to an individual as righteousness (ותחשב לו לצדקה) was previously reserved for Abraham when he believed God's promise to him (Gen 15:6).

Conclusions

this issue by suggesting it broke out as a result of YHWH's anger soon after the idolatry started. Yet another example of this phenomenon arises with Psalm 105's rendition of the plagues' narrative in Ps 105:28–36, which evidently reorders and reduces the plagues from Exodus. In doing so, the psalmist creates a fluid account that avoids difficulties raised in the source concerning the deaths of *all* the cattle on three separate occasions—during the plagues of pestilence, hail, and striking of the firstborn.[16]

Evidence of Editorial Activity in Arrangement

Before examining how the editors and arrangers of the Psalter sought to influence the meaning of the individual psalms, the literary building blocks from which they worked, it is first prudent to review the indications of deliberate positioning. This study reveals clear signs of purposeful arrangement by uncovering instances of rare words and phrases found between juxtaposed psalms,[17] clusters of more common words repeated between the psalms,[18] similar themes,[19] and chronological sequencing.[20] Before reviewing examples of the above, it is important to recall that Psalms 136 and 137 fail to exhibit repeated words or phrases linking the two works together. This fact alone strengthens the argument that in the forthcoming examples, the existence of such phenomenon is not incidental.

---

16. Another example of psalmists adapting their sources' traditions to address a perceived lacuna deserves mention here, even if it does not include the exodus motif. The account of Joseph in Psalm 105 explains why he had to suffer at the hands of the wicked. The psalm implies that the suffering was necessary in order to purify and test Joseph in some way, preparing him for the task that lay before him.

17. See, for example, Rofé, מבוא לשירה המזמורית, 21, who quotes the example of מלאך יהוה ("Angel of the Lord") as a deciding factor in the juxtaposition of Psalms 34 and 35; and Keil and Delitzsch, *Psalms*, 21, who classify this phenomenon as "external association."

18. Cassuto discusses this phenomenon, which concerns a number of biblical texts (see "Sequence and Arrangement" and "The Arrangement of the Book of Ezekiel").

19. See Keil and Delitzsch, *Psalms*, 21, who suggest that the theme of "sacrifice" links Psalms 50 and 51.

20. Nasuti, "Sequence and Selection," specifically raises this as a potential strategy in the organization of certain psalms; and as a general principle for organization; see Rofé, "The Arrangement," who adduces the arrangement of the Torah and Deuteronomic history as evidence of this rationale.

From Bards to Biblical Exegetes

With respect to rare words, Pss 105:23, 27, and 106:22 constitute the only two places in the Bible containing the phrase ארץ חם ("the Land of Ham"). Psalm 106 further links with Psalm 107 via the word ישימון, which occurs four times in the Psalter, but is only found in juxtaposed psalms here (Pss 106:14 and 107:4). Also linking these psalms is the phrase מרה עצה ("to rebel against advice"), which, with respect to the Hebrew Bible, only appears in Pss 106:43 and 107:11. Just like the rare words and phrases, certain groups of words similarly appear together in juxtaposed psalms. The words, יהוה, שמח, שיח, זמר, and שיר, (YHWH, rejoice, meditate, make music, and sing) appear together at the end of Psalm 104 and the beginning of Psalm 105, creating a smooth transition between the two works. Additionally, Psalm 135 links to Psalm 134 via the phrases ברך יהוה מציון, עבדי יהוה עמדים בבית יהוה, ברך את יהוה, and עשה שמים וארץ ("bless YHWH, servants of YHWH standing in the house of YHWH, bless YHWH from Zion, and maker of heaven and earth"), and also connects with Psalm 136 through vv. 10–12, which more or less replicate 136:17–22.[21]

Concerning common themes, it is no coincidence that each of the selected psalms, broadly speaking, juxtaposes another psalm containing the exodus motif. As we have already witnessed, Psalm 105 sits next to 106, and 135 next to 136. Such broad associations, however, form only a small part of the connections between the psalms. At this point, it should be noted that the ordering of the aforementioned psalms is

---

21. Concerning the potential degree of influence the editors and arrangers may have had on individual psalms, there are three possible scenarios. First, the psalms may have remained unaltered during the process of arrangement. The editor would then have selected psalms sharing common vocabulary from a vast repository of poetry, and juxtaposed them when compiling his collection of compositions. Second, it is possible that in selecting psalms for inclusion into a smaller assemblage, the arrangers possessed the authority to alter certain words within the psalm in order to forge a stronger association with its neighbors. Thus, they would have actively sought to change isolated words in each psalm to create, or accentuate connections to the juxtaposed psalms. Third, some of the Psalter's arrangers were themselves psalmists and poets who wrote certain compositions as a response to works with which they were previously familiar; thus, they actively created compositions in order to address issues in older works, or expound themes they deemed important in established psalms. Within this scenario, the arrangers would have possessed the freedom to borrow vocabulary and motifs from certain psalms and rework them into their own composition, addressing problems or developing ideas as they saw fit. Although none of the aforementioned possibilities is mutually exclusive, the results patently suggest the Psalter's editors and arrangers acquired an intimate familiarity with the songs in their available corpora, and positioned them with deliberate plans and purposes in mind.

chronological, that is to say, the second of the juxtaposed works usually contains later historiographical data than its predecessor, although some overlap might exist.

On a wider scale, another sign of editorial activity concerns the positioning of Psalms 105 and 106. These compositions appear together at the end of Book IV and represent the only exodus psalms mentioning Moses' role in the proceedings.[22] The positioning of these psalms here represents an apparent desire by an editor to complete an inclusion around Book IV. Psalm 90 opens Book IV with a mention of Moses in the title, and Psalms 105 and 106 close the book with another mention of Israel's esteemed leader.[23]

Motivations for Juxtaposing Psalms

From the evidence presented in the selected psalms, there are three possible motivations that influenced the Psalter's editors and arrangers to juxtapose psalms. First, the arranger may have sought to correct or influence the meaning of another work. Evidence of this appears in the positioning of Psalms 135 and 136. The former describes the nature of foreign gods as idols that are impotent, wielding neither power nor breath. This knowledge sets the tone for Psalm 136, which acknowledges the existence of other gods. The very phrase לאלהי האלהים ("to the God of gods," v. 2) suggests at least two tiers of gods—lesser deities and YHWH himself who presides over such deities. By first reading Psalm 135, the arranger demonstrates to the reader the exact nature of such gods; in reality they are merely idols.

Second, the juxtaposition of psalms functions as a tool for addressing implicit or explicit questions arising from a particular work.[24] For example, Psalm 106 consists of a confession of sins, and a plea to YHWH for deliverance from exile; it closes with a request for him to gather the exiles from the nations in which he has scattered them, וְקַבְּצֵנוּ מִן־הַגּוֹיִם, ("And gather us from the nations," v. 47). The implicit question arising from this composition is: "How did God respond to the plea?" Following this psalm, Psalm 107, a song of thanksgiving, distinctly states that God has gathered people from foreign lands, וּמֵאֲרָצוֹת

---

22. See section on juxtaposition for Psalm 106.

23. See the discussion on the Book of Moses in the Excursus.

24. This idea is by no means new; Zakovitch, "Juxtaposition," cites examples from the Abraham narratives.

קִבְּצָם מִמִּזְרָח וּמִמַּעֲרָב מִצָּפוֹן וּמִיָּם, ("And from the lands you have gathered them, from the east, from the west, from the north and from the south [literally, the sea]," v. 3). By placing them in this particular order, the editor uses the latter psalm to answer a question in the former.

Third, juxtaposition of psalms permits the development of ideas and themes. The positioning of Psalms 104–106 exemplifies this idea. A consecutive reading reveals a development in historical continuity from creation (Psalm 104) through to the exodus, up to the southern kingdom's exile (Psalm 106). In a similar vein, the juxtaposition of Psalms 134 and 135 develop the idea of praise. The first one, only three verses long, exhorts the listeners to praise God but fails to detail any of his works.[25] As a logical development to this, Psalm 135 continues by listing numerous factors that exalt YHWH over the gods of the nations, and thus provides a rationale for worshiping him.

・・・

Among the activities performed by the psalmists and redactors mentioned throughout the present study are lucid examples of inner-biblical interpretation, the process by which a biblical author knowingly and actively influences the meaning or perception of his source text when transferring it into a new context.[26] Each psalmist would have read and understood his source one way, and, to varying degrees, altered the meaning when rewriting it. As shown, sometimes these alterations were relatively minor, and at other times they were more significant. The earlier paragraphs of the current section demonstrate that the editors and redactors of the Psalter employed a similar process of interpretation. Instead of using individual verses from a repository of biblical literature, however, the editors of the Psalter drew from complete psalms. Although they were probably limited in their ability to alter their source material, they still apparently changed isolated words and phrases, and positioned their sources in such a way as to affect their readers' understanding of the text. Thus, both the psalmists and the

---

25. These two concepts are often found together in hymns; see Gunkel and Begrich, *Introduction to the Psalms*, 26–34.

26. McKenzie, "Inner-Biblical Interpretation," 338, similarly defines inner-biblical interpretation as, "The process of reuse, reinterpretation, and reapplication of previous texts from within the Hebrew Bible." His definition clearly resonates with the examples mentioned above.

editors of the Psalter should be classified as biblical exegetes, and their works be defined as inner-biblical interpretation.

THE PSALMISTS' USE OF THE EXODUS MOTIF

Shared Conceptions of the Exodus

In addition to the numerous alterations and adaptations made by the psalmists, each author also held fundamental conceptions about the exodus motif. Irrespective of how these ideas were expressed in individual psalms, each composer recognized three aspects of the exodus motif: first, it was a miraculous event in which YHWH intervened directly into the realms of men; second, the benefits of the intervention were exclusively bestowed to Israel; third, the interventions on Israel's behalf were undeserved.

Concerning the miraculous and supernatural acts in the exodus, each author recognized that they were initiated by YHWH as an expression of undeserved favor. The desired response to this undeserved favor varied for each work. Psalm 136, for example, used it to encourage gratitude and induce an attitude of praise, whereas Psalm 105 employed it to encourage obedience. Although each psalmist used it for a different purpose, the element of undeserved kindness is nevertheless ever-present. Regarding the relationship between these acts and the nation of Israel, each of the selected works reflects, to one degree or another, that God performed the deeds exclusively for the sake of his people. The psalms portrayed in this study patently reveal that the exodus was an event benefitting Israel only, and other nations are therefore portrayed as enemies and obstructers of YHWH's plans for his people. For the most part, the role of the other nations was reflected by Egypt and the Canaanites, but Psalm 105 also alludes to individuals such as Laban and the king of Gerar. In every instance, however, the non-Israelites are constantly portrayed as being rebuked, plagued, or killed.

The Relationships between the Psalmists and the Exodus

In each of the selected compositions, the psalmists sought to be associated and identified with the exodus generation. A lucid example of the close association between the psalmists and their generation and the exodus generation appears in Psalm 106. Within this composition, the psalmist conceives a timeless continuum and chain of behavior that began with the Israelites' stay in Egypt, and continued through to his present reality. No distinction arises between the desert generation and his own, a fact made evident by v. 6, חָטָאנוּ עִם־אֲבוֹתֵינוּ הֶעֱוִינוּ הִרְשָׁעְנוּ ("we have sinned with our fathers, we have committed iniquity, we have acted wickedly"). Here, the first-person common plural verbs closely associate the psalmist's sinful generation with their transgressing forefathers. For the psalmist, all of Israel, past and present, is united together as a people who inherently rebel against God in spite of all he does for them. Because of the psalm's confessional purposes, it was essential for the psalmist to link intimately all of Israel's generations in this way.

Implications of the Exodus

Although the relationships between the psalmists and their audiences vary between the psalms, the events of the exodus are significant in each composition and carry concrete implications. Such implications are reflected in each psalm's purpose. Because the close reading performed in the body of the research has already detailed the purposes of each composition, only a brief summary is presented here.

In Psalm 105, because YHWH had employed supernatural acts to deliver Israel from Egypt and lead them to Canaan, it was incumbent upon the psalmist's generation to obey all of God's commands as a response to the benevolence YHWH showed the psalmist's forefathers. In Psalm 106, the exodus constituted a history of sin and rebellion that began in Egypt and continued to the psalmist's day. As a result, the psalmist himself stood before God, as Moses and Phinehas had, to confess the sins of his generation in the hope that YHWH would show himself merciful and return Israel from captivity. YHWH's past faithfulness and mercy forms the basis of the psalmist's plea for the nation's deliverance. Psalm 135 employed the exodus as an example of God's omnipotence and supremacy over the gods of the nations. YHWH's dominance over creation generally, and Israel's enemies specifically, were starkly contrasted with the inabilities of the nations' idols. For the psalmist, here, the biggest implication came to his generation: in light of the comparison, they now were forced to choose whom they should serve. In the last of the selected psalms, Psalm 136, the past events of the exodus primarily formed the basis for God's eternally merciful disposition towards his people Israel and for motivation of the psalmist's generation to praise God for what he has done. In each instance cited

Conclusions

above, a lucid cause-and-effect relationship appears between the events of the exodus and the psalmist and his generation.

The Exodus as a Didactic Motif

From the research on the selected psalms, it is reasonable to conclude that three of the psalmists have employed the exodus motif as a means of imparting wisdom to its readers (only Psalm 136 lacks associations to wisdom literature). Thus, the selected psalms can, to a certain degree at least, be associated with Wisdom literature. Within the context of this study, the term is used in its broadest sense to refer to literature that provides a guide by which its readers may conduct their lives.[27] Within such literature, according to Clifford, the authors "sought to instruct the next generation, to solve specific problems . . . hand on ancestral traditions."[28] Although the degree to which three of the selected psalms correspond to the above definition vary, the associations are nevertheless evident.

Psalm 105 contains scant vocabulary specifically linked to wisdom traditions. In spite of this, its overall message resonates with wisdom ideals.[29] Psalm 105 teaches Israel why YHWH manipulated individuals, nations, and creation to grant them the land of Canaan. However, these were conditional acts; Israel also had a responsibility to obey his laws. Consequently, it is possible to understand the psalm as an incentive to live righteously, according to God's laws. Psalm 106 only contains a single word, אשרי (blessed, v. 3), associating it to Wisdom literature, but it employs the exodus motif as a negative behavioral example demonstrating an ungrateful response to God's benevolence. Because the psalm lucidly demonstrates that persistent disobedience ultimately leads to exile, the psalm serves as an incentive to contemporaneous and future generations to be fully obedient to God's laws and to always remember the miraculous deeds he performed on their behalf by responding accordingly.

---

27. See Fohrer, *Introduction*, 313–14, who describes Psalm 78's connection to wisdom literature in these terms.

28. See Clifford, "In Zion and David," 8. According to this broad definition, all of the selected psalms could be described as wisdom literature because they all hand down ancestral traditions to future generations.

29. Incidentally, both Fohrer, *Introduction*, 313–15, and Eissfeldt, *The Old Testament*, 125, include Psalm 105 as belonging to the genre of Wisdom poetry.

Finally, Psalm 135 bears the weakest association to Wisdom literature, and yet its message, particularly with regards to its structure, resonates with wisdom ideals. Via a comparison between the abilities of YHWH and those of the nations' idols, the psalm presents its listeners with a choice. They must decide whether to choose YHWH, and be blessed as a result, or choose the idols of the nations, that are impotent and whose followers are as useless as them (v. 18). In presenting the readers with this choice, the psalm recalls the two paths of the righteous and the wicked that often appear in Wisdom literature. The righteous ultimately progress to a blessed future, whereas the wicked are destined for destruction. Perhaps the best example of these destinies appears in Psalm 1, which similarly recalls the fates of the wicked and the righteous (those who follow YHWH) as an incentive to obedience. Although Psalm 135 is not specific in employing the terminology of Wisdom literature, the connection is nevertheless evident.

Restricted Usage of the Exodus Motif

At this point, it is only appropriate to mention two purposes for which the exodus motif is *not* used. The first constitutes the antithesis of what we have already discussed with regard to the shared conceptions of the exodus. Just as the psalmists all conceived the exodus as a community affair, it is worthwhile mentioning explicitly that the event is never employed to state or describe a process that takes place in the life of an individual. Although it may initially seem strange that an author would take a community event and transform it to apply to an individual, this exact process takes place in later literature. In the New Testament, clear echoes of the exodus tradition that relate to a corporate experience are adopted and applied to Jesus individually.[30]

Second, and perhaps more surprising, is that the exodus motif never adopts an eschatological meaning for the psalmists. This is more surprising because in the Second Temple period there was an intense atmosphere of messianic expectation,[31] and the inauguration of a messianic kingdom. Admittedly, a very slight eschatological theme can be detected from Psalm 105's merging of the Egyptian exodus with the Babylonian exodus. Realistically, however, the psalmist is simply

---

30. See Matt 2:15, which alludes to Hos 11:1 describing God leading Israel out of Egypt.

31. See Mitchell, "Lord Remember David," 529.

Conclusions

reflecting his own historical reality in which God has already been faithful in returning the remnants of Israel to their land. In the New Testament again, however, elements of the Exodus plagues' tradition are recast into a context describing future events. Revelation 16 recalls: sores (v. 2), the sea turning to blood (v. 3), darkness (v. 10), frogs (v. 13), and hail (v. 21).

Relationships between Creation and Exodus

Because none of the selected psalms exclusively depends on the exodus motif, a number of other motifs and allusions to other biblical traditions frequently arise. The most prominent of these is creation, which should not come as a total surprise because biblical literature frequently unites the two.[32] With respect to the selected psalms, associations with the creation motif appear in different formats with varying degrees of intensity. In Psalm 105, the first hint of the motif appears in the psalmist's reorganization of the plagues into a sequence that partially reflects the creation order. By placing darkness first and the killing of the firstborn last, the psalmist recalls the order of God first dispelling darkness, and forming man last during the six days in which God established the earth. Another link to creation concerns the placement of Psalm 104—a psalm celebrating YHWH's work in the event—immediately before Psalm 105, an exodus psalm. In this instance, an arranger of the Psalter forged the nexus. Psalm 135:7 explicitly details God's work in founding the earth, although the specific aspect of creation differs from the previous example because it depicts YHWH's ongoing work, raising clouds and making lightning for the rain. Like Psalm 135, Psalm 136 additionally includes a reference to creation within the body of the psalm. The latter psalm devotes five verses to the motif, vv. 5–9, as opposed to one, and references God's primordial work in creation.

---

32. Often in biblical literature authors portray the events of the exodus, especially the crossing of the sea, in terms reminiscent of a creation myth. The description found in Psalm 77, before the amendment in the last verse, relates first to creation, but was adjusted to create an exodus psalm. Concerning Psalm 77:16–19, Tate, *Psalms 51–100*, 275, states, "The language of v. 17 reflects the ancient motif of a divine struggle with chaotic forces in bringing forth creation." Similar examples of authors combining these motifs occur in Exod 15:5–10; Isa 51:9–11; 63:12–14; and Ps 114:3–5 (concerning Psalm 114, see Allen, *Psalms 100–150*, 142). Furthermore, Nehemiah 9 directly links the two themes in a single prayer.

With the associations between creation and the selected psalms established, a more pressing question arises: how do the psalmists use creation to support the exodus motif? In Psalm 105, the creation motif supports the idea of an unraveling of the cosmic order that YHWH initiated against Egypt. Although the plagues are depicted in a relatively harmless manner in this psalm, the depth and meaning of the work YHWH performed is intensified because he is portrayed as reversing the creation order against the Egyptians. Instead of setting order to chaos, as in the creation account, he returns their land to primordial chaos by removing the rules that define and maintain the created order in their lives. This imagery enhances the plagues' narrative and demonstrates the extent to which God was willing to act on behalf of his people: he was willing to undo creation for their sake. For the redactor, the further association between Psalms 104 and 105 sets the exodus events, as well as the earlier patriarchal narratives, into its correct historical context. Moreover, it strengthens the comparison between the order instigated in creation and the disorder wrought in the lives of the Egyptians as a result of the exodus.

In Psalm 135, the psalmist recalls God's work in creation in what could be described as part of a *curriculum vitae* listing YHWH's achievements. Adding to those achievements, the psalmist cites YHWH's work in the exodus to exemplify God's power and abilities. Such credentials constitute a critical part of the psalmist's work as he constructs a case to emphasize and prove YHWH's might and superiority over the idols of the nations. Thus, for the psalmist, creation represents an act of power and might that is comparable to that of the exodus, establishing YHWH's preeminence among the gods. Another function of creation in Psalm 135 is to serve as a warrant for God's further actions in the psalm. By including the fact that YHWH bears sole responsibility for sustaining the created order, the psalmist justifies God's authority to apportion land as he sees fit, e.g., bestowing the land of Og and Sihon to Israel as an inheritance (Ps 135:12).

Just as the creation story in Genesis can be understood as setting a literary stage for the events of the exodus, it also creates a background for the exodus events in Psalm 136. By partially recounting creation events, ending with the creation of nocturnal celestial bodies, the psalmist creates a nighttime scene that recalls the night that the angel of death passed through the midst of Egypt smiting their firstborn.

Conclusions

Thus, the darkness of night constitutes a literary nexus between the two motifs and establishes the setting for the striking of Egypt's firstborn. Additionally, the inclusion of creation extends the timeframe covered in the composition. Instead of recalling acts from the exodus to the psalmist's era, God's works are described as reaching all the way back to the dawn of time. In extending the temporal framework, the psalmist better conveys the eternal aspect of God's grace, the primary purpose for writing the psalm.

Rejected Traditions

A notable observation concerning the psalmists' use of the exodus is that they fail to recall all of the accounts and secondary motifs included in Israel's deliverance and the desert wandering period.[33] At this point, one can only hypothesize potential reasons for these omissions. With respect to the rebellion instigated by Aaron and Miriam against Moses in Numbers 12, its omission is relatively easy to understand because it did not constitute an instance of national rebellion, but an isolated incident in which Aaron and Miriam worked alone. A similarly understandable omission concerns that of Bilaam and Balak in Numbers 22–24. Within this narrative, Israel does not actively participate in events, and the incident unfolds without their knowledge of it.

With regards to Israel's complaining in Numbers 21 that led to the people being punished by God with poisonous snakes, it is possible to see how this narrative would resonate with the message of Psalm 106, which recalls instances of national rebellion. However, the reason for its omission probably relates to the means of Israel's deliverance, the bronze snake. Throughout the psalm, idolatry constitutes a sin that is heavily denounced (see Ps 106:19–23, 28–31, 34–42); consequently, it seems counterproductive for the psalmist to mention an image resembling an idol as a means of Israel's deliverance.

Although an allusion to the provision of water in the desert appears in two of the selected psalms, none of them recalls the incident at Marah (Exod 15:22–26), when the bitter waters were made potable through the intervention of Moses and God. Two possible reasons exist to explain why an author would fail to recall it. First, the account is not presented as a serious instance of rebellion, but as a test that God

---

33. See the introduction for a list of the main secondary motifs.

designed to encourage the Israelites to trust him for future assistance. As such, it is not entirely suitable for Psalm 106, which focuses on national rebellion. Second, the event is portrayed more as a *natural* phenomenon. Moses, albeit through God's direction, solves the problem of an undrinkable water supply by throwing wood into the river. This incident is far less dramatic and indicative of divine power than that of YHWH causing an abundant water supply to materialize from a dry rock in the desert.

When one reads the exodus tradition as it appears in the Pentateuch from beginning to end, perhaps the most dominant aspect of the account is the lawgiving at Sinai, during which the physical descendants of Abraham enter into a covenant with YHWH, and the nation of Israel receives its legal and cultic rules for establishing its society in the promised land. In many ways, this incident constitutes the crux of the Pentateuchal account. However, none of the selected psalms specifically narrates the event—the process in which God presents the covenant agreement to Israel and they agree to its terms. Yet it is evident that the lawgiving at Sinai was known to each of the psalmists because faint reflections of it appear in three of the selected psalms (Psalms 105, 106, and 135). In spite of this, the event does not dominate the various psalmists recital of events.

Israel's battle with Amalek (Exod 17:8–16), which never appears in the selected exodus psalms,[34] is notable because opportunities arise in which the battle could have been successfully employed in at least one psalm. On one hand, it could be viewed positively as an example of YHWH assisting Israel in battle, even though his presence during the incident is somewhat muted.[35] Consequently, we would expect to see the account in Psalms 105, 135, or 136. On the other hand, one could interpret the event as a punitive measure by God to punish the

---

34. In fact, none of the exodus psalms recalls the incident.

35. The text alludes to God's presence when it depicts Moses ascending a hill with the staff of God (מטה האלהים, 17:9) in his hand. Additionally, at the end of the incident, God declares future vengeance on the descendants of Amalek. Cassuto, *A Commentary*, 204, also interprets God as fighting for his people in Exodus 17, stating: "The purpose of this passage is to show that just as the Lord was concerned to deliver the children of Israel from every danger to which they were subjected by the forces of inanimate nature, even so He was concerned to deliver them from the power of human beings who rose up in hostility."

Conclusions

Israelites for doubting his presence among them (Exod 17:7).[36] Within this scenario, Psalm 106 could have adopted the account to contribute towards the picture of Israel's persistent rebellion and punishment. In either event, one would expect at least an allusion to the tradition in one of the psalms.

The final omission concerns the account of the God-fearing midwives in Exod 1:15–21. Rather than obey Pharaoh's command to kill all of the male Hebrew children, the midwives preserve them, and YHWH subsequently rewards their actions. This omission is notable because the account does appear among the sectarian writings of Qumran. The scroll 4Q422[37] extensively utilizes Psalms 78 and 105 to retell the exodus, including a reference to the midwives account. Of all the psalms examined in this study, Psalm 105 was best suited for the inclusion of account because it emphasized the protection of the patriarchs and Israel from numerous forms of harm. Yet the psalmist failed to include it in his composition. One can only speculate that the psalmist's overwhelming emphasis on depicting YHWH's acts for Israel caused him to exclude an account in which the efforts of man enabled deliverance for God's people.

---

36. For proponents of this view, see Rashi (see Katzenelenbogen, ספר שמות, 215), followed by Zakovitch, מבוא לפרשנות פנים-מקראית, 37–38.

37. This scroll, also known as *4QParaphrase of Genesis and Exodus*, recounts a series of events from creation through to the striking of the Egyptians' firstborn. Among the more notable incidents it includes are: the creation of the world, the fall, the flood, the righteous midwives, the commissioning of Moses, and the plagues. In addition to Genesis and Exodus, as mentioned above, the scroll also relies on Psalms 78 and 105 for its recital of events. See Martínez, *The Dead Sea Scrolls*, 2:855–56.

Appendix A

Psalm 105

וַיָּבֹא יִשְׂרָאֵל מִצְרָיִם וְיַעֲקֹב גָּר בְּאֶרֶץ־חָם	Ps 105:23
וְאֵלֶּה שְׁמוֹת בְּנֵי יִשְׂרָאֵל הַבָּאִים מִצְרָיְמָה אֵת יַעֲקֹב אִישׁ וּבֵיתוֹ בָּאוּ	Exod 1:1
וַיֶּפֶר אֶת־עַמּוֹ מְאֹד וַיַּעֲצִמֵהוּ מִצָּרָיו	Ps 105:24
וּבְנֵי יִשְׂרָאֵל פָּרוּ וַיִּשְׁרְצוּ וַיִּרְבּוּ וַיַּעַצְמוּ בִּמְאֹד מְאֹד וַתִּמָּלֵא הָאָרֶץ אֹתָם	Exod 1:7
הָפַךְ לִבָּם לִשְׂנֹא עַמּוֹ לְהִתְנַכֵּל בַּעֲבָדָיו	Ps 105:25
וַיֻּגַּד לְמֶלֶךְ מִצְרַיִם כִּי בָרַח הָעָם וַיֵּהָפֵךְ לְבַב פַּרְעֹה וַעֲבָדָיו אֶל־הָעָם וַיֹּאמְרוּ מַה־זֹּאת עָשִׂינוּ כִּי־שִׁלַּחְנוּ אֶת־יִשְׂרָאֵל מֵעָבְדֵנוּ	Exod 14:5[1]
שָׂמוּ־בָם דִּבְרֵי אֹתוֹתָיו וּמֹפְתִים בְּאֶרֶץ חָם	Ps 105:27
וַאֲנִי אַקְשֶׁה אֶת־לֵב פַּרְעֹה וְהִרְבֵּיתִי אֶת־אֹתֹתַי וְאֶת־מוֹפְתַי בְּאֶרֶץ מִצְרָיִם	Exod 7:3
שָׁלַח חֹשֶׁךְ וַיַּחְשִׁךְ וְלֹא־מָרוּ אֶת־(דְּבָרוֹ) [דְּבָרָיו]	Ps 105:28
וַיֹּאמֶר יְהוָה אֶל־מֹשֶׁה נְטֵה יָדְךָ עַל־הַשָּׁמַיִם וִיהִי חֹשֶׁךְ עַל־אֶרֶץ מִצְרָיִם וְיָמֵשׁ חֹשֶׁךְ	Exod 10:21
הָפַךְ אֶת־מֵימֵיהֶם לְדָם וַיָּמֶת אֶת־דְּגָתָם	Ps 105:29
וַיַּעֲשׂוּ־כֵן מֹשֶׁה וְאַהֲרֹן כַּאֲשֶׁר צִוָּה יְהוָה וַיָּרֶם בַּמַּטֶּה וַיַּךְ אֶת־הַמַּיִם אֲשֶׁר בַּיְאֹר לְעֵינֵי פַרְעֹה וּלְעֵינֵי עֲבָדָיו וַיֵּהָפְכוּ כָּל־הַמַּיִם אֲשֶׁר־בַּיְאֹר לְדָם וְהַדָּגָה אֲשֶׁר־בַּיְאֹר מֵתָה	Exod 7:20–21
שָׁרַץ אַרְצָם צְפַרְדְּעִים בְּחַדְרֵי מַלְכֵיהֶם	Ps 105:30
וְשָׁרַץ הַיְאֹר צְפַרְדְּעִים וְעָלוּ וּבָאוּ בְּבֵיתֶךָ וּבַחֲדַר מִשְׁכָּבְךָ וְעַל־מִטָּתֶךָ וּבְבֵית עֲבָדֶיךָ וּבְעַמֶּךָ וּבְתַנּוּרֶיךָ וּבְמִשְׁאֲרוֹתֶיךָ	Exod 8:3 [7:28]
אָמַר וַיָּבֹא עָרֹב כִּנִּים בְּכָל־גְּבוּלָם	Ps 105:31
וַיַּעַשׂ יְהוָה כֵּן וַיָּבֹא עָרֹב כָּבֵד בֵּיתָה פַרְעֹה וּבֵית עֲבָדָיו וּבְכָל־אֶרֶץ מִצְרַיִם תִּשָּׁחֵת הָאָרֶץ מִפְּנֵי הֶעָרֹב	Exod 8:24 [20]

---

1. Even though this verse speaks of slightly different circumstances, the common words still forge a viable link between the Psalm and the Exodus events recorded. See also the quote from Exod 7:3 below.

Appendix A

וַיַּעֲשׂוּ־כֵן וַיֵּט אַהֲרֹן אֶת־יָדוֹ בְמַטֵּהוּ וַיַּךְ אֶת־עֲפַר הָאָרֶץ וַתְּהִי הַכִּנָּם בָּאָדָם וּבַבְּהֵמָה כָּל־עֲפַר הָאָרֶץ הָיָה כִנִּים בְּכָל־אֶרֶץ מִצְרָיִם	Exod 8:17 [13]
נָתַן גִּשְׁמֵיהֶם בָּרָד אֵשׁ לֶהָבוֹת בְּאַרְצָם וַיַּךְ גַּפְנָם וּתְאֵנָתָם וַיְשַׁבֵּר עֵץ גְּבוּלָם	Ps 105:32-33
וַיַּךְ הַבָּרָד בְּכָל־אֶרֶץ מִצְרַיִם אֵת כָּל־אֲשֶׁר בַּשָּׂדֶה מֵאָדָם וְעַד־בְּהֵמָה וְאֵת כָּל־עֵשֶׂב הַשָּׂדֶה הִכָּה הַבָּרָד וְאֶת־כָּל־עֵץ הַשָּׂדֶה שִׁבֵּר	Exod 9:25
אָמַר וַיָּבֹא אַרְבֶּה וְיֶלֶק וְאֵין מִסְפָּר	Ps 105:34
וַיַּעַל הָאַרְבֶּה עַל כָּל־אֶרֶץ מִצְרַיִם וַיָּנַח בְּכֹל גְּבוּל מִצְרָיִם כָּבֵד מְאֹד לְפָנָיו לֹא־הָיָה כֵן אַרְבֶּה כָּמֹהוּ וְאַחֲרָיו לֹא יִהְיֶה־כֵּן	Exod 10:14
וַיֹּאכַל כָּל־עֵשֶׂב בְּאַרְצָם וַיֹּאכַל פְּרִי אַדְמָתָם	Ps 105:35
וַיְכַס אֶת־עֵין כָּל־הָאָרֶץ וַתֶּחְשַׁךְ הָאָרֶץ וַיֹּאכַל אֶת־כָּל־עֵשֶׂב הָאָרֶץ וְאֵת כָּל־פְּרִי הָעֵץ אֲשֶׁר הוֹתִיר הַבָּרָד וְלֹא־נוֹתַר כָּל־יֶרֶק בָּעֵץ וּבְעֵשֶׂב הַשָּׂדֶה בְּכָל־אֶרֶץ מִצְרָיִם	Exod 10:15
שָׂמַח מִצְרַיִם בְּצֵאתָם כִּי־נָפַל פַּחְדָּם עֲלֵיהֶם	Ps 105:38
תִּפֹּל עֲלֵיהֶם אֵימָתָה וָפַחַד בִּגְדֹל זְרוֹעֲךָ יִדְּמוּ כָּאָבֶן עַד־יַעֲבֹר עַמְּךָ יְהוָה עַד־יַעֲבֹר עַם־זוּ קָנִיתָ	Exod 15:16
שָׁאַל וַיָּבֵא שְׂלָו וְלֶחֶם שָׁמַיִם יַשְׂבִּיעֵם	Ps 105:40
וַיֹּאמֶר יְהוָה אֶל־מֹשֶׁה הִנְנִי מַמְטִיר לָכֶם לֶחֶם מִן־הַשָּׁמָיִם וְיָצָא הָעָם וְלָקְטוּ דְּבַר־יוֹם בְּיוֹמוֹ לְמַעַן אֲנַסֶּנּוּ הֲיֵלֵךְ בְּתוֹרָתִי אִם־לֹא	Exod 16:4
פָּתַח צוּר וַיָּזוּבוּ מָיִם הָלְכוּ בַּצִּיּוֹת נָהָר	Ps 105:41
וְלֹא צָמְאוּ בָּחֳרָבוֹת הוֹלִיכָם מַיִם מִצּוּר הִזִּיל לָמוֹ וַיִּבְקַע־צוּר וַיָּזֻבוּ מָיִם	Isa 48:21
וַיּוֹצִא עַמּוֹ בְשָׂשׂוֹן בְּרִנָּה אֶת־בְּחִירָיו	Ps 105:43
וּפְדוּיֵי יְהוָה יְשׁוּבוּן וּבָאוּ צִיּוֹן בְּרִנָּה וְשִׂמְחַת עוֹלָם עַל־רֹאשָׁם שָׂשׂוֹן וְשִׂמְחָה יַשִּׂיגוּן נָסוּ יָגוֹן וַאֲנָחָה	Isa 51:11

Appendix B

Psalm 106

וַיִּגְעַר בְּיַם־סוּף וַיֶּחֱרָב וַיּוֹלִיכֵם בַּתְּהֹמוֹת כַּמִּדְבָּר	Ps 106:9
מוֹלִיכָם בַּתְּהֹמוֹת כַּסּוּס בַּמִּדְבָּר לֹא יִכָּשֵׁלוּ	Isa 63:13
וַיּוֹשִׁיעֵם מִיַּד שׂוֹנֵא וַיִּגְאָלֵם מִיַּד אוֹיֵב	Ps 106:10
בְּכָל־צָרָתָם (לֹא) [לוֹ] צָר וּמַלְאַךְ פָּנָיו הוֹשִׁיעָם בְּאַהֲבָתוֹ וּבְחֶמְלָתוֹ הוּא גְאָלָם וַיְנַטְּלֵם וַיְנַשְּׂאֵם כָּל־יְמֵי עוֹלָם	Isa 63:9
וַיְכַסּוּ־מַיִם צָרֵיהֶם אֶחָד מֵהֶם לֹא נוֹתָר	Ps 106:11
וַיָּשֻׁבוּ הַמַּיִם וַיְכַסּוּ אֶת־הָרֶכֶב וְאֶת־הַפָּרָשִׁים לְכֹל חֵיל פַּרְעֹה הַבָּאִים אַחֲרֵיהֶם בַּיָּם לֹא־נִשְׁאַר בָּהֶם עַד־אֶחָד	Exod 14:28
וַיַּאֲמִינוּ בִדְבָרָיו יָשִׁירוּ תְּהִלָּתוֹ	Ps 106:12
וַיַּרְא יִשְׂרָאֵל אֶת־הַיָּד הַגְּדֹלָה אֲשֶׁר עָשָׂה יְהוָה בְּמִצְרַיִם וַיִּירְאוּ הָעָם אֶת־יְהוָה וַיַּאֲמִינוּ בַּיהוָה וּבְמֹשֶׁה עַבְדּוֹ אָז יָשִׁיר־מֹשֶׁה וּבְנֵי יִשְׂרָאֵל אֶת־הַשִּׁירָה הַזֹּאת לַיהוָה וַיֹּאמְרוּ לֵאמֹר אָשִׁירָה לַיהוָה כִּי־גָאֹה גָּאָה סוּס וְרֹכְבוֹ רָמָה בַיָּם	Exod 14:31; 15:1
וַיִּתְאַוּוּ תַאֲוָה בַּמִּדְבָּר וַיְנַסּוּ־אֵל בִּישִׁימוֹן	Ps 106:14
וְהָאסַפְסֻף אֲשֶׁר בְּקִרְבּוֹ הִתְאַוּוּ תַּאֲוָה וַיָּשֻׁבוּ וַיִּבְכּוּ גַּם בְּנֵי יִשְׂרָאֵל וַיֹּאמְרוּ מִי יַאֲכִלֵנוּ בָּשָׂר	Num 11:4
וַיְקַנְאוּ לְמֹשֶׁה בַּמַּחֲנֶה לְאַהֲרֹן קְדוֹשׁ יְהוָה	Ps 106:16
וַיִּקָּהֲלוּ עַל־מֹשֶׁה וְעַל־אַהֲרֹן וַיֹּאמְרוּ אֲלֵהֶם רַב־לָכֶם כִּי כָל־הָעֵדָה כֻּלָּם קְדֹשִׁים וּבְתוֹכָם יְהוָה וּמַדּוּעַ תִּתְנַשְּׂאוּ עַל־קְהַל יְהוָה	Num 16:3
תִּפְתַּח־אֶרֶץ וַתִּבְלַע דָּתָן וַתְּכַס עַל־עֲדַת אֲבִירָם	Ps 106:17
וַתִּפְתַּח הָאָרֶץ אֶת־פִּיהָ וַתִּבְלַע אֹתָם וְאֶת־בָּתֵּיהֶם וְאֵת כָּל־הָאָדָם אֲשֶׁר לְקֹרַח וְאֵת כָּל־הָרְכוּשׁ וַיֵּרְדוּ הֵם וְכָל־אֲשֶׁר לָהֶם חַיִּים שְׁאֹלָה וַתְּכַס עֲלֵיהֶם הָאָרֶץ וַיֹּאבְדוּ מִתּוֹךְ הַקָּהָל	Num 16:32–33
וַתִּבְעַר־אֵשׁ בַּעֲדָתָם לֶהָבָה תְּלַהֵט רְשָׁעִים	Ps 106:18
וְאֵשׁ יָצְאָה מֵאֵת יְהוָה וַתֹּאכַל אֵת הַחֲמִשִּׁים וּמָאתַיִם אִישׁ מַקְרִיבֵי הַקְּטֹרֶת	Num 16:35
וַיְהִי הָעָם כְּמִתְאֹנְנִים רַע בְּאָזְנֵי יְהוָה וַיִּשְׁמַע יְהוָה וַיִּחַר אַפּוֹ וַתִּבְעַר־בָּם אֵשׁ יְהוָה וַתֹּאכַל בִּקְצֵה הַמַּחֲנֶה	Num 11:1

Appendix B

יַעֲשׂוּ־עֵגֶל בְּחֹרֵב וַיִּשְׁתַּחֲווּ לְמַסֵּכָה	Ps 106:19
וָאֵרֶא וְהִנֵּה חֲטָאתֶם לַיהוָה אֱלֹהֵיכֶם עֲשִׂיתֶם לָכֶם עֵגֶל מַסֵּכָה סַרְתֶּם מַהֵר מִן־הַדֶּרֶךְ אֲשֶׁר־צִוָּה יְהוָה אֶתְכֶם	Deut 9:16
וַיֹּאמֶר לְהַשְׁמִידָם לוּלֵי מֹשֶׁה בְחִירוֹ עָמַד בַּפֶּרֶץ לְפָנָיו לְהָשִׁיב חֲמָתוֹ מֵהַשְׁחִית	Ps 106:23
וָאֶתְנַפַּל לִפְנֵי יְהוָה אֵת אַרְבָּעִים הַיּוֹם וְאֶת־אַרְבָּעִים הַלַּיְלָה אֲשֶׁר הִתְנַפָּלְתִּי כִּי־אָמַר יְהוָה לְהַשְׁמִיד אֶתְכֶם	Deut 9:25
וָאֲבַקֵּשׁ מֵהֶם אִישׁ גֹּדֵר־גָּדֵר וְעֹמֵד בַּפֶּרֶץ לְפָנַי בְּעַד הָאָרֶץ לְבִלְתִּי שַׁחֲתָהּ וְלֹא מָצָאתִי	Ezek 22:30
וַיִּמְאֲסוּ בְּאֶרֶץ חֶמְדָּה לֹא־הֶאֱמִינוּ לִדְבָרוֹ	Ps 106:24
וּבַדָּבָר הַזֶּה אֵינְכֶם מַאֲמִינִם בַּיהוָה אֱלֹהֵיכֶם	Deut 1:32
וַיֵּרָגְנוּ בְאָהֳלֵיהֶם לֹא שָׁמְעוּ בְּקוֹל יְהוָה	Ps 106:25
וַתֵּרָגְנוּ בְאָהֳלֵיכֶם וַתֹּאמְרוּ בְּשִׂנְאַת יְהוָה אֹתָנוּ הוֹצִיאָנוּ מֵאֶרֶץ מִצְרָיִם לָתֵת אֹתָנוּ בְּיַד הָאֱמֹרִי לְהַשְׁמִידֵנוּ	Deut 1:27
וַיִּשָּׂא יָדוֹ לָהֶם לְהַפִּיל אוֹתָם בַּמִּדְבָּר	Ps 106:26
בַּמִּדְבָּר הַזֶּה יִפְּלוּ פִגְרֵיכֶם וְכָל־פְּקֻדֵיכֶם לְכָל־מִסְפַּרְכֶם מִבֶּן עֶשְׂרִים שָׁנָה וָמָעְלָה אֲשֶׁר הֲלִינֹתֶם עָלָי אִם־אַתֶּם תָּבֹאוּ אֶל־הָאָרֶץ אֲשֶׁר נָשָׂאתִי אֶת־יָדִי לְשַׁכֵּן אֶתְכֶם בָּהּ כִּי אִם־כָּלֵב בֶּן־יְפֻנֶּה וִיהוֹשֻׁעַ בִּן־נוּן	Num 14:29-30
גַּם־אֲנִי נָשָׂאתִי אֶת־יָדִי לָהֶם בַּמִּדְבָּר לְהָפִיץ אֹתָם בַּגּוֹיִם וּלְזָרוֹת אוֹתָם בָּאֲרָצוֹת	Ezek 20:23
וּלְהַפִּיל זַרְעָם בַּגּוֹיִם וּלְזָרוֹתָם בָּאֲרָצוֹת	Ps 106:27
גַּם־אֲנִי נָשָׂאתִי אֶת־יָדִי לָהֶם בַּמִּדְבָּר לְהָפִיץ אֹתָם בַּגּוֹיִם וּלְזָרוֹת אוֹתָם בָּאֲרָצוֹת	Ezek 20:23
וַיִּצָּמְדוּ לְבַעַל פְּעוֹר וַיֹּאכְלוּ זִבְחֵי מֵתִים	Ps 106:28
וַיִּצָּמֶד יִשְׂרָאֵל לְבַעַל פְּעוֹר וַיִּחַר־אַף יְהוָה בְּיִשְׂרָאֵל	Num 25:3
וַיַּכְעִיסוּ בְּמַעַלְלֵיהֶם וַתִּפְרָץ־בָּם מַגֵּפָה	Ps 106:29
וַיָּבֹא אַחַר אִישׁ־יִשְׂרָאֵל אֶל־הַקֻּבָּה וַיִּדְקֹר אֶת־שְׁנֵיהֶם אֵת אִישׁ יִשְׂרָאֵל וְאֶת־הָאִשָּׁה אֶל־קֳבָתָהּ וַתֵּעָצַר הַמַּגֵּפָה מֵעַל בְּנֵי יִשְׂרָאֵל וַיִּהְיוּ הַמֵּתִים בַּמַּגֵּפָה אַרְבָּעָה וְעֶשְׂרִים אָלֶף	Num 25:8-9
וַיַּעֲמֹד פִּינְחָס וַיְפַלֵּל וַתֵּעָצַר הַמַּגֵּפָה	Ps 106:30
וַיָּשָׁב אַהֲרֹן אֶל־מֹשֶׁה אֶל־פֶּתַח אֹהֶל מוֹעֵד וְהַמַּגֵּפָה נֶעֱצָרָה	Num 16:50 [17:15]
וַיַּרְא פִּינְחָס בֶּן־אֶלְעָזָר בֶּן־אַהֲרֹן הַכֹּהֵן וַיָּקָם מִתּוֹךְ הָעֵדָה וַיִּקַּח רֹמַח בְּיָדוֹ	Num 25:7
וַתֵּחָשֶׁב לוֹ לִצְדָקָה לְדֹר וָדֹר עַד־עוֹלָם	Ps 106:31
וְהֶאֱמִן בַּיהוָה וַיַּחְשְׁבֶהָ לּוֹ צְדָקָה	Gen 15:6

Appendix B

וַיִּשְׁפְּכוּ דָם נָקִי דַּם־בְּנֵיהֶם וּבְנוֹתֵיהֶם אֲשֶׁר זִבְּחוּ לַעֲצַבֵּי כְנָעַן וַתֶּחֱנַף הָאָרֶץ בַּדָּמִים	Ps 106:38
וְלֹא־תַחֲנִיפוּ אֶת־הָאָרֶץ אֲשֶׁר אַתֶּם בָּהּ כִּי הַדָּם הוּא יַחֲנִיף אֶת־הָאָרֶץ וְלָאָרֶץ לֹא־יְכֻפַּר לַדָּם אֲשֶׁר שֻׁפַּךְ־בָּהּ כִּי־אִם בְּדַם שֹׁפְכוֹ	Num 35:33

Appendix C

Psalm 135

כִּי־יַעֲקֹב בָּחַר לוֹ יָהּ יִשְׂרָאֵל לִסְגֻלָּתוֹ	Ps 135:4
כִּי עַם קָדוֹשׁ אַתָּה לַיהוָה אֱלֹהֶיךָ בְּךָ בָּחַר יְהוָה אֱלֹהֶיךָ לִהְיוֹת לוֹ לְעַם סְגֻלָּה מִכֹּל הָעַמִּים אֲשֶׁר עַל־פְּנֵי הָאֲדָמָה	Deut 7:6
כִּי עַם קָדוֹשׁ אַתָּה לַיהוָה אֱלֹהֶיךָ וּבְךָ בָּחַר יְהוָה לִהְיוֹת לוֹ לְעַם סְגֻלָּה מִכֹּל הָעַמִּים אֲשֶׁר עַל־פְּנֵי הָאֲדָמָה	Deut 14:2
שֶׁהִכָּה בְּכוֹרֵי מִצְרָיִם מֵאָדָם עַד־בְּהֵמָה	Ps 135:8
וְעָבַרְתִּי בְאֶרֶץ־מִצְרַיִם בַּלַּיְלָה הַזֶּה וְהִכֵּיתִי כָל־בְּכוֹר בְּאֶרֶץ מִצְרַיִם מֵאָדָם וְעַד־בְּהֵמָה וּבְכָל־אֱלֹהֵי מִצְרַיִם אֶעֱשֶׂה שְׁפָטִים אֲנִי יְהוָה	Exod 12:12
שָׁלַח אֹתוֹת וּמֹפְתִים בְּתוֹכֵכִי מִצְרָיִם בְּפַרְעֹה וּבְכָל־עֲבָדָיו	Ps 135:9
לְכָל־הָאֹתוֹת וְהַמּוֹפְתִים אֲשֶׁר שְׁלָחוֹ יְהוָה לַעֲשׂוֹת בְּאֶרֶץ מִצְרָיִם לְפַרְעֹה וּלְכָל־עֲבָדָיו וּלְכָל־אַרְצוֹ	Deut 34:11
שֶׁהִכָּה גּוֹיִם רַבִּים וְהָרַג מְלָכִים עֲצוּמִים	Ps 135:10
לְמַכֵּה מְלָכִים גְּדֹלִים כִּי לְעוֹלָם חַסְדּוֹ	Ps 136:17
וַיַּהֲרֹג מְלָכִים אַדִּירִים כִּי לְעוֹלָם חַסְדּוֹ	Ps 136:18
לְסִיחוֹן מֶלֶךְ הָאֱמֹרִי וּלְעוֹג מֶלֶךְ הַבָּשָׁן וּלְכֹל מַמְלְכוֹת כְּנָעַן	Ps 135:11
לְסִיחוֹן מֶלֶךְ הָאֱמֹרִי כִּי לְעוֹלָם חַסְדּוֹ	Ps 136:19
וּלְעוֹג מֶלֶךְ הַבָּשָׁן כִּי לְעוֹלָם חַסְדּוֹ	Ps 136:20
וְנָתַן אַרְצָם נַחֲלָה לְיִשְׂרָאֵל עַמּוֹ	Ps 135:12
וְנָתַן אַרְצָם לְנַחֲלָה כִּי לְעוֹלָם חַסְדּוֹ	Ps 136:21
נַחֲלָה לְיִשְׂרָאֵל עַבְדּוֹ כִּי לְעוֹלָם חַסְדּוֹ	Ps 136:22

Appendix D

Psalm 136

וַיּוֹצֵא יִשְׂרָאֵל מִתּוֹכָם כִּי לְעוֹלָם חַסְדּוֹ	136:11
אוֹ הֲנִסָּה אֱלֹהִים לָבוֹא לָקַחַת לוֹ גוֹי מִקֶּרֶב גּוֹי בְּמַסֹּת בְּאֹתֹת וּבְמוֹפְתִים וּבְמִלְחָמָה וּבְיָד חֲזָקָה וּבִזְרוֹעַ נְטוּיָה וּבְמוֹרָאִים גְּדֹלִים כְּכֹל אֲשֶׁר־עָשָׂה לָכֶם יְהוָה אֱלֹהֵיכֶם בְּמִצְרַיִם לְעֵינֶיךָ	Deut 4:34[2]
בְּיָד חֲזָקָה וּבִזְרוֹעַ נְטוּיָה כִּי לְעוֹלָם חַסְדּוֹ	136:12
אוֹ הֲנִסָּה אֱלֹהִים לָבוֹא לָקַחַת לוֹ גוֹי מִקֶּרֶב גּוֹי בְּמַסֹּת בְּאֹתֹת וּבְמוֹפְתִים וּבְמִלְחָמָה וּבְיָד חֲזָקָה וּבִזְרוֹעַ נְטוּיָה וּבְמוֹרָאִים גְּדֹלִים כְּכֹל אֲשֶׁר־עָשָׂה לָכֶם יְהוָה אֱלֹהֵיכֶם בְּמִצְרַיִם לְעֵינֶיךָ	Deut 4:34
וְנִעֵר פַּרְעֹה וְחֵילוֹ בְיַם־סוּף כִּי לְעוֹלָם חַסְדּוֹ	136:15
וַיֵּט מֹשֶׁה אֶת־יָדוֹ עַל־הַיָּם וַיָּשָׁב הַיָּם לִפְנוֹת בֹּקֶר לְאֵיתָנוֹ וּמִצְרַיִם נָסִים לִקְרָאתוֹ וַיְנַעֵר יְהוָה אֶת־מִצְרַיִם בְּתוֹךְ הַיָּם	Exod 14:27
לְסִיחוֹן מֶלֶךְ הָאֱמֹרִי כִּי לְעוֹלָם חַסְדּוֹ	136:19
קוּמוּ סְּעוּ וְעִבְרוּ אֶת־נַחַל אַרְנֹן רְאֵה נָתַתִּי בְיָדְךָ אֶת־סִיחֹן מֶלֶךְ־חֶשְׁבּוֹן הָאֱמֹרִי וְאֶת־אַרְצוֹ הָחֵל רָשׁ וְהִתְגָּר בּוֹ מִלְחָמָה	Deut 2:24
וּלְעוֹג מֶלֶךְ הַבָּשָׁן כִּי לְעוֹלָם חַסְדּוֹ	136:20
וַיִּתֵּן יְהוָה אֱלֹהֵינוּ בְּיָדֵנוּ גַּם אֶת־עוֹג מֶלֶךְ־הַבָּשָׁן וְאֶת־כָּל־עַמּוֹ וַנַּכֵּהוּ עַד־בִּלְתִּי הִשְׁאִיר־לוֹ שָׂרִיד	Deut 3:3
וְנָתַן אַרְצָם לְנַחֲלָה כִּי לְעוֹלָם חַסְדּוֹ נַחֲלָה לְיִשְׂרָאֵל עַבְדּוֹ כִּי לְעוֹלָם חַסְדּוֹ	136:21–22
לְהוֹרִישׁ גּוֹיִם גְּדֹלִים וַעֲצֻמִים מִמְּךָ מִפָּנֶיךָ לַהֲבִיאֲךָ לָתֶת־לְךָ אֶת־אַרְצָם נַחֲלָה כַּיּוֹם הַזֶּה	Deut 4:38

2. See the section on sources concerning this semantic marker.

Bibliography

Allen, Leslie C. *Psalms 101–150*. WBC 21. Waco, TX: Word, 2002.
Alter, Robert. *The Art of Biblical Narrative*. New York: Basic, 1981.
———. *The Art of Biblical Poetry*. New York: Basic, 1985.
Amit, Yairah. גלוי ונסתר במקרא. Tel Aviv: Yedioth Ahronoth and Chemed, 2005.
Anderson, Arnold. *The Book of Psalms: Volume 2*. NCB. London: Oliphants, 1981.
Anderson, Arnold A. "Historic Psalms." In *It Is Written: Scripture Citing Scripture, Essays in Honour of Barnabas Lindars, SSF*, edited by D. A. Carson and H. G. M. Williamson, 56–67. Cambridge: Cambridge University Press, 1988.
Anderson, Francis I. *Spelling in the Hebrew Bible*. Rome: Biblical Institute, 1986.
Anderson, George W. "Canonical and Non-Canonical." In *The Cambridge History of the Bible: From the Beginnings to Jerome*, edited by Peter R. Ackroyd and C. F. Evans, 113–59. Cambridge: Cambridge University Press, 1969.
Andrews, D. K. "Yahweh the God of the Heavens." In *The Seed of Wisdom: Essays in Honour of T. J. Meek*, edited by William S. McCullough, 5–58. Toronto: University of Toronto Press, 1991.
Avishur, Yitzhak. עיונים בשירת המזמורים העברית והאוגריתית. Jerusalem: Magnes, 1989.
Barton, John. "Intertextuality and the Final Form of the Text." In *Congress Volume: VTS* 80, 33–37. Leiden: Brill, 1998.
Bauer, Uwe F. W. "Eine Literarische Analyse Von Psalm CXIV." *VT* 51.3 (2001) 289–311.
Bazak, Jacob. "The Geometric-Figurative Structure of Psalm CXXXVI." *VT* 35 (1985) 130–38.
Beentjes, Pancratius. "Inverted Quotations in the Bible: A Neglected Stylistic Pattern." *Biblica* 63 (1982) 506–23.
Bellinger, W. H. *Psalms: Reading and Studying the Book of Praises*. Peabody, MA: Hendrickson, 1990.
Ben-Porat, Ziva. "The Poetics of Literary Allusion." *PTL: A Journal for Descriptive Poetics and Theory of Literature* 1 (1976) 105–28.
Berlin, Adele. *The Dynamics of Biblical Parallelism*. Bloomington, IN: Indiana University Press, 1985.
———. *Poetics and Interpretation of Biblical Narrative*. Winona Lake, IN: Eisenbrauns, 1994.
———. "Psalms." In *The Jewish Study Bible*, edited by Marc Zvi Brettler, 1280–1446. Oxford: Oxford University Press, 2004.
———. "Psalms and the Literature of the Exile; Psalms 137, 44, 69, and 78." In *The Book of Psalms: Composition and Reception*, edited by Peter Flint and Patrick D. Miller, 65–86. Leiden: Brill, 2005.
Berman, Yael. "פרק קו." In עולם התנ״ד ב: תהלים, edited by Gershon Galil, 132–35. Tel Aviv: Dodson Eti, 1999.
Bernstein, Moshe. "A Jewish Reading of the Psalms." In *The Book of Psalms: Composition and Reception*, edited by Peter W. Flint and Patrick D. Miller, 476–504. Leiden: Brill, 2005.

Bibliography

Black, Jeremy, Andrew George, and Nicholas Postgate, eds. *A Concise Dictionary of Akkadian*. Santag 5. Wiesbaden: Harrassowitz, 1999.

Block, Daniel I. *The Book of Ezekiel: Chapters 1–24*. Grand Rapids: Eerdmans, 1997.

Booij, Thijs. "The Role of Darkness in Psalm 105:28." *VT* 39.2 (1989) 209–14.

Braun, Roddy. *1 Chronicles*. WBC 14. Waco, TX: Word, 1986.

Briggs, Charles A. *A Critical and Exegetical Commentary on the Book of Psalms: Vol. 2*. Edited by S. R. Driver, A. Plummer, and C. A. Briggs. ICC. Edinburgh: T. & T. Clark, 1969.

Bright, John. *A History of Israel*. 3rd ed. Chatham, UK: SCM, 1998.

Brooke, George J. "Psalms 105 and 106 at Qumran." *RevQ* 14.2 (1989) 267–92.

Brown, Francis, Charles Briggs, and Samuel Driver. *A Hebrew and English Lexicon of the Old Testament*. 2nd ed. 1907. Reprint. Oxford: Clarendon, 1974.

Brueggemann, Walter. *The Psalms and the Life of Faith*. Minneapolis: Fortress, 1995.

Buber, Martin. דרכו של המקרא. Jerusalem: Bialik, 1997.

Budd, Philip J. *Numbers*. WBC 5. Waco, TX: Word, 1984.

Butler, Trent C. "A Forgotten Passage from a Forgotten Era (1 Chr. 16:8–36)." *VT* 28.2 (1978) 142–50.

Buttenwieser, Moses. *The Psalms: Chronologically Treated with a New Translation*. The Library of Biblical Studies. New York: Ktav, 1969.

Campbell, Antony F., and Mark A. O'Brien. *Sources of the Pentateuch: Texts, Introductions, Annotations*. Minneapolis: Fortress, 1993.

Carroll, R. P. "Psalm LXXVIII: Vestiges of a Tribal Polemic." *VT* 21 (1971) 133–50.

Carson, D. A., and H. G. M. Williamson, eds. *It Is Written: Scripture Citing Scripture, Essays in Honour of Barnabas Lindars, SSF*. Cambridge: Cambridge University Press, 1988.

Cassuto, Moshe, ed. אנציקלופדיה מקראית: אוצר הידיעות על המקרא ותקופתו. 8 vols. Jerusalem: Bialik, 1950.

———. פירוש על ספר שמות. Jerusalem: Magnes, 1987.

Cassuto, Umberto. "The Arrangement of the Book of Ezekiel." In *Biblical and Oriental Studies: Vol. 1*, 277–40. Jerusalem: Magnes, 1973.

———. *Biblical and Oriental Studies*. Translated by Israel Abrahams. 2 vols. Jerusalem: Magnes, 1973.

———. *A Commentary on the Book of Exodus*. Translated by Israel Abrahams. Jerusalem: Magnes, 1967.

———. "The Sequence and Arrangement of the Biblical Sections." *Biblical and Oriental Studies: Vol. 1*, 1–6. Jerusalem: Magnes, 1973.

———. "מעשה בני האלהים ובנות האדם." In vol. 1, ספרות מקראית וספרות כנענית, 98–107. Jerusalem: Magnes, 1972.

———. "שירת העלילה בישראל." In vol. 1, ספרות מקראית וספרות כנענית, 62–90. Jerusalem: Magnes, 1972.

Ceresko, Anthony R. "A Poetic Analysis of Ps 105, with Attention to Its Use of Irony." *Biblica* 64.1 (1983) 20–46.

———. *Psalmists and Sages*. Indian Theological Studies Supplements 2. Bangalore: St. Peter's Pontifical Institute, 1994.

Childs, Brevard S. "Anticipatory Titles in Hebrew Narrative." In *Isaac Leo Seeligmann Volume: Essays on the Bible and the Ancient World*, edited by Alexander Rofé and Yair Zakovitch, 57–65. Jerusalem: E. Rubinstein's Pub. House, 1983.

———. *The Book of Exodus: A Critical, Theological Commentary*. Philadelphia: Westminster, 1974.

———. "Deuteronomic Formulae of the Exodus Tradition." In *Hebräische Wortforschung: Festschrift Zum 80. Geburtstag Von Walter Baumgartner*, 30–39. Leiden: Brill, 1967.

———. *Introduction to the Old Testament as Scripture*. London: SCM, 1979.

Chisholm, Robert B. *From Exegesis to Exposition: A Practical Guide to Using Biblical Hebrew*. Grand Rapids: Baker, 1998.

Christensen, Duane L. *Deuteronomy 1:1–21:9*. WBC 6A. Nashville, TN: Thomas Nelson, 2001.

Clarke, Ernest G. "Targum Pseudo-Jonathan: Numbers." In *The Bible in Aramaic: Vol. 4*, edited by Kevin Cathcart, Michael Maher, and Martin McNamara, 185–294. Collegeville, MN: Liturgical, 1995.

Clements, Ronald E. "The Book of Deuteronomy." In *NIB*, vol. 2, edited by Leander E. Keck, Thomas G. Long, Bruce C. Birch, et al., 269–538. Nashville, TN: Abingdon, 1994.

———. "Style and Purpose in Psalm 105." *Biblica* 6.3–4 (1979) 420–22.

Coats, George W. "Despoiling the Egyptians." *VT* 18 (1968) 450–57.

———. *Rebellion in the Wilderness: The Murmuring Motif in the Wilderness Traditions of the Old Testament*. Nashville, TN: Abingdon, 1968.

Cody, Aelred. "When Is the Chosen People Called a *Goy*?" *VT* 14 (1964) 1–6.

Cohen, Menachem, ed. *Psalms: Part II, Mikra'ot Gedolot 'Haketer': A Revised and Augmented Scientific Edition of 'Mikra'ot Gedolot': Based on the Aleppo Codex and Early Medieval Manuscripts*. Ramat Gan, Israel: Bar Ilan University, 2003.

Craigie, Peter C. *Psalms 1–50*. WBC 19. Waco, TX: Word, 1983.

Crenshaw, James L. *The Psalms: An Introduction*. Grand Rapids: Eerdmans, 2001.

Croft, Steven J. L. *The Identity of the Individual in the Psalms*. JSOTSup 44. Sheffield, UK: JSOT, 1987.

Cross, Frank Moore. *Canaanite Myth and Hebrew Epic*. 1973, Reprint. Cambridge: Harvard University Press, 1997.

Curtis, Edward L. *A Critical and Exegetical Commentary on the Book of Chronicles*. ICC. Edinburgh: T. & T. Clark, 1910.

Dahood, Mitchell S. J. "Hebrew-Ugaritic Lexicography." *Biblica* 45.3 (1964) 393–412.

———. *Psalms I: Introduction, Translation and Notes*. Edited by William F. Albright and David N. Freedman, AB 16. Garden City, NY: Doubleday, 1965.

———. *Psalms II: Introduction, Translation and Notes*. Edited by William F. Albright and David N. Freedman, AB 17. Garden City, NY: Doubleday, 1970.

———. *Psalms III: Introduction, Translation and Notes*. Edited by William F. Albright and David N. Freedman, AB 17A. Garden City, NY: Doubleday, 1981.

———. "Two Pauline Quotations from the Old Testament." *CBQ* 17 (1955) 19–24.

Davies, G. Henton. "The Ark in the Psalms." In *Promise and Fulfilment: Essays Presented to Professor S. H. Hooke in Celebration of His Ninetieth Birthday, 21st January, 1964*, edited by F. F. Bruce, 51–61. Edinburgh: T. & T. Clark, 1963.

Davies, G. I. "Sinai, Mount." In *ABD: Vol. 6*, edited by David N. Freedman, Gary A. Herion, David F. Graf and John D. Pleins, 647. Garden City, NY: Doubleday, 1992.

Day, John. "A Case of Inner Scriptural Interpretation: The Dependence of Isaiah XXV 13—XXVII 11 on Hosea XIII 4—XIV 10 (Eng. 9) and Its Relevance to Some Theories of the Redaction of the 'Isaiah Apocalypse.'" In *Writing and Reading the*

Bibliography

Scroll of Isaiah: Studies of an Interpretive Tradition, edited by Craig C. Broyles and Craig A. Evans, 399–491. Leiden: Brill, 1997.

———. "The Destruction of the Shiloh Sanctuary and Jeremiah VII 12, 14." In *Studies in the Historical Books of the Old Testament*, 87–94. Leiden: Brill, 1979.

———. "How Many Pre-Exilic Psalms Are There?" In *In Search of Pre-Exilic Israel: Proceedings of the Oxford Old Testament Seminar*, edited by John Day, 225–50. London: T. & T. Clark, 2004.

de Boer, Pieter A. "Psalm 81, 6a: Observations on Translation and Meaning of One Hebrew Line." In *In the Shelter of Elyon: Essays on Ancient Palestinian Life and Literature in Honor of G. W. Ahlström*, edited by W. Boyd Barrick and John R. Spencer, 67–80. Sheffield, UK: Sheffield Academic, 1984.

del Olmo Lete, Gregorio, and Joaquin Sanmartin. *A Dictionary of the Ugaritic Language in the Alphabetic Tradition*. Translated by Wilfred G. E. Watson. 2 vols. Handbook of Oriental Studies 67. Leiden: Brill, 2002.

DeVries, Simon J. *1 Kings*. WBC 12. Waco, TX: Word, 1985.

Dirksen, Peter B. *1 Chronicles*. Translated by Antony P. Runia. Historical Commentary on the Old Testament. Leuven: Peeters, 2005.

Driver, Godfrey R. "Abbreviations in the Masoretic Text." *Textus* 1 (1960) 112–31.

Driver, Samuel R. *An Introduction to the Literature of the Old Testament*. 9th ed. ITL. 1891. Reprint. Edinburgh: T. & T. Clark, 1972.

———. *A Treatise on the Use of the Tenses in Hebrew and Some Other Syntactical Questions*. Edited by Astrid B. Beck and David N. Freedman. The Biblical Resource Series. 1874. Reprint. Grand Rapids: Eerdmans, 1998.

Duhm, D. Bernhard. *Die Psalmen*. Tübingen: Mohr (Siebeck), 1922.

Durham, John I. *Exodus*. WBC 3. Waco, TX: Word, 1987.

Eaton, John H. "Psalms." In *Dictionary of Biblical Interpretation: K–Z*, edited by John H. Hayes, 324–29. Nashville, TN: Abingdon, 1999.

———. "The Psalms in Israel's Worship." In *The Psalms in Israel's Worship*, edited by G. W. Anderson, 238–73. Oxford: Clarendon, 1997.

Ehrensvärd, Martin. "Why Biblical Texts Cannot Be Dated Linguistically." *HS* 4 (2006) 177–89.

Eichrodt, Walther. *Ezekiel*. OTL. London: SCM, 1970.

Eissfeldt, Otto. *The Old Testament: An Introduction*. Translated by Peter R. Ackroyd. 1965. Reprint. Oxford: Blackwell, 1966.

Emerton, John A. "Are There Examples of Enclitic *Mem* in the Hebrew Bible?" In *Texts, Temples, and Traditions: A Tribute to Menahem Haran*, edited by Michael V. Fox, Avi Hurvitz, Victor A. Hurowitz et al., 321–38. Winona Lake, IN: Eisenbrauns, 1996.

Enns, Peter E. "Creation and Recreation: Psalm 95 and Its Interpretation in Hebrews 3:1—4:13." *Westminster Theological Journal* 55.2 (1993) 255–57.

Eslinger, Lyle. "Inner-Biblical Exegesis and Allusion: The Question of Category." *VT* 42.1 (1992) 47–58.

Fabry, Heinz-Joseph. "עצב." In *TDOT* 11, edited by G. Johannes Botterweck and Helmer Ringgren, 281–84. Grand Rapids: Eerdmans, 1990.

Fensham, Frank C. "Neh 9 and Pss 105, 106, 135 and 136: Post-Exilic Historical Traditions in Poetic Form." *Journal of Northwest Semitic Languages* 19 (1981) 35–51.

Fishbane, Michael. *Biblical Interpretation in Ancient Israel*. Oxford: Clarendon, 1985.

———. *The Garments of Torah: Essays in Biblical Hermeneutics*. Indiana Studies in Biblical Literature. Bloomington, IN: Indiana University Press, 1989.

———. *Text and Texture: Close Reading of Selected Biblical Texts*. New York: Schocken, 1979.

———. "Types of Biblical Intertextuality." In *Congress Volume: VTS 80*, 39–44. Leiden: Brill, 1998.

Flint, Peter. "Three Psalms from Qumran: The Preliminary Editions of 4QPs-1 and 4QPs-N." *JNSL* 24.2 (1998) 35–44.

Fohrer, Georg. *Introduction to the Old Testament*. Translated by David Green. London: SPCK, 1974.

Follis, Elaine R. "Sea." In *ABD: Vol. 5*, edited by David N. Freedman, Gary A. Herion, David F. Graf and John D. Pleins, 1058–59. Garden City, NY: Doubleday, 1992.

Foster, Benjamin R. "Enuma Elish." In *Context of Scripture: Canonical Compositions from the Biblical World*, edited by William W. Hallo, 390–402. Leiden: Brill, 1997.

Freedman, David N. "Archaic Forms in Early Hebrew Poetry." *ZAW* 72 (1960) 101–107.

———. *Pottery, Poetry, and Prophecy: Studies in Early Hebrew Poetry*. Winona Lake, IN: Eisenbrauns, 1980.

Fretheim, Terence E. *The Book of Genesis*. In *NIB*, vol. 1, edited by Leander E. Keck, Thomas G. Long, Bruce C. Birch, et al., 319–674. Nashville, TN: Abingdon, 1994.

———. "The Plagues as Ecological Signs of Historical Disaster." *JBL* 110.3 (1991) 385–96.

Gamble, Harry Y. "Canon." In *ABD: Vol.1*, edited by David N. Freedman, Gary A. Herion, David F. Graf and John D. Pleins, 837–61. Garden City, NY: Doubleday, 1992.

Garsiel, Moshe "פרק קלו." In תהלים ב, edited by Gershon Galil, 243–47. Tel Aviv: Divrei HaYamim, 1999.

———. "פרק קלה." In תהלים ב, edited by Gershon Galil, 240–43. Tel Aviv: Divrei HaYamim, 1999.

Gelb, Ignace J., A. Leo Oppenheim, and Thorkild Jacobsen, eds. *The Assyrian Dictionary of the Oriental Institute of the University of Chicago*. 21 vols. Chicago: The Oriental Institute, 1956–2011.

Gibson, John C. L. *Canaanite Myths and Legends*. Edinburgh: T. & T. Clark, 1977.

———. *Davidson's Introductory Hebrew Grammar—Syntax*. 4th ed. Edinburgh: T. & T. Clark, 1994.

Ginzberg, Louis. *The Legends of the Jews*. Vol. 3. *Moses in the Wilderness*. Translated by Paul Radin. Philadelphia: Jewish Publication Society, 1968.

Goulder, Michael D. *The Psalms of the Return (Book V, Psalms 107–150)*. Edited by David J. A. Clines and Philip R. Davies. JSOTSup 258: Studies in the Psalter 4. Sheffield, UK: Sheffield Academic, 1998.

———. *The Psalms of the Sons of Korah*. JSOTSup 20. Sheffield, UK: JSOT, 1982.

Gray, John. *1 & 2 Kings: A Commentary*. OTL. London: SCM, 1970.

———. *The Biblical Doctrine of the Reign of God*. Edinburgh: T. & T. Clark, 1979.

———. "Cultic Affinities between Israel and Ras Shamras." *ZAW* (1950) 207–20.

Greenberg, Moshe. *Ezekiel 1–20*. AB 22. Garden City, NY: Doubleday, 1983.

———. "Hebrew *Segulta*: Akkadian *Sikiltu*." In *Studies in the Bible and Jewish Thought*, 172–74. Philadelphia: Jewish Publication Society, 1995.

Gunkel, Hermann. *Die Psalmen: Übersetzt Und Erklärt*, Göttinger Handkommentar Zum Alten Testament. Göttingen: Vandenhoeck & Ruprecht Göttingen, 1926.

Bibliography

———. *The Psalms: A Form Critical Introduction*. Translated by Thomas H. Horner, Philadelphia: Fortress, 1967.

Gunkel, Hermann, and Joachim Begrich. *Introduction to Psalms: The Genres of the Religious Lyric of Israel*. Translated by James D. Nogalski. Mercer Library of Biblical Studies. Macon, GA: Mercer University Press, 1998.

Hacham, Amos. ספר תהלים. מקרא דעת פירוש עם כתובים נביאים תורה. Vol. 14. Jerusalem: Mosad Rav Kook, 1981.

Hammer, Reuven. *The Classic Midrash*. The Classics of Western Spirituality. New York: Paulist, 1995.

Hatch, Edwin, and Henry Redpath. *A Concordance to the Septuagint and Other Greek Versions of the Old Testament*. 2nd ed. Grand Rapids: Baker, 1988.

Hays, Richard B. *Echoes of Scripture in the Letters of Paul*. New Haven: Yale University Press, 1989.

Held, Moshe. "Marginal Notes to the Biblical Lexicon." In *Biblical and Related Studies Presented to Samuel Iwry*, edited by Ann Kort and Scott Morschauser, 93–104. Winona Lake, IN: Eisenbrauns, 1985.

Herrmann, Siegfried. "Ephraim." In *ABD: Vol. 2*, edited by David N. Freedman, Gary A. Herion, David F. Graf, and John D. Pleins, 551–56. Garden City, NY: Doubleday, 1992.

Hill, Andrew E. "Patchwork Poetry or Reasoned Verse: Connective Structure in 1 Chronicles XVI." *VT* 33 (1983) 97–101.

Hoffman, Yair. "A North Israelite Typological Myth and a Judaean Historical Tradition: The Exodus in Hosea and Amos." *VT* 39.2 (1989) 169–82.

———. יציאת מצריים באמונת המקרא. Tel Aviv: The Chaim Rozenberg School for Jewish Studies University, 1983.

———. "פרק קה." In תהלים ב, edited by Gershon Galil, 129–32. Tel Aviv: Divrei HaYamim, 1999.

———. "פרק קו." In תהלים ב, edited by Gershon Galil, 132–35 Tel Aviv: Divrei HaYamim, 1999.

Hoffmeier, James K. "Egypt, the Plagues In." In *ABD: Vol. 2*, edited by David N. Freedman, Gary A. Herion, David F. Graf and John D. Pleins, 374–76. Garden City, NY: Doubleday, 1992.

Hossfeld, Frank-Lothar, and Erich Zenger. *A Commentary on Psalms 51–100*. Translated by Linda M. Maloney. Edited by Klaus Baltzer. Hermeneia. Minneapolis: Fortress, 2005.

Howard, David M. "A Contextual Reading of Psalms 90–94." In *The Shape and Shaping of the Psalter*, edited by J. Clinton McCann, 108–23. Sheffield, UK: JSOT, 1993.

———. "Editorial Activity in the Psalter: A State-of-the-Field Survey." In *The Shape and Shaping of the Psalter*, edited by J. Clinton McCann, 52–70. Sheffield, UK: JSOT, 1993.

———. *The Structure of Psalms 93–100*. Biblical and Judaic Studies 5. Winona Lake, IN: Eisenbrauns, 1997.

Humphries, Walter Lee. *Joseph and His Family: A Literary Study*. Columbia, SC: University of South Carolina Press, 1988.

Hurvitz, Avi. "Can Biblical Texts Be Dated Linguistically? Chronological Perspectives in the Historical Study of Biblical Hebrew." In *Congress Volume: VTS 80*, 143–60. Leiden: Brill, 1998.

———. "The Chronological Significance of Aramaisms." *IEJ* 18 (1968) 234–40.

———. "Dating the Priestly Source in Light of the Historical Study of Biblical Hebrew." *ZAW* 100 (1988) 88–100.

———. "The History of a Legal Formula." *VT* 32.3 (1982) 255–67.

———. *A Linguistic Study of the Relationship between the Priestly Source and the Book of Ezekiel: A New Approach to an Old Problem*. Paris: Gabalda, 1982.

———. "Originals and Imitations in Biblical Poetry: A Comparative Examination of 1Sam 2:1–10 and Psalm 113:5–9." In *Biblical and Related Studies Presented to Samuel Iwry*, edited by Ann Kort and Scott Morschauser, 115–21. Winona Lake, IN: Eisenbrauns, 1985.

———. "The Recent Debate on Late Biblical Hebrew." *HS* 47 (2006) 191–210.

———. בין לשון לשון: לתולדות לשון המקרא בימי בית שני. Jerusalem: Bialik, 1972.

Jacobs, Jonathan. "מידה כנגד מידה באמצעי ספרותי ואידיאולוגי בסיפור המקרא." PhD diss., Bar-Ilan University, 2002.

Janowski, Bernd. "Psalm CVI:28–31 Und Die Interzession Des Pinchas." *VT* 33.2 (1983) 237–44.

Japhet, Sara. *I & II Chronicles: A Commentary*. London: SCM, 1993.

Jastrow, Marcus. *A Dictionary of the Targumim, the Talmud Babli and Yerushalmi, and the Midrashic Literature*. Jerusalem: Horeb, 1984.

Jenni, Ernst. "עת." In *TLOT: Vol. 2*, edited by Ernst Jenni and Claus Westermann, 951–61. Peabody, MA: Hendrickson, 1997.

Jenni, Ernst, and Klaus Westermann, eds. *TLOT*. 3 vols. Peabody, MA: Hendrickson, 1997.

Jirku, Anton. *Die Älteste Geschichte Israels Im Rahmen Lehrhafter Darstellungen*. Leipzig: Deichert, 1917.

Johnson, A. R. "The Psalms." In *The Old Testament and Modern Study: A Generation of Discovery and Research*, edited by Harold H. Rowley, 162–209. Oxford: Clarendon, 1951.

Johnstone, William. *1 and 2 Chronicles: Volume 1*. Edited by David J. A. Clines and Philip R. Davies. JSOTSup 253. Sheffield, UK: Sheffield Academic, 1997.

Joosten, J. *People and Land in the Holiness Code: An Exegetical Study of the Ideological Framework of the Law in Leviticus 17–26*. Leiden: Brill, 1996.

———. "Review of Young, Ian and Robert Rezetko, with the Assistance of Martin Ehrensvärd, Linguistic Dating of Biblical Texts. An Introduction to Approaches and Problems." In *Bibel Und Babel 6*. (forthcoming).

Joüon, Paul, and T. Muraoka. *A Grammar of Biblical Hebrew*. Translated by Takamitsu Muraoka. 2 vols. Subsidia Biblica. Rome: Editrice Pontificio Istituto Biblico, 1996.

Kang, Sa-Moon. "The Authentic Sermon of Jeremiah in Jeremiah 7:1–20." In *Texts, Temples, and Traditions: A Tribute to Menahem Haran*, edited by Michael V. Fox, Avi Hurvitz, Victor A. Hurowitz, et al., 147–62. Winona Lake, IN: Eisenbrauns, 1996.

Katzenelenbogen, Mordechai L., ed. תורת חיים, ספר שמות: שמות־יתרו. Jerusalem: Mosad Rav Kook, 1993.

Kaufmann, Yehezkel. *The Religion of Israel: From Its Beginnings to the Babylonian Exile*. Translated by Moshe Greenberg. Jerusalem: Sefer Ve Sefel, 2003.

Kautzsch, Emil. *Gesenius' Hebrew Grammar*. Translated by Cowley Arthur E. 2nd ed. 1910. Reprint. Oxford: Clarendon, 1957.

Keil, Karl Friedrich. *Introduction to the Old Testament*. Translated by George C. M. Douglas. 2 vols. Peabody, MA: Hendrickson, 1988.

Bibliography

Keil, Karl Friedrich, and Franz Delitzsch. *The Pentateuch*. Translated by James Martin. Vol. 1 (III). Commentary on the Old Testament in Ten Volumes. Grand Rapids: Eerdmans, 1981.

———. *Psalms*. Translated by James Martin. Vol. 5. Commentary on the Old Testament in Ten Volumes. Grand Rapids: Eerdmans, 1982.

Kimhi, David. הפירוש השלם על תהלים. Edited by Avraham Dror. Jerusalem: Mosad Rav Kook, 1971.

Kissane, Edward J. *The Book of Psalms: Translated from a Critically Revised Hebrew Text. With Commentary*. Dublin: Browne and Nolan, 1964.

Kittel, Rudolf, ed. *Biblia Hebraica Stuttgartensia*. Stuttgart: Deutsche Bibelgeselllschaft, 1990.

Klein, Ralph W. *1 Chronicles*. Hermeneia. Minneapolis: Fortress, 2006.

Klingbeil, Martin. *Yahweh Fighting from Heaven: God as Warrior and as God of Heaven in the Hebrew Psalter and Ancient Near Eastern Iconography*. Orbis Biblicus Et Orientalis 169. Göttingen: Vandenhoeck & Ruprecht, 1999.

Klopfer, Richard. "Zur Quellenscheidung in Exod. 19." *ZAW* 18 (1898) 197–235.

Koehler, Ludwig, and Walter Baumgartner. *The Hebrew and Aramaic Lexicon of the Old Testament*. Translated by M. E. Richardson. Revised by Walter Baumgartner and Johann J. Stamm. 5 vols. Leiden: Brill, 1995.

Kohlenberger, John R., ed. *The Parallel Apocrypha*. Oxford: Oxford University Press, 1997.

Kraus, Hans-Joachim. *Psalms 1–59: A Commentary*. Translated by Hilton C. Oswold. Minneapolis: Augsburg, 1988.

———. *Psalms 60–150: A Commentary*. Translated by Hilton C. Oswold. Minneapolis: Augsburg, 1988.

Kroll, Woodrow M. *Psalms: The Poetry of Palestine*. Lanham, MD: University Press of America, 1987.

Kropat, A. *Die Syntax Des Autors Der Chronik Verglichen Mit Der Seiner Quellen*. BZAW 16. Giessen: Töpelmann, 1909.

Kugel, James L. *The Bible as It Was*. Cambridge: Harvard University Press, 2000.

———. *The Idea of Biblical Poetry: Parallelism and Its History*. New Haven: Yale University Press, 1981.

———. *In Potiphar's House: The Interpretive Life of Biblical Texts*. New York: Harper Collins, 1990.

———. *Traditions of the Bible: A Guide to the Bible as It Was at the Start of the Common Era*. Cambridge: Harvard University Press, 1998.

Kutscher, Eduard Y. *A History of the Hebrew Language*. Edited by Raphael Kutscher. Jerusalem: Magnes, 1982.

———. מילים ותולדותיהן. Jerusalem: Kiryat-Sepher, 1974.

———. "בשולי המילון המקראי." לשוננו 32 (1967–68) 343–73.

Lauha, Aarre. *Die Geschichtsmotive in Den Alttestamentlichen Psalmen*. Helsinki: Suomalainen Tiedeakatemia, 1945.

———. "Genesis 1 and the Plagues Tradition in Psalm CV." *VT* 40.3 (1990) 257–63.

Lehrman, S. M., ed. *Midrash Rabbah*. Vol. 3. *Exodus*. London: Soncino, 1961.

Leonard, Jeffrey M. "Identifying Inner-Biblical Allusions: Psalm 78 as a Test Case." *JBL* 127.2 (2008) 241–65.

Leslie, Elmer A. *The Psalms: Translated and Interpreted in the Light of Hebrew Life and Worship*. New York: Abingdon-Cokesbury, 1949.

Levine, Baruch A. *Numbers 1–20*. Edited by William F. Albright and David N. Freedman. AB 4a. Garden City, NY: Doubleday, 1993.
Licht, Jacob. הניסיון במקרא וביהדות של הבית השני. Jerusalem: Magnes, 1973.
Liddell, Henry G., and Robert Scott. *A Greek–English Lexicon*. 9th ed. Oxford: Clarendon, 1977.
Limburg, James. "Psalms, Book of." In *ABD: Vol. 5*, edited by David N. Freedman, Gary A. Herion, David F. Graf, and John D. Pleins, 522–36. Garden City, NY: Doubleday, 1992.
Liver, Jacob. "Korah, Dothan and Abiram." In *Scripta Hierosolymitana VIII*, edited by Chaim Rabin, 189–217. Jerusalem: Magnes, 1961.
Loewenstamm, Samuel E. *The Evolution of the Exodus Tradition*. Translated by Baruch J. Schwartz. Jerusalem: Magnes, 1992.
———. "The Number of Plagues in Psalm 105." *Biblica* 52.4 (1971) 34–38.
———. "רשף." In אנציקלופדיה מקראית, edited by Umberto Cassuto, 437–41. Jerusalem: Bialik, 1976.
Lohfink, Norbert, and Erich Yenger. *The God of Israel and the Nations: Studies in Isaiah and the Psalms*. Translated by Everett R. Kalin. Collegeville, MN: Liturgical, 2000.
Lord, Albert B. *The Singer of Tales*. Harvard Studies in Comparative Literature 24. Cambridge: Harvard University Press, 1964.
Ludwig, Theodore M. "Traditions for Establishing the Earth." *JBL* 92 (1973) 345–57.
Lust, Johan, Erik Eynikel, and Katrin Hauspie. *A Greek–English Lexicon of the Septuagint*. 2 vols. Stuttgart: Deutsche Bibelgesellschaft, 1992.
Mare, W. Harold. "Zion." In *ABD: Vol. 6*, edited by David N. Freedman, Gary A. Herion, David F. Graf and John D. Pleins, 1096. Garden City, NY: Doubleday, 1992.
Margulis, Baruch. "The Plagues Tradition in Ps 105." *Biblica* 50.4 (1969) 491–96.
Martínez, Florentino Garcia, and Eibert J. C. Tigchelaar, eds. *The Dead Sea Scrolls Study Edition*. 2 vols. Leiden: Brill, 1997–98.
Mays, James L. *Hosea*. OTL. Philadelphia: Westminster, 1969.
McCann, J. Clinton. "Psalms." In *NIB*, vol. 4, edited by Leander E. Keck, Thomas G. Long, Bruce C. Birch, et al., 639–1280. Nashville, TN: Abingdon, 1996.
———, ed. *The Shape and Shaping of the Psalter*. JSOTSup 159. Sheffield, UK: JSOT, 1993.
McNamara, Martin. *Targum Neofiti 1: Genesis*. Edited by Kevin Cathcart, Michael Maher, and Martin McNamara. The Aramaic Bible 1A. Collegeville, MN: Liturgical, 1992.
———. *Targum Neofiti 1: Numbers and Pseudo-Jonathan: Numbers*. Edited by Kevin Cathcart, Michael Maher, and Martin McNamara. The Bible in Aramaic 4. Collegeville, MN: Liturgical, 1995.
Meier, Samuel A. *Speaking of Speaking: Marking Direct Discourse in the Hebrew Bible*. VTS 46. Leiden: Brill, 1992.
Meyers, Carol. "Temple, Jerusalem." In *ABD: Vol. 6*, edited by David N. Freedman, Gary A. Herion, David F. Graf, and John D. Pleins, 350–69. Garden City, NY: Doubleday, 1992.
Middleburg, C. H. "The Mention of Vine and Fig Tree in Psalm 105." *VT* 28 (1978) 480–81.
Milgrom, Jacob. "The Alleged 'Hidden Light.'" In *The Idea of Biblical Interpretation: Essays in Honor of James L. Kugel*, edited by Hindy Najman and Judith H. Newman, 41–44. Leiden: Brill, 2004.

Bibliography

———. *Leviticus 1-16: A New Translation*. AB. Garden City, NY: Doubleday, 2001.
———. *Leviticus 23-27: A New Translation*. AB. Garden City, NY: Doubleday, 2001.
———. "Priestly ('P') Source." In *ABD: Vol. 5*, edited by David N. Freedman, Gary A. Herion, David F. Graf and John D. Pleins, 454-61. Garden City, NY: Doubleday, 1992.
Mitchell, David. "Lord Remember David: G. H. Wilson and the Message of the Psalter." *VT* 56 (2006) 526-48.
Mowinckel, Sigmund. *The Psalms in Israel's Worship*. Translated by D. R. Ap-Thomas. 2 vols. Oxford: Blackwell, 1962.
Mrozek, Andrzej. "The Motif of the Sleeping Divinity." *Biblica* 80 (1999) 415-19.
Muilenburg, James. "Form Criticism and Beyond." *JBL* 89 (1969) 1-18.
———. "The Linguistic and Rhetorical Usages of the Particle כי in the Old Testament." *HUCA* 32 (1961) 135-60.
Mulder, Martin J. *1 Kings*. HCOT. Leuven: Peeters, 1998.
Myers, Jacob. *1 Chronicles*. AB. Garden City, NY: Doubleday, 1965.
Nasuti, Harry P. *Defining the Sacred Songs: Genre, Tradition, and the Post-Critical Interpretation of the Psalms*. JSOTSup 218. Sheffield, UK: Sheffield Academic, 1999.
———. "The Interpretive Significance of Sequence and Selection in the Book of Psalms." In *The Book of Psalms: Composition and Reception*, edited by Peter Flint and Patrick D. Miller, 311-39. Leiden: Brill, 2005.
———. *Tradition History and the Psalms of Asaph*. SBLDS 88. Atlanta: Scholars, 1988.
Nielsen, Kirsten. "Intertextuality and the Hebrew Bible." In *Congress Volume: VTS 80*, 17-31. Leiden: Brill, 1998.
Noble, Paul R. "Esau, Tamar, and Jacob: Criteria for Identifying Inner-Biblical Allusion." *VT* 52.2 (2002) 219-52.
Noordtzij, Arie. *Numbers*. Translated by Ed van der Maas. Grand Rapids: Zondervan, 1983.
Norin, Stig I. L. *Er Spaltete Das Meer: Die Auszugsüberlieferung in Psalmen Und Kult Des Alten Israel*. Coniectanea Biblica Old Testament Series 9. Lund: Gleerup, 1977.
Noth, Martin. *The Deuteronomistic History*. Edited by David J. A. Clines and Philip R. Davies. 2nd ed. JSOTSup 15. Sheffield, UK: JSOT, 1991.
———. *Exodus: A Commentary*. Translated by J. S. Bowden. OTL. Philadelphia: Westminster, 1962.
———. *A History of Pentateuchal Traditions*. Translated by B. W. Anderson. Englewood Cliffs, NJ: Prentice Hall, 1972.
———. *Leviticus: A Commentary*. Translated by J. E. Anderson. OTL. London: SCM, 1965.
———. *Numbers: A Commentary*. Translated by James D. Martin. London: SCM, 1968.
Oesterley, William O. E. *The Psalms: Translated with Text-Critical and Exegetical Notes*. London: SPCK, 1962.
Palmoni, Ya'akov. "ארבה." In אנציקלופדיה מקראית, edited by Umberto Cassuto, 520-26. Jerusalem: Bailik, 1976.
Parker, Simon B., ed. *Ugaritic Narrative Poetry*. SBL Writings from the Ancient World 9. Atlanta, GA: Scholars, 1997.
Paul, Shalom. "Hosea 7:16: Gibberish Jabber." In *Pomegranates and Golden Bells: Studies in Biblical, Jewish, and Near Eastern Ritual, Law, and Literature in Honor of*

Jacob Milgrom, edited by David P. Wright, David N. Freedman, and Avi Hurvitz, 707–12. Winona Lake, IN: Eisenbrauns, 1995.

Pfeiffer, R. *The First and Second Book of Chronicles*. The Interpreter's Bible 3. Nashville, TN: Abingdon, 1962.

Phillips, Anthony. *Deuteronomy*. Cambridge: Cambridge University Press, 1973.

Pietersma, Albert, ed. *Septuagintal Exegesis and Superscriptions of the Greek Psalter*. VTS 99. Leiden: Brill, 2005.

Polzin, Robert. *Late Biblical Hebrew: Towards an Historical Typology of Biblical Hebrew Prose*. Harvard Semitic Monographs 12. Missoula, MT: Scholars, 1976.

Pritchard, James B., ed. *Ancient Near Eastern Texts Relating to the Old Testament: Volume 1. An Anthology of Texts and Pictures*. 1958. Reprint. Princeton: Princeton University Press, 1973.

Propp, William H. *Exodus 1–18*. AB 2. Garden City, NY: Doubleday, 1999.

———. "Massah and Meribah." In *ABD: Vol. 4*, edited by David N. Freedman, Gary A. Herion, David F. Graf, and John D. Pleins, 600–601. Garden City, NY: Doubleday, 1992.

Raabe, Paul R. "Deliberate Ambiguity in the Psalter." *JBL* 110.2 (1991) 213–27.

Rad, Gerhard von. *Genesis: A Commentary*. OTL. London: SCM, 1972.

———. *The Problem of the Hexateuch and Other Essays*. Translated by E. W. Trueman Dickens. London: Oliver & Boyd, 1966.

———. *Wisdom in Israel*. Translated by James D. Martin. London: SCM, 1975.

Reddish, Mitchell G. "Heaven." In *ABD: Vol. 3*, edited by David N. Freedman, Gary A. Herion, David F. Graf and John D. Pleins, 90–91. Garden City, NY: Doubleday, 1992.

Reiterer, F. "פרק." In *TDOT 12*, edited by G. Johannes Botterweck, Helmer Ringgren, and Heinz-Joseph Fabry, 111–14. Grand Rapids: Eerdmans, 2003.

Rendsburg, Gary. "Some False Leads in the Identification of Late Biblical Hebrew Texts: The Cases of Genesis 24 and 1 Samuel 2:27–36." *JBL* 121 (2002) 23–46.

———. "A Comprehensive Guide to Israelian Hebrew: A Grammar and Lexicon." *Orient* 38 (2003) 5–35.

———. "Hurvitz Redux: On the Continued Scholarly Inattention to a Simple Principle of Hebrew Philology." In *Biblical Hebrew: Studies in Chronology and Typology*, edited by Ian Young, 104–28. London: T. & T. Clark, 2003.

———. *Linguistic Evidence for the Northern Origins of Selected Psalms*. SBLMS. Atlanta: Scholars, 1990.

Rendtorff, Rolf. *The Old Testament: An Introduction*. Translated by John Bowden. London: SCM, 1985.

Richardson, Niel H. "Psalm 106: Yahweh's Succoring Love Saves from the Death of a Broken Covenant." In *Love and Death in the Ancient Near East*, edited by John H. Marks and Robert M. Good, 191–203. Guilford, CT: Four Quarters, 1987.

Ringgren, Helmer. "ים." In *TDOT 6*, edited by G. Johannes Botterweck and Helmer Ringgren, 87–98. Grand Rapids: Eerdmans, 1990.

Robbins, K. *Exploring the Texture of Texts*. Philadelphia: Trinity, 1996.

Robertson, David A. *Linguistic Evidence in Dating Early Hebrew Poetry*. SBLDS 3. Missoula, MT: University of Montana, 1972.

Rofé, Alexander. "The Arrangement of the Laws in Deuteronomy." *Ephemerides Theologicae Lovanienses* 64.4 (1988) 265–87.

Bibliography

———. "Enquiry into the Betrothal of Rebekah." In *Die Hebräische Bibel Und Ihre Zweifache Nachgeschichte: Festschrift Für Rolf Rendtorff Zum 65. Geburtstag*, edited by Erhard Blum, Christian Macholz, and Ekkehard W. Stegemann, 27–39. Neukirchner-Vlyun: Neukirchener, 1990.

———. *Introduction to the Composition of the Pentateuch*. The Biblical Seminar 58. Sheffield, UK: Sheffield Academic, 1999.

———. מבוא לשירה המזמורית ולספרות החכמה שבמקרא. Jerusalem: Carmel, 2004.

Rom-Shiloni, Dalit. "אלהים בעידן של חורבן וגלויות." PhD diss., Hebrew University, 2000.

Rooker, Mark F. *Biblical Hebrew in Transition*. JSOTSup 30. Sheffield, UK: Sheffield Academic, 1990.

Sáenz-Badillos, Angel. *A History of the Hebrew Language*. Translated by John Elwolde. Cambridge: Cambridge University Press, 1993.

Saidel, Moshe. "מקבילות בין ספר ישעיה לספר תהלים." *Sinai* 32 (1956) 149–82, 229–42.

Sanders, James A., ed. *The Psalms Scroll of Qumran Cave 11*. DJD 4. Oxford: Clarendon, 1965.

Sarason, Richard S. "Midrash." In *Dictionary of Biblical Interpretation: K–Z*, edited by John H. Hays, 155–57. Nashville, TN: Abingdon, 1999.

Sarna, Nahum, ed. ספר תהלים ב, עולם התנ"ך. Tel Aviv: Divrei HaYamim, 1999.

———. "Notes on the Use of the Definite Article in the Poetry of Job." In *Texts, Temples, and Traditions: A Tribute to Menahem Haran*, edited by Michael V. Fox, Avi Hurvitz, Victor A. Hurowitz, et al., 279–84. Winona Lake, IN: Eisenbrauns, 1996.

———. "Psalm 89: A Study in Inner-Biblical Exegesis." In *Studies in Biblical Interpretation*, 377–94. Philadelphia: Jewish Publication Society, 2000.

Schaefer, Konrad. *Psalms*. Berit Olam. Collegeville, MN: Liturgical, 2001.

Schmidt, Werner. *Introduction to the Old Testament*. London: SCM, 1984.

Schniedewind, William M. "Are We His People or Not? Biblical Interpretation in Crisis." *Biblica* 76.4 (1995) 540–50.

Schökel, Luis Alonso. *A Manual of Hebrew Poetics*. Subsidia Biblica 11. Rome: Editrice Pontificio Istituto Biblico, 1988.

Schoors, Antoon. "(Mis)Use of Intertextuality in Qoheleth Exegesis." In *Congress Volume: VTS 80*, 45–59. Leiden: Brill, 1998.

Seeligman, Isaac L. "גבורות האדם וישועת האל: הסיבתיות הכפולה בחשיבה ההיסטורית של המקרא." In מחקרים בספרות המקרא, edited by Avi Hurvitz, Sara Japhet and Emanuel Tov, 62–81. Jerusalem: Magnes, 1996.

Segert, Stanislav. *A Basic Grammar of the Ugaritic Language*. Los Angeles: University of California Press, 1984.

Seow, Choon L. "Hosea, Book of." In *ABD: Vol. 3*, edited by David N. Freedman, Gary A. Herion, David F. Graf, and John D. Pleins, 291–97. Garden City, NY: Doubleday, 1992.

Seybold, Klaus. *Die Psalmen*, Handbuch Zum Alten Testament. Tübingen: Mohr (Siebeck), 1996.

———. *Introducing the Psalms*. Translated by R. Graeme Dunphy. Edinburgh: T. & T. Clark, 1990.

Sheppard, Gerald T. "Canonical Criticism." In *ABD: Vol.1*, edited by David N. Freedman, Gary A. Herion, David F. Graf, and John D. Pleins, 861–66. Garden City, NY: Doubleday, 1992.

Shinan, Avigdor, and Yair Zakovitch. ךלא כך כתוב בתנ״ך. Tel Aviv: Yedioth Ahronoth and Chemed, 2006.

Simkins, Ronald A. *Creator & Creation: Nature in the Worldview of Ancient Israel*. Peabody, MA: Hendrickson, 1994.

Ska, Jean Louis. *Our Fathers Have Told Us: Introduction to the Analysis of Hebrew Narratives*. Subsidia Biblica 13. Rome: Pontificio Istituto Biblico, 1990.

Sommer, Benjamin. "Exegesis, Allusion and Intertextuality in the Hebrew Bible: A Response to Lyle Eslinger." *VT* 46.4 (1996) 497–89.

———. *A Prophet Reads Scripture*. Stanford: Stanford University Press, 1998.

Sparks, Hedley F. D., ed. *The Apocryphal Old Testament*. Oxford: Clarendon, 1989.

Speiser, Ephraim A. "The Creation Epic." In *Ancient Near East Texts Relating to the Old Testament*, edited by James B. Pritchard, 60–72. Princeton: Princeton University Press, 1969.

———. *Genesis: Introduction, Translation and Notes*. AB. Garden City, NY: Doubleday, 1964.

Spencer, Aída Besançon. "שרירות as Self Reliance." *JBL* 100.2 (1981) 247–48.

Sperber, Alexander, ed. *The Bible in Aramaic: Based on Old Manuscripts and Printed Texts*. 4 vols. Leiden: Brill, 1959.

Stec, David M. *The Targum of Psalms: Translated, with a Critical Introduction, Apparatus and Notes*. The Aramaic Bible 16. London: T. & T. Clark, 2004.

Steck, Odil Hennes. *Old Testament Exegesis: A Guide to the Methodology*. Translated by James D. Nogalski. SBL Resources for Biblical Study 39. Atlanta: Scholars, 1998.

Sternberg, Meir. *The Poetics of Biblical Narrative: Ideological Literature and the Drama of Reading*. Bloomington, IN: Indiana University Press, 1985.

Swanson, Steven R. "Hallel." In *ABD: Vol. 3*, edited by David N. Freedman, Gary A. Herion, David F. Graf and John D. Pleins, 30. Garden City, NY: Doubleday, 1992.

Sweeney, Marvin A. *The Twelve Prophets*. Edited by David W. Cotter. Berit Olam: Studies in Hebrew Narrative and Poetry 1. Collegeville, MN: Liturgical, 2000.

Talmon, Shemaryahu. "Double Readings in the Massoretic Text." *Textus* 1 (1960) 144–85.

Tanner, Beth L. *The Book of Psalms through the Lens of Intertextuality*. Studies in Biblical Literature 26. New York: Lang, 2001.

Tate, Marvin E. *Psalms 51–100*. Edited by David A. Hubbard and Glen W. Barker. WBC 20. Dallas, TX: Word, 1990.

Terrien, Samuel. *The Psalms: Strophic Structure and Theological Commentary*. Grand Rapids: Eerdmans, 2003.

Thompson, Yaakov. "A Missing Hexateuchal Narrative Concerning Child Sacrifice." *Dor Le Dor* 15.1 (1986) 35–51.

Tigay, Jeffrey. "On Evaluating Claims of Literary Borrowing." In *The Tablet and the Scroll: Near Eastern Studies in Honor of William W. Hallow*, edited by M. E. Cohen, D. C. Snell, and D. B. Weisberg, 250–55. Bethesda, MD: CDL, 1993.

Tourney, Raymond J. *Seeing and Hearing God with the Psalms: The Prophetic Liturgy of the Second Temple in Jerusalem*. Translated by J. Edward Crowley. JSOTSup 118. Sheffield, UK: Sheffield Academic, 1991.

Tov, Emanuel. "Did the Septuagint Translators Always Understand Their Hebrew Text?" In *The Greek and Hebrew Bible: Collected Essays on the Septuagint*, edited by H. M. Barstad, Phyllis A. Bird et. al., 203–18. Leiden: Brill, 1990.

Bibliography

———. *The Text-Critical Use of the Septuagint in Biblical Research.* Jerusalem Biblical Studies 8. 2nd ed. Jerusalem: Simor, 1997.

———. *Textual Criticism of the Hebrew Bible.* Minneapolis: Fortress, 1992.

Treves, Marco. *The Dates of the Psalms: History and Poetry in Ancient Israel.* Pisa: Giardini, 1988.

Trible, Phyllis. *Rhetorical Criticism: Context, Method, and the Book of Jonah.* Guides to Biblical Scholarship. Old Testament Series. Minneapolis: Fortress, 1994.

Tucker, W. "Revisiting the Plagues in Psalm CV." *VT* 55.3 (2005) 401–11.

Tuell, Steven S. *First and Second Chronicles.* Louisville: John Knox, 2001.

Unterman, Jeremiah. "The Social-Legal Origin for the Image of God as Redeemer גואל of Israel." In *Pomegranates and Golden Bells: Studies in Biblical, Jewish, and Near Eastern Ritual, Law and Literature in Honor of Jacob Milgrom,* edited by David P. Wright, David N. Freedman, and Avi Hurvitz, 399–405. Winona Lake, IN: Eisenbrauns, 1995.

van Leeuwen, C. "עד." In *TLOT* 2, edited by Ernst Jenni and Claus Westermann, 838–46. Peabody, MA: Hendrickson, 1997.

Vermes, Geza. *Post-Biblical Jewish Studies.* Edited by Jacob Neusner. Studies in Judaism in Late Antiquity 8. Leiden: Brill, 1975.

Wagner, Norman E. "רנה in the Psalter." *VT* 10 (1960) 435–41.

Wagner, S. "בקש." In *TLOT* 2, edited by G. Johannes Botterweck, Helmer Ringgren and Heinz-Joseph Fabry, 229–41. Grand Rapids: Eerdmans, 1975.

Waltke, Bruce K., and M. O'Connor. *An Introduction to Biblical Hebrew Syntax.* Winona Lake, IN: Eisenbrauns, 1990.

Warning, Wilfried. *Literary Artistry in Leviticus.* Biblical Interpretation Series 35. Brill: Leiden, 1998.

Watson, Wilfred G. E. "Chiastic Patterns in Biblical Poetry." In *Chiasmus in Antiquity: Structures, Analyses, Exegesis,* edited by John W. Welch, 118–68. Hildesheim, Germany: Gerstenberg, 1981.

———. *Classical Hebrew Poetry: A Guide to Its Techniques.* JSOTSup 26. Sheffield, UK: JSOT, 2001.

———. "Internal Parallelism in Classical Hebrew Verse." *Biblica* 66.3 (1985) 363–83.

———. *Traditional Techniques in Classical Hebrew Verse.* JSOTSup 170. Sheffield, UK: Sheffield Academic, 1994.

Weinfeld, Moshe. *Deuteronomy 1–11: A New Translation with Introduction and Commentary.* Edited by William F. Albright and David N. Freedman. AB 5. Garden City, NY: Doubleday, 1991.

———. *Deuteronomy and the Deuteronomic School.* Winona Lake, IN: Eisenbrauns, 1972.

Weiser, Artur. *The Psalms.* Translated by Herbert Hartwell. OTL. London: SCM, 1965.

Weiss, Meir. *The Bible from Within: The Method of Total Interpretation.* Jerusalem: Magnes, 1984.

———. אמונות ודעות במזמורי תהילים. Jerusalem: Bialik, 2001.

———. המקרא כדמותו : שיטת מחקר והסתבלות במקרא על־פי עיקרי מדע־הספרות החדש. Jerusalem: Bialik, 1962.

———. המקרא כדמותו: שיטת האינטרפרטאציה הכוליית. 1962. Reprint. Jerusalem: Bialik, 1967.

———. המקרא כדמותו: הכוליית שיטת האינטרפרטאציה. 1967. Reprint. Jerusalem: Bialik, 1987.

Bibliography

Wente, Edward F. "Egyptian Religion." In *ABD: Vol. 2*, edited by David N. Freedman, Gary A. Herion, David F. Graf, and John D. Pleins, 552. Garden City, NY: Doubleday, 1992.

Westermann, Claus. *Genesis 12–36: A Commentary*. Translated by John J. Scullion. Minneapolis: Ausburg, 1985.

———. *The Living Psalms*. Translated by Joshua R. Porter. Edinburgh: T. & T. Clark, 1989.

Whiston, William, ed. *The Works of Josephus: Complete and Unabridged*. Peabody, MA: Hendrickson, 1995.

Whitelam, Keith W. "King and Kingship." In *ABD: Vol. 4*, edited by David N. Freedman, Gary A. Herion, David F. Graf and John D. Pleins, 350–69. Garden City, NY: Doubleday, 1992.

Williams, Ronald J. *Hebrew Syntax: An Outline*. Toronto: University of Toronto Press, 1996.

Wilson, Gerald H. *The Editing of the Hebrew Psalter*. SBLDS 76. Chico, CA: Scholars, 1985.

———. "Evidence of Editorial Divisions in the Hebrew Psalter." *VT* 34.3 (1984) 337–52.

———. "Shaping the Psalter: A Consideration of Editorial Linkage in the Book of Psalms." In *The Shape and Shaping of the Psalter*, edited by J. Clinton McCann, 72–82. Sheffield, UK: JSOT, 1993.

———. "Understanding the Purposeful Arrangement of Psalms in the Psalter: Pitfalls and Promise." In *The Shape and Shaping of the Psalter*, edited by J. Clinton McCann, 42–51. Sheffield, UK: JSOT, 1993.

———. "The Use of Royal Psalms at the 'Seems' of the Hebrew Psalter." In *The Poetical Books*, edited by David J. A. Clines, 73–83. Sheffield, UK: Sheffield Academic, 1977.

———. "The Use of 'Untitled' Psalms in the Hebrew Psalter." *ZAW* 97 (1985) 401–13.

Yaron, Shlomit. "הנסים במקרא ובספריות המזרח הקדום." Phd diss., Haifa University, 1997.

Young, Ian. *Diversity in Pre-Exilic Hebrew*. Forschungen Zum Alten Testament 5. Tübingen: Mohr (Siebeck), 1993.

Young, Ian, Robert Rezetko, and with the assistance of Martin Ehrnsvärd. *Linguistic Dating of Biblical Texts*. 2 vols. London: Equinox, 2008.

Zakovitch, Yair. *And You Shall Tell Your Son: The Concept of the Exodus in the Bible*. Jerusalem: Magnes, 1991.

———. *The Concept of the Miracle in the Bible*. Tel Aviv: Ministry of Defense, 1987.

———. "Juxtaposition in the Abraham Cycle." In *Pomegranates and Golden Bells: Studies in Biblical, Jewish, and Near Eastern Ritual, Law and Literature in Honor of Jacob Milgrom*, edited by David P. Wright, David Noel Freedman, and Avi Hurvitz, 509–24. Winona Lake, IN: Eisenbrauns, 1995.

———. "Psalm 82 and Biblical Exegesis." In *Sefer Moshe: The Moshe Weinfeld Jubilee Volume*, edited by Chaim Cohen, Avi Hurvitz, and Shalom Paul, 213–28. Winona Lake, IN: Eisenbrauns, 2004.

———. "אחת דבר אלהים שתים זו שמעתי: מבעים דו משמעיים בספרות המקרא." In *In Memory of Professor Meir Weiss*, 21–68. Jerusalem: Institute of Jewish Studies, 1999.

———. "הדגם הספרות שלושה וארבע במקרא." PhD diss., Hebrew University, 1977.

———. מבוא לפרשנות פנים־מקראית. Even-Yehuda: Reches, 1992.

Bibliography

———. מקראות בארץ המראות. Tel Aviv: Hakibbutz Hameuchad, 1995.
———. "על נהרות בבל" : תהילים קל"ז – זכרון בצל הטראומה." In: מחקרים: תשורה לשמואל בעולם המקרא, edited by Zipporah Talshir, Shamir Yonah and Daniel Sion, 184–204. Jerusalem: Bialik, 2001.
———. על תפיסת הנס במקרא. Tel Aviv: Ministry of Defense, 1987.
Zobel, Hans–Jürgen. "יעקב." In *TLOT 6*, edited by G. Johannes Botterweck and Helmer Ringgren, 185–208. Grand Rapids: Eerdmans, 1990.

Scripture Index

Genesis

1	86
1:3	58, 217
1:6	216
1:15	216
1:16	216
1:16	218
1:28	164n159
2:2–3	58n73
2:3	31
4:10	127
6:13	36, 114
7:22	193
8:17	227
9:11	227
9:15	134
9:16	35
9:22	50
10:6	50
11:1–9	164n159
12:2	30, 175
12:8	30n6
13:17	40
14:22	180n21
15:6	18n68
15:13	50n57
15:17	221
15:18	36, 38
17:6	43, 186n38
18:19	95n11
18:25	34n16
18:28	114
20:7	43, 43n42
20:9	41
20:16	42
23:4	40
25:23	68n93
26:3	36
26:11	42
26:25	30n6
27:40	227
27:42	191n49
29:32	133
30:2	129
31:7	43
31:18	48
31:42	41
34:29	135
34:30	39
34:31	128
34:35	191
37:6–11	46
37:10	100
37:17	45
37:18	52
37:27	45
37:35	191
38:15	128
39:2	45
40:1	214n10
41:14	47, 48
41:33–39	49
41:35	136
41:56	44
42:1–3	44
42:10	48, 214n10
42:17	49
43:3–14	45
43:20	48
45:7	45
45:8	48
48:11	120n68
49:3	61

Scripture Index

Exodus

1–4	76
1–14	243
1:1	50
1:7	50, 249
1:9–11	52
1:15–21	263
1:18	44
1:20	51
1:22	52
2:24	134
2:25	133
3:8	102, 114
3:9	131
3:15	189
3:20	31, 98
4:14	129n87
4:21	33n14, 51, 54
6:5	134
6:6	231n46
6:8	116
7:2	58n73
7:3	33n14, 51, 54
7:5	99, 220
7:19	220
7:20–21	56
8:2–15 [7:27—8:11]	79
8:3 [7:28]	57
8:5 [1]	220
8:12	58
8:20	58
8:21 [17]	202
9:3–4	55n66
9:13–34	185
9:14	119
9:18	80
9:22	220
9:23	59, 80
9:25	59
9:29	80
10:1–20	80
10:2	53n62
10:12	220
10:14	60
10:15	60, 61
10:21	55
11:1—12:32	81
11:2	62n85, 82
11:9–10	33n14
11:35	82
12:12	184, 190, 202, 205
12:12	219
12:23	114
12:29	61
12:29	184n35, 202, 218
12:31	234n53
12:35	62n85
12:36	82
12:38	148
12:41	62
13:13	231n46
13:21	82, 221
14:4	99
14:28	102
14:10–12	145
14:12	98
14:13	95
14:16	220
14:19–20	64
14:27	221, 234, 236
14:31	112
14:31—15:1	144
15	243
15:1	103
15:5–10	259n32
15:13	32
15:16	63
15:22–26	261
15:24	190n47
16	83
16:4	66
16:21	243
17	84
17:1–7	66, 163
17:2	105, 148
17:3	148
17:7	122n72, 263
18:11	179, 202

Exodus (cont.)

19:5	179, 202
19:9	169
20:1–2	70
20:11	215
23:19	200n70
23:33	125
27:19	224n24
28:36	107
29:7	42n40
31:16	95n11
31:17	181
32–34	114
32:8	104, 110
32:10	129
32:11–14	113
32:12	134
32:23–25	191n50
33:9	169
34:15	128n85
38:18	64
39:3	216n12, 230
39:30	108
40:5	64

Leviticus

4:5	42
5:4	123
6:11 [18]	189n44
7:36	189n44
15:26	128
16:31	46n50
16:32	42
17:3	9
18:5	94
18:6	9
18:21	126
23:14	189n44
25:25	132n93, 231n46
25:35	132n93
25:39	132n93
25:47	132n93
26:26	44
26:44	135
26:44–45	134
26:45	133
27:8	132n93

Numbers

8:17	219
11	147
11–14	243
11:1	129n87
11:1–3	109
11:4	104, 159n153
11:20	106, 148
12	144, 261
12:8	52
13:20	61
14	190n47
14:8	114
14:22	105, 148
14:31	114
15:32–40	145
16	149, 243
16:5	108
16:11	106
16:35	109
16:39 [17:4]	216n12
16:50 [17:15]	156
17:5	52
17:15	156, 247
20–21	243
20:1–12	143
20:1–13	157
20:10	248n12
20:24	122n72
21	261
21:23–24	224
21:24–25	223
21:33–35	224
22–24	261
25	154–55, 243
25:1	128n84
25:3	117
25:7	119
25:8	156

Scripture Index

Numbers (*cont.*)

25:12	120
27:8	188
27:13	122n72
27:14	55n66, 143
30:3	37n24
30:14	46n50
33:4	202, 219
35:33	127
36:7	38

Deuteronomy

1:1	143
1:4	233n52
1:15	231n46
1:22–40	150–51
1:27	115
1:32	115
1:34–37	158n150
1:37	248n12
2:24	236
2:24—3:3	232
2:24—3:7	233
3:1–7	224
3:26	248n12
4:8	69n98
4:16–18	110
4:20	67n91
4:25–28	237
4:26	75
4:27	40n33
4:28	124
4:29	32
4:32–38	233
4:34	219, 232
4:34–38	225
4:38	188, 207n87, 232
5:15	220n16, 232n50
5:26	118
6:22	54n65, 185, 202
7:6	179, 202, 205, 249
7:8	37
7:9	36n22
7:13	61
7:16	125
7:19	54, 220n17, 232n50
8:5	222
8:8	59n78
8:15–18	164
9	152
9:1	207n87
9:7	121
9:19	143
9:22	121
10:10	114
10:17	214, 243n3
10:18	227n37
11:2	220n17, 232n50
11:17	75
12:31	126
13:14 [15]	65
13:16 [17]	136
13:18	134
13:18 [19]	95n11, 115
14:2	179, 202, 205
14:23	205
15:4	188, 232
17:8	31
17:19	69n98
18:9	124
19:10	188
21:17	61
21:18	115
24:4	188, 232
25:19	188
26:1	188
26:14	115, 118n64
27:10	115
27:15	124
28:31–32	41
29:8 [7]	188
30:3	136
30:10	69n98
31:27	98n23
32:16	118
32:17	126

Scripture Index

Deuteronomy (cont.)

32:21	107n44
32:28	96n14
32:36	191, 243n3
32:37	249
32:51	143, 157
33:6	40n33
33:8	143n120
33:9	69n97
33:19	53
34:4	37
34:5	52, 175
34:11	202

Joshua

1:1	52
7:9	30
7:19	29n5
9:24	123
10:20	187
11:9	123
12:7	187
14:4	48
18:4	41n36
18:7	52
22:5	52
24:25	37n24
24:29	175

Judges

2:8	175
2:12	107n44, 118
2:14	130
2:20	96n14
3:25	214n10
3:30	131
5:7	230n42
5:12	176n5
5:10	31
5:31	93n7
6:5	60
7:4	47
16:26	41

17:7–9	40n34

1 Samuel

1:11	133
1:27	105
2:25	119
6:4	119
7:13	131
11:7	63
12:3	41, 42
12:15	115
14:45	95
18:21	125
20:30	129
24:15 [16]	190
25	164n159
25:42	103n35
28:10	132
30:6	113

2 Samuel

1:4	116
3:30	223
5:6–7	197
7:14	42n39
8:13	175
16:17	36
20:8	117
21:6	34n17
22:43	216
24	119
24:21	156

1 Kings

2:16	105
4:25 [5:5]	59n78
6:38	58n74
8	135n96
8:1	197
8:28	133
8:37	133
8:47	96

293

Scripture Index

1 Kings (*cont.*)

8:50	134
9:1	180
10:8	93
10:21	191
21:26	129
22:20	116

2 Kings

6:11	230n42
7:9	132
9:3	42n40
10:34	93
11:12	67n91
11:18	200n68
13:12	93
13:23	37
17:17	118
17:20	130
19:21	197
21:5	176n7
4:24	60n79, 123

1 Chronicles

5:20	199n64, 230n43
15:4	196
16	23n81
16:8–22	26n1
16:16	36
16:34	213
16:35	136
17:14	72n104
21:17	123
23:24	200
24:20	200
27:27	230n43, 199n64
28:21	224n24
29:3	178

2 Chronicles

2:5 [4]	179n20, 180
5:13	213
6:32	232
7:3	213
9:8	72n104
23:7	200n68

Ezra

2:2	39n32
3:11	19, 213
8:17	200
8:20	199n64, 230n43

Nehemiah

1:1—12:42	11n43
3:5	214n10
4:14 [8]	33
5:13	234n54
9	259n32
9:10	54n65, 185, 202
9:18	109n49
9:26	132
10:32–39	200
10:36	200n70
10:40	196

Esther

1:17	60n79, 123
2:11	40
7:6	102
8:17	63

Job

3:21	103
5:2	224
5:17	93
7:11	31
26:12	220n17
27:3	193
34:15	227
37:5	31
39:19	93n7
40:12	131n91

Job (cont.)

42:3	31
42:6	114n61
42:15	38

Psalms

2:1	68n93
2:10	97n20
5:5	178
5:12 [13]	94n9
6:4–5 [5–6]	177n9
7:6 [7]	33
8	1, 1n1
9:5	93
9:6	100
9:8 [9]	190n45
10:43	74
12:1 [2]	177n9
13:5 [6]	213n8
14:7	197
15:4	196
17:7	98n21
18:1	175
18:30 [31]	47
19:6 [7]	182
20:1 [2]	197
21:2	32
21:13 [14]	31, 93n7
22	2n6, 3n7
22:23 [24]	197
24	1n1
24:2	1
24:6	32
25:11	99
25:12	196
25:16	177n9
28:4	129
28:9	188
29:7	59n76
31:21 [22]	197n60
32:1	93
33	1n1
33:5–6	218
33:6	193, 215
33:7	182n29
33:11	189
33:12	129, 188
33:18	98
34	251n17
34:2 [3]	31
35	251n17
35:13	46n50
35:25	49
38:1 [2]	121
40:12 [13]	86
44	2n6, 3n7
44:2	68n93
46:6 [7]	41n37
47:1	248
48:1	248
49:1	248
50	251n19
50–51	11n40
50:19	117
51	251n19
52–22	11n40
54:1 [3]	190
54:6 [8]	177
54:8	175
57:7 [8]	31
61:2 [3]	182
62–68	11n40
62:10 [11]	41
65	1n1
66	2n6, 3n7
66:3	32
66:6	30, 101n31
66:20	197n60
68	2n6
68:8	167n164
68:19 [20]	197n60
68:35 [36]	197n60
69:6 [7]	31
69:17 [18]	177n9
70:4	32
71:6	32n13
72:11	186

295

Scripture Index

Psalms (cont.)

73:14 [15]	59
74	1n1, 2n6, 3n7
74:13	32
77	2n6, 3, 139
77:7–11 [8–12]	213n8
77:11 [12]	215
77:12 [13]	30
77:16–19	259n32
77:19 [18]	183
77:20 [21]	107, 107n45, 169
78	2n6, 3, 243n2
78:4	93, 215
78:5	178
78:11	31
78:13	221
78:14	33
78:15–20	66
78:16	67n91
78:17	98n24
78:18	65, 105
78:24	66
78:32	215
78:38–39	225n33
78:40	167n164
78:42	102n33
78:43	54, 185
78:44	56
78:44–51	244 n6
78:45	57
78:46	60
78:47	59
78:51	50, 61, 74, 81, 112, 162n155, 219
78:61	32n12
78:70	139
79:6	41n37
79:9	99
80	2n6, 3n7
81	2n6, 3, 243n2
81:5	178
82:8	40
83:14 [15]	59n76
84:10 [11]	176
85:6	189
89	10n36, 170
89:3 [4]	36
89:8–9 [9–10]	220n17
89:18–38 [19–39]	1n2
89:20 [21]	43n40
90	169, 253
90:13	134
92:1 [2]	177
92:13 [14]	176
93:1	170n169
94:10	49
95	3, 16n62, 97, 170, 243n2
95:3	170n169, 180
96:4	180
96:10	170n169
97:4	183
98	2n6, 3n7
98:1	31n8
98:6	170n169
99	2n6, 3n7
99:1	170n170
99:7	169
102:12 [13]	189
102:15 [16]	186n38
103	2n6, 3n7
103:7	170
104	29n3, 85, 86, 260
104–106	254
104:6–7	181n24
104:7	100
104:13, 16, 28	86
104:24	215n11
105	161–65
105–106	253
105:1–15	26n1
105:2–36	81
105:8	225
105:11	80
105:12–15	247n10
105:14	79
105:15	242
105:17	249n13
105:23	222, 252

Psalms (cont.)

105:24	102n33, 227n36, 249
105:26	107, 250n15
105:27	185, 252
105:28	86
105:28–36	244, 251
105:34–35	80
105:36	219
105:37	82, 250
105:38	82
105:39	244
105:40	105
105:41	74, 244
105:43	133
106	2n6, 3, 4, 169, 170, 255, 161–65
106:34–42	261
106:5	96n14
106:9	22n80, 101n31, 222, 244n5, 250
106:9	
106:12	144
106:14	148, 252
106:15	65
106:16	250n15
106:16–18	248
106:19–23	154, 261
106:22	31, 74, 215, 252
106:23	156n147
106:28–31	261
106:29	250
106:31	18n68
106:32	69
106:34	60n79
106:37–38	244
106:43	252
106:45	225n33
107	2n6, 3n7, 165–68, 104n38
107:4	252
107:11	252
109:26	98n21
111	2n6, 3n7
111:9	36
112:6	45n48
113:1	175, 247n10
113:2	175
114	2n6, 3, 243n2
114:1	178
114:3–5	259n32
115	195n58
115:3	181, 182
115:5–6	194
115:6	193n54
119:12	197n60
119:24	104
119:106	94
119:163	129n89
119:169	133
121	1n1
122:4	174
125:1	197n61
126:1	197n61
128:1	196
128:5	197n61
129:5	197n61
132	1
132:13	197n61
132:14	104
133:3	197n61
134	1n1
134–135	254
134:1	203
134:3	197n61, 203
135–136	238–40, 253
135	2n6, 3, 4, 92, 95, 256
135:1	247n10
135:4–9	245
135:7	247n10, 259
135:8	219
135:9	53n62, 221
135:10–12	243
135:11	250
135:12	260
135:14	243n3, 249
135:15	124
135:15–17	117
135:16	192n51

Scripture Index

Psalms (cont.)

135:19	196
136	2n6, 3, 4, 95, 255, 256
136–137	240–41
136:2–3	243n3
136:5	244n7
136:10–12	252, 250
136:13–16	100n29
136:15	101n31, 234
136:16	232
136:17–18	186
136:17–22	243, 244, 252
136:19–20	250
137:3	135
138:6	225
143:7	103n35
143:10	106
143:12	133
144:1	197n60
145:5	53
146:7	228n37
147	2n6, 3n7
147:5	86
147:15	47
148:5	175
149:8	48

Proverbs

3:11	114n61
3:13	93
3:19	215
3:31	107
5:2	69n97
6:16–17	127
6:22	31
6:26	128
8:34	93
10:7	189
11:27	32
12:18	123n75
14:28	106n41
14:34	68n93
25:14	182

Ecclesiastes

1:11	199n64, 230n43
2:8	178
5:12 [11]	41
8:2–3	181
10:18	132
10:6	231

Isaiah

1:4	96n14
3:4	59n75
4:5	64, 83
5:14	46n49
6:3	96n15
7:9	213n9
10:11	125n76
10:16	106
10:19	39
12:4	30, 247n10
26:9	33
27:1	220n17
29:23	178
34:1	68n93
40:19	216
41:2	186n38
41: 8	34, 178
41:16	96
42:4	228
42:5	230
42:24	178
44:1	34, 178
44:24	181n25, 216n12, 230
45:1	42
45:4	34
46:10	181
47:14	59n76
48	243
48:10	47n10
48:13	181n25
48:20	66, 167n163
48:21	74, 244
49:26	227
51	243

Scripture Index

Isaiah (*cont.*)

51:9	181n24
51:9–10	220n17
51:9–11	84, 259n32
51:11	68, 74
58:5	46n50
61:2	94n9
62:12	167n163
63	145n125
63:7	82
63:7–14	145n125
63:9–13	244n5
63:12–14	259n32
63:13	62, 101
63:17	130
65:1	32, 65
66:23	227

Jeremiah

1:10	187n43
1:18	224n24
2:6	66
2:11	110
3:1	128n85
3:2	128
3:19	114, 151n136
4:28	181n25
5:21	192
7:16	133
7:22	1n3
7:31	126
8:19	107n44
9:11 [10]	59n75
10:3	124
10:12	215
10:13	183, 247n10
10:16	130
11:5	37
14:20	96
18:7	187n43
18:21	186
19:4–5	127
19:14	176n7
21:5	232
22:17	127
26:2	176n7
31:21	176n5
31:32	1n3
32:35	126
33:11	19
33:26	34
33:26	36n23
46:23	60
48:21	33
50:3	206
50:4	32
50:12	66n90
51:20	41n37

Lamentations

5:5	41
5:8	227, 230n46

Ezekiel

4:16	44
5:3	128
5:16	44
8:16	176n7
10:15	98n24
12:27	196
14:13	44
20	244
20:1–26	151
20:1–2	151n137
20:6	1n3
20:7–9	99n25
20:13	98n23
20:23	117
20:30–31	128
22	244
22:15	151n137
22:30	113, 143, 154, 247
23:8	87
31:4	181
38:12	48
39:21	33
39:25	107n44
40:46	200

Scripture Index

Daniel

8:24	186
9:16	97n17
11:14	72n104

Hosea

2:5	66n90
3:5	32
4:17	125n76
5:3	128, 128n83
7:6	109
7:10	32
8:4	125n76
10:4	36
11:1	258n30
13:2	191

Joel

1:2	93n6
1:4	60n81
1:19	109
2:18	107n44
2:25	60n81
3:16 [4:16]	9

Amos

1:2	9, 197
5:12	178
5:21	180n21
5:25	196
7:4	181
7:9	36
7:16	36

Jonah

2:4 [5]	46
2:5 [6]	181
3:4	44

Micah

2:10	69
4:10	167n163

Nahum

1:4	100
3:19	32n13

Habakkuk

3:10	181n24

Zephaniah

1:6	32
2:9	95n12
3:8	187n43

Zechariah

1:14	107n44
7:14	114
7:14	151n136
13:9	47n10
14:12	119

Malachi

1:2	178
3:16	197

Matthew

2:15	258n30
7	1n3
7:9–16	49

Romans

9:10–15	179

Hebrews

11:27	1n3

Jude

1:5	1n3